D0206177

Yugoslavia

Yugoslavia
A History of its Demise

Viktor Meier
translated by Sabrina P. Ramet

London and New York

First published as *Wie Jugoslawien verspielt wurde*
in 1995 by Viktor Meier

First published in English 1999
by Routledge
11 New Fetter Lane, London EC4P 4EE

Simultaneously published in the USA and Canada
by Routledge
29 West 35th Street, New York, NY 10001

Routledge is an imprint of the Taylor & Francis Group

© C.H. Beck'sche Verlagsbuchhandlung, Munich 1995

Typeset in Baskerville by
The Florence Group, Stoodleigh, Devon
Printed and bound in Great Britain by
Clays Ltd, St Ives plc

British Library Cataloguing in Publication Data
A catalogue record for this book is available
from the British Library

Library of Congress Cataloguing in Publication Data
  Meier, Viktor, 1929–
    [Wie Jugoslawien verspielt wurde. English]
    Yugoslavia: a history of its demise / Viktor Meier:
      translated by Sabrina Ramet
      p. cm.
    "First published as 'Wie Jugoslawien verspielt wurde' in 1995 by
Viktor Meier" – CIP t.p. verso.
    Includes bibliographical references and index.
    ISBN 0–415–18595–5. ISBN 0–19596–3 (pbk).
    1. Yugoslavia–History–1980–1992.   2. Former Yugoslav republics.
3. Yugoslav War, 1991–1995–Causes.   I. Title.
DR1307.M4513 1999
949.702'4–dc21   98–32356
                  CIP

ISBN 0–415–18595–5 (hbk)
ISBN 0–415–18596–3 (pbk)

Contents

Foreword   vii
Preface to the English edition   xi
Preface   xiii
Chronology of events   xv
Glossary   xix
Maps
(i) Yugoslavia before summer 1991   xx
(ii) The area of former Yugoslavia at the end of
       1998   xxi

1 Fateful weaknesses after Tito's death   1

2 The turning point: 1986–87   35

3 The beginning of the end   60

4 Western Yugoslavia reacts   101

5 Irreconcilable positions   138

6 Unwanted independence – the fate of Macedonia
   and Bosnia-Herzegovina   181

7 From the Yugoslav tragedy to the tragedy of the West   215

Epilogue   244
Bibliography   246
Notes   250
Index of Names   271
Subject index   276

Foreword

Sabrina P. Ramet

The outbreak of war in Yugoslavia encouraged many persons who had been previously unfamiliar with that country or whose knowledge and understanding of that country's culture and politics were at best superficial to offer their interpretations, in print, in the broadcast media, and on lecture circuits. In the process, certain myths having no basis in fact gained wide circulation, some of them even attaining to the status of "conventional wisdom". In consequence, it is especially welcome to have Viktor Meier's *Yugoslavia: A History of its Demise* available. Dr Meier, a veteran observer of the Yugoslav scene for the *Neue Zürcher Zeitung* and the *Frankfurter Allgemeine Zeitung*, has always shown a keen understanding of Balkan politics and many of us have been deeply indebted to his articles for the *Frankfurter Allgemeine* for helping us to sort out the sundry complexities of socialist Yugoslavia's politics. In this book, which has already won wide acclaim in the German-speaking world, Dr Meier provides a unique insight into the deliberations and intra-party disputes which underlay the growing crisis in Yugoslavia in the late 1980s and early 1990s. Grounding his analysis in archival research, interviews with many of the leading parties to the crisis, and memoirs by a number of participants, Dr Meier shatters the myth favored by relativists that all sides were more or less blameworthy and pins the blame for the break-up of Yugoslavia squarely on Milošević and the army leadership, while noting also the importance of the complicitous actions taken by Stipe Šuvar (a Croat), Lazar Mojsov (a Macedonian), and others. Of course, Borisav Jović helped to instrumentalize the crisis during his year as president of the collective presidency, but Jović's role is not a point stressed in this account.

As Meier shows, the turning point came in 1989, when Serbia snuffed out the autonomy of the provinces but pocketed their votes in the state presidency (even though logic would have dictated that if the provinces no longer enjoyed autonomy, they could not have a claim to separate votes in the presidency, least of all votes controlled by Serbia). With that, the state presidency forfeited any possibility of passing measures which did not enjoy Milošević's favor.

Meier explodes other myths as well, including the myth that the Slovenes unnecessarily provoked the breakup of the country out of a combination of self-congratulatory nationalism and economic self-seeking, the myth that the Western state community dealt with the Yugoslav crisis and the outbreak of war in a competent and responsible manner, the myth that England and France were neutral in the conflict, and the myth that Germany was some-how "to blame" for having advocated recognition of Slovenian and Croatian independence. It strikes me, personally, as I reflect on this book that, at least from my standpoint, underlying all of these myths is a failure to grasp the essential difference between legitimate governments (which respect human rights and promote tolerance among the inhabitants of their societies) and illegitimate regimes (which do not respect human rights and which, on the contrary, promote intolerance and hatred among the members of their societies). In sketching the difference between legitimate and illegitimate governments in this way, I am highlighting the moral aspects of legitimacy. In my view, at least, legitimacy may be viewed triadically, as consisting of moral, political, and economic aspects. Under moral legitimacy we may consider whether a government respects natural rights, whether it endeavors to frame its laws in accord with Natural Law (as translated, for example, in the Universal Declaration of Human Rights) and whether it fosters tolerance of difference, among other things. Under political legitimacy, we may consider whether office-holders gain office in accord with procedures which are widely accepted within the given society. Under economic legitimacy, we may consider whether the system protects the weak against exploitation, whether there is a commitment to social justice, whether, indeed, the economic system is, in some sense, compatible with Natural Law.[1] Under the moral criteria entailed in this vision – which lie at the heart of the classical liberal agenda outlined by John Locke, Immanuel Kant, Thomas Jefferson, James Madison, J. S. Mill, and Joseph Raz – Slovenia and Croatia had every right to bid for independence, not because of some purported and self-contradictory "right of national self-determination", which is incapable of consistent application, but because all people and peoples have the right to defend themselves against tyrannies and, failing to overthrow tyrants, have the right to secede and to establish legitimate governments.[2] To affirm this is to say no more than is enshrined in the American Declaration of Independence.

Legitimate governments and illegitimate regimes do not act in the same way, either internally or externally in relations with other states, because their internal dynamics, needs, information, and support mechanisms are fundamentally different. Nor should it come as any surprise that illegitimate regimes gravitate toward other illegitimate regimes, following a pattern already identified by Thucydides in his *Peloponnesian Wars*, even if the venerable Greek placed his stress on *forms* of government, rather than on such differences in legitimacy as may be associated with formal differences. Moreover, while legitimate governments encourage their citizens to behave in responsible ways, illegitimate regimes do the very opposite – as shown in the Serbian government's encouragement of ethnic Serbs to organize mass demonstrations *against* the 1974 constitution, even while banning mass demonstrations in support of the then-still-valid 1974 constitution by ethnic Albanians. When it becomes illegal to support the constitution, it is obvious that one can no longer speak of legitimate politics in the system in question.

For Britain, France, the Netherlands, and other states to rebut the Slovenian and Croatian politicians and to lend their support to Serbia's Milošević thus not only revealed a blindness to the reality of illegitimate politics but also betrayed a surprising willingness to apply a double standard *vis-à-vis* the Balkans: liberalism may be fine for us, but it is unnecessary in the Balkans – or so the politicians in these states seemed to be thinking.

Of course there were other, more trivial considerations which entered into the picture too, as Meier points out, ranging from the diplomats' comfort with their connections in Belgrade and unwillingness to travel much outside the capital, to an ingrained inability to adjust to the pace of change in Yugoslavia and an attachment to, bordering on affection for, the unified Yugoslav state, to lack of information about and understanding of the Slovenian and Croatian points of view. But even with these encumbrances, the diplomats and political leaderships of the Western states should have been able to establish that the Milošević government was already doing violence to the human rights of Albanians, that it had behaved illegally and in ways contrary to the constitution (as exhaustively documented in this book), and that the so-called "national question" in Yugoslavia ultimately revolved around the Serbs. There were, thus, no problems between Slovenes and Croats or between Hungarians and Croats (in the Vojvodina), while the later conflict between Croats and Muslims in Bosnia was not yet on the horizon. Even the problems between Macedonia's numerically dominant Macedonians and minority Albanians had not yet come into the open. To the extent that there was a "national question" in socialist Yugoslavia, it could be reduced to a growing conflict between Serbs and non-Serbs (whether Slovenes or Croats or Bosnian Muslims or Muslims of the Sandžak or Hungarians or Albanians or even, from time to time, Macedonians and autonomist Montenegrins), a conflict, indeed, being actively promoted by Milošević and his supporters.

Relativism is beguiling, because it seems so "fair". But relativism is also facile, offering the appearance of wisdom for those who lack either the time or the patience to sort out the facts. Viktor Meier's *Yugoslavia: A History of its Demise* makes a major contribution toward torpedoing relativist analyses about the Yugoslav crisis.

In closing, I would like to express my gratitude to Heather McCallum at Routledge for her enthusiastic support of this project, and to Gisela Kwast,

Renate Piasek-Lenz, and Andreas Piasek-Lenz for assistance in connection with the translation of certain passages. Finally, I should like to say what a pleasure it has been working with the author, with whom I share the satisfaction of seeing this book reach an English-speaking audience.

Sabrina P. Ramet
Kyoto, Japan

Preface to the English edition

Some passages were abridged for the English edition of this book, but the text has also been enhanced with the addition of some allusions to evidence which has since come to light or to recently published literature. The character of the book as a discussion and analysis of the collapse of Yugoslavia has remained the same and I did not attempt to include the later period of the war in Bosnia. Only in a short epilogue do I try to summarize my views concerning the present situation of the still open-ended questions of Bosnia-Herzegovina and Kosovo.

I would like to thank the translator, Professor Sabrina P. Ramet, for her not always easy work, and Heather McCallum of Routledge for her interest in this project. I also wish to thank the institutions which, through their generous support, made possible the translation of this book and its publication in English, specifically, the Friedrich Naumann Stiftung, the Nova Ljubljanska Banka in Ljubljana, and the Fazit Stiftung of the *Frankfurter Allgemeine* newspaper.

Viktor Meier

Preface

This book was written at the end of a nearly 35-year-long career as a journalist and political observer of Southeast Europe – first with the *Neue Zürcher Zeitung* (until 1966), then for a pool of German regional newspapers, and finally, beginning in 1975, for the *Frankfurter Allgemeine*. My first contact with this part of the world, and with Yugoslavia in particular, came when I was already a student and doctoral candidate; the theme of my dissertation, "The New Yugoslav Economic System", still seemed meaningful and relevant in the 1950s.

Yugoslavia did not seem to me either then or later to be an artificial creation, but at the moment that the state formation became unrealistic and politically unsustainable, it became necessary to draw the appropriate conclusions. As of summer 1991, Yugoslavia had become uninhabitable for the country's non-Serbian nations and nationalities. This book undertakes to inquire into the reasons for Yugoslavia's collapse and to identify those responsible. I did not write this book as a historian, but rather as a contemporary witness and observer. The book is not the first to treat of these events; nor will it be the last. But I hope that I have been able to contribute something unique to the understanding of the tragic events in the former Yugoslavia. I was always aware of the extent to which the past has affected the present in this country.

In writing this book, I made use of the archival materials kept in the Republic of Slovenia, above all of the records of the presidium of the Central Committee of the League of Communists of Yugoslavia, of its Central Committee, and of the presidency of the Republic of Slovenia. The first two sets of records were federal materials, which were delivered to the republics; the third consisted of purely Slovenian documents. These materials were very voluminous but the essential information could be consulted. The protocols of the Yugoslav state presidency were not deposited in republic archives and were not available to me, but I talked once again with persons in positions of power, who had taken part in the events that constitute the tale herein. In addition, I made use of the records of my earlier interviews, observations, and accounts (especially those published in the *Frankfurter Allgemeine*).

The reader may find that Slovenian perspectives and interpretations are given ample space in this book. The explanation for that lies in the situation itself. Even in the days when there was little understanding in Yugoslavia of the need for objective reporting, information in Slovenia was relatively open. I must concede that I always felt a sympathy for the aspirations of the Slovenian people to live, within or outside Yugoslavia, according to their own ways and that, to me as a Swiss citizen, federalism seemed plausible and useful.

In my view, the principal source of the implosion of Yugoslavia is to be sought in the abandonment, by Serbia, of the principles of equality, democracy, and tolerance. In addition, one should note also the responsibility of the army leadership which, for not entirely clear reasons, designated Slovenia as its chief "enemy", and which, with a dogmatic arrogance of power, put a strain on the cohesion of the joint state. The machinations of the army leadership had not always been clearly visible in the years preceding the final collapse of socialist Yugoslavia, since in this sphere, the proclivity of the military to secrecy was especially marked. Responsibility must also be borne by those communist functionaries in higher echelons of the federal nomenklatura of Yugoslavia, who obstructed reforms and democratization alike. Here I am thinking of people like Stipe Šuvar, Lazar Mojsov, or Raif Dizdarević, among others, who, instead of putting the brakes on Yugoslavia's ruinous skid to perdition, actually accelerated it.

It remains for me to say a few words of thanks to the institutions and persons who have generously provided me with the opportunity to look back once more over the last 15 years of my professional activity. I am grateful to the Stiftung Wissenschaft und Politik in Ebenhausen (Germany) which, in a manner of speaking, took over the patronage for this book. I owe an equally great debt of gratitude to the Fritz Thyssen Foundation, which provided generous support for this book project. I also wish to thank all those persons who granted me interviews, as well as those institutions which supported me in other ways, especially the Republic of Slovenia and its president, Milan Kučan. I would also like to thank the School of Advanced International Studies (SAIS) of the Johns Hopkins University in Washington D.C., which made it possible for me to conduct research there as well. I owe heartfelt thanks also to the large number of personal friends in all parts of the former Yugoslavia, who helped me in various ways. Finally, I would like to express my deep gratitude to my wife, Rosmarie, who, during my entire career, as well as during the writing of this book, including during countless absences, displayed great patience and understanding and who helped me in my work.

Viktor Meier
Esslingen, Switzerland

Chronology of events

4 May 1980 Josip Broz Tito dies.

August 1980 Political trials in Croatia (against Tudjman and others).

11 March 1981 The first unrest in Kosovo.

May 1981 Milka Planinc succeeds Veselin Djuranović as head of the government.

October 1982 Introduction of the "border tax" for foreign trips.

February 1985 Branko Mikulić becomes new head of the government.

February 1986 Slobodan Milošević becomes Serbian party chief.

April 1986 Milan Kučan becomes Slovenian party chief and Azem Vllasi becomes party chief in Kosovo.

May 1986 Stanko Stojčević becomes party chief in Croatia.

End of September 1987 Slobodan Milošević becomes sole ruler in Serbia, at the Eighth Plenum of the Central Committee of the Serbian communist party.

25–26 March 1988 Unsuccessful attempt by the army leadership to intervene in Slovenia.

31 May 1988 Arrest of four journalists in Slovenia on the order of military justice.

May 1988 Kaqusha Jashari becomes party chief in Kosovo.

June 1988 Veljko Kadijević replaces Branko Mamula as Defense Minister.

End of July 1988 The Kosovo Serbs establish a committee for the organization of mass demonstrations throughout Yugoslavia, in support of Slobodan Milošević.

5 October 1988 The leadership of Vojvodina resigns after a mass demonstration in Novi Sad.

19 November 1988 Milošević extracts changes in the leadership of Kosovo, by means of mass demonstrations.

30 December 1988 The Mikulić government loses a vote of no confidence in the parliament and resigns. Ante Marković becomes the new Prime Minister.

11 January 1989 After mass demonstrations by Milošević's supporters in Titograd, the Montenegrin leadership resigns.

24 January 1989 Demonstrations in Priština after the passage of the new, centralistic constitution of Serbia in the Serbian parliament.

27 February 1989 After new demonstrations, a state of emergency is declared in Kosovo.

2 March 1989 Azem Vllasi and other leading figures among the Albanians of Kosovo are arrested.

28 March 1989 Serbia proclaims a new constitution which, for all practical purposes, abrogates the autonomous status of the provinces. There are demonstrations in Priština.

2 April 1989 Janez Drnovšek is elected Slovenia's representative in the Yugoslav state presidency and assumes the chairmanship of that body on 15 May.

28 June 1989 At the commemoration of the 600th anniversary of the Battle of Kosovo Milošević threatens new "fights, even armed conflicts".

26 September 1989 Passage of the new Slovenian constitution, against the opposition of the Serbian leadership and the army.

30 October 1989 Beginning of the trial of Vllasi and his co-defendants.

1 December 1989 A demonstration planned for Ljubljana by Milošević's supporters is thwarted.

12/13 December 1989 A change of power in Croatia. Ivica Račan becomes the new party chairman.

18 December 1989 Prime Minister Ante Marković announces his reform program.

20/21 January 1990 The Fourteenth and last Congress of the LCY. The departure of the Slovenes brings an end to the party on the federal level.

8 April 1990 The first free elections in Slovenia.

22 April 1990 The first free elections in Croatia.

15 May 1990 Borisav Jović (a Serb) becomes new chairman of the Yugoslav state presidency.

17 May 1990 The army leadership confiscates the weapons of the territorial defense forces in the republics, having only partial success in Slovenia, however.

28 May 1990 Prime Minister Marković announces the establishment of his own political party.

2 July 1990 Serbian police prevent the deputies of the parliament of Kosovo from entering the parliamentary building. Thereupon, the latter, sitting in front of the entrance to the building, proclaim the establishment of the "Republic of Kosovo".

18 August 1990 The Serbs in Croatia hold a referendum about autonomy. Unrest breaks out in many Serb-inhabited districts of Croatia.

4 November 1990 The establishment of an army party, under the name "League of Communists – Movement for Yugoslavia".

11 November 1990 The first free elections in Macedonia.

18 November 1990   The first free elections in Bosnia-Herzegovina.

9 December 1990   The first free elections in Serbia, Milošević's victory, election boycott by the Albanians.

22 December 1990   The Croatian *Sabor* endows Croatia with "sovereignty".

23 December 1990   The plebiscite in Slovenia concerning independence.

End of December 1990   Serbia's "invasion" into the Yugoslav monetary system.

25 January 1991   The army leadership is prevented from intervening in Croatia, but enters into conflicts at the local level.

12–15 March 1991   Session of the state presidency in Belgrade. The army does not receive authorization for a general intervention, but threatens independent action. On 13 March, Kadijević and Jović make a secret trip to Moscow.

16 March 1991   Milošević induces Jović to resign from the state presidency. The Serbian parliament does not accept Jović's resignation, however, and Jović soon withdraws his resignation.

25 March 1991   Tudjman and Milošević meet at Karadjordjevo.

15 May 1991   Serbia renders the state presidency incapable of functioning, by refusing to recognize the accession of Croatian representative, Stipe Mesić, as the new chairman.

25 June 1991   Slovenia and Croatia declare independence.

27 June 1991   The army attacks Slovenia on authorization by Prime Minister Marković.

7 July 1991   A troika of EU representatives (in Brioni) obtains a "moratorium" in the actualization of Slovenian and Croatian independence and an agreement concerning the reinstitution of the state presidency.

September/October 1991   Conference in The Hague. This ends with the rejection by Serbia of the final draft by Lord Carrington on 5 November 1991.

26 October 1991   The last soldiers of the Yugoslav People's Army leave Slovenia, but there are difficult conflicts in Croatia.

16 December 1991   The Council of Ministers of the EU decides to recognize Croatia and Slovenia on 15 January 1992, though Germany declares its recognition already on 18 December 1991.

2 January 1992   A truce for Croatia is signed in Sarajevo.

Early April 1992   Outbreak of war in Bosnia-Herzegovina.

Glossary

ASNOM	Anti-fascist Assembly of the People's Liberation of Macedonia
AVNOJ	Anti-fascist Council for the People's Liberation of Yugoslavia
CC	Central Committee
CP	Communist Party
ELAS	Greek People's Liberation Army
FAZ	*Frankfurter Allgemeine Zeitung*
HDZ	Hrvatska Demokratska Zajednica (Croatian Democratic Community)
IMRO/VMRO	Internal Macedonian Revolutionary Organization
JNA	Jugoslovenska Narodna Armija (slovenian Jugoslovenska Ljudska Armada) Yugoslav People's Army
KOS	Kontraobaveštajna Služba (Counter Espionage Service)
LC	League of Communists
LCY	League of Communists of Yugoslavia
P	Presidency
SANU	Serbian Academy for Sciences and Arts
SAWPY	Socialist Alliance of Working People of Yugoslavia
SFRY	Socialist Federal Republic of Yugoslavia
SNOF	Slavo-Macedonian People's Liberation Front
TO	Teritorijalna Odbrana (slovenian Teritorialna Obramba) Territorial Defence Force

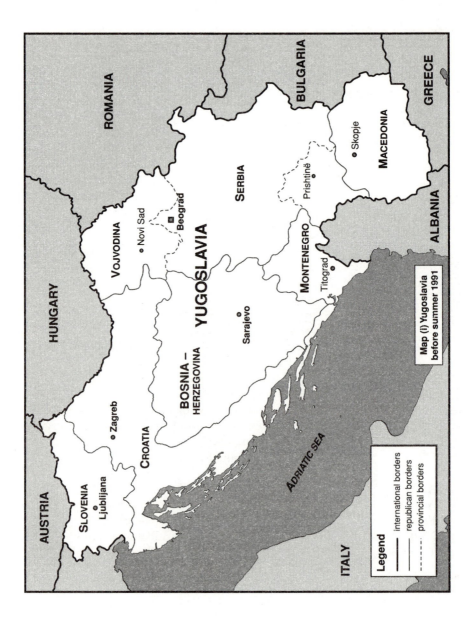

AUSTRIA

HUNGARY

ROMANIA

BULGARIA

GREECE

ALBANIA

ITALY

SLOVENIA
Ljubiljana

CROATIA
Zagreb

BOSNIA –
HERZEGOVINA
Sarajevo

VOJVODINA
Novi Sad

Beograd

YUGOSLAVIA

SERBIA

Prishtinë

Skopje

MACEDONIA

MONTENEGRO
Titograd

ADRIATIC SEA

Map (I) Yugoslavia
before summer 1991

Legend

international borders

republican borders

provincial borders

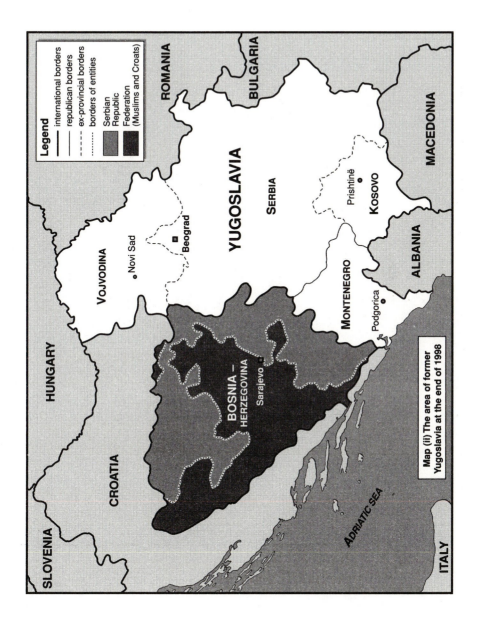

Map (ii) The area of former Yugoslavia at the end of 1998

Legend

— international borders
— republican borders
--- ex-provincial borders
···· borders of entities

Serbian Republic
Federation (Muslims and Croats)

SLOVENIA

CROATIA

HUNGARY

ROMANIA

BULGARIA

VOJVODINA

• Novi Sad

Beograd

YUGOSLAVIA

SERBIA

Prishtinë •

KOSOVO

MACEDONIA

BOSNIA – HERZEGOVINA

Sarajevo

MONTENEGRO

Podgorica •

ALBANIA

ADRIATIC SEA

ITALY

1   Fateful weaknesses after Tito's death

Tito's political legacy

On 4 May 1980, Josip Broz Tito, President of the Socialist Federated Republic of Yugoslavia, died. An American professor, who had known Tito since the Second World War, had the opportunity to ask the Yugoslav president, during his last trip to America (in 1978), what he, Tito, considered to have been his greatest political failure. Tito answered that his greatest failure was to have failed to bring together the peoples of Yugoslavia in a real community.[1]

Tito's great and widely acknowledged political accomplishments had their deficiencies and distortions. The Yugoslav marshal was a practical politician. Economics was foreign to him. Even after the introduction of the system of self-management and the socialist market economy, he always resolved such issues as arose from the tension between demands for economic freedom for the enterprises and the political monopoly of the party in favor of the latter. In this behavior, he enjoyed the support of his close collaborator, Slovene Edvard Kardelj; the latter composed numerous treatises concerning self-management and socialist democracy but never found his way out of the dilemma posed by the dual aspiration to party dictatorship and democracy.

The Law on Associated Labor, adopted in 1976 under Kardelj's influence, was supposed to transform the principles of self-management, and aimed above all at the atomization of the economic enterprises and at their control through complicated institutions. This was supposed to prevent the enterprises or banks from developing into "centers of alienated power" and to prevent their managers from becoming rivals to the party functionaries. This system, developed during almost two decades, came to be known as "contract economy" (*dogovorna ekonomija*). Its organizational principle had notched some successes in the late 1950s and 1960s, insofar as it signified a liberalization of the hitherto Stalinist planned economy. Later on it became a factor for stagnation. Kardelj's amateurish pedantry made it difficult to introduce rational management in Yugoslav enterprises or a rational investment policy.

Although not without personal magnanimity, Tito had a low opinion of political democracy. Until his last years, he could not reconcile himself to his expulsion from the Soviet camp; he saw in the "communist family" a uniquely serious form of power politics. Included in this was also the technique of playing potential opponents against each other. Tito's political style showed the stamp of his experience working in the Comintern. Indeed, he remained, to the end, a Comintern man who could not make peace with the subordination of the Comintern to the interests of the Soviet Union and Stalin. A Slovenian politician, Mitja Ribičič, who collaborated with Tito over a long period, would state in retrospect that whenever there was a rapprochement between Tito and the given leadership in Moscow, democratization and reform in Yugoslavia were set aside. That was the case in 1955 and after 1965, and in a weaker form also after 1971.[2]

Until the summit meeting of the nonaligned states in Havana in 1979, Tito's leadership among the nonaligned had been founded on the aspiration to restrain Third World countries from "capitalist error" and to lead them to the altar of world socialism. Only when Fidel Castro tried to hem his leadership role and to promote the thesis that the nonaligned were "natural allies of the socialist camp" did Tito decide on a completely independent foreign policy. Among the Western states, he basically respected only the United States, whose power he recognized even though he did not comprehend the country and its ways. Aside from that, he cherished, from the war years, a respectful affection for certain people in England. He considered the Western social democrats to be babblers and disdained them. This attitude entailed, among other things, a certain neglect of the emerging European Economic Community. .

Tito's political power system rested, until well after his death, on the "trinity" of party, police, and army. These three elements were supposed to serve to hold the federalized state structure, which Tito had reluctantly accepted, in check. This was not successful. One should take into account also the way in which the entire Yugoslav system rotated around the person of Tito. The oft-used term, "Titoist Yugoslavia" (*Titova Jugoslavija*), was supposed to encapsulate everything which characterized Yugoslavia as a state and power system, from the Partisan tradition to socialist self-management, to state federalism and to the nonaligned policy. The strong emphasis on Tito's person is partially responsible for the fact that "Yugoslav consciousness" showed itself to be utterly void, soon after Tito's death.[3] Tito's personal authority could not be replaced. This was understood even in his lifetime, as indicated in the proclamation of the principle of "collective leadership" as the mechanism for succession. But this would develop in a direction entirely contrary to the original intention.

The Communist Party of Yugoslavia, renamed the League of Communists of Yugoslavia (*Savez komunista Jugoslavije*) in 1952, retained the political monopoly until the end of the 1980s, despite all its professions of democratization. Its "leading role" was anchored also in the constitution of 1974

(Preamble VIII). In certain areas, above all in the law on emergency, the party's role was formally acknowledged. The instrument of the party's dominion was "democratic centralism". This signified that all decisions which were reached in party organs, regardless at what level, were binding on the members of these organs and for all party members concerned, even if they had voted against the decision and did not approve of it. This "Leninist" principle of democratic centralism entailed also an obligation for party members in state and communal organs, for example in enterprises, to vote and work in accordance with party decisions. For the constitutional life of the Yugoslav federal state, this signified that important decisions were always taken in the highest party organs, in the Party Presidium or in the Central Committee, and were then supposed to be binding on the state and administrative organs. In the final phase, this principle continued to work only to a limited degree, although party leaders tried to maintain this principle until the actual death of the LCY in early 1990.

Mitja Ribičič said that democratic centralism and its role already stood in contradiction to the constitution of 1963, insofar as it attempted to concede an independent role to the parliaments at both federal and republic levels. Until almost the end, democratic centralism and the ban on factions were used to exert a pressure on the republics.[4] The first great error on the part of Milovan Djilas consisted in the fact that he earnestly believed that the Sixth Party Congress of 1952, with its renaming of the party, was an honest effort in the direction of liberalization and democratization.

For all that, there were certain special developments within the Yugoslav communist party. These showed themselves already at the time of the Second World War, insofar as the Partisan struggle had to be conducted on a decentralized basis reflecting the multiethnic composition of Yugoslavia. There was an effort during the early period of democratization to revive some of these developments, which had been most marked in Slovenia, Croatia, and Macedonia. They were largely eliminated after 1945, but the party apparatchiks in the republics retained considerable organizational independence. These relatively independent apparatchiks created, on the other hand, independent power bases for the leaders in the republics and provinces.[5] The federalization of the party was in this way practically pre-programmed. It assumed practical form as a certain identity of interest between leadership and population developed, first in the economic sphere, subsequently also in the political and national domain.

After the death of Tito there developed a vacuum of authority also in the central party apparatus. To be sure, there continued to be a central party apparatus, but it retained real power only within circumscribed limits. Political life shifted to the republics and provinces (Kosovo and Vojvodina). The political life in the federal League of Communists consisted almost entirely of in-fighting between representatives of the republics in its sundry organs. Compromises were reached which often evaporated before the functionaries from the republics and provinces had even reached the Belgrade airport or railroad station to begin the trip home. Djilas committed the second great error of his life when he thought that the problem of democracy in Yugoslavia could be solved after the English prototype through the establishment of a general dualism of ruling party and opposition. There was, quite simply, no general Yugoslav framework any more which could have made possible such a path. Those politicians who tried to make their careers in the central apparatus, such as Slovene Stane Dolanc or certain functionaries from Croatia, ended up shipwrecked.

The central organs of the party were the Central Committee, with about 110 to 120 members, and the Party Presidium, with 23 members at the end. The members of both organs were elected in the republics and provinces. The Central Committee had a somewhat liberal face in the last phase of Yugoslavia but could not really determine policy. The Presidium consisted of three members from each republic and two from each province, along with the party chiefs of the federal units ex officio. A representative of the army leadership completed the composition. The principle of consensus, anchored on the state level in the federal constitution of 1974, did not hold in the party organs. The party decided by majority vote. Equally important was the constant rotation of cadres, a principle introduced in the name of collective leadership and more marked in federal organs than in the republics. For an elective party post, the usual mandate was four years, but for the chairs of the party and also in the state organs, a one-year mandate was customary.

The police, the second pillar of the regime, found itself largely under the control of republic and provincial party leaderships after Tito's death. This was not true merely of the ordinary police, but also of the political police, generally called UDBa (short for *Uprava Državne Bezbednosti*, or Administration of State Security). This development began in 1966 with the overthrow of Security Chief Aleksandar Ranković. To be sure, there continued to be a federal UDBa, but it occupied itself above all with relations with abroad and with foreigners. Serbs predominated in its ranks; the federal apparatus of UDBa maintained relations with the police apparatchiks of other communist states and, up to a point, with international terrorists.

The decentralization of the political police did not improve the situation, but made the police dependent upon concrete relationships in the individual republics and provinces. The entire police apparatus was oriented to the maintenance of communist rule and saw in the West the chief enemy. The police moved especially repressively in Croatia, as part of the consequences of 1971. People were imprisoned there for singing patriotic Croatian songs, while similar Serbian songs had long belonged to the repertoire of coffee-house orchestras in Belgrade. The situation in Bosnia-Herzegovina was even worse. In that republic, authorities sought a solution by fighting with equal brutality all national stirrings among any of the three peoples living in the republics. *Gastarbeiter* living abroad saw themselves exposed to especial repression. They were interrogated when they returned home on visits and were maltreated in other ways. Police authorities conducted active terror against emigrants.

Tito's real darling was the army, officially named the Yugoslav People's Army (*Jugoslovenska Narodna Armija*, or JNA). Tito accorded it the status of a state within a state. The Slovene Mitja Ribičič believed that the favoritism which Tito displayed toward his army, which he bound in obligation to himself personally and whose officers he overwhelmed with privileges, was the most evil and most grave legacy of Tito's dominion. It had the consequence that the army, i.e., its leadership, considered itself a kind of collective successor to Tito and viewed socialism and the unified Yugoslav state as the prerequisite for its own existence. The problem was sharpened by the fact that the officer corps was not only communist and centralist in orientation, but also predominantly Serbian and Montenegrin (60 per cent of the officer corps consisted of Serbs and Montenegrins).[6] These two factors began to become mixed in the final phase of Yugoslavia. Only at the highest command posts was a certain minimum of national parity maintained.

The army was not only a military but also a political and economic factor and even served as a surrogate police force. Mitja Ribičič, who himself spent time in the police apparatus but who later developed into a reform-oriented politician, reported from his own experience that as the police developed into instruments of republic leaderships, the army developed its counter-espionage service *(Kontraobaveštajna Služba,* or KOS) as its own political police, with the assignment of keeping an eye on the political forces of the republics and provinces.[7] Many conflicts between individual republic leaderships and the Army were, in fact, conflicts with KOS. As important was the fact that the army had control of a considerable arms industry which, in the late 1980s, totalled some 56 enterprises, with about 70,000 employees. Four-fifths of these enterprises lay in Bosnia-Herzegovina. As long as weaponry constituted an important part of Yugoslavia's exports – above all to nonaligned states – this factor strengthened the political weight of the Army, especially where the budget was concerned. Later, however, when the relaxation of tensions resulted in a decline in arms exports, this became a debit.

It was difficult to oppose the financial demands of the army, which had long insisted on obtaining 6 per cent of the national income. Ribičič considered it a great success that, between 1969 and 1972, he was able to obtain the abolition, in spite of Tito's opposition, of the so-called extraordinary state budget. Another politician from Slovenia, Janko Smole, considered it a great success that he was able to reduce the army's budget in 1970 to 5.6 per cent of the national income.[8]

The Soviet invasion of Czechoslovakia in 1968 provided a certain validation of the army's importance, but, on the other hand, provoked reflections on the tradition of the Partisan war and on the concept of people's defense, embodied mainly in the so-called Territorial Defense Forces *(Teritorijalna Obrana* in Serbo-Croatian; *Teritorialna Obramba* in Slovenian). Ribičič said that this concept was not Tito's idea, but had to be wrested out of him. The fear that these reserve units would develop into instruments of power of the republics was on the minds of army leaders from the start. In reality, the republic leaderships did not have complete control over the Territorial Defense Forces or over their weapons, and especially not over any heavy weaponry. But the organization was, strictly speaking, subordinate to the republics.

The legal basis for the functioning of Yugoslavia as a state in the late- and post-Tito era was the new constitution adopted in 1974. Viewed juristically, it was a pastiche of imprecisions and contradictions. Its most important "father", Edvard Kardelj, had conceived it chiefly as an ideological tract concerning self-management. Viewed politically, it was of great significance, for it attempted to constitute Yugoslavia as a federal state with democratic outlines, as it would have functioned if ever the political monopoly of the communist party had been cast aside. Its core element was the new definition of the republics and provinces as constituent units of the joint state. The constitution of 1974 pointed rather unambiguously also in the direction of confederation; it constituted Yugoslavia, as one of its critics remarked, as a kind of midpoint between federation and confederation, as a "Yugoslav exception".[9]

In contrast to the earlier constitutions, the constitution of 1974 defined the republics explicitly as states (Article 3) and made them into independent agents of political decision-making, who could not be outvoted. Both of the provinces in union with the Republic of Serbia – Kosovo and Vojvodina – were, indeed, not defined as states, but were given equality with the republics at the level of the common state. Both houses of the Yugoslav Federal Assembly *(Skupština SFRJ-e)* – the Federal Chamber *(Savezno veće)* and the Chamber of Republics and Provinces *(Veće republika i pokrajina)* – were in fact bodies representing the republics and provinces; it is of note that the Federal Chamber did not provide a direct representation of the citizens. The members of both houses of the Federal Assembly were appointed by the parliaments of the republics or provinces or by other republic organs.

Legislative procedure and the procedure in all important affairs were based on the principle of consensus among the republics and provinces. This signifies, formulated in reverse, that every republic or province enjoyed a veto right in practically all affairs of any importance. Even for the Federal Chamber, for which majority rule had been foreseen, Article 294[10] stipulated in all matters "of general interest for a republic or province or for the equality of peoples and nations" a special procedure which, for all practical purposes, provided a veto right for the republics and provinces. The Chamber of Republics and Provinces, even in formal terms, expressly represented the parliaments of the republics and provinces, and in its work it observed the principles of consensus and the narrowing of differences (*uskladjivanje stavova*, literally, the harmonization of viewpoints) between the republics and provinces. In all affairs of importance, the Federal Chamber and the Chamber of Republics and Provinces were given equal power. The principle of consensus was moderated solely by the provision for the possibility of having resort to emergency measures, on which the state presidency essentially had the last word.

The political leadership organ of the common state was the presidency (*Predsedništvo SFRJ*), to which each republic and each province sent a deputy. As long as Tito lived, he held the post of President of the Republic; afterwards, the appropriate articles of the Constitution automatically went out of force. The state presidency was supposed to exercise collective authority over the army. According to Article 330 of the Constitution, the state presidency should have likewise operated in accordance with the principle of consensus, but in the same article, it is stated that the presidency "decides" in accord with standing orders. These were issued at a time when there was not yet much trace of democracy; the state presidency itself had decided on them, so to speak, for internal use.

The protocols of the sessions were never turned over to the deputies or even to the republics. Procedures stipulated that consensus was required on certain specified subjects, while a simple or qualified majority vote could suffice on other questions. When Borisav Jović, as representative of Serbia, as will be shown, claimed in mid-May 1991 that the state presidency did not need to decide by consensus, he was pitting himself simultaneously against both the constitution and the procedural rules. The sequence in which the office of the President of the Presidency was to be filled by the representatives of individual republics and provinces, in accordance with Article 327, was laid down only in the procedural rules.[11] This would later become as much a problem as the fact that only the President of the Presidency could convene sessions. He had certain operative authorization in connection with the execution of decisions of an often thoroughly vague nature which had been taken by the presidency. This concerned also questions related to the deployment of the army. For military affairs, a council for national defense was attached to the presidency, but its competence was not clearly regulated. It was possible to draw in other personalities to sessions of the presidency, such as the presidents of the republics or high-ranking military figures. These persons did not enjoy a vote in the presidency's deliberations, however.

It may seem noteworthy that this partly federal, partly confederal constitution was adopted in Yugoslavia in 1974, just three years after the mass movement in Croatia, which had been demanding just such provisions, had been forcefully suppressed. One can only explain this by observing that Tito himself had come to the conclusion that it was necessary to make some concessions to the strengthened national consciousness of the peoples of Yugoslavia. On the other hand, however, he was, as already mentioned, convinced that the surviving central institutions, i.e., party and army, together with his own personal prestige, would suffice to provide a counterweight to state federalism. One should by no means overestimate Tito's federal engagement, according to Mitja Ribičič, to whom the constitution of 1974 did not seem, in spite of everything, sufficiently federal.[12]

When the constitution was discussed and came into force, there was no big dispute about its content, because at that time the Yugoslav system still functioned in tune with Tito's thinking. The problems began as soon as the constitution took on life, when its content was taken seriously, and one began, even within the party, to take its individual stipulations seriously. In the wink of an eye certain circles began to feel uncomfortable with the notion of a "communist nomocracy". The military took a leading role in this criticism. For General Veljko Kadijević, the Defense Minister at the time of Yugoslavia's collapse, the constitution of 1974 was only the final consequence of a decision taken by Tito and Kardelj as early as 1962 to move the system in the direction of federalism and self-management; with that decision, in his view, the seeds of all the evils which would later bedevil Yugoslavia had been sown.[13]

There is no denying that the constitution of 1974 made great concessions to the independence of the republics and provinces. Later, when people took the constitution seriously, there were even federalist-oriented politicians who discovered that certain provisions were in need of revision in the interest of a better functioning of the joint state.[14] The argument that the state needed to function better was soon misused by Serb hegemonists and centralists, however; they demanded an "effective federation", when what they really meant was a centralized state dominated, if possible, by the Serbs. Despite the proclaimed statehood of the republics, the constitution did not lay down a procedure for secession. Only in the preamble was there a mention of the Leninistically-inspired "right of separation", assured not to the republics, but to the peoples of Yugoslavia. A procedure for exercising this supposed right was not stipulated either. Republic boundaries coincided with demographic distribution only in the case of Slovenia.

For the Republic of Serbia, there was the special problem of the autonomous provinces of Kosovo and Vojvodina, which existed within Serbia's boundaries. In principle these provinces had existed since the end of the Second World War, but only the constitution of 1974 gave them the status of nearly equal partners in federal administration. Their representatives, whether in the federal state organs or in the party, voted independently of those from the Republic of Serbia. Nevertheless, the republics were territorial parts of the Republic of Serbia; they participated in the legislative process at the republic level, where they even enjoyed the right of veto, while on the other hand the authority of the republic organs in the affairs of the two provinces was curtailed. The autonomous province of Kosovo had been established because the Albanians constituted a majority there. Vojvodina, on the other hand, had a Serbian majority, but also a tangible Hungarian minority; the Serbs of Vojvodina upheld an autonomist tradition dating back to Austro-Hungarian times. It may be conceded that the constitutional and juridical situation for Serbia was uncomfortable and even illogical. The Serbian leadership of that time had assembled its reservations in 1977 in a so-called *Blue Book* but had not offered any essential resistance to the new constitution. One cannot say that the Republic of Serbia would have lost the character of a state because of the provinces, though this would later be claimed by Serbian politicians. There would have been a number of possibilities for a peaceful solution of the problems of the provinces, but the Serbian government would have nothing to do with any of them. Kosovo at least would never have declined to be granted the status of a republic. Instead, the demand for republic status was criminalized by Serbs and portrayed as "damaging to the integrity of Yugoslavia".

Until the very end, the concept of *nationality (narodnost)*, unclear in the Yugoslav constitutional system, remained in contrast to the concept of *people (narod)*. In the constitution of 1974, there was no indication what the difference is between a *people* and a *nationality*. Unofficially, *peoples* were understood to be ethnic formations whose ethnic centers lay within the boundaries of Yugoslavia, while *nationalities* had their ethnic centers outside Yugoslavia. With regard to Kosovo and the Albanians, there was a glaring discrepancy. In 1981, there were more than 1.7 million Albanians living in Yugoslavia, but only about 570,000 Montenegrins and 1.3 million Macedonians. In spite of that, the Albanians were considered a "nationality", while the others were classified as "peoples" and therefore endowed with correspondingly greater rights.

The government (or administration), officially the Federal Executive Council (*Savezno Izvršno Veće*), had a weak position in the constitutional system. In practical terms, its authority as a body was limited to economic policy. (The ministries for Defense, Foreign and Internal Affairs were more or less directly subordinate to the state presidency.) Neither the functionaries of the state presidency nor officials in party organs were eager to take responsibility for overseeing the economy. Tito's natural antipathy toward the economy continued under the collective leadership. The last prime minister, Ante Marković, on the other hand, stubbornly refused to get involved in any political problem outside the economy. In view of the circumscribed role of the government and its chief in the Yugoslav system, it was strange that Western diplomacy and politics placed so much stock in Prime Minister Marković.

All in all, the constitution of 1974 was undoubtedly in accord with the prevailing views of that time and also fulfilled the wish of the Yugoslav nations to lead their own national, political, and even economic existence within the common state. It was unrealistic to insist, as the Serbs would

later do, that the constitution of 1974 could not lay claim to any legitimacy, because it was, in the first place, a "communist thing" and because
it had, secondly, come about in an "undemocratic way". If the constitution had been born in entirely free circumstances, it would have ended
up, without any doubt, even more federal, anti-centralist, and democratic.
The constitution regulated above all the position of the member states in
a positive sense, but devoted less attention to the individual rights of the
citizens. Even so, it could have provided the foundation for the guaranteed further existence of the Yugoslav state in conformity with the wishes
of the majority of its peoples and in conformity with the objective, admittedly complex national relationships. The presupposition for its success
would have been that those concerned would have adhered to and defended
the constitution.

The opposition to economic and political reform

When Tito died, Yugoslavia found itself already in a serious economic
crisis. The economy labored under a trade deficit and a deficit in the
balance of payments, as well as a rapidly growing foreign debt. In 1979,
the deficit in the balance of payments, counting receipts from tourism and
remittances from *Gastarbeiter*, came to $3.6 billion; the foreign debt reached
$15 billion in early 1980 and its servicing ate up 15 per cent of all foreign
currency earnings.[15] The inflation rate came to 20 per cent per year.

In Yugoslavia, the question would always be raised later why the country,
which in the 1960s had experienced considerable prosperity, could find
itself in a crisis of that kind in the second half of the 1970s. The answer
may well be that after the oil crisis of 1973, the authorities refused to
accept the consequences of that crisis and to pass them on to the population. Instead, they went on as if nothing had happened; they refused to
introduce effective reform steps and, instead, settled the balance of
payments deficit and the investment deficit with foreign credits. This situation went so far that, under the pretext that one now had a convertible
dinar, foreign credits in foreign currency were simply converted into dinars
and were used to cover current expenses. The price of oil was, for political reasons, left as it was before the crisis, although, as a result of the
price hikes, oil finished by accounting for one-third of Yugoslavia's outlays
for imports.

In 1985, the Belgrade magazine *NIN* published a revealing and much-
noted article about the practice of debt accumulation.[16] In the course of
things, the magazine asked, how could a Yugoslav debt of $5.7 billion in
1975 have risen to $19.2 billion by the end of 1981? The answer was
ready: the so-called social plan for the period 1976–80 had been stitched
together from the sundry and often unrealistic demands of the republics
and provinces. Because the federation had little money on hand at that
time, it simply covered the deficit by taking out foreign loans. In this way,

some $11.5 billion in debt were acquired, which, as a result of changes in the rate of exchange, grew to $13.5 billion.

As Yugoslavia struggled toward a convertible dinar, it had to face a second source of trouble. This lay in the system. In the 1960s, enterprises operating under the system of workers' self-management had been able to share in the general economic boom in the West. Now, however, after 1973, in spite of massive export subsidies, they could no longer keep pace. Their costs for "social management", i.e., for all the complicated taxes which had to be paid not only to the state and agencies of social insurance but also to support the mostly purposeless structures of self-management, were simply too high. This drove up the prices excessively, especially of industrial products, whether for the domestic market or for export. Thus Yugoslavia was unable to derive any advantages from its low level of salaries. As a result, calls for comprehensive reform grew steadily louder after 1981.

Here the post-Tito leadership failed seriously for the first time. There were, of course, functionaries who recognized the necessity of reforms. Among their number was Kiro Gligorov, later to become President of the independent Republic of Macedonia, who was relieved of all his duties in 1978.[17] By and large, however, it was peripheral figures in the system, such as certain more or less independent economics professors, like Branko Horvat in Zagreb or Alexandar Bajt in Ljubljana, who criticized the regime's fear of liberalization and privatization and demanded change.

But it soon became clear that the agents of the political system were not prepared to undertake reforms in the direction of the liberalization of the economic system. Responsible persons in the party attempted, on the contrary, to renounce any responsibility for economic policy and to attribute all negative developments to the organs of workers' self-management or to the state functions.[18]

This behavior was sharply expressed, in particular, at the Twelfth Party Congress in June 1982, the first such congress since Tito's death, when the long-range program of economic stabilization, drawn up by an expert commission headed by Sergej Kraigher, came up for discussion. Despite the high credentials of the commission, its findings and recommendations were treated in a patronizing fashion by both the party presidium and the state presidency. Ribičič, who was elected chair of the federal party organization at this congress, recalls the debates staged on that occasion and concedes that the decision to turn the matter over to the state presidency was connected with the party's unwillingness to take responsibility for economic policy. The congress merely adopted a minor and very lukewarm resolution on economic policy, straining at a compromise.[19]

The regime's response to calls for liberal reforms was largely limited to purely technical measures and efforts to obtain new foreign credits. At the beginning of June 1980, the dinar was devalued by 30 per cent. The consequent decline in imports led, in the course of the summer, to serious problems in the supplies of coffee, detergent, soap, oil, and other products; the supply bottleneck was only intensified by the administratively decreed price freeze in the domestic market. The Yugoslav population received the impression that the relatively modest gains which they had hammered out in the course of the preceding two decades might now be retracted.

The reactions of Western regimes, banks, and international finance institutions to the requests for new credits were altogether positive. The Federal Republic of Germany, too, responded favorably, and soon a credit package of DM 1.4 billion was under discussion; it was approved on the occasion of a visit on the part of Prime Minister Veselin Djuranović to Bonn in February 1981. In retrospect, it seems almost spooky how readily the Western governments and the world of finance satisfied the repeated financial requests of the Yugoslav government, without paying any attention to the overall situation in the country or, for the most part, even to the concrete uses to be made of the funds extended. From the German credit package alone, DM 600 million were available without restrictions of any kind. Had the banks taken their usual care, nothing of the sort would have happened. Certainly, general credits for the communist states were in the spirit of the times. Wherever a state was prepared to guarantee repayment, that was, at the time, considered to provide nearly 100 per cent security.

Yugoslavia profited at the time from the frankly romantic affection which it enjoyed in the West. Neither the German nor any other government thought to demand of Yugoslavia any kind of reciprocation or commitment to specific behavior. The World Bank even supported quite deliberately the socialist sector, especially in the agricultural sphere, with its credits.[20] The new credits contracted in the period 1980/81 worked merely to further increase the foreign debts of the country, without bettering the economy in any way.[21]

The absolute refusal of the regime to set reforms in motion resulted in a certain resignation on the part of economists to the continued reliance on exclusively technical measures. Among these "technical measures", the manipulation of the rate of exchange had a prominent place. But recourse to this measure inevitably compromised the policy of maintaining a stable dinar; in consequence, the rate of inflation became ever greater. In summer 1981, matters reached the point where exports to the West were strongly curtailed and price controls became necessary to deal with the waxing inflation. The swollen federal budget contributed ever more powerfully to this situation. Individual republics grasped for measures of self-protection, endeavoring to set up their own hard currency accounts and confronting the difficulties experienced by local enterprises by encouraging their banks to provide "transition credits".

Necessity inspired Belgrade's bureaucrats to become inventive. In order to tax the flow of hard currency, they developed for the first time, in the second half of 1981, the idea of a toll for every border crossing. According to an early draft, each Yugoslav citizen would have had to pay a sum of 1,500 dinars (at that time, around DM 100) upon departure. This draft was indignantly rejected by the western republics, especially Slovenia. In Ljubljana, the border with Italy and Austria was proudly hailed as "Europe's most open border", in Tito's phrase. Slovenia did not want to let itself be isolated.[22] Belgrade authorities countered the move towards openness, since the Yugoslav National Bank was skeptical about another devaluation, many goods were cheaper in neighboring countries and many Yugoslavs were availing themselves of these favorable terms to make shopping trips across the border. At the end of October, new regulations concerning hard currency and customs came into effect, which toughened conditions for border tariffs. At the borders, people had to wait for hours on end. This affected, above all, the *Gastarbeiter;* one even had the impression that this had been consciously anticipated.

In early 1982, Croat Milka Planinc was expected to assume the prime ministership from the outgoing Montenegrin, Djuranović. She put together a new governmental team in the course of weeks of consultations, selecting persons from whom expert economic policy could be expected. In the economic departments, Slovenes were in the majority. At the same time, Slovene Stane Dolanc became Minister of the Interior, while Admiral Branko Mamula took over as Defense Minister from General Nikola Ljubičić, who was transferred to the Serbian state presidency. A new currency law established that 16 per cent of all hard currency remittances had to be deposited in a special account at the National Bank, in order to cover the obligations of the federation. This currency law reflected the optimistic mood of the time; it seemed to have realized the interpretation that the overcoming of the crisis was the common concern of the whole country. Since Slovenes were strongly represented in the new government, Slovenes too pinned their hopes on federal policy.[23]

In addition, the state presidency tasked the Kraigher Commission to work out a long-range program of economic stabilization. Macedonian Kiro Gligorov was the chair of the most important subgroup. The program was completed in two parts in July and August 1983. It advocated reforms, and acknowledged the market and the need for a realistic exchange rate; it demanded the free development of private farmlands and small enterprises as well as the reduction in the state's portion of the social product, a system of pay based on performance, and a better tax system.[24] The recommendations of the Kraigher Commission were reasonable and appropriate, even if it was stated that they should be carried out inside the existing socialist system.

But nothing came of the anticipated "new beginning". The main reason for this is that the Planinc administration was pressed from the beginning by acute problems and was seduced into solving them with administrative remedies rather than through a thorough liberalization. With this, the new administration designed relations from which there was no easy escape. Milka Planinc herself was closely linked with the traditional mentality of the system's functionaries. She had been installed as party chief in Croatia in late 1971, after the crushing of the "Croatian spring", and tried, on the occasion of being appointed prime minister, to bring some outspokenly dogmatic politicians into high positions. From the beginning, the long-term stabilization program of summer 1983 came up against the opposition of dogmatic politicians. Among these, Branko Mikulić, a Bosnian Croat and representative of Bosnia-Herzegovina in the state presidency, would soon become prominent.

In autumn 1982, Yugoslavia's continued financial solvency came into question for the first time, necessitating a moratorium on repayment of the Yugoslav debt. The tourist season had been poor. The government introduced a price freeze, in hopes of limiting inflation to 30 per cent. There was even talk of a general public loan and a wage freeze. Once again, there were supply problems, this time above all for gasoline. This showed that the problems were not merely the product of a shortage of currency, but also the result of disturbances in the traffic between enterprises in different republics.

In mid-October 1982, the government took a fateful step, which for the first time seriously shook people's feeling of solidarity with the federal state, especially in Slovenia. After a long discussion, the Yugoslav Assembly decided that, in the future, every Yugoslav who wanted to make a private trip abroad had to deposit 5,000 dinars in the bank for the period of a year for the first trip, and 2,000 dinars for each additional trip within the given calendar year. The amount corresponded to the average monthly income. In addition, certain limitations were introduced concerning the access by private citizens to their hard currency accounts, which had reached a value of about $9 billion, and which the Yugoslav banks had largely mortgaged for foreign credits. There were new customs restrictions aimed above all at Yugoslav *Gastarbeiter*. On All Souls' Day 1982, the border crossing points were, within a matter of hours, littered with television sets and washing machines – discarded by returning *Gastarbeiter* who were unable to pay the import duties.

A visit to Slovenia a short while later revealed an angry mood. Certainly, the Slovenian ministers in Belgrade and the Slovenian deputies had themselves approved of these federal measures, but this did not earn them any prestige back home. High functionaries in Ljubljana now admitted that they had not been clear about the consequences of these measures; they had simply gone along with the new laws out of solidarity and a feeling of duty. Now, however, confronted with the practical consequences of these measures, they had the feeling of having fallen into a "Balkan trap". Slovenia was now, for all practical purposes, cut off from its Western neighbors. The "customs raid" against the *Gastarbeiter* was due to a mistake; three days later, the Ministry of Foreign Trade in Belgrade, headed by

Serb Milenko Bojanić, had to allow that most of the *Gastarbeiter* would have been allowed to bring their confiscated goods into the country under normal procedures.[25] The deposit for the right to cross the border lost its edge when inflation drove down the value of the dinar, but it was only finally abolished at the end of 1984.

The political débâcle was emphasized when the Republic of Croatia also felt itself affected by the economic measures. The Zagreb leadership of that day had an anti-national and politically reactionary orientation, but in economic matters it had to take into account the interests of the republic. Croatia had not only absorbed a large part of the foreign credits in order to build up its tourist industry, but had also taken out short-term loans abroad, again chiefly for investment in the tourist sector.[26] In consequence of all the restrictions, *Gastarbeiter* held back remittances to a significant extent, hurting Croatia's economy. Yugoslav Finance Minister Jože Florijančič explained that the obstructive measures of autumn 1982 had reduced the outflow of cash by a billion dollars, but the country lost almost as much by reduced remittances from *Gastarbeiter* abroad.

In the following period, nothing much changed. Outlays to service the debt had long ago reached the critical threshold of 25 per cent of hard currency intake; with such a ratio it was practically inconceivable that the economy could once more be restored to health. Payments and interest per year amounted to more than $5 billion, against overall exports which brought in between $10 and $15 billion. Since this was too much, Yugoslavia tried, from 1984 onwards, to reach an agreement with the World Bank and its creditors on a long-term regulation of its debts, in practice a permanent moratorium, but found little enthusiasm for this idea.[27] On the contrary, in March 1984, the International Monetary Fund energetically demanded, for the first time, the adoption of serious reforms as a precondition for a new agreement on debts. At first, some Yugoslav functionaries sat on their high horses: Yugoslavia, so they said, would not permit any "interference" in its internal system. But a little while later, they gave in, and in March 1984, important steps in the direction of a market economy were taken in execution of the debt conversion agreement, such as the elimination of price controls, a restoration of hard currency reserves, and a return to a free exchange rate, even if this should once more stimulate inflation. Even the government was satisfied; the International Monetary Fund had helped to overcome the resistance of dogmatic politicians.[28]

Resistance to reform was ever more clearly localized and personalized. One center of resistance was Zagreb, where ideological arguments could be heard. In July 1984, a member of the Croatian leadership, Milutin Baltić, for example, characterized the endeavor to revise Kardelj's 1976 Law on Associated Labor, as "counterrevolutionary".[29] That law, which had thoroughly atomized the Yugoslav enterprises, was for some functionaries an especially important instrument for the preservation of their power. Another center of dogmatism was Bosnia-Herzegovina. Certain large industrial concerns, including arms industries, were located there. In this republic, neither "atomization" nor self-management had been really introduced; instead, a state-run economy prevailed. The chief exponent of this system was Branko Mikulić, who would assume the office of Prime Minister in 1986.

Alexandar Bajt, who worked as adviser in the Planinc administration, held that during 1985, a stabilization of economic relationships had slowly begun and that, had the Planinc administration been allowed to continue its program, it might with time have restored the system to health. After the stabilization of debts and an improvement in exports, it might have been possible to get a grip on the inflation (then running at 60 per cent per year) and carry out some reforms. But then Mikulić, at the time Bosnia's representative in the state presidency, entered the scene. Exploiting his prestige as the chief organizer of the 1984 Winter Olympic games in Sarajevo and supported by Deputy Prime Minister Janez Zemljarič (from Slovenia), he endeavored to thwart any further movement of the regime in the direction of a market economy and reform. The state presidency and party presidium aligned themselves with Mikulić. Milka Planinc wanted, as a result, to resign in October 1985, but her resignation was not accepted.[30]

Interest was an especially difficult question. The International Monetary Fund set great store, in all its negotiations, on the real interest rates, which should exceed the rate of inflation. However, this was hardly realizable, because under the existing system, the Yugoslav enterprises had to work almost exclusively with capital assigned to them in the form of loans on interest. The interest burden was thus ruinous for them; and the greater the inflation became, the worse the problem became. It was not entirely without reason that Mikulić, upon assuming the prime ministership in May 1986, wanted above all to shake off the "interest servitude" of the International Monetary Fund.

The Planinc administration was not entirely inactive during 1985. One of its principal efforts related to a new law on hard currency, which had a centralist inspiration and which would later prove to be an essential element in the process of decay of Yugoslavia. The proposal foresaw that the enterprises would again sell the largest part of their earned hard currency to the National Bank, as they had before 1976, and buy hard currency back, no longer according to administrative procedures, however, but according to supply and demand. The new law did not allow any room for the republics to retain portions of their own hard currency earnings. There was a lot of political pressure in Croatia and Slovenia on this account, parallel with attempts to revise the constitution along centralist lines. As to why the Slovenes softened their position on the question of hard currency retention, in spite of their veto right, I was told in Ljubljana that it was not easy and, besides, not always safe for Slovenes to stand alone and play the opposition in isolation.

The Slovenian politicians saw themselves confronted with a dilemma, because they had to concede that as long as Yugoslavia had to function as a unified state, there had to be a unified economic policy. The interference of the republics, according to Bajt, could, under the circumstances, only do damage. As it did so often, the Belgrade administration gave the new currency law a much tougher interpretation than had been anticipated. The Yugoslav National Bank, which now received all hard currency in its hands, hesitated to settle Slovenian obligations with foreign countries. Earlier, Slovenian enterprises had received short-term or long-term credits from time to time, because there was confidence in the republic or at least in its biggest bank, Ljubljanska Banka. This factor now disappeared. Besides, it turned out that, as a result of the general shortage of hard currency and the tendency of the Yugoslav National Bank to give Serbian enterprises preferential treatment, the "purchase" of hard currency to cover import needs became, especially for Croatian and Slovenian enterprises, an administrative matter, rather than a question of supply and demand.[31]

As Mikulić took over the administration in May 1986, he had little good to say in his program about the activity of his predecessor. The gross social product had risen 2 per cent since 1982, while exports were 2 per cent lower than in 1982.[32] The new prime minister did not want to say how much the real income of the population had declined in the preceding period; estimates at the time pegged the decline at 25–30 per cent. In other respects, the new program revealed the expected bias toward administrative measures. Yugoslavs were traveling abroad too much, said Mikulić.

Planinc had already said, in the last phase of her administration, that the government could only be as good as it was allowed to be. By that she was referring, in the first place, to the increasing weight of the republics.[33] Mikulić took up this theme in his cabinet address, in spite of the adoption of the law on hard currency, and believed that it would be ever more difficult to synchronize the views of the republics and provinces. This would lead, or so he said, to the depreciation of the federal organs. All in all, his cabinet address offered few new ideas. His assumption of office can be seen as the beginning of the end of all efforts to reform the system.

In general, the outbreak of unrest in the largely Albanian province of Kosovo in spring 1981 is considered the beginning of the Yugoslav existential crisis. In retrospect, one may attribute to the then less noticed confrontations in which the communist regime became entangled in Croatia soon after Tito's death considerable blame for the fate of the common state. In Croatia, it was almost clearer than in Kosovo how the officials provoked conflicts and how they repudiated any democratic opening. There was little comprehension in the West, at that time, just how serious and potentially explosive the situation in Croatia was. Even in liberal circles in the West, there was a certain reserve towards Croatia. In most regions of Yugoslavia "dissidents" were persecuted, in Croatia and Kosovo these being "nationalists" – or so the mass media in Western Europe and America reported.

The suppression of the nationally accented "Croatian spring" in 1971 had ushered in an atmosphere of repression in Croatia, in which everything national, insofar as it was Croatian, was a priori treated with suspicion. More than a dozen of the spiritual leaders of the alleged "mass movement", excluding the demoted leaders of the Croatian communist party, were given prison terms. According to statements by Croatian dissidents, about 32,000 persons were "persecuted, discriminated against, or harassed", mostly through the loss of their jobs. Officially, it was conceded that criminal procedures were introduced against 1,156 persons.[34]

The situation in Croatia became aggravated by the fact that Serb members of the new leadership, Dušan Dragosavac and especially Milutin Baltić, took the lead in pushing for further repression. The Zagreb daily, *Vjesnik*, which they controlled, demonized Djilas and oppositionists in general as "maggots". To be sure, the Croatian party leaders of Croatian ethnicity – Jure Bilić, Josip Vrhovec, and even Milka Planinc – played their parts in this understanding of "democracy", but among the Serbs, there was often, in addition, an element of national extortion present, tending to accuse the entire Croatian nation of collective guilt and to characterize Croatian national feeling as "fascistoid".[35]

A typical example was the issue of the steadily magnified estimates of the number of victims in the *Ustaša* concentration camp at Jasenovac during the Second World War. In the immediate post-war period, official estimates in Zagreb had referred to 50,000 to 70,000 victims, but later the figure was pumped up without any appropriate documentation. Historians in Zagreb who opposed this revisionism were reprimanded. In the 1982 edition of Tito's works, 800,000 persons were said to have died at Jasenovac, and soon afterwards, a Serbian general claimed that more than a million persons had lost their lives at the camp. Meanwhile, the official figure provided by the Yugoslav government of the number of overall casualties in the Second World War remained constant at 1.7 million.[36]

The Serbian element in the Republic of Croatia was, on account of developments in the Second World War, significantly more strongly bound to the communist regime than were the Croats. In the Serb-inhabited western Krajina, Tito had found important, possibly decisive sources of support for the war effort, as a result of the persecutions experienced by Croatian Serbs beginning in 1941 at the hands of the *Ustaše*. In the entire communist era, the Serbs of Croatia, who comprised 14 per cent of the population, represented 30 per cent of the communist party members in the republic. Serb overrepresentation in the Croatian police force was even more blatant: up to 60 per cent of police in Croatia, it was said, were Serbs, and the figure was about the same in the political police.[37] But Serbs pointed out that the communist leaders of Croatian nationality gladly used the Serbs as helpmates, in order to defend their power positions.

Besides, the high representation of Serbs in the police force was also a consequence of the lower level of economic development in the Serb-inhabited districts.

The first new criminal proceedings initiated after Tito's death came in August 1980, and involved Franjo Tudjman, a former partisan soldier, retired general, and historian, later to be elected President of Croatia, and novelist Vlado Gotovac, chief editor of the weekly *Hrvatski tjednik* at the time of the "Croatian spring" and one of the chief ideologues of the "mass movement". Both had already been condemned after 1971, but after their release from prison, they came forward time and again with public declarations, in which they criticized the injury done to Croatia and the lack of democracy. The authors of the repressive course in Zagreb felt an especial rancour toward Tudjman. They had already had the intention in 1971 of putting him up as the principal defendant in a show trial against the "Croatian spring", but Tito had forbidden this.[38] Now Tito was dead and the intriguers in Zagreb wanted to avenge their earlier setback.

The trials began only in the first half of 1981. Tudjman received three years in prison, Gotovac was given two years. At the same time, student Dobroslav Paraga, later a leader of the nationalist Croatian Party of the Right, was also sent to prison. He received a three-year prison sentence, because he had circulated among intellectuals a petition for greater freedom of discussion. In September 1981, an especially questionable trial handed down an 11-year prison sentence to opposition politician and intellectual Marko Veselica. This sentence was considered outrageous even in communist circles and was reduced by a superior court.[39]

The political intrigues were capped with a campaign against the Catholic Church. The Church in Croatia was the only institution after 1971 which expressed the national feeling of Croats. It had become, even more, the national embodiment of Croatianhood. Later, after the Church had stabilized its strength on this basis, it expanded its scope of activity into impressive mass meetings always connected with the national idea. The Archbishop of Zagreb and chair of the Yugoslav Bishops' Conference, Franjo Cardinal Kuharić, was resolved, from the beginning, that in the contemporary atmosphere of anti-Croat agitation and general repression, the Church could not allow itself to be sucked into any kind of compromise. That earned him the usual criticism from short-sighted Western diplomats in Belgrade, but his strategy would prove correct. In his Christmas sermon of 1980, he openly took the side of political prisoners.

The conflict between Church and state escalated at the end of January 1981, when Jakov Blažević, the formal state president of Croatia, on the occasion of the publication of his reminiscences, fired off some verbal volleys against Alojzije Stepinac, the former Archbishop of Zagreb, who had been condemned in 1946 and who had died in 1960, exiled in his village. Blažević had been the prosecutor in Stepinac's trial and considered it necessary to justify his conduct in that trial. The attacks brought this issue once more into the political foreground. Blažević's attacks provoked sharp protests from the Church. Blažević finally had to concede that his line in the court had been rather exactly prescribed for him.[40]

As Archbishop of Zagreb and *de facto* primate of the Catholic Church in Croatia during the Second World War, Stepinac had a difficult, nearly impossible assignment. It is historically documented that the majority of Croats, including Stepinac, welcomed the proclamation of the independence of Croatia in April 1941. The Archbishop admitted as much during his trial. This was the consequence of the oppressive Serbian policy of hegemonism in the first Yugoslav state. Croats were less pleased about the fact that the state had to be established under foreign occupation. Croats were even more upset when they saw that their state had fallen into the hands of the terrorist *Ustaša* movement, which enjoyed Mussolini's support. The *Ustaša* had many adherents in western Herzegovina and was imprinted with a fanatical national and also religiously oriented concept of Croatia. The Archbishop of Zagreb had to undertake to walk the tightrope, and may not always have been up to this difficult situation. It is known that he protested against the persecution of the Serbs by the *Ustaša*. It is also true that as the war drew to a close, after the rise of the communist Partisan movement, communism seemed to him a greater danger than the exhausted *Ustaša* government. The communism with which Stepinac found himself confronted was not the mellow communism of latter-day "self-managing socialism", but hard-boiled Stalinism. On this point, the communists also made mistakes, as they would later admit. If Stepinac had really been what the communists would claim, he would have been brought to trial already in 1945 and the communists would never have tried to establish a cooperative relationship with him. Arrest and indictment came only in 1946, after the Archbishop somewhat unrealistically criticized certain communist measures, such as the inclusion of Church property in the land reform, and thereby made an enemy of the new regime.

The campaign against the Catholic Church reached a new high point when, in mid-summer 1981, alleged apparitions of the Blessed Virgin in the Herzegovinan mountains near Medjugorje became public. The local Franciscans, who had played a special, historical role in those regions, had the apparition in their hands, as it were. The Bosnian regime, with the active involvement of ethnic Croatian politicians such as Branko Mikulić and Franje Herljević, took direct measures against these apparitions, but soon had to admit failure.

Bosnian political scientist Zdravko Grebo wrote at the beginning of 1994 that a calmer analysis might perhaps reveal that Yugoslavia fell apart because it was undemocratic and not so much because it was a multinational state.[41] The question is interesting. For the first half of the 1980s, it could be said that these elements were often linked and influenced each other reciprocally. In Croatia, the repression was general and specifically directed against the Croatian nation as well; in Bosnia-Herzegovina, all three nations were repressed, on the pretext of the "fight against nationalism". There was a liberal patch on the political map of Yugoslavia in that day and this was Serbia, or at least Belgrade. The Belgrade weekly magazine, *NIN*, and the newspaper *Politika*, as well as other Serbian news organs, and the Belgrade intellectual circles in general not only enjoyed a large amount of maneuvering room, but also pushed hard for even freer discussion. In this they were not exactly supported by the Serbian party leadership headed by the cautious Draža Marković, but neither were they obstructed too much by the leadership.

Quite early on, however, and especially in connection with the situation in Kosovo, one could see that, among the Serbs, liberalism and nationalism very often went together. Intellectuals belonging to the Praxis group later made the switch to one-sided Serbian nationalism; some of them joined Dobrica Ćosić's team when the Serbian novelist became "Yugoslav" President. I remember the heartfelt sigh of a Slovenian intellectual in the early 1980s: "God protect us from the Serbian liberals." In the West, their Janus-like character was not always understood, and, especially in the United States, they were treated as "dissidents" on a par with Djilas, although Šešelj, for example, with his thesis that the Muslims were not a nation, anticipated much of what would happen later.[42]

Among the advocates and agents of the repressive course, there were those who proceeded from Yugoslav positions and believed that in repression lay the only remedy for the growing revival of particularist nationalisms. One found such people in the federal government as well as in the republics. One of these was Stane Dolanc. When he became the new Yugoslav Minister of the Interior, replacing Herljević in May 1982, it was generally believed, including in Western circles, that he would make an end of arbitrary behavior on the part of the police. In this regard, he was a disappointment. Dolanc soon proved to be a quintessential embodiment of the police mentality. Shortly before he stepped down in spring 1984, it was admitted that there were 18,000 convicts in Yugoslavia, as compared with 13,000 in 1969.[43] Political prisoners comprised a large portion of this number; most prominent among these were the Albanians, who were often physically abused. Only in January 1984 did Dolanc warn the police establishment against assuming political pretensions.[44]

Some of the Zagreb politicians of Croatian nationality increasingly aligned themselves with this repressive "Yugoslavism". Albanian political leader Azem Vllasi would later make it clear that he had allowed himself to be guided by primarily "Yugoslav" standpoints in pursuing his repressive course in Kosovo. In Bosnia-Herzegovina, the politicians of that time viewed their republic as a "Yugoslavia" in miniature; nationalism, they thought, could have especially explosive consequences here. The mistake made by all these people was that they overlooked how little could be accomplished with naked repression. The repressive course which prevailed in Yugoslav domestic policy in the first five years after Tito's death presented nationalists with ready arguments on a silver platter.

At this point, some politicians in Croatia exceeded all limits. Stipe Šuvar, who as Croatian Minister of Education had, at one time, pushed through a school reform which had practically eliminated the humanities from the high school curriculum, went on a rampage against opposition elements, above all cultural life, in May 1984. Shortly after launching this campaign, he released a kind of "White Book", full of hostile attacks on intellectuals, above all in Serbia, but also including some Slovenes.

An especially fateful act of repression took place in Sarajevo in July 1983: it was nothing less than a reckoning, of sorts, with revived Islam. From approximately the beginning of 1982, reports multiplied about a renaissance of Islam in Bosnia-Herzegovina where, according to the census of 1981, some 39.52 per cent of the republic's 4.13 million inhabitants had declared themselves ethnic Muslims. On a percentage basis, this was roughly the same figure as had been recorded in the census 10 years earlier. The result was not entirely clear, because in the same time span, the number of those who called themselves "Yugoslavs" rose from 43,800 to 326,300 (or 7.91 per cent of the total).[45] Muslims constituted the largest part of this "Yugoslav" category.

The revived strength of Muslim self-consciousness in Bosnia coincided with the economic upswing in the 1960s and early 1970s. It was accomplished, on the one hand, in the religious sphere, through the *medressahs* in Sarajevo, the newspaper *Preporod* (Rebirth), and through the building of many new mosques in the villages, often paid by *Gastarbeiter* working abroad. On the other hand, the process was realized on the basis of Muslim cultural inheritance and signified nation-building in the modern sense.

The communist power-holders in Sarajevo felt that it was necessary to counter this process. In April 1983, they arrested 13 persons in all, whipped up a massive propaganda campaign against them, and sentenced them to heavy prison terms in a big trial in August 1983. Among the condemned was Alija Izetbegović, later the President of the Republic of Bosnia-Herzegovina, who received 14 years in prison, because he had written an "Islamic Declaration" ten years earlier. In it he had attempted to bring Islamic principles into harmony with the demands of modern Western civilization.[46]

The trial was conducted in the style of a Stalinist show trial, i.e., the authorities endeavored to link people and groups who had nothing to do with each other, in order to extend charges applicable to one person or group to others. The leitmotiv of the trial was that the accused had acted in the spirit of Islamic fundamentalism and wanted to turn Bosnia into an Islamic state. Such attacks were surprising in that Yugoslavia still considered the policy of nonalignment to be the foundation-stone of its foreign policy. And Islamic countries occupied an important position within the nonaligned movement.

In reality, the charges, at least insofar as they were applied against people like Izetbegović, were unjustified. The "Islamic Declaration" which he had written a decade earlier was theoretical and general. The agents of the so-called Islamic renaissance in Bosnia were, as they emphasized both then and later, in favor of a European, "rational" Islam; they emphatically contrasted their position with radical tendencies in the Middle East. In conversations one would often hear the argument that Europe could do well to use "its" Islam as a counterweight to fundamentalist tendencies in the East.

Izetbegović and his fellow accused did not have to serve out their terms, but they were in prison when, in February 1984, the Winter Olympics took place in Sarajevo. Many people in Bosnia expected, at the time, that the games would usher in greater openness in their republic and moderate the dogmatic and xenophobic instincts of the political leadership. This happened only in part.

The cancer in Kosovo

On 11 March 1981, student unrest broke out in the cafeteria of the University of Priština, quickly spreading to the streets. On 26 March, reports emerged concerning further difficult incidents. After the Yugoslav media had published complaints about deficient information, Minister of the Interior Dolanc felt induced on 6 April to concede that they were dealing with events of considerable proportions and that these had spread to other parts of Kosovo. A state of emergency was imposed throughout the province.[47] Dolanc had the usual labels immediately at hand: on his account, alleged "pro-fascist groups" were implicated, which operated from centers in "Stuttgart, Brussels, and other places in Europe", or alternatively, "Cominformist" groups. Dolanc was careful about leveling any direct accusations at Albania.

The events agitated the Yugoslav public, especially in Belgrade. With the supplementary information which appeared in certain newspapers and magazines, the question emerged: how could an embargo on information concerning such important events have been justified? The weekly magazine *NIN* put itself in the forefront of those criticizing the restrictive information policy of the authorities.[48] Slovenian politician Jože Smole, then chair of the Foreign Policy Commission of the Central Committee of the LC Slovenia, considered it necessary, on the other hand, to look for the roots of these events not only in "the activity of hostile elements both domestically and abroad", but also in the "insufficient development of the political system" in Yugoslavia; he also disputed the claims registered by some that there was "too much democracy" in the country.[49]

Certainly, there had been some small incidents already in 1979, when Tito made his last visit to the region, but now the events were serious. The functionaries were at a complete loss. Typical was the reaction of an old follower of Tito, Macedonian Lazar Koliševski: "How was it possible that after three decades of building socialist self-management . . . such an intense outbreak of Albanian nationalism and irredentism could take place in Kosovo?"[50] The enemy was now found also in Tirana.[51] Then came the scapegoats. On 5 May 1981, Mahmut Bakalli, party chief in Kosovo since 1971, was removed from office; his predecessor, Veli Deva, though older than Bakalli, once more took the reins in the Kosovo party apparatus. More serious efforts to explain the outbreak of Albanian nationalism in terms of bad economic performance followed.

Kosovo and the Metohija region (Dukaqin, in Albanian) formed, in the fourteenth century, the center of the medieval Serbian kingdom. The greatest Serbian emperor, Dušan the Mighty, was buried near Prizren in a monastery later destroyed by the Turks. In 1389, a battle took place in Kosovo Polje, between Serbs and Turks, which initiated the end of the medieval Kingdom of Serbia and introduced the 400-year Turkish lordship over Serbia. At that time, most Albanians lived, practically speaking only in Metohija, and even there, they were not densely settled.[52] The immigration of Albanians, above all from the northern districts of today's Albania, assumed large proportions only in the eighteenth century, after a portion of the Serbian population had migrated northward to Vojvodina. This Serb migration was led by Patriarch Arsenije III Čarnojević of Peć after the failure of the Austrian campaign against the Turks in 1690. The Albanian new-arrivals worked, for the most part, on the Turkish feudal estates and allowed themselves to be islamicized. As late as 1939, the proportion between Serbs and Albanians in Kosovo was still about 40:60. According to the census of 1981, Albanians constituted 77.5 per cent of the population of Kosovo.[53] According to estimates in 1991 – Albanians did not take part in that census – Albanians constituted 82.2 per cent of the provincial population.[54]

Within Yugoslavia, Albanians lived not only in Kosovo but also in Macedonia (374,000, according to the census of 1981), Montenegro (about 40,000), and in districts in southern Serbia (another 20,000). The total number of Albanians in Yugoslavia, according to the census of 1981, came to 1.7 million; in the meantime, the number may have grown to more than 2 million.

The large number alone – there were, after all, only about 3 million Albanians in Albania as of 1994 – suggested that those Albanians living in Yugoslavia should be viewed, not as a "minority" but as the "smaller half" of the Albanian nation. The Albanians, who are of Indo-European stock and who view themselves as the descendants of the ancient Illyrians, could thank the two Balkan wars of 1912–13 for the division of their nation. This development had not been entirely unexpected. The Albanians had tried for the first time in 1878, through the League of Prizren, to counter the division of their demographic area among the rising Christian national states. On the Serbian side, it would later be claimed that the

League of Prizren was "reactionary" and "anti-emancipation", because it did not aim at national liberation, supporting instead the preservation of Turkish dominion in the Balkans. The League sought at most autonomy for the Albanians. To this, the Albanian side replied that this was the only way to prevent the partition of the Albanian demographic zone. It was true that the Albanian nation, even though the oldest nation in the Balkans, had been late in creating a modern national identity. This was connected with the fact that the majority of Albanians were Muslim, and that they therefore did not feel a fundamental need to break out of the Ottoman empire.[55]

Serbia viewed its return to Kosovo in 1912 as the vindication of a national trauma. The return of the Serbs was, however, accompanied by massacres of Albanians and Turks. In 1989, under the aegis of Slobodan Milošević, Serbia celebrated once more its "return" to Kosovo. This rally, staged on 28 June ("Vidovdan" or St Vitus' Day) on the field where the battle had taken place in 1389, was a one-sided affront to the Albanians. The anti-Albanian orientation which these festivities displayed was historical nonsense, because the Albanians had not been the Serbs' enemies on the Field of the Blackbirds. On the contrary, at least two Albanian feudal lords had fought with their troops alongside the Serbs.[56]

The division of the Albanian nation in two halves – since 1991 the fragmentation of Yugoslavia has further divided it – has always given the modern Albanian national movement aspects of a movement for unification. The moment of unification came in April 1941, when Yugoslavia was occupied by the Axis powers and carved up. The largest parts of Kosovo and western Macedonia were assigned to the Italian zone of occupation. In summer 1941, Italy had allowed the unification of these districts with the Albanian state it had occupied in 1939; the result was a "Greater Albania". The most capable and most touted Albanian politician of that era, Xhaver Deva, came from Kosovo – not specifically from the Italian zone but from Kosovska Mitrovica, which the Germans had kept for themselves because of its silver and lead deposits in Trepča.[57]

Even high-up Yugoslav functionaries such as Svetozar Vukmanović-Tempo conceded, in their writings, that the Albanians in Yugoslavia had reason to view the events of April 1941 as a national liberation and that the change in sovereignty opened possibilities for political and national development which they had not had before.[58] The Albanians in Yugoslavia found themselves in an entirely different situation from that in which Albania's Albanians were operating; the latter experienced the Italian occupation of 1939 as an injury to their national pride.

The nationalist-ruled Great-Albanian state functioned badly; one could already see then that the two halves of the Albanian people had developed differently. The nationalists from Kosovo were, in Tirana just as they were in Kosovo, the leading force under the Italians as, later, under the Germans. The communists in Kosovo faced enormous difficulties;[59]

they remained a small, politically hardly credible, and rather isolated group. Where the national question was concerned, they saw that every propaganda effort which was oriented to restoration of Yugoslavia found no resonance at all. At the turn of the year 1943/44, the Kosovo communists in Bujan put on a conference, under the protective umbrella of Enver Hoxha's partisans. This conference resolved that Kosovo should, in principle, be united with Albania, according to the Leninist principle of self-determination up to the point of secession.[60] Among the 49 participating delegates there were six Serbs. One of the participants was Fadil Hoxha, later a close collaborator of Tito and a leading politician in Kosovo.

For Tito, this entire question was rather delicate. Shortly before, in November 1943, in the resolutions of AVNOJ (the acronym being derived from the Serbo-Croatian for the Anti-Fascist Council for the People's Liberation of Yugoslavia), Kosovo had been granted autonomous status in the projected new Yugoslav state. On the other hand, the resolution passed in Bujan proceeded on the assumption of a close cooperation, even association, between Yugoslavia and Albania in the post-war period. Rumors and speculations were already circulating about a federation of Balkan states. However, one had to take into account the feelings of the Serbs and the Serbian communists. Tito's answer to the Bujan conference, on 28 March 1944, was cautious and ambiguous. In essence, so the message stated, nothing should be undertaken for the time being, which could prejudice the relations between Albania and Yugoslavia in the future; moreover, the credentials of the delegates in Bujan were open to question.[61] Later, it would be regularly attempted, by the Serbian side, to paint the conference in Bujan as an act of separation and to criminalize those Albanian communists who were present there.[62]

From 1943, when the eventual victory of the Allies became clear, the communists in Kosovo grew in strength. Meanwhile, as the so-called liberation really occurred in November 1944, something rather unusual happened in Kosovo: there was an uprising against the communists, in the course of which not a few Partisan units went over to the nationalists.[63] One reason for this seems to have been that the communists wanted to send these units to the frontlines in Syrmia. Another reason was that the Partisan units from Macedonia had perpetrated some atrocities against Albanians.[64] The deeper roots must, however, be sought in the fact that the Albanians of Kosovo simply did not want to hear anything about a reincorporation into Yugoslavia or, above all, Serbia. The Yugoslav historian and constitutional lawyer of Albanian nationality, Hajredin Hodža, writes that it was still openly debated at the time whether one really had to follow the Soviet example of incorporating autonomous regions into one or another republic.[65] The battles continued through the winter. On 8 February 1945, martial law was declared throughout Kosovo; in March 1945, the communist district secretary Miladin Popović was murdered in Priština. Only in June 1945 could the district committee dare to revise the resolution of Bujan in any form and to resolve on the incorporation of Kosovo as an autonomous region (comprising Kosovo and Metohija) into the Republic of Serbia.[66]

Tito took the position that, in spite of the uprising, Kosovo should be subjected to only a modest amount of repression. There remained, however, the largely negative attitude of the entire Yugoslav security apparatus, over which the Serb Aleksandar Ranković presided, *vis-à-vis* all Albanians. In the course of the years, there were various anti-Albanian acts of violence which Tito did not combat. From 1951, many Yugoslav Albanians (especially in Macedonia) were induced to declare themselves Turks and to request emigration to Turkey. Between 1953 and 1966, 231,000 persons emigrated from Yugoslavia to Turkey, among them allegedly more than 80,000 Albanians.[67] In winter 1955/56, the police staged an ambitious campaign to confiscate private firearms throughout Kosovo, on a concocted pretext, in the course of which more than 30,000 persons were threatened and manhandled. Approximately 100 persons were murdered in prisons.[68] In 1956, trials were staged in Prizren, at first against the Dervishes, and later against Albanian communist cadres at the middle and lower echelons, who had been implicated, Stalinist-style, in the trial of the Dervishes. The security organs acted partly against the will of the province's leading political personalities of Albanian nationality. The police, almost entirely controlled by the Serbs, even drew up a list of subscribers to the official communist newspaper in the Albanian language, *Rilindja*.[69] The year 1964 saw a new series of trials, involving *inter alia* an alleged organization said to be operating under the name of the National Movement for the Annexation of Kosovo to Albania, under the leadership of the pan-Albanian novelist, Adem Demaqi. At the conclusion of this trial, Demaqi was sentenced to 15 years in prison.

After Ranković's overthrow in July 1966, the situation in Kosovo began to change; a Serbian author described the changed atmosphere as an "opening of the vents".[70] To be sure, revelations concerning the crimes of the security organs were slow in coming, because some of the Albanian communist leaders probably had known more than they were prepared to admit, but also because Tito himself did not want to force the criminal prosecution of UDBa personnel. In spite of everything, many convicted persons were freed, rehabilitated, or, as in Demaqi's case, had their prison terms reduced.

Now Albanians took over key positions in the party and state, as well as in the police, in proportion to their demographic strength. At the same time, open discussions began, not only concerning the configuration of interethnic relations in Kosovo, but also about the future shape of the federation generally, and the status which Kosovo should have in it. Hajredin Hodža, then a member of the special Constitutional Commission of the province, was the first to demand that the two autonomous provinces of Serbia be elevated to the status of full-fledged "federal units", on a par with the republics. The valid Yugoslav constitution, so he argued, prescribed in Article 2 that the country consisted "of six republics and two provinces".[71] In practice, this had been interpreted as if Yugoslavia consisted "of five republics plus Serbia, in which there were two provinces". At the same time, Hodža proposed that the concept of "nationality" (*narodnost*) – formerly, "minority" – be expurgated and that one speak in the future only of the "Yugoslav peoples". He alluded to the fact that, shortly before, the parliament of the Republic of Bosnia-Herzegovina had proclaimed that three distinct peoples were living there: Serbs, Croats, and Muslims. If one could grant the Bosnian Muslims such status, Hodža argued, one could do the same for the numerically by no means inconsequential Albanian community.

These demands found a wide echo among the Albanians of Kosovo. Officially, there was no public demand for raising Kosovo to the level of a republic. But there were indirect comments from the Albanian side to the effect that republic status could already have been granted in 1945.[72]

In November 1968, Albanians demonstrated in Priština and other towns, and shortly thereafter also in the Macedonian town of Tetovo. Certainly the slogans went in part beyond the official standpoints but, as even Serbian author Miloš Mišović had to concede, they did not include a formal demand for a "Republic of Kosovo".[73] The demand came to the surface, however, as a slogan in the unrest of 1981. This demand was denounced by Albanian communists and Serbs alike, as well as by spokespersons of the federal government, as "hostile", "counterrevolutionary", and "directed against the integrity of Yugoslavia".[74] Properly viewed, these characterizations were utterly capricious, because it is a generally accepted principle that the constitution of every state should be considered open to revision. From a political standpoint, moreover, it was absurd to describe as illegal a postulate which had been a real object of debate.

The new Albanian leadership was deeply embarrassed by the demonstrations of 1968. Tito viewed these demonstrations as an opening of the vents and did not interpret them as dangerous or as pointing to a special relationship with Albania; they could also open the doors to an open discussion of two decades of repression in Kosovo. Finally, it was conceded by the Serbian side that the "deformation" in the work of the state organs in Kosovo had been more difficult than elsewhere.[75] Tito warned against overestimating the importance of the demonstrations in Kosovo.[76] They were also a reminder to the communist functionaries not to be forever congratulating themselves self-righteously that the national questions in Yugoslavia had been solved as a result of the "international" spirit of communist ideology and of "self-management".

The Serbian leaders of that day did not like the new constitution, with its federative structure and with its provision for an independent position for the two autonomous provinces, but they did not offer any open resistance. Only two years later, when the provinces began to assert their constitutional rights, especially in terms of practical equality with the republics on the federal level, did Serbia's leaders raise their voices, collecting their demands in the so-called "Blue Book". But they did not get anywhere with these demands in Tito's time.[77] As early as 1969, a new statute for Kosovo had been issued, with the complete assent of the then-liberal leadership of Serbia; under its provisions, Kosovo would continue to be a constituent part of Serbia, but at the same time, its autonomy would be guaranteed and, for the first time, it would be described as "a part of the federal structure of Yugoslavia". The price of this compromise was that the Albanian leadership in Kosovo, with Veli Deva as party chief, to be replaced in 1971 by Mahmut Bakalli (hitherto city secretary for Priština), had to hold to a middle position between the radical Albanian demands and the insistence on the part of Serbs and Montenegrins on holding on to the old order. The leadership accepted the Yugoslav federal system in which the Albanian nation was entitled to its own habitat. To the direct question of whether Kosovo should finally obtain the status of a republic, Bakalli answered in 1978 that the province was now a "constituent factor" of Yugoslavia with all the rights pertaining thereto; the real issue was the actual situation and not the formalities; the rest had to be left for the future.[78]

In spite of many interviews and conversations over the years, I have not succeeded in establishing with absolute clarity what the Albanian demonstrators in March and April 1981 actually wanted. The Albanians felt acknowledged as a national group in Yugoslavia and were gratified that the province of Kosovo was described as a "constituent factor" of Yugoslavia. The then-authoritative Albanian politicians in Kosovo, a more or less functioning combination of older and younger people, profited from the infusion of funds from the center. Through the Federal Fund for the Economically Underdeveloped Republics and Provinces considerable resources flowed into Kosovo, which, within the framework of this financial arrangement, was unambiguously privileged in comparison with the other lesser developed regions of Yugoslavia.[79] Of course, there were already at that time arguments that the financial resources flowing into the province were being put to poor use. Priština was built up as a showcase. Behind the ambitious edifices one could detect the aspiration of the new intellectual stratum of Kosovo to see Priština develop into a center of the Albanian nation, co-equal with Tirana. The hasty construction of the University of Priština had special significance; as early as 1979 the university already boasted nine faculties and had an enrollment of 24,000 students, among them 17,700 Albanians.[80]

On the other hand, it is correct that the economic development of Kosovo, in spite of all the abovementioned financial donations, continued to lag behind the Yugoslav average and that the disparity between Kosovo and the developed republics of Yugoslavia had become even greater. The high rate of population increase was to blame above all for that result.

Between 1971 and 1981 the population of Kosovo increased by 27.4 per cent, compared with 8.9 per cent for Yugoslavia as a whole.[81] There were always Albanians who considered the high birthrate a weapon in the struggle for national validation. As a consequence of this unbridled population growth, the number of unemployed in Kosovo remained very high. In 1979, there were 107 employed for every 1,000 inhabitants in Kosovo, as compared with 253 in Yugoslavia as a whole.[82] However, the social structure of Kosovo must be taken into consideration; agriculture absorbed a large portion of the working-age population, and in larger families the notions of "employed" and "unemployed" lost any absolute meaning. But economics played only a subordinate role in sparking conflicts in socialist Yugoslavia. On the contrary, it would be erroneous to seek the roots of the demonstrations of 1981 in economic discontent. It was precisely those who first began demonstrating, the students of the University of Priština, who had the least to complain about economically.

Azem Vllasi, who rose as the new political star in the Kosovar firmament after 1981, always claimed as an especially passionate defender of the "Yugoslav" line among Kosovo's Albanians – until the Serbian threat became overwhelming – that the demonstrations of 1981 had been organized by outspokenly sectarian, partly reactionary-communist, partly reactionary-nationalist groups, combining their own peculiar visions of communism with romantic views about national unification. They had taken for their model the stone-age communism of Albania's Enver Hoxha, without even understanding it. They believed that by taking over this model and through the unification of Albanians, the economic and national questions of all Albanians could be solved.[83]

It was not the authorities in Kosovo who opposed the contacts with Albania. In 1972, the representatives of Kosovo agreed, at the all-Albanian Orthography Congress in Tirana, to adopt the Tosk literary language which was used in Albania. In the late 1970s, a group of professors from Tirana, mainly in the natural sciences, was teaching at the University of Priština. It was the regime of Enver Hoxha in Albania which was against any widening of contacts; the Hoxha regime was concerned lest the freer, more open atmosphere in Kosovo, where religious practice was free, could have a disintegrative effect on Albania. Refugees from Kosovo were isolated and locked up in Albania, and often turned over to the Yugoslav authorities.

In the course of a visit to Albania in 1982, I was able to verify that a verbally duty-conscious national solidarity with Kosovo was being professed, but that the atmosphere was characterized by distrust and aversion. Sofokli Lazri, the former chief editor of the party organ *Zeri i Popullit* and later director of the Institute for Foreign Policy, said that Mahmut Bakalli himself had told him that Tito had given the Kosovar Albanians a free hand in the development of relations with Albania; in this regard, Bakalli observed that the construction of this relationship had to be accompanied by a general improvement in relations between Albania and

Yugoslavia. This had awakened the suspicion in Tirana that Tito wanted to use the Kosovar Albanians to soften the regime in Albania. The result was distrust in the relationship. Albania – as Lazri said – did not want to get directly involved in Kosovo; this problem had to be solved within the framework of Yugoslavia, and Albania was interested in a stable Yugoslavia. It was not possible to confirm any direct sympathies on the part of the demonstrators in Kosovo for the Enver Hoxha regime; the national impulse was decisive.[84]

From whatever side one considered things, one was driven to the conclusion that it was hard to characterize the Kosovo demonstrations of 1981, in contrast to those of 1968. Meanwhile, these latter demonstrations had a catastrophic effect on the situation of Kosovo's Albanians, as well as on the entire subsequent development of Yugoslavia. The reaction of the Albanian leadership in Kosovo was equally catastrophic. In their firm faith in a federal, socialist Yugoslavia and in their categorical view that the future of Kosovo was indissolubly linked with socialist Yugoslavia, they reacted to the irrational mutiny of parts of their younger elite against the Yugoslav path with counterforce. The province's leaders believed they could wash the "stain" of the demonstrations from their garments, in order to rejoin the Yugoslav socialist ranks once more. The leadership's administrative methods weakened the solidarity and thus also the capacity for political resistance on the part of the Kosovar Albanians within the province's political structures. It later turned out that socialist Yugoslavia lacked the will to defend either the constitutional status of Kosovo or the rights of the Albanian community.

The first step toward disaster came during the second wave of demonstrations in March 1981, when the security chief of Kosovo, Rahman Morina, later a Serbian toady, called in special units of Serbian police over the heads of the regional leadership. Under pressure from Belgrade for Bakalli to be made accountable, he was relieved of his job as provincial party secretary. This was accompanied by a series of arrests and the first trials of alleged "nationalists". "Nationalism" became the label which the authorities would insist on associating with the Albanians. The more time passed, the more extravagant the court verdicts became; the highest court in Kosovo felt obliged on a regular basis to reduce the sentences imposed. By 1984, the number of convicted had reached 2,000, including those condemned to administrative punishments (maximum of 60 days).[85] The Albanian functionaries of Kosovo who wanted to be tough could verify that, in spite of the then relatively liberal leadership in Serbia, a pressure emanated from Belgrade in the form of collective suspicions, against which it was difficult to organize opposition. In a similar way, many Serbs wanted to see a tough line *vis-à-vis* Croatia. In addition, the relations between the Republic of Serbia and the two autonomous provinces incorporated within it was not clearly regulated on either the state or the party level, so that political pressure could rather easily be exerted. The young intellectuals and teachers were, above all, identified as the agents of Albanian nationalism; they were, according to Serbian voices, agitating young people to embrace demands for a "Kosovo Republic" and an "ethnically pure Kosovo".[86] With this mode of argumentation, the Serbian side tried to divide the Albanian communists in Kosovo from Albanian intellectuals, and brought a factor into play which would prove important for the future development of the province: the existential *Angst* of Serbs and Montenegrins living in Kosovo. The political leadership of Kosovo had failed, it was argued.[87]

The fear among these Serbs and Montenegrins of being driven out by the Albanians was based mostly on demographic developments. The share of Albanians in the population of the province had increased from 67.1 per cent in 1961 to 77.5 per cent in 1981, while the share of Serbs and Montenegrins had dwindled from 27.4 per cent to 14.9 per cent.[88] It is undeniable that the "Albanian renaissance" in Kosovo was matched by a steady out-migration of Serbs and Montenegrins. The only question is why this occurred. Soon Serbian propaganda began to talk of violence, threats, expulsion, and similar things, all of which justified Serbian officials in marshalling force against Kosovo.

The fact is that the Serbian out-migration from Kosovo increased after 1966 as a by-product of the reduction in the abnormally high representation of Serbs and Montenegrins in the power apparatus in the wake of Ranković's fall from power. Later, economic pressures contributed to the process, compounded by the Albanian population's growing involvement in both state and economy. It was difficult for many young Serbs in Kosovo in the 1970s to find a position, because the Albanian "quota" had to be filled. The out-migration of Serbs and Montenegrins involved some 112,600 persons between 1961 and 1981, according to Serbian figures.[89] Of course, many Albanians also migrated from Kosovo, some of them going to other parts of Yugoslavia, others taking temporary employment abroad.

The demonstrations of 1981 had no tangible effect on the process of out-migration, contrary claims by the Serbian side notwithstanding. In autumn 1984, the magazine *NIN* reported that since the events of 1981 some 20,000 Serbs and Montenegrins had left Kosovo.[90] In 1983, only 4,377 Serbs and Montenegrins had left, according to *NIN*, while later the number was estimated at 3,000 per year. Among other things, it must be taken into account that the price of land in Kosovo was significantly higher than elsewhere in Yugoslavia. A Serb who sold his property in Kosovo could buy significantly more land elsewhere in Yugoslavia and in a more civilized environment. Of course, there were also instances of indirect dislodgement. Albanians bought houses in Serbian neighborhoods, eventually becoming the local majority. These Albanians were, for the most part, Muslims and they had different customs. Soon there were difficulties with the Serbian schools. The Serbian intellectuals in the cities left; their departure left remaining Serbs feeling culturally isolated.

There were rarely real instances of violence. I tried to investigate such instances in the vicinity of Vučitrn in July 1982.[91] It soon became obvious that there were two kinds of Serbs in Kosovo: the long-established Serbs, who were used to living with Albanians, and the newcomers, whose families had come to Kosovo only after the Balkan wars of 1912–13. In the interwar period many of the latter had been settled as "colonists" on land confiscated from Albanian feudal families. Tito had declined to allow a general return of the colonists to Kosovo after 1945, but many property questions from the war and the immediate post-war period remained unsolved.

Interrogations in Serbian villages of Kosovo in all the following years elicited more or less the same formula. First came endless tirades about rapes, robberies, property damage, harassments, and so forth; typically, the University of Priština was identified as the source and refuge of the trouble-makers. To the question whether any of these things had really taken place nearby, the answer usually came that this was not the case, but that one could not just wait until they actually occurred.[92] There were of course troubling incidents, but there were also myths, such as the example so often cited on Belgrade television of nuns from a Serbian convent who allegedly needed to carry rifles in order to get around. To that Vllasi, at the time President of the People's Front of Kosovo, said that the nuns could also have mentioned that the Albanians, mainly Catholics in that region, had for generations regularly performed work for them without remuneration.

This remained more or less the line along which the debates in and about Kosovo developed. The Albanian cadres of socialist-Yugoslav orientation carried out a witch hunt against "nationalists" among the Albanian population, without being able to mention that there were comparable problems also on the Serbian side. They began to carry out "differentiations" (a euphemism for purges) in cultural institutions, schools, and educational institutions. At the end of 1985, an allegedly underground organization was ferreted out and about 100 Albanians were taken into custody in towns around Kosovo and Macedonia.[93] It was claimed that with this operation the "center of irredentism" had finally been suppressed. That was not the case, however, because there was no such center. But against the ever tougher pressure there developed ever stronger bonds of solidarity among the region's Albanians, against the Serbs as well as against their own leaders.

In December 1984, on the occasion of a visit to Kosovo, I received the impression that the policy of differentiation carried out by the Albanian leadership among the ranks of Albanians had miscarried and had failed to accomplish anything. Moreover, the Serbian side no longer even reckoned on the Albanians "pacifying" Kosovo themselves. One heard ever more frequent arguments that Serbs had to take care of the situation themselves. For such agitation any and all instruments were acceptable. To the question of why the court judgments against Albanian "nationalists" had gradually lost all sense of proportion, Vllasi answered that there was "something at stake".[94] By this he ostensibly meant the autonomy of the province as such.

Between 1981 and 1986, about 4,000 young Albanians were sent to prison.[95] Even the Belgrade newspaper *Politika* judged, in 1986, that this policy could only multiply the state's enemies. The paper did not, however, draw the conclusion that one should therefore call a halt to the repression, but argued instead that it was necessary to engage the enemy at his hearth, viz., at the university and in general in the ranks of Kosovar intellectuals.[96] According to official data at the time, more than 800 teachers and professors had already been relieved of their posts since 1981. The Serbian side, as it seemed, wanted to carry this process to its logical conclusion and deprive the Albanians in Kosovo of both their intellectual elite and their educational opportunities; these policies would later be carried out by the Milošević regime.

2 The turning point: 1986–87

Milošević, Kučan, Vllasi – the new protagonists

In retrospect, one can establish that as early as 1985 those elements which would later tear apart the Yugoslav state were already visible. The communist regime set itself against genuine democratization as well as against any earnest reforms of the economic system. The new administration of Branko Mikulić did not even want to hear anything more about the macro-economic adjustments with which the previous administration of Milka Planinc had occupied itself. One could readily argue that the level of debt now reached, of about $20 billion, had rendered fundamental reform impossible. Serbian policy *vis-à-vis* Kosovo was, moreover, pushing the country in a direction holding great danger both for the constitutional order and for the country's non-Serbian peoples. While the democratization process in Serbia and Montenegro stagnated and nationalist extremism gathered strength, people in the western part of Yugoslavia, and especially in Slovenia, watched with growing concern. The army, finally, was not prepared, under any circumstances, to give up its privileged position.

In the course of 1986, the political and personal constellations in most of the republics crystalized, assuming the shapes which would determine the subsequent course of confrontations and political antagonisms. Slovenia took the first step by retiring its conservative "old guard" at its Tenth Congress in mid-April; Milan Kučan, a young adherent of the liberal wing of the Slovenian party, was elected Slovenian party chief. The Slovenian liberals had been in the political wilderness for 15 years, ever since Stane Kavčič had been removed from power by Tito and Kardelj at the end of 1971. In the intervening years, the political scene in Slovenia had been dominated by generally older and dogmatic communists, such as Tito-loyalist, France Popit. They defended the economic and national interests of Slovenia, but also felt themselves to be a part of the general Yugoslav regime, and, in any case, wanted nothing to do with any kind of democratization in Slovenia.

The election of then-45-year-old Milan Kučan as party president did not signify a revolution, though a new spirit was soon felt in the now mixed political leadership. Kučan had been born in 1941, i.e., during the war, in the Prekmurje area which had belonged to Hungary before the First World War. His father, a teacher, lost his life in the Partisan struggle. Kučan's family was Protestant. Kučan studied law and began his political ascent by taking part in the communist party's university committee and holding office in the official League of Communist Youth of Slovenia. Although he sympathized with Kavčič's ideas, he did not want to leave office in 1971. He is said to have confided in a trusted colleague that he thought he could accomplish more inside the apparatus than outside it. Especially important for his later undertakings was his lengthy experience in Belgrade as a Slovenian representative in various organs of the federal party.

One month after Kučan's election, viz., in mid-May 1986, Croatia likewise experienced a political transition. The pragmatically oriented party president Mika Špiljak had been pushing for a scuttling of radicalism even before the Croatian Tenth Party Congress, but the party leadership was divided and constantly embrangled in polemics. Upon stepping down, Špiljak, who no longer harbored any personal ambitions, put new voting procedures into effect which, in combination with a secret ballot, would ensure that a number of the old party big-wigs would no longer be elected to high office. That did not please everyone, but it worked. The three most venomous demagogues of the post-1971 epoch – the Serbs Milutin Baltić and Dušan Dragosavac, together with Croat Jure Bilić – were removed from their offices. Moreover, Josip Vrhovec and Milka Planinc, two other prominent Croatian party figures who had risen to prominence in the wake of Tito's attack on the "Croatian spring", were not elected to the offices which they had sought.[1] Stanko Stojčević, a colorless Serb born in 1929, was elected new party president, while Drago Dimitrović, a young Croat from Split, became the new secretary of the Croatian party presidium.

One could not call the new leadership team in Zagreb reform-oriented, but it was at least pragmatic. Ante Marković, who had served as Croatian prime minister since 1982 and who would later serve as Yugoslav prime minister, was made a member of the Croatian presidency. Marković, a Croat by nationality, had been born in Bosnian Konjica in 1924 and had spent the war engaged in illegal work in the communist youth organization in Dubrovnik. He received his diploma as an electrical engineer at the University of Zagreb in 1954, and became General Director of the Rade Končar electrical firm (in Zagreb) in 1961. In this role, he took a position clearly antagonistic toward the so-called nationalists of the "Croatian Spring". He played only a marginal part in the political fights in Croatia at this time; his main interest was the economy. The more economic issues dominated the agenda in Croatia, the stronger Marković's position became, until he was finally called, in 1982, to take the leadership post in the Croatian government. How much Marković actually contributed to political liberalization in Croatia is debatable. In Zagreb people said he had already at that time a clear propensity to restrict his active involvement to economics and to leave political decision-making to others.

After the Tenth Croatian Party Congress in May 1986, the Croatian party leadership stopped playing the role of guardian of the holy grail of Tito's legacy. Certainly Croatia's representatives in federal organs, in both the state and party hierarchies, continued to support this legacy, while Stipe Šuvar, the anti-reform chief ideologue of the LCY, committed himself to making sure that none of the necessary economic and political reforms were carried through. Šuvar, who enjoyed the partial, if less committed, support of Josip Vrhovec, Croatia's representative in the state presidium, demanded at the beginning of May 1987 that the party repudiate more sharply the "main danger" for society – "bourgeois rights". Of course, he paid lip service to market laws, but only under the control and supervision of planning instruments. Class interests, according to Šuvar, had to have primacy over national interests in Yugoslavia, and – in his view – the primary assignment of self-management was not to produce economic successes, but to vouchsafe the realization of socialism.[2]

Šuvar could not carry out his ideas. The new Slovenian party chief, Kučan, opposed Šuvar's demand for a "permanent purge". Šuvar's thesis of the primacy of class interests was a "mask for a unitarist and centralist distribution of surplus value", according to Kučan. The younger generation of Yugoslavia demanded a modern progressive program; young people had had their fill of socialism as a "just sharing of poverty" and were no longer satisfied that the Yugoslav living standard was higher than that of Albania.[3]

For Croatia itself, a new epoch was beginning, which was characterized both within the republic and elsewhere in Yugoslavia as "silent Croatia". That was in fact an improvement. But when it came to defending interests Croatia shared with Slovenia, nothing had changed; all too often the Slovenes had to step forward alone in defense of their common interests and shared viewpoints.

Even before the Croatian Party Congress, the Fourteenth Conference of Communists in Kosovo (in late April 1986) elected 38-year-old Azem Vllasi, erstwhile party secretary in Priština, to succeed Kolj Shiroka as provincial party chief. The party conference also brought about the final departure from office of 70-year-old Fadil Hoxha, a political veteran and friend of Tito's. From the old guard of Kosovar Albanian politicians, only Ali Shukrija, Sinan Hasani, and Kolj Shiroka remained in the leadership. Vllasi, who had been leader of the League of Communist Youth of Yugoslavia (SKOJ) for a long time, now found himself at the pinnacle of power in Kosovo. He could not imagine then that just four years later he would be brought to court in handcuffs, beneath the portrait of his idol, Tito. One month after the party conference in Priština, Sinan Hasani, who had represented Kosovo in the Yugoslav presidency, became President of the collective presidency and thereby ceremonial head of state of Yugoslavia.

The prevailing opinion among the Albanians of Kosovo at the time was that Vllasi and his people had realized that in the long run they could not fight a two-front war against their own people, on one side, and against the Serbs, on the other, and that threats from Belgrade had reached the point where even the position of the Albanian politicians in Kosovo was endangered. Of course, it was still rare to hear politicians in Belgrade openly call for the dissolution of the province's autonomy, but repeated references to the need to "regulate" relations within the Republic of Serbia were not without their significance. On this point, the Serbs found support among members of the federal organs, such as Stane Dolanc, who, in an interview with the Slovenian newspaper *Telex*, openly endorsed the Serbian position.[4]

Nevertheless, under Vllasi, the leadership in Priština won some maneuvering room. The Kosovar leaders had the mettle, shortly before the party conference, to arrest Kosta Bulatović, one of the noisier "anti-bureaucratic" rabble-rousers among the Kosovar Serbs. In the village of Batus near Priština, one of the centers of extreme Serbian agitation, their organizers talked for a while of abandoning their village altogether on account of an alleged threat from local Albanians, calling off this migration at the last minute. I had the occasion to visit Batus a few months later and the only concrete "threat" in evidence was that two Albanians had bought houses on the street connecting the village with the main street to Priština and Serbs could not avoid passing by those houses.[5]

The most extreme Serbian elements staked everything on blocking the stabilization of conditions in Kosovo. The Milošević era was dawning. In February 1986, Slobodan Milošević, chair of the party committee of Belgrade, was proposed as the new party president of Serbia. The previous office-holder, the relatively measured Ivan Stambolić, who had to give up his post as part of a rotation at the Serbian party congress in May 1986, recommended Milošević to the Serbian Central Committee, with the thought that one needs people who "can get things done and not waste a lot of time talking".[6] Some months later, Milošević turned on his protector, Stambolić, and pushed him out of office.

Milošević was in fact elected Serbian party chief in May 1986, at the Congress of the League of Communists of Serbia, but this was not yet the turning point, which only came more than a year later. The Milošević faction did not have a majority in 1986 and the new party chief did not yet exercise personal control over Serbian television and over the daily newspaper *Politika*. In general, Milošević presented himself at the time rather as a young technocrat who, in the view of many Western diplomats stationed in Belgrade, wanted to set Yugoslavia on a modern foundation. He spoke tolerable English and, after his law studies, was active not only as a political functionary but also as an economic manager. Among other things he was, from 1978 to 1983, President of the Bank of Belgrade *(Beogradska banka)*. Born in Požarevac in 1941, he was the son of an Orthodox priest. It seems that there were some problems in his family, and the wide gulf between his father's sacerdotal calling and his own communist career cannot have been without influence on his character.[7]

Milošević would marry Mirjana Marković, a Professor of Marxism at the University of Belgrade.

The intensified nationalist agitation blowing out of Serbia dominated the Thirteenth Yugoslav Party Congress in mid-July 1986. Under Serbian pressure, it was decided even before the congress to adopt unprecedented extraordinary measures in Kosovo: the appointment of a mixed commission, consisting of representatives from the province, the Republic of Serbia, and the federal government. This commission was supposed to verify that legislative acts, especially in regard to the sale of land, were correctly applied *vis-à-vis* the Serbian minority. Aside from that, the judicial and educational reforms were also supposed to be reviewed. Moreover, the authorities imposed a moratorium until 1990 on all sales of property owned by Serbs.[8] This was the first curtailment of Kosovo's autonomy. It followed a "spontaneous" rally of Kosovar Serbs, which adhered to the pattern of Milošević's later "agitation meetings".

The Yugoslav party congress itself yielded few results; indeed, it was entirely incapable of producing much of anything. Prime Minister Mikulić promised reforms, for example the extension of a further credit to enterprises. Defense Minister Admiral Mamula thought it was necessary to confront the growing criticism of the army, especially in Slovenia. As for Kosovo, there was relatively little discussion of the problems there; that subject was supposed to be treated at a special meeting of the Central Committee.

This meeting took place only a year later, at the end of June 1987, in Belgrade. While the highest party organ sat in deliberation, several thousand Serbs, among them many from Kosovo, demonstrated outside, demanding "finally" some security. As a result of the demonstrations, the Central Committee ended its work a day early.[9] It had had to endure a veritable tidal wave of Serbian attacks, accusations, and demands. For the first time, an army spokesperson entered into the débâte with the argument that the Kosovo problem was a "defense problem" for Yugoslavia. Serbian demands centered concretely on the "unification of the Republic of Serbia". Milošević himself had spoken along these lines already at the Central Committee session of mid-January 1987: state and party in all of Serbia should, in future, be unified.[10] The Central Committee did not satisfy this twin demand. On the contrary, as shown in the closing statement of CC chair Milenko Renovica, a Bosnian Serb, there was rather a tendency to view Kosovo as an issue for all of Yugoslavia.[11] But there was also another tendency, especially marked among representatives of the western republics (i.e., Slovenia and Croatia in particular), to take little interest in the Kosovo problem, because taking a position in the face of voluble Serbian agitation could only lead to conflict with Serbia and was not likely to be of much practical benefit to anyone.

The dam broke at the end of September 1987. After painstaking political preparation, which had given him control of the state television as well as of the newspaper *Politika*, Milošević set out to strip the rival faction in the Serbian party, under Ivan Stambolić, of power. He did not imme-diately attack Stambolić, however, but concentrated his fire on Belgrade party secretary Dragiša Pavlović, a moderate liberal very much in the spirit of Belgrade party tradition. Milošević himself had had to comport himself as a liberal when he had held this office, and his attacks on Pavlović now disappointed many people.

The city committee at first did not want to eject Pavlović from office. So the affair was taken before the Serbian party Central Committee. Here Milošević's adherents fired endless salvoes with ever weightier and more malicious reproaches. The style of this fateful Eighth Plenum of the Serbian Central Committee on 23 and 24 September 1987 was open intimidation of the opponents of Milošević's faction and of those who were still unde-cided in this contest. The two factions were originally about equally matched. Milošević's side claimed that Stambolić's adherents had betrayed the interests of the Serbian people, by taking a soft line in Kosovo. Pavlović had in fact warned about the extravagant agitation by Serbs in Kosovo. There was also talk at the session of a letter sent by Stambolić to the Belgrade city committee. In it, the head of the Serbian Republic had asked for democratic proceedings against Pavlović. The letter was now charac-terized as "interference" and, ironically, was used against Stambolić himself. Finally, not only was Pavlović forced to resign, but the entire liberal faction in the Serbian Central Committee was defeated. Stambolić himself was removed from the office of Serbian state president in December 1987.[12]

At the end of this quasi-Stalinist power struggle, Milošević stood as the *de facto* sole ruler of Serbia. An ideological platform and mobilizable street columns stood ready to be used in the service of his extreme politics. The ideological platform was the so-called "Memorandum", prepared by a group of academics in the Serbian Academy of Sciences and Art in the course of 1986. Its harmless title concealed an explosive document. Here was a Serbian national program calling for either the consolidation of Serbian hegemony in a new, (re)centralized Yugoslavia or – in the event that this could not be achieved – the creation of a Greater Serbia, to be constructed on the ruins of the existing state structure. The existence of this document was already known at the time that Milošević took power,[13] but it had not yet been published and no one knew for sure just what was actually written there. The essential parts of the Memorandum were first published in summer 1989.[14] Stambolić and his adherents criticized the document as "nationalist". Milošević maintained his silence, but later used their criticism of the Memorandum against Stambolić and Pavlović.

Milošević's stormtroopers on reserve were the incited Serbs of Kosovo, who would later bring his "anti-bureaucratic revolution" to the very doorsteps of federal organs in Belgrade and local organs in Vojvodina and Montenegro, and who would try to do the same thing in Slovenia.[15]

Milošević had carried out a dress rehearsal in Kosovo during summer 1987. Already, on 24 April, he had gone over the heads of the Kosovo party leadership to promise local Serb demonstrators, "No one will ever beat you again." One of the ringleaders of the demonstrators would later say that they had deliberately provoked the clashes with the police in order to induce Milošević to intervene, but that it had taken no great effort to obtain this result. From September 1987 on, Yugoslav politics was played out "on the streets" and federal organs should have taken steps to restrain Milošević and his methods. Political scientist Dušan Bilandžić said in the Zagreb weekly magazine, *Danas*, that it was already unfortunately well known that a large segment of the Yugoslav leadership was not up to facing "the spirit of the times and its attendant problems".[16] But just as important would have been a correct assessment abroad of the Milošević phenomenon. I recall conversations with diplomats in Belgrade who were inclined, at the time, to the belief that Milošević's centralism was possibly better for Yugoslavia than no centralism at all. The then-US ambassador in Belgrade, John Scanlan, unequivocally took Milošević's side. Scanlan would later serve as manager of the Belgrade branch of the pharmaceutical firm of Milan Panić, the future Prime Minister of "new" Yugoslavia. The pro-Milošević phase in American foreign policy ended only in March 1987 with the arrival of Warren Zimmermann as the new ambassador. He had been given the assignment, quite explicitly, of taking a critical stance *vis-à-vis* Milošević's politics.[17]

In September 1987, political relationships in hitherto dogmatic Bosnia-Herzegovina became destabilized. This did not happen as a result of liberalization, however, but as a by-product of a finance scandal. For years, the large Bosnian agro-firm "Agrokomerc" had operated throughout Yugoslavia as well as abroad. The firm was headquartered in the west Bosnian city of Velika Kladusa near Bihać and was managed by Fikret Abdić, a Muslim politician. Within Yugoslavia, the firm was able to exert a decisive influence on the domestic market through large-scale deliveries in various centers, above all by supplying products at a relatively low price. Through deliveries abroad, above all in the Middle East, Agrokomerc gave Yugoslavia the wherewithal to purchase oil and other products. Cazin Krajina, in which the firm had its headquarters, was inhabited overwhelmingly by Muslims; it was here that, in 1950, the only open revolt against Tito's program of agricultural collectivization had taken place.

With the gathering economic uncertainty, Agrokomerc's business dealings began to include financial speculation. This, in turn, led to losses; these were concealed by uncovered promissory notes which were accepted as collateral for credits by various banks, including Ljubljanska Banka, along with some Bosnian banks. Finally, in 1987, this house of credit collapsed when several banks, including Ljubljanska Banka, could not or would not continue to underwrite Agrokomerc. Now the strong links between Bosnian politics and Agrokomerc became visible. The brother of Hamdija Pozderac, Bosnia's representative in the state presidency, was heavily involved in the concealment of Agrokomerc's losses and was soon arrested. This had the consequence that Hamdija had to resign his posts. Shadows were even cast on Prime Minister Mikulić. The affair severely damaged the prestige of the regime in Sarajevo.[18] The scandal assumed an additional dimension insofar as the opinion gained ground among the Muslim population of Bosnia that the entire affair was a "conspiracy" against the Muslims.[19] The political popularity which Fikret Abdić later won – after spending a few years in prison – was grounded, to a considerable extent, on these notions of conspiracy.

A review of these two fateful years, 1986 and 1987, would not be complete without some mention of the fact that the leadership of the Yugoslav People's Army made its political views obvious, views which were of an unambiguously dogmatic and centralist inspiration. The army, as Slovenian President Kučan put it in early November 1987, had, in this regard, no economic or national affiliation and was therefore politically weak. This made it thoroughly incapable of acting as a political factor, as long as political factors dominated the scene. As a result of demographic developments, there was an ever growing discrepancy between the composition of its officer corps (60 per cent Serb and Montenegrin) and that of the rank and file. This discrepancy had some implications for military preparedness.[20]

One should not neglect to mention that the dogmatic and centralist attitude of the army's higher echelons brought the army politically ever closer to Milošević. The army's image of itself as the "guarantor of Yugoslav unity" was shaken in autumn 1987 by the shooting spree of an Albanian soldier, Aziz Kelmendi, in the Paraćin barracks, in which four soldiers died, with six more wounded.[21] This event, together with other developments, impelled the Yugoslav authorities to send about 400 federal police to Kosovo at the end of 1987.

By that point, the lines of polarization which would push the country to its eventual collapse were already well established. Perhaps it might have been possible to reverse this process, had the Mikulić government been able to come up with some stabilizing measures. But this was not the case. On the contrary, Mikulić held fast to a dogmatic economic policy. The opening months of his government were characterized by administrative measures. These were in fact not inspired by socialist teaching, but were concepts which were then being tested in France. Mikulić tried to create stability at three pressure points – wages, prices, and rates of exchange. He could not get anywhere with wages, however, and the attempt to stabilize them collapsed after a few months, as did efforts to shake off the "tutelage" of the International Monetary Fund and to reach a long-term regulation of Yugoslav debts.[22] A period of uncontrolled *"laissez-faire – laissez-aller"* resulted, which was only further heated by inflation.

In Yugoslavia, the suspicion prevailed that Mikulić was doing all of this deliberately, in order to justify a strong arm policy.[23] Only toward the end of 1987 did his administration develop an active anti-inflation program;

discontent had, in the meantime, spread in all the republics, and Mikulić came under personal attack. But political relationships had also changed fundamentally. Slovenia and soon Croatia and even Serbia did not want to hear anything further about centralist measures or the curtailment of republic sovereignty. The unsuccessful economic policy of the regime worked to catalyze centrifugal tendencies.

The first year of Mikulić's government discouraged everyone who had believed in reforms and renewal on the Yugoslav level and who had believed in the reformability of the Yugoslav system. The recommendations of the Kraigher Commission were finally scattered by the wind. The Yugoslav regime as a whole had shown that it did not want any real reforms. One can not overestimate the significance of the realization of this fact which hit people in many parts of the country around the end of 1987. Kučan told me in autumn 1994 that he began to doubt Yugoslavia's future when he saw the work of the Kraigher Commission finally swept aside by Mikulić. The attitude of the party base, or at least of its majority, was clearly oriented backwards. Warnings about a "bourgeois restoration", as Šuvar put it, made a big impression. A survey conducted in February 1987 found that half of all LCY members wanted to see once again "a party of the old style".[24]

Diverse interests came into the picture. The reform-oriented Macedonian Kiro Gligorov, in the course of a discussion of a reform of constitutional provisions dealing with the economy, criticized the fact that relations between municipalities and enterprises had not been taken up, the character of those relations standing in the way of reforms too.[25]

Serbia between Yugoslav hegemonism and Greater Serbia

As Milošević assumed power in Serbia in autumn 1987, he faced opposition from half of the Serbian Central Committee, the Belgrade middle class, the liberal intellectual milieu in Belgrade, those Serbs whose families had been living for a long time in Vojvodina, and at least half of the Montenegrins – quite apart from practically all non-Serbs in Yugoslavia. Ten years later, Milošević seemed to a strong majority of Serbs to be the best guarantor of Serbian national interests, despite his use of troops against the Serbian opposition in March 1991, despite his authorization of the arrest of his political rival Vuk Drašković in June 1993, and despite his having "sold out" Croatian Serbs in 1995.

How was Milošević relatively easily able to mobilize the Serbian public for his extreme-nationalist line and to turn the Serbian people, both inside and outside Serbia, into a nearly unreflective instrument of his own ambitions? Milošević's rule rested, certainly, to a great extent on his roughly 100,000 police, including many refugees from Bosnia, as well as on the fact that he was able to Serbianize the Yugoslav Army after June 1991 and often to exploit the weaknesses of western policy to his own interest.

Most Serbs do not blame Milošević and his policies for their difficulties; they blame the alleged hostility of the West.

But all of that is not sufficient to explain his success. There had to be a predisposition in the political thinking of a large part of the Serbian people to "solutions" along the lines of what he represented. This in turn leads one to the conclusion that the problem is not Milošević at all, but rather the political dispositions among people in Serbia itself. For a long time, Western policy-makers, both European and American, tried to close their eyes to this fact. They therefore placed their hopes on a "better Serbia", on the Serbian opposition, the students, or even on a man such as Milan Panić, who served temporarily as "Prime Minister" of the new so-called Yugoslavia. This went on for years.

In winter 1996/97, the opposition coalition "Zajedno" became the focus of western hopes, and in the second half of 1997, Biljana Plavšić and later Milorad Dodik in the Bosnian "Serbian Republic" seemed, in western eyes, to don the mantle of moderation. I myself must confess that I too hoped, in the late 1980s, that countervailing forces, first in Yugoslavia, then within Serbia, would finally block Milošević. For the most part these conjectures and hopes proved to be false and stillborn.

The new Serbia did not arise where the old kingdom had existed, but rather further to the north, in the so-called Pašaluk of Belgrade, in the region of Šumadija. The area had been extensively depopulated in the course of the Austro-Turkish wars at the end of the seventeenth and early eighteenth centuries. The Serbs from the south who migrated there brought with them a new flexible, enterprising mentality; they fashioned, at their new places of residence, forms of self-administration such as hardly existed elsewhere in the Turkish empire. They also brought their myths, which revolved around the lost medieval empire which had aspired at one point to take the place of the Byzantine Empire. Their epic heroic songs had, after the fact, transformed the Battle of Kosovo (1389), which had ended to the detriment of the Serbs, into a victory, or, at least, flying in the face of historical truth had tried to pin the blame for Serbia's defeat on the alleged "betrayal" on the part of Vuk Branković. Vasa Čubrilović was quite correct when he said that the new Serbian settlers in the Belgrade Pašaluk wanted from the beginning to make a connection with their old statehood and dreamt of a new strong state in the Balkans.[26]

The first rebellion under Karadjordje from 1804 to 1815 miscarried, but in 1815, another representative of the local Serbian ruling stratum, Miloš Obrenović, obtained a precarious autonomy from the Turks, which, in 1830, he was able to solidify and ground in international recognition. With this, the time had come for the young Serbian ruling class to be able to form their ideas concerning the future development, purpose and goal of their state. The most important adviser to Prince Miloš Obrenović, Ilija Garašanin (1812–1874), undertook in 1844 to summarize these ruminations in a Serbian state program, the so-called "Načertanje"; in this he could build on the "expertise" which Polish Prince Adam Czartoryski, then living in Turkish exile, and a Czech artillery officer named Franjo Zach, who had entered Serbian service, had contributed.[27]

The basic thesis of Garašanin held that only a strong state could survive in this position in the Balkans. Serbia was called upon to create such a state. The small principality was not sufficient for this purpose; as a result, it had to expand, absorbing the other Serbs and even other South Slav peoples. In this aspiration, Serbia would encounter enemies. Of course, the Ottoman Empire would soon expire but Austria and even Russia would have no particular interest in seeing a powerful new state arise in the stead of the sunken Ottoman state, that would evade their influence. Serbia's natural allies were, therefore, France and England. Garašanin left it open as to whether the new Serbian "empire" would be defined as "Serbian" or as "Slavic". Garašanin had nothing against the incorporation of other South Slavs; he wrote off only the Bulgarians, because they lived too close to the Turkish center to be able to liberate themselves by their own power and were looking with hope to Russia. Nonetheless, it was without question for Garašanin that the new Slavic empire, which he wanted to see arise in the Balkans, would always primarily have a Serbian name and be under the political domination of Serbia.

A program, thus, for a Greater Serbia? Not entirely. Garašanin's concept arose from national thinking which was not yet undergirded, as it would be later, by the ideas of bourgeois nationalism. His nationalism had an imperial dimension; it was, certainly, associated with the Serbian name and the Serbian tradition, but there was no place in his concept for any national "exclusivism", let alone for "ethnic cleansing". One may identify, in the body of ideas expressed in the "Načertanje", an important precursor of later Yugoslav concepts, even if markedly from a Serbian point of view. Without doubt, Serbian policy over all the decades until the collapse of the first Yugoslavia in 1941 followed, more or less, the lines sketched by Garašanin. In this sense, the "Načertanje" had something of a prophetic quality. For a long time, its contents were kept secret for the most part; only in 1906 was it published in full for the first time.[28]

Even the Serbian Left operated on the premise of Garašanin's frame of reference. When, in the course of the 1860s, an exclusivist nationalism insinuated itself into Serbian political thought, Svetozar Marković (1846–1875) opposed this narrow concept of a "Greater Serbia", not unrealistically, with the argument that this would inevitably bring Serbia into conflicts with all of its neighbors.[29] As an alternative he proposed, in keeping with the spirit of the times, not the return to an "imperial" model, but a "federation" of free, revolutionary communities covering the entire Balkan peninsula. He could thereby fasten onto ideas which had already been developed in Habsburg-ruled Vojvodina by Mihailo Polit-Desančić.[30] How much even Marković had, in the meantime, been influenced by Serbian messianism is shown in his glorification of old Serbian institutions such as the *zadruga* (rural commune), in which he saw the model for his Balkan communes.[31]

The annexation of Bosnia-Herzegovina by Austria-Hungary in 1908, which Serbia had to accept, closed its path westwards, but, as if in compensation, a path southward opened up in the course of the two Balkan Wars, 1912–13. For the then-dominant Serbian politician, Nikola Pašić (1845–1926), the confrontation with the Danube Monarchy and the First World War came too soon after the difficult Balkan wars, indeed quite inopportunely, but it was politically impossible for him to retreat before Austria's provocation. The promises which the Allies made to Italy to obtain its entry into the war induced Serbia to publish its war aims and, for the first time, to think about including Croats and Slovenes in a new common state. The year 1917 brought the signing, on Corfu, of a joint declaration with the Yugoslav Committee, which had been established in London shortly before the war's inception.

Serbian national policy now faced a dilemma. Certainly, Pašić was enough of a statesman to realize that the planned new South Slav state could not be seen simply as an expansion of the old Serbia, with all of its institutions, or merely in terms of the unification of all Serbs in one state – as not a few of his countrymen wanted – but he could not and did not want to run from political reality either. His rival, Stojan Protić, who wanted to build a new state on a federal foundation from the beginning, had no chance. It probably suited Pašić just fine that unitaristic tendencies prevailed in the Yugoslav Committee. He could therefore concede the demand of Croats and Slovenes for "equality" under the banner of unitarism, but after the establishment of the state on 1 December 1918, he immediately tried to inject the unitarist body politic with the lifeblood of Serbian hegemonism.

For all that, multinationalism was a reality in the new state. The more far-sighted among the Serbian politicians realized this. Pašić tried in 1926 to reach an understanding with the Croatian leader, Stjepan Radić, but death cut short his efforts in this direction. King Alexander displayed no such far-sightedness. After the murder in the National Assembly in 1928, he reacted, contrary to the advice he was being given, not with concessions to the non-Serbian peoples but with the coup of 6 January 1929, which nominally replaced Serbian hegemony with a pseudo-Yugoslav unitarism, but in practice, Serbian hegemonism became all the more pronounced. Shortly after the proclamation of the dictatorship, the leading Croatian and Slovenian politicians were interned, along with Svetozar Pribičević, leader of the largest Serbian opposition party. In 1934, King Aleksandar paid for this policy with his life.

The question is often raised as to whether the first Yugoslavia, had it been allowed to operate beyond 1941, could not have finally solved its internal problems. The question seems justified, for the events of 1928–34 had kindled some critical thinking and, in addition, the signs of danger on the international horizon were beginning to appear. Milan Stojadinović, a tough-minded politician with authoritarian tendencies, did not want to change the institutional infrastructure of the country, but he encouraged a pluralism of nationally-based parties. Prince-Regent Paul, to whom Greater Serbian thinking was completely foreign, then went a step further and initiated, though without altering the country's constitution, the *Sporazum* (agreement) of 20 August 1939, which brought about the establishment of the semi-autonomous Banovina Hrvatska (Governate of Croatia). The agreement was signed by the new prime minister, Dragiša Cvetković, and the leader of the Croatian Peasant Party, Vladko Maček.[32] The *Sporazum* did not introduce a federal arrangement, but it was the first step in this direction. But one could not overlook the fact that important circles in Serbia as well as the army leadership remained opposed to the agreement. One has the impression, thus, that the Belgrade *putsch* of 27 March 1941 was directed as much against the *Sporazum* as against Yugoslavia's accession, under great pressure, to the Tripartite (Axis) Pact.[33]

Something should be said about those Serbs, about 4 million strong, who lived outside the principality and later kingdom of Serbia. They were usually called "Prečani Serbs", from the Serbian word for "across". As a rule, the concept was, for the most part, applied only to the Serbs of the Vojvodina who literally lived across the Danube and Sava rivers. These Serbs had, for the most part, come to the area from the south in the eighteenth century, but in Vojvodina they found themselves, from the beginning, under Habsburg rule. They were, in part, organized in the system of military frontiers, in part not. The Vojvodina, which originally bore the name "Serbian Vojvodina", became the cultural center of the Serbian nation in the eighteenth and nineteenth centuries. This cultural development took place as a result of the region's inclusion in the Habsburg Empire, under Central European conditions.

The situation of Serbs in Bosnia was quite different. They were practically Turkish "raja", i.e., vassals, until the Austrian occupation in 1878. They lived together with a strong Muslim population which lived, in great part, in the cities and who had earlier (prior to 1878) constituted the ruling class of Bosnia-Herzegovina. Again there were those Serbs who lived on the Austrian side of the frontier; practically all of them had been organized as border guards in the so-called Military Frontier (*Vojna Krajina*). Personally they were free, but under military discipline. Only in the nineteenth century were they gradually incorporated into the regular Croatian civil state structure, which did not please them at all. Croatia belonged, at the time, to the Hungarian half of the empire.

The Serbs of the Vojvodina had their own political parties, which were organized in a notably democratic way. After the turn of the century, the Serbs in Croatia and Dalmatia mostly supported the Yugoslav-oriented Croat-Serb coalition. After the establishment of Yugoslavia, the Prečani Serbs could usually be found, together with the Bosnian Serbs, in the unitarist-inspired party of Svetozar Pribičević. Their Yugoslav unitarism reflected the fact that they considered that the more Yugoslavia functioned as a unified state, the better they would be able to protect their Serbian culture and their links with the rest of the Serbs. They did not uncondi-tionally view Serbia, with its institutions, as their own state. Pribičević was almost permanently in opposition to the regime and court; when, under Stojadinović, the Croatian Peasant Party became the fulcrum for the crys-tallization of all opposition forces in the state, Pribičević discovered, in support of it, a love for federalism.[34] He accused the power-holders in Belgrade at the time of having always abused those Serbs living outside Serbia, since the very establishment of Yugoslavia, in their fight against "Croatian separatism". It did not take much to persuade those Serbs to be supportive in this fight. As the autonomy of the Banovina of Croatia was being set up, the majority of Serbs in Knin and in the bordering areas immediately demanded that they be conjoined with the Vrbaška Banovina, which was to continue to be fully integrated into the state structure; the capital of Vrbaška Banovina was Banja Luka.

After the occupation of Yugoslavia in 1941, the majority of Bosnian and Croatian Serbs were at first Chetniks. The Italians got along well with the Chetniks in their zone of occupation, because they considered them as much rivals to the communists as a resistance force *vis-à-vis* the *Ustaše*. After the Italian capitulation in September 1943, these Serbs for the most part entered the ranks of the Partisans. Their brigades helped to liquidate democracy and the bourgeoisie in Belgrade in 1944–45 – a fact well remembered even now by some of Belgrade's older residents. After the war, many of the members of these brigades were settled, as a reward, in villages formerly inhabited by Germans in eastern Slavonia and the Vojvodina. These were the same Serbs, who in the summer of 1991 carried out the first grave massacres against the Croats in Dalj, Borovo, and neighboring towns.

The view is widespread in Serbia today that the creation of federative Yugoslavia by the victorious communists was a Comintern conspiracy directed against the Serbian people. This claim is backed up with the argument that the Comintern had supported the idea of a Balkan feder-ation in the 1930s. This conspiracy theory was given authoritative expression in the previously mentioned Memorandum of the Serbian Academy of Sciences and Art of September 1986 (as published in the magazine *Duga* in 1989). The authors of the Memorandum complained throughout about the (alleged) slighting of Serbs under the Tito regime, but totally neglected to say anything about the disproportionately large role played by Serbs, especially from Bosnia and from the Croatian *Krajina*, in the communist regime, and in the army. In some republics, for instance in Croatia and Bosnia-Herzegovina, Serbs exerted control over important departments. The quotas, which fixed the representations of individual republics and provinces in the federal organs, were, in Croatia, Bosnia, and Vojvodina, heavily filled by Serbs. Tito's deputy for internal security, Aleksandar Ranković, was a Serb. In the immediate post-war period, he bore primary responsibility for the rounding up of disaffected Chetniks and the smashing of the Belgrade bourgeoisie, but when he was removed from office in 1966, this was viewed in all of Serbia as "a blow against Serbdom". In any case, the repressive post-war policy of the communists affected the bourgeoisie and peasantry not only in Serbia, but also in other regions of the country.

Nevertheless, the authors of the Memorandum advanced the thesis that ever since the Second World War, Serbs had been "systematically and deliberately" injured by the "revanchist politics" of an "anti-Serbian coalition".[35] This coalition was put together by Croats and Slovenes; it was embodied in the cooperation between Tito and Kardelj. The discriminatory policies against Serbia and the Serbs were allegedly pushed forward under the slogan, "a weak Serbia means a strong Yugoslavia". This went so far, in the words of the Memorandum, that "the Serbian nation does not even have the right to its own state". The authors substantiated this not only by reference to the establishment of two autonomous provinces within Serbia but also by noting the large numbers of Serbs living in other republics who "in contrast to the national minorities are not able to organize themselves culturally and to develop the unified culture of their people, to serve their alphabet and language".

The great evil for Serbs, in the eyes of the authors of the Memorandum, was the constitution of 1974, which not only divided Serbia practically in three, but also led to the "genocide" of the Serbs in Kosovo. In this way, the Memorandum also hurled reproaches against Serbs living outside Serbia-proper. With their "disinformation" they shared in the guilt for these "unsolved problems". This referred to the Serbs of Vojvodina, or at least to the old settlers there, who strongly supported the autonomy of their region. That these two provinces appear in the constitution of 1974 as "constituent elements" of Yugoslavia was especially disturbing to the authors of the Memorandum. The "restoration of the complete national and cultural integrity of the Serbian people, regardless of which republic or region they may inhabit, is their historic democratic right". The revision of the 1974 constitution was, in the eyes of the Memorandum's authors, absolutely necessary.

The Memorandum's authors stated their case adroitly. They went on for pages cataloguing grievances associated with the communist regime. With the thesis that the communist regime had become "bureaucratized", the Memorandum provided Milošević with his cue, inspiring him to represent his drive for power as an "anti-bureaucratic revolution". Only in the final section of the Memorandum did its authors reveal their actual aspirations for a 'Greater Serbia'. They tried to varnish this by claiming that Serbia did not oppose the federal constitution of 1946, but that the constitution of 1974 was, in fact, "confederative".

The Memorandum registered a formal demand for the revision of the constitution and the creation of a "federative" common state, which would assure the "equality" of Serbia and the "cultural and spiritual unity of the Serbian people". But this could only be understood as a call to return to the old Serbian idea of hegemonism. Publicly, they inclined to the view that the other peoples of Yugoslavia would never accept such a new state, because they did not want to return to the conditions of the pre-war era. Less openly, they looked toward the consolidation and expansion of the Serbian state; about the rights of the other nations, republics, and regions they had practically nothing to say. In their view, the self-determination of the Serbian nation should be realized through a "referendum of the Serbian people", to be conducted without regard to borders or the sovereign rights of the republics. That the authors of the Memorandum intended this to apply to the entire Serbian nation is clear from the fact that they wanted Serbs to exercise their "sovereignty" also in regions where they were living intermixed with other peoples, including where they were in the minority. Even today it is hard to establish who stood behind this unsigned, never properly finished document, which was always designated as a "draft". Parts of it appeared in newspapers or circulated in photocopies. The incarnation cited above (pp. 48–9) which appeared in the magazine *Duga* in summer 1989 was never disputed. Among the most important collaborators were novelist Antonije Isaković and Professor Mihajlo Marković, one of the leading figures in the Praxis group, which had passed as so liberal in the West. Professor Kosta Mihajlović was responsible for the economic section of the Memorandum. The collaboration of novelist Dobrica Ćosić, the later president of the Federal Republic of Yugoslavia, is undisputed.

When one places the Memorandum of the Serbian Academy in the context of political developments among Serbs, one obtains a clear impression of political and moral decline. Where earlier any reference to the leadership role of Serbia in the broader region in which Serbs lived was accompanied by reflections of a more extensively prepared policy and even statesmanship, the Memorandum comes across as a composite of tearful self-pity, aggressiveness, and animosity toward all the other inhabitants of Yugoslavia. Aside from its claim to an exclusive prioritization of the alleged rights of Serbs, the realization of which was demanded in the most uncompromising way, there is no sign in the Memorandum of any broader political conception. In the hands of a brutal and cunning politician such as Milošević, the Memorandum could serve as an ideal ideological program. Some observers are of the opinion that the evil in today's Serbia was sown in 1972 with the removal from office of the liberal-communist leaders of Serbia, Marko Nikezić and Latinka Perović.[36] But the ease with which the Memorandum transformed Serbian politics demonstrates that ultimate responsibility for what followed must be sought in a broader context.

Slovenia defends federalism

By contrast with the Serbs, the two million Slovenes had neither a state tradition nor a state mythology. The Socialist Republic of Slovenia, which originated after the communist victory in 1945 within the framework of the new Yugoslavia, was the first Slovene state in history. The Carantanian principality of Borut and Cheitmar, which existed between 730 and 800 CE, left hardly any traces. It had been a part of the Holy Roman Empire in medieval times. Besides, its center was not the area corresponding to today's Slovenia, but rather the area corresponding to today's Carinthia.

The communists and the Slovenian Left as a whole tried to deduce from what one may read about peasant uprisings in the late Middle Ages and in the time of the Reformation some notion of a Slovenian political tradition, as they had done also in Croatia under peasant leader Matija Gubec. Edvard Kardelj's book about the Slovenian national question, which was published under the pseudonym "Sperans" before the Second World War, constructed a veritable cult around these peasant uprisings, which were quite common also in other parts of Europe.[37] Djilas writes about his visit during the Partisan war in Slovenia, as Kardelj and Boris Kidrić, viewing a burning castle, commented emotionally, "The castle goes up in flames, the baron takes to flight." That era, as Djilas notes, clearly left a deep impression on the Slovenes.[38] In reality, the Slovenes view this epoch today less in terms of its socio-political than of its cultural aspects. Protestantism temporarily gained an observable foothold in the Slovene lands. The translation of the Bible, produced by Primož Trubar, a Ljubljana scholar, represented the first codification of a Slovenian literary language and provided an important foundation for the later modern national awakening.

The process of this awakening, initiated in the eighteenth century with the emancipation of the peasants, the early beginnings of a modern economic system, and the Enlightenment, had to be carried forward without an indigenous noble class. The leadership role was filled, much as it was in Bohemia, by the young bourgeoisie and the intelligentsia, at least as long as they did not embrace German culture or simply move to Vienna. The national defection of young elites was a problem even later, until 1918. Even today some Slovenian intellectuals worry that the nation could be culturally absorbed by the larger neighboring nations.

The modern Slovenian national movement took off rather slowly; it gave greater emphasis to cultural and economic aspects than to political goals until the outbreak of the First World War. The Slovenian core area, the Duchy of Krain, recorded a Slovene majority in the Landtag (Diet) for the first time in 1877.[39] The Slovenian national movement obtained its first strong reinforcement when the peasantry became actively involved in political and social processes. They were brought together by their village priests, though with time the higher ecclesiastical hierarchy would also prove important in this regard. From this symbiosis, the clerical People's Party arose, around the turn of the century, later becoming the dominant political force in Slovenia.

Kardelj reproached the Slovenian bourgeoisie and its political ideology, liberalism in all its variants from the Illyrists to the first Yugoslavists, that they always allowed themselves to be guided by their class interests, to the neglect of the national element.[40] This is an ideologically conditioned exaggeration. Without the preparation of bourgeois liberalism, the emancipation of the Slovenian peasantry would not have been possible. Their leading representative, Janez Krek (1865–1917), saw in the establishment of cooperatives the means to the solution of Slovenia's most salient problems. The Social Democrats played, however, only a very limited role in Slovenian politics prior to the First World War.

The Slovenian national movement was also characterized by a multiplicity of often petty disputes among various groups and their exponents. Intellectuals played an important role in these disputes; not even the two foremost national poets of the Slovenes, Franc Prešeren at the time of Illyrism and Ivan Cankar in the second half of the nineteenth century, should be left out.

Another problem for the Slovenian national movement, from its Illyrist origins until the turn of the century, was the differentiation of Slovenes from Croats. The Slovenes did not want to be "Alpine Croats", as some Croatian exponents gladly put it. The question was clarified with the further consolidation of the Slovenian literary language and Slovene culture. Politically the problem was solved in the Ausgleich of 1867, when Croatia was assigned to the Hungarian half of the empire, Slovenia to the Austrian half.

The primary political goal of the Slovenian national movement until the First World War was the unification of all Slovene areas into one Austrian crownland. Besides the Duchy of Krain, Slovenes also inhabited Styria, Carinthia, and the coastal region surrounding Trieste. Despite their common assignment to the Austrian half of the empire,[41] the Slovenes felt constrained and wronged by this political fragmentation, since outside Krain they were everywhere in a minority. They supported federalist tendencies within the monarchy, and later tried to advance the cause of trialism. Not even the outspoken Yugoslavists, who advocated union with Croats and Serbs, offered an alternative outside the monarchy. Those who today look back to the Habsburg monarchy with nostalgia often forget that this monarchy was also one of such missed opportunities.

Slovenian politicians and intellectuals periodically summarized their demands in so-called national programs.[42] But there was always a contradiction between the demand for the greatest possible autonomy and the fear of standing alone as a small nation. Once more, in February 1987 – at the beginning of the dissolution of Yugoslavia – a "national program" of this sort was published yet again, this time in the journal *Nova Revija*, edited by later Foreign Minister Dimitrij Rupel.[43]

The growing tendencies of Greater German and Greater Italian imperialism, which manifested themselves during the First World War, induced the Slovenes, in spite of their grievances, to favor even more the maintenance of the Habsburg Monarchy. Kardelj's reproach that Slovenian politics was too passive during the First World War and never managed to escape an outdated "Austroslavism" appears incomprehensible. The London agreement of 1915 between the Allied Great Powers and Italy promised Italy, as recompense for its entry into the war on the side of the Allies, not only portions of Dalmatia but also regions which were inhabited by Slovenes. The Slovenes had fought for the unification of their regions for more than a hundred years. This explains the decidedly pro-Austrian politics of Ivan Šušteršić, then clerical leader and district captain of Krain. Any pro-Allied policy, including any pro-Serbian policy, on the part of Slovenia would, as Prunk rightly notes, have been utterly impossible in view of the London agreement.[44] The Slovenian soldiers, as is confirmed on all sides, fought with particular vigor against the Italians and played a large role in the Austrian breakthrough at Caporetto in 1917.

In the course of 1917, of course, the certainty that the days of the monarchy were numbered could no longer be repressed. Slovenes had to adapt to the changing reality and they would have to do so quickly. It was clear to all that such adaptation could only mean reassociation along the lines of a South Slav solution. A younger representative of the Slovenian clergy, Anton Korošec, was prepared to move in this direction. The result of his efforts was the "May Declaration" of the Club of South Slav Deputies in the Vienna *Reichstag*.[45] Korošec, the chairman of this club, drew up the declaration himself. This document declared that those deputies associated with the club demanded, "on the basis of the national principle and of the Croatian state right", the unification of all Slovenes, Croats, and Serbs living in regions of the monarchy to form an independent, democratic state, "under the scepter of the Habsburg-Lorraine dynasty".

Whether the reference in the "May Declaration" to the House of Habsburg was meant in earnest is debatable. For tactical reasons, no other formulation would seem to have been possible. All evidence suggests that the signatories, among whom the deputies of the Croat-Serb coalition were also to be found, simply wanted to keep all options open. Even Serbian historian Momčilo Zečević admits that the reproach that the "May Declaration" remained encrusted in old Austro-Slavic thinking resulted above all from political rivalry with the Slovenian clerics.[46] It was important that the South Slav deputies within the monarchy committed themselves to cooperation and joint action. Certain reactions on the Austrian side showed that people there understood the significance of this step.[47] In January 1918, US President Woodrow Wilson proclaimed the national right of self-determination. The Slovenian People's Party was united and organized; it was the Croats who were fragmented and divided. But it was not easy for a people such as the Slovenes, or for their political leaders, to bid farewell to Central Europe, as it were. So one had to wait for developments to dictate an appropriate reaction.

This came soon enough. On 5 October 1918, in anticipation of the impending collapse of the monarchy, a National Council of Slovenes, Croats, and Serbs was formed in Zagreb; on the Slovenian side, deputies from Trieste, Graz, and Carinthia participated. At the same time, Korošec made one final attempt, in Vienna, to sound out possibilities for an Austrian solution. His absence from Zagreb had the consequence that the National Council was dominated by members of the Croat-Serb coalition, who not only decided on union with Serbia but also adopted a Yugoslav-unitarist orientation and sketched a state union without historic rights and autonomous zones.[48] The Slovenes were not entirely pleased about this solution; for them, the national unity of all Slovenes still had the highest priority.

On 28 October 1918, the monarchy finally dissolved itself, and in Zagreb, the State of Slovenes, Croats, and Serbs was proclaimed, with the intention, on the part of its founding fathers, that it would embrace all South Slav regions of the monarchy. This newborn "state" now openly sought union with Serbia. For Slovenian politics, the connection with Serbia meant stepping into a new world. Korošec set out for Geneva, where he conducted difficult negotiations with Serbian politicians, above all Nikola Pašić, the erstwhile Serbian prime minister. Apparently Korošec did not make an entirely realistic assessment of Serbian hegemonist pretensions. In any event, under pressure from Belgrade and the Yugoslav unitarists of the Croat-Serb coalition, the Kingdom of Serbs, Croats, and Slovenes was established on 1 December 1918 on a strictly unitarist basis.

For all that, it can be said that until April 1941 the Slovenian People's Party of Korošec adopted a positive attitude toward the Yugoslav state and considered the link with the Serbs a guarantee of Slovenia's national existence. *Straža*, a newspaper published in Maribor, took this position in August 1919 with regard to the charge that Korošec had sold the Slovenes down the river: the monarchy had disappeared, *Straža* noted, and in view of German and Italian imperialism, the notion of a national state cherished by some liberal politicians was simply not realistic; the only solution, *Straža* concluded, was to join with Serbia, an affiliate of the wartime *Entente*, who embraced the Slovenian nation now as its "ill-begotten brother".[49] The future leader of the Croatian Peasant Party, Vladko Maček, would later cite a conversation with Korošec, who said that, in spite of all his understanding for the Croatian standpoint, he could not embrace it as his own, since all in all Slovenia profited considerably from association with Yugoslavia, whether one spoke of its security or its national achievements or the founding of Slovenia's own university.[50]

But the disappointments were none the less great. The denial of regional autonomy within the framework of a unitarist and Serb-dominated state apparatus was only the beginning. The Slovenes were also struck by the fact that even Serbia's status as an *Entente* affiliate did not suffice to prevent the assignment of large swathes of unambiguously Slovene territory to Italy, on the basis of the 1915 agreement. Only in regard to Dalmatia were there any corrections to the peace treaty. Thus, the old *Küstenland* up to and including Postojna were assigned to Italy. After the fascist conquest of power, and especially after 1927, a policy of forcible denationalization was undertaken by Rome, under the slogan, "Drain the border!"[51] There was at the time no shortage of rebukes from Slovenes that the Yugoslav delegation at the peace negotiations had not defended Slovenia's territorial interests sufficiently energetically. In southern Carinthia, a referendum conducted on 10 October 1920 yielded a majority for remaining with Austria (22,025 against 15,279). The unstable relationships in the new South Slav state seem to have played an essential role in producing this outcome. In consequence, the Slovenes, whose whole national movement had been oriented to state unity, now found themselves more fragmented after the establishment of the Yugoslav state than ever before.

Serbian arrogance and ineptitude gradually managed to repel even the Slovenian politicians. King Alexander provided the proverbial final straw when, after the proclamation of his personal dictatorship at the beginning of 1929, he interned Korošec, in spite of his positive attitude toward the state. Korošec later took part in the Stojadinović government as Minister of the Interior. At the request of Prince-Regent Paul he was, however, included in Stojadinović's fall from power in 1939 as the refusal to solve the Croatian question on the basis of autonomy seemed increasingly risky not only to the Prince-Regent but also to the Slovenes. Korošec is said to have remarked that even the worst Yugoslavia was better for Slovenia than none at all. It should, however, also be said that toward the end of his life, Korošec became deeply concerned as to whether Serb-ruled Yugoslavia was really in a position to defend the interests and existence of the Slovenian people.[52]

After the April 1941 war, Slovenia's long-nurtured fears seemed to come true, as German and Italian imperialism divided Slovenia between themselves. The German occupying authorities wanted not only to occupy the Slovenian regions of lower Styria and southern Carinthia (Gorenjska) but to annex them outright. Nationally conscious Slovenes were persecuted, and in May, occupation authorities began deporting thousands of Slovenes to Serbia, Croatia, and also to the German Reich. Ferenc cites a total number of 54,000.[53] The deportations were halted in summer 1942, however, and some sources mention lower figures. The Italians allowed Slovenes in their *Provincia di Lubiana* a certain degree of self-administration, which, because of the activity of the Partisans, did not get very far. Marko Natlačen, the earlier Ban of the Drava Banovina whom the Italians installed as chief of a *Consulta*, resigned in September 1941 in protest against Italian repression. He was later murdered by the communist Partisans. The clerics, shocked by the communists' tactics in the war, agreed to an Italian proposal to establish village guards (*vaške straže*), though these were largely liquidated after the Italian capitulation in September 1943.

Now the relationships were inverted. The Germans tried to pursue a pro-Slovenian policy in the former Italian zone, even while continuing to display unbridled hostility toward Slovenes within their original zone of occupation – a policy supported by many *Volksdeutsche* in the area.[54] The Germans installed Leon Rupnik as President of the Ljubljana region, to which the Slovenian districts formerly occupied by Italy were now attached; Rupnik, a former general in the Yugoslav Army, had already served as mayor of Ljubljana, under the Italian occupation authorities. This Slovenian administrator was supported by nationally-oriented politicians, above all by right-wing clerics, led by Professor Lambert Ehrlich until he was murdered by the communists in May 1942. After his death, Bishop Gregorij Rožman of Ljubljana, who would flee the country after the war, became the soul of the anti-communist resistance movement. This movement originated from the fact that the communists, who were in complete command of the Partisan movement, were concerned not so much about national liberation as such, as about eliminating their political rivals, carrying out their "social revolution", and seizing power. As Slovene nationalist politician Čiril Žebot notes,[55] all the actions undertaken by the communists were, from the beginning, directed toward the achievement of these final objectives.

Soon the Germans allowed the establishment of the Slovenian *Domobranci* (Home Guards), who were entrusted with maintaining order and combating the communists. Their great disadvantage was that they had to carry out their struggle on the side of the Germans, who, on the other hand, did not hesitate to force them into compromising actions, for example, to take an oath to Hitler. As a result, they and their political exponents were branded as collaborators, to the benefit of the communists, who wanted them out of the way. Without a doubt, there were, among the *Domobranci*, some elements of open collaboration. But in general, the officers and troops were Slovenian nationalists, who became inconvenient also to the Germans from time to time. Some *Domobranci* officers were, moreover, arrested by the Germans and removed to the concentration camp at Dachau.

The end of the *Domobranci* movement was a tragedy which retains its sting even today and which, in spite of all efforts at national reconciliation, remains a source for internal factions. Janez Janša, who served as Slovenian Defense Minister 1990–94, came from a *Domobranci* family, as did also the first Prime Minister of independent Slovenia, later Foreign Minister, Lojze Peterle. The *Domobranci* retreated to Carinthia in the final days of the war in 1945 and were forcibly returned to Yugoslavia by the British, in not very noble conditions. Most of them, something over 11,000 in all, were killed by the communists in several locations, meeting the same fate as that awaiting Croatian soldiers and *Ustaša* militias sent back by the British.[56]

The communists had been less numerous in pre-war Slovenia and had had little influence even in intellectual circles. When they decided on action after the German attack on the Soviet Union, they had to attract people to their Liberation Front. They had some success recruiting from a circle of left-oriented Christian Socialists associated with novelist Edvard Kocbek, a left-oriented wing of the earlier Sokol, a group of left-wing writers and artists associated with Josip Vidmar, as well as some people from the then Italian coast, who identified with the Liberation Front, either out of feelings of national repression or from direct sympathy with the communists. This did not amount to a very broad base, but it was in any event broader than what the communist-sponsored liberation fronts elsewhere in Yugoslavia could boast.

The communist organizations, led by physician Boris Kidrič and former trade union functionary Franc Leškovšek, set about their work very ably. Edvard Kardelj joined them later, coming out of his exile in Moscow via Belgrade. In the German zone, the communists used people's opposition to national repression and deportation; in the Italian zone they fought above all against domestic and political rivals and amply exploited the greater maneuvering room they enjoyed under the Italians. Within the Liberation Front the communists grabbed the organizational initiative everywhere, reserved the key functions, including control of political propaganda, for themselves, removed people who contested their leadership, and deftly shifted emphasis between national and social factors, according to each region and its specific relationships. They led the Partisan struggle in Slovenia as a Slovenian, but also pro-Yugoslav, affair. The *Domobranci* drove them to desperate straits on several occasions. What finally gave them the upper hand was the general course of the war and abandonment of the idea of a Balkan landing by Allied troops. With their entry into Trieste and southern Carinthia in May 1945, the Partisans were able to pose as champions of long-cherished Slovenian territorial goals.

Communist rule in Slovenia was by no means any milder or more moderate than elsewhere. There may have been communists who regretted the end of the Slovenian Partisan war in centralized Yugoslav post-war communism, but there was no real resistance against those tendencies for centralization. Certainly, neither Trieste nor Carinthia became Slovenian, but most of the hitherto Italian districts inhabited entirely or in part by Slovenes were transferred to Yugoslavia, and thus to Slovenia. The so-called Zone B of the never realized Free Territory of Trieste remained under Yugoslav administration and brought Slovenia a port – Koper (Capodistria). In 1954, this zone was provisionally assigned to Yugoslavia in the Trieste Memorandum; in 1975, the Osimo Accords confirmed this assignment, to Slovenia's benefit.

From the standpoint of domestic politics, however, the picture was sadder. The Five-Year Plan introduced in 1947, which according to the famous SANU Memorandum of 1986 had allegedly wronged Serbia, actually discriminated against Slovenia, in that it placed its emphasis on satisfying the demands of the less developed parts of the country. Together with the well-known weaknesses of the communist system, this had the consequence that, during the entire period of its association with Yugoslavia after 1945, Slovenia had to live in conditions which fell short of its potential.

The Liberation Front was soon only a memory in Slovenia. Kocbek, the Christian-Socialist writer, told me around 1980 how, when he was serving as a minister in Belgrade, his communist colleagues at first withheld information from him concerning the fate of the Slovenian *Domobranci* returned by England and then lied openly about it. Between 1948 and 1951, the communists engaged in outright Stalinist police methods. The most notorious case involved the so-called Dachau trials. About 20 to 30 communist Slovenes, former inmates at Dachau, were publicly accused, without any real basis, and under torture, of having betrayed fellow citizens and party comrades in the Dachau camp. The death penalty was handed down in all cases, and carried out in ten.[57]

From about 1958, the communist leadership in Ljubljana, whether directly or through its ministers in Belgrade, increasingly engaged itself on behalf of the economic interests of Slovenia. As a result, in contrast to Croatia, Slovenia was able to advocate its interests effectively even within the framework of the communist system, and in consequence, the Catholic Church in Slovenia had no reason to step forward as the protector of the nation, as the Church did in Croatia. National emotions were also present, to be sure, in the Slovenian renewal movement. Thus Spomenka Hribar, writing in the pages of the February 1987 issue of *Nova Revija*, advanced the dubious thesis that had Tito not turned so one-sidedly to the Soviet Union after the war, Trieste and Carinthia would almost surely be Slovenian today.[58] A short while later, novelist Matej Bor stepped forward with a national-romantic thesis which originated in the nineteenth century, that in contrast to the other South Slavs, the Slovenes were not late immigrants to the region, but descendants of the old Venetians, who allegedly had been Slavs – thus "old settlers". Serious Slovenian historians such as Bogo Grafenauer rejected such ideas as arrant nonsense.[59]

The Slovenian "national program" of 1987 took a direction entirely different from that of its aggressive and xenophobic Serbian counterpart.[60] It tried to define Slovenia's position inside Yugoslavia and to draw conclusions from the present unsatisfactory situation. Sociologist Veljko Rus, an important advocate of democratization in Slovenia, wrote that one had to finally break with Bolshevism in order to move toward democratic socialism. Jože Pučnik, later chair of the Social Democratic Party, argued that Slovenia was moving through a liberal phase, but that liberalism was not yet secure. Spomenka Hribar repeated, in a retrospective glance at the liquidation of the *Domobranci*, her thesis about national reconciliation. Ivan Urbančič took aim at the almost extralegal status of the army in Yugoslavia, in which he saw a great danger for the democratization process as well as the sovereignty of Slovenia. The right of the republics to be consulted in military questions was practically nonexistent, and in this regard, Slovenia approximated an occupied country. *Nova Revija*'s chief editor, Dimitrij Rupel, concluded that the heavy burdens which Slovenia had to bear for the rest of Yugoslavia could deny Slovenia a better future.

In this "program", the existence of Yugoslavia was nowhere called into question. The thrust of the argument was that Yugoslavia needed to be restructured so as not to obstruct Slovenia's path toward democracy or to prevent its developing otherwise along "European" lines. This was the first suggestion that Slovenia's inclusion in Yugoslavia might be contingent; national self-determination took precedence. The publication of this controversial issue of *Nova Revija* also bore witness to important transformations of viewpoints during the years since 1945. Back in 1945, the reestablishment of the Yugoslav state had assured Slovenes of national unity within their own state structures, even if those structures were integrated into communist Yugoslavia. Aside from that, the protective function of communist Yugoslavia, which had proven illusory in the Second World War, was once more made believable.

More than 40 years later, the borders of Slovenia were fixed and there was neither a German nor an Italian imperialism which might prove dangerous to Slovenes; thus the Slovenes placed the demand for democracy and inclusion in Europe in the foreground and wanted – and this was especially the case among the young people of Slovenia – nothing more to do with the Balkan ways which prevailed in other parts of Yugoslavia. The hope took hold that the interests of Slovenia could, however, still be realized within the framework of a new and restructured Yugoslavia.

This conception also penetrated the upper echelons of the Slovenian party itself. For them, the "national program" might have come at an inopportune time, because the contributors to *Nova Revija* anticipated the events, but the national program stood by no means in fundamental contradiction with their own way of thinking. The cautious Jože Smole, as chair of the Socialist Alliance, indicated that he could not agree with "some of the theses".[61] Party chairman Kučan kept silent.

3 The beginning of the end

The army against Slovenia

The extreme nationalist platform which Milošević took over from the Memorandum of the Serbian Academy had its effects. But the polarization which resulted from the political activity of the Yugoslav People's army, or rather of its leadership, was less obvious then to political observers. This was connected with the fact that relatively little information concerning the political influence of army circles reached the public. Outwardly, there was the appearance that the political leadership – until the end of 1989, primarily the party presidium and after that the state presidency – held the threads of power in its hand. That was not actually the case, according to Slovenian President Milan Kučan.[1] Already, in 1987, Milošević was partly indebted for his victory at the Eighth Plenum of the Serbian party to the former Defense Minister General Ljubičić, then chair of the Serbian state presidency. The chairmen of the Yugoslav party presidium in those critical years were Boško Krunić of Vojvodina from June 1987 to June 1988 and Stipe Šuvar of Croatia from June 1988 to June 1989; both Krunić and Šuvar maintained the closest contact with the army leadership. Otherwise, or so Kučan thought, they could not have carried out the duties of their office effectively. On almost every occasion, they took into account the views of the army leadership and, where possible, complied with its wishes. This had bad results for Kosovo and constituted a permanent danger for Slovenia.

The question to what extent the views and interests of the army leadership coincided with those of Milošević is, in this connection, important. From the beginning, an element of political collaboration was evident. Borisav Jović, a vassal of Milošević, testifies to this phenomenon in many places in his memoirs.[2] One may argue, however, that while Milošević's program was, after the Eighth Plenum, primarily oriented to Serbian interests, the army leadership continued to think in terms of a united Yugoslavia. But the two orientations did not necessarily contradict each other. In the SANU program adopted by Milošević, the erection of a strong and unified Serbia took precedence, but this Serbia should, if possible, constitute at the same time the core of a new Yugoslavia, in which other peoples could live, so long as they subordinated themselves to Serbian hegemony. The conception of a unified, centralized, Serbian-run Yugoslavia corresponded also to the interests of most generals.

At the end the army could no longer function properly anywhere. This was because the army was itself a part of the Yugoslav system, bureaucratized and strained by national tensions. As long as it wanted to be Yugoslav, it had to hold itself to certain basic rules of the game. But this did not prevent it from adopting a position of hostility *vis-à-vis* the constitution of 1974 and seeking the transformation of Yugoslavia into a centralized socialist state.[3]

The army leadership's pretension to be the collective successor of Tito, the custodian of the Holy Grail of socialism and the ultimate guarantor of Yugoslavia seems to have led some individual generals to engage in personal power politics. This was clearest in the case of Admiral Mamula, who served as Minister of Defense until June 1988. It did not seem, however, that Mamula's aspirations were taken too seriously in political circles.

Foreign observers, including diplomats and military attachés, did not always correctly assess the special character of the Yugoslav People's army. Too often they saw the army only as a professional institution and overlooked the fact that it was completely politicized. As a result, the army did not enter the equation as an ultimate arbiter in the country's inner conflicts, much to the disappointment of some Westerners. On the contrary, insofar as it aspired to a political role, the army tended rather to become just one more party to the conflict. Both within and outside Yugoslavia there were hopes that Veljko Kadijević, who succeeded Mamula as Defense Minister in June 1988 and who had completed his studies in the United States, would undertake to effect the de-politicization of the army. These expectations were not at all fulfilled. On the contrary, Kadijević maneuvered the army establishment directly into political confrontations; in his memoirs,[4] he reveals unmistakable anti-democratic, anti-Western, pro-Soviet, and communist-dogmatic attitudes. The only enduring legacy of his stay in the United States, evidently, was his haughty arrogance. He may be seen as one of the most culpable for the collapse of Yugoslavia.

The suspicion has sometimes been voiced that Slovenian opposition figures, above all the later Defense Minister Janez Janša and the circle associated with the magazine *Mladina*, began a campaign against the army in early 1988 because they deliberately wanted to destroy that "ultimate arbiter" of Yugoslavia in order to prepare the way for Slovenian independence. This interpretation seems vastly exaggerated. Criticism of the army as a centralized institution lying almost entirely beyond the control of the republics can already be found in the journal *Nova Revija* in early 1987; this criticism reflected the growing contradictions between the democratic, pro-federalist orientation of Slovenia and Balkan centralism, as embodied in the army.[5]

The first provocative attack on Slovenia from Belgrade may have been the somewhat delayed letter from the federal prosecutor Miloš Bakić to the Slovenian state prosecutor on 18 January 1988, in which he characterized the "national program" essays published in *Nova Revija* as an instance of "the crime of hostile propaganda" and, in the name of legal equality for all of Yugoslavia, demanded that criminal proceedings be initiated.[6] The argument of "legal equality" for all of Yugoslavia would be cited often in the months ahead, in order to attack the achievements of the democratization process in Slovenia. The Slovenian state prosecutor rejected the argumentation of the federal prosecutor and held that this opinion amounted to an abuse of the provisions of the law; moreover, if federal authorities wanted to pass judgment on the relatively mild Slovenian "national program", they should also – to be consistent – pass judgment on the more radical and infinitely more hostile Memorandum of the Serbian Academy.[7]

In the first days of February 1988, the Slovenian newspaper *Delo* published highly critical reports concerning a visit by Defense Minister Mamula to Ethiopia. The purpose of the visit was to sell Yugoslav-manufactured weaponry to Addis Ababa, and this at a time when Western countries were organizing relief efforts to alleviate widespread hunger in the East African country. On 12 February 1988, there appeared in *Mladina*, officially still the news-organ of the Slovenian Youth Association, an editorial with the headline, "Mamula Go Home". Criticism was also directed against the development of a new fighter aircraft and against the construction of a luxurious villa at the seaside for the army commander-in-chief.

The army leadership was speechless. Criticism of this sort was unprecedented in communist Yugoslavia. The army newspaper *Narodna armija*, supported by the Serbian press, reported on 18 February that there was an open "anti-Yugoslav campaign" which needed to be "energetically" countered. Moreover, according to the interpretation of the army news-organ, the campaign was directed toward the achievement of an independent Slovenian state. The Slovenian leadership viewed the *Mladina* article with discomfort; Jože Smole, chair of the Socialist Alliance of Slovenia and, at the time, the second most important politician in Slovenia (after Kučan), characterized the public discussion of the development of Yugoslavia's new combat aircraft as "premature".[8] The presidency of the Central Committee of the League of Communists of Slovenia held, however, in a position adopted on 3 March 1988, that *Mladina* 's criticism of the army had to be seen in the context of the fast unfolding democratization process in Slovenia.[9]

On 25 March 1988, a momentous session of the Military Council, to which the leading members of the army high command belonged, took place in Belgrade at the Defense Ministry. The Military Council constituted a kind of coordinative body for the political activity of the military establishment. This organ assigned General Svetozar Višnjić, then commander of the Ljubljana

Military District, the task of communicating the next day with the Slovenian Minister for Internal Affairs, Tomaz Ertl, and informing him that the army leadership considered the attacks against it tantamount to "counter-revolutionary activity" and believed that it had roots not merely in the respective editorial offices. The general was assigned to ask the Slovenian Interior Minister how Slovenian authorities would react in the event that it should prove necessary to arrest a number of Slovenian intellectuals and, above all, whether they were in a position to make an end to expected demonstrations. The army offered its "assistance" to the Slovenian authorities.[10]

The conversation between Ertl and Višnjić actually took place on 26 March. The astonished Ertl realized at once that he could not speak authoritatively on matters of such gravity. He cut short the conversation, therefore, and informed the highest authorities in the republic. The conversation was continued in Planica in the afternoon in the presence of Kučan and Stane Dolanc in his capacity as Slovenia's representative in the Yugoslav state presidency, as well as the head of State Security in Slovenia, Ivan Erzen. Kučan and Dolanc replied decisively that such things simply could not be discussed with representatives of the army, as this was incompatible with the constitutional position of Slovenia. Furthermore, there was the question of the constitutional competence of the Defense Ministry's Military Council itself.

The behavior of the military and the events which followed indicate that the army leadership felt called upon to launch a broad, coordinated "purge" of the political sphere throughout the country and to apply some sort of "emergency measures" in order to discipline individual party leaderships, above all in Kosovo and Slovenia, but, naturally, not in Serbia. This objective was obvious also in other ways. The murder committed by a soldier of Albanian ethnicity in the Paračin barracks on 3 September 1987 was dramatized by the military in early 1988, in a highly dubious way, as if it were symptomatic of a broad conspiracy against the army.[11] The army was, predictably, given solid support in the Serbian press, which did not want to miss a chance to make a "common front" against the Albanians. In Priština, the representatives of Albanian human rights organizations began to complain, from this point on, of bad treatment of soldiers of Albanian nationality.

At the end of February or beginning of March 1988, the federal prosecutor tried to file an indictment against *Mladina* and *Teleks*, but because of the unclear division of jurisdiction between federal and republic prosecutors, did not know exactly how to proceed. The Slovenian state prosecutor refused to cooperate; as for certain accusations against Admiral Mamula in connection with the construction of a villa at government expense, the prosecutor was willing, at most, to investigate this "insult" to the army.[12] But this would have entailed bringing the affair before the public. The federal prosecutor gave notice that he was prepared to go over the head of the Slovenian state prosecutor.[13] The Serbian press continued to publish bitter attacks on Slovenia. On the other hand, the army leadership decided to eliminate the Ljubljana Military District and to attach it to the Fifth Army District in Zagreb. This measure, as was suspected at the time in Slovenia, was intended to curtail the Slovenian leadership's control over the Territorial Defense Forces.[14]

It later became clear that the entire operation had been carefully prepared beforehand. On 21 March, the Federal Council for the Protection of the Constitutional Order (*Savezni savet za zaštitu ustavnog poretka*), a kind of permanent commission under the chairmanship of a member of the state presidency, had published a "document". In this document, it was alleged that the attacks on the army emanating from Slovenia displayed a tendency which was threatening to the constitutional order. "Strong counter-measures" were demanded; among other things the federal UDBa should "identify" the agents of this "special war" against Yugoslavia and its constitutional order.[15]

Apparently brought into line by this summons, one of the working groups of the party presidium offered a proposal to resolve the crisis which, after its acceptance in the federal party presidium and contingently in the Central Committee, would have given the green light for concerted action in Slovenia, perhaps even for the proclamation of a state of emergency.[16] The document referred specifically to "attacks on the sovereignty and integrity of Yugoslavia" and to an "abuse of democracy". The document also took aim at those who had opened up public space "for such attacks", which is to say, the leadership of Slovenia. In conclusion, it called for "decisive action" and "differentiation", including against those who bore "responsibility" for creating the possibility of such attacks taking place.

The situation with which Kučan saw himself confronted at the secret 29 March session of the LCY Presidium was grave. The Presidium presented a more difficult challenge than the Central Committee in that the former was dominated by dogmatic thinking and pro-army sympathies, which one could not say of the Central Committee as a whole. Kučan could cite two points in his defense against dogmatic figures such as Pančevski, Krunić, Lazar Mojsov, and Raif Dizdarević, who took the army's side. First, as he noted at the very beginning of his report,[17] an expanded session of the Slovenian communist Central Committee, in which representatives of the trade unions and other organizations also took part, had agreed to reject the insinuations of the documents emanating from Belgrade. The Slovenian communists, according to Kučan, rejected the assessment contained in the document; it was, in their view, unacceptable, not objective, not real. The Slovenian communists could not accept responsibility for, or answer for the consequences of, such assessments which were embraced by the term "counter-revolutionary"; moreover, the document seemed inclined to some rather facile generalizations about "all Slovenes". One had to see the criticism of the army in Slovenia in the total context, above all in connection with the miserable economic situation.

The second point, which Kučan made the pivot of his report, had to do with the behavior and standpoint of the Military Council. The party presidium should expressly concern itself with this, said Kučan. What were the legal provisions which empowered precisely the Military Council to issue such wide-ranging political assessments and even to call for specific actions? That was a "new quality" in the political discussion. The assessments in the Military Council were distinct from those of the leading political organs. What did it mean when, in the Military Council, Yugoslavia was defined as a "unified federal country"? Krunić, like Mojsov, had assured him that they had not heard anything about the session of the Military Council or about the consequent intervention of the military commander in Ljubljana. "I protest energetically against such a procedure," Kučan replied. One should imagine, Kučan continued, what kind of impression a military *putsch* in Yugoslavia would make abroad, above all in the neighboring states.

With this report, Kučan was able to block passage of a resolution. He told me later[18] that then, as on other occasions, the isolated Slovenes had concentrated on preventing a vote. Whether with long speeches or by raising procedural questions, they succeeded in this; they talked filibuster-style, until the other members became tired and just wanted to go home. In any case, the general aversion to voting in communist organs was a party tradition of long standing; this had its origin in the fact that the fate of minorities in communism was in general not an enviable one.

The question as to whether the events of March 1988 were really connected with a *putsch* attempt or were merely a bluff, can be answered today with considerable certainty, in that it seems that the army leadership did not actually intend to carry out a military *putsch* as such. There were practical and organizational reasons why the army leaders could not do this. But they did hope to carry out a kind of political or institutional *putsch*, i.e., an intervention under a state of emergency, on which the highest political leadership of the party was supposed to confer legitimation and which could then be carried out by the army, by force if necessary. For such purposes, an appropriate political document was needed – ideally something from the LCY Presidium; on the basis of this document the subordinate organs, including those of the state, could have been induced, with an allusion to "democratic centralism", to collaborate. According to Kučan, there were no direct preparations, however, such as lists of intellectuals who should be arrested.[19]

The Slovenian leadership was perplexed. Already the most modest beginning of criticism and incipient democratization had confronted the republic with the threat of armed intervention by the military and had subjected it to an unbelievable smear campaign in the Serbian press. The federal leadership, including both the party presidium and the state presidency, had lined up on the side of the interventionists and had been dissuaded from this position only with effort. The situation was, thus, unpleasant, because in the party presidium, a simple majority, not a consensus, would have sufficed to ratify a decision. The Slovenian leadership now knew what its country could expect from the continuation of efforts at democratization. The army, denied the realization of its plans, now thought in terms of revenge. That the affair was in earnest was shown in the almost desperate attempts of the LCY Presidium to keep it secret. Under the circumstances, the Slovenian leadership had to adopt a cooperative demeanor. Fourteen days after these events, the Slovenian leadership prevented an article entitled "Night of the Long Knives" from appearing in *Mladina*. At the end of May 1988, Kučan's speech became known, which gave rise to an enormous amount of agitation in Ljubljana. That was shortly before the arrest of the four out-of-favor Slovenian publicists (p. 67). KOS agents found a copy of Kučan's speech in Janez Janša's desk in the editorial offices of *Mladina*.

At first the political leadership did nothing after Kučan's speech, however. On 8 April, a delegation of the LCY Presidium, headed by Krunić, arrived in Ljubljana, to mediate or negotiate. The delegation met with the Slovenian party presidium for an expanded session. "Some sort of document," as Montenegrin Vidoje Žarković put it almost pleadingly, had to be issued; one was discussing this subject for the fourth time already. Krunić thought that if some document could not be issued, the party would suffer a loss of prestige.[20]

On 31 May 1988, as Janez Janša relates in his memoirs,[21] his doorbell rang in the early morning. At the door were officials of the Slovenian political police. Janša was arrested, and was asked, by the Slovenian police, how a state secret such as Kučan's speech had come to be in his desk drawer at *Mladina'*s editorial offices. Then military justice took over the case. Also arrested was Sgt Ivan Borštner, an active-duty soldier serving in Ljubljana, who was accused of having stolen an army document. This concerned a rather unimportant report about the level of military preparedness of certain units in Slovenia. David Tasić, a *Mladina* journalist, was likewise arrested, while Franc Zavrl, senior editor of the magazine, evaded arrest by fleeing to a hospital. The charge was betrayal of a state secret.

Janša and many others both then and later expressed the suspicion that Slovenian organs and politicians had actively cooperated with the army in his arrest. Janša implicated the Slovenian political police, which carried out arrests of civilians, as well as some Slovenian politicians, above all Dolanc, Andrej Marinc, Jože Smole, Interior Minister Ertl, and Ivan Erzen, chief of political security. Other than that, he also claimed that the editor-in-chief of *Mladina*, Robert Botteri, had been a KOS agent.[22]

Without a doubt, the procedures now initiated against Janša, ostensibly on the demand of Defense Minister Mamula, placed not only the Slovenian politicians, but also the accessories in the Slovenian police, in a quandary. The Administration for State Security in the Slovenian Ministry for Internal Affairs had, against the background of certain rebukes, declared that it was, in any event, obliged to provide legal assistance for military justice. It did not have the right to decide as to whether the charges were justified; this was a matter for military justice.[23] For his part, Kučan held that it had been impossible for him or any other leaders of Slovenia to intervene in these proceedings; one had to await the results of the investigation and trial. Later, when open conflict had broken out between him and Kučan, Janša would accuse the Slovenian president of complicity in his arrest.[24] But one may note that in his memoirs, published in 1992, Janša did not make such direct accusations against Kučan. In any event, the relationship between Slovenian UDBa and KOS had long been one of mutual distrust, in which each kept close watch over the other. Kučan, for his part, considered it unlikely that Botteri had ever been a KOS agent.[25]

The news of the arrests provoked widespread indignation in Slovenia. The spontaneous and organized demonstrations alike, as well as political activities which now followed, provided concrete impetus for full democratization, and ultimately energized the movement for state independence.[26] Immediately after the arrests, a Committee for the Protection of Human Rights was formed, which was supposed to coordinate all future protest actions, and in which one could see the precursor of the later political coalition, Demos. Among the 30 founding members of this Committee were Igor Bavčar, a personal friend of Janša's, later to serve as Slovenian Minister of the Interior, and Lojze Peterle, later to serve as (Christian-Democratic) Prime Minister and subsequently as Foreign Minister. They were joined by France Bučar, the future President of the Parliament, and other personalities of Slovenian intellectual life.

On 21 June 1988, the Committee organized a rally with 15,000 participants in downtown Ljubljana. The trial and the entire agitation by the army, its attempted *putsch* (which had by now become public knowledge in all its aspects), and the activities of certain federal organs together with the general tone of the Serbian press convinced many Slovenes that they were under threat from the Yugoslav center.

At the same time, in June 1988, there were some significant changes in the principal actors in the Yugoslav drama which was unfolding. Stipe Šuvar, a Croat, who now took Krunić's place as chair of the LCY Presidium, was a complex personality of considerable intellectual prowess mixed with cynicism, who continued nonetheless to adhere to almost primitive dogmatic Marxist beliefs. The divided Central Committee of the LC Croatia had left it to the LCY Presidium to choose between two candidates, who represented rival factions within the Croatian party. The LCY Presidium showed its dogmatic proclivities by picking, by a wide margin, Šuvar over Ivica Račan, the champion of the "liberal" wing of the Croatian communist party. During his earlier campaign against the intellectuals, when he served as Minister of Education in Croatia, Šuvar had said that one good platoon of soldiers would suffice to disperse all critical Yugoslav intellectuals.

There was also the aforementioned change in the Ministry of Defense (p. 61) when, in mid-May, Gen.-Col. Veljko Kadijević succeeded Branko Mamula as Minister of Defense (and hence, as *de facto* Supreme Commander of the army). Like Mamula, Kadijević was a Serb from Croatia, having been born in 1925 near Imotski in the so-called Dalmatian hinterland. In the Partisan war he served largely as a political commissar; later he made his career at army headquarters.

In the same way, following the rules of rotation, former Foreign Minister Raif Dizdarević, now representing Bosnia-Herzegovina in the state presidency, was elected to a one-year term as chair of this body, succeeding the Macedonian representative, Lazar Mojsov. As a communist Bosnian Muslim, he was inclined toward centralism; as a former police functionary he thought along dogmatic lines. His opportunism, conjoined with fearfulness, would prove fatal on a number of occasions.

Finally, at the beginning of June 1988, Janez Stanovnik, head of the European Division of the UN, succeeded France Popit, who as a member of an earlier generation no longer understood the world, at the helm of the Slovenian presidency. Stanovnik represented the transition to a multiparty, democratic state; he had not made his career in the communist apparatus and this fact gave him credibility. His dignified appearance kindled in the minds of many Slovenes the hope of independent statehood, even though Stanovnik, in all his conversations with me in 1988 and 1989, always underlined that he could not imagine Slovenia existing outside Yugoslavia; maybe young people saw things differently. In this regard he was of the same mind as Jože Smole.

The Slovenian leadership, which at that point in time could not yet afford to ignore the legal situation, focused, where the trial of Janša was concerned, on two points: First, the leadership demanded a speedy end to the investigation; and second, it seconded the demand of the public demonstrators that the trial be held in Slovenian, rather than in Serbo-Croatian. This was not a purely military affair, in which the language of command, Serbo-Croatian, should be used, Kučan argued.[27] This issue brought the Slovenian leadership and the so-called opposition together. "The Slovenes," Kučan told the Central Committee at the end of June, "cannot accept a state which does not guarantee them the use of their mother tongue and their equality, and in which the freedom, sovereignty, and equality of the Slovenian people are not safeguarded." Kučan spoke these words after conducting utterly fruitless talks with General Kadijević,[28] and after the Yugoslav state presidency headed by Dizdarević had expressly rejected the Slovenian demand that the Slovenian language be used in proceedings of military courts on the territory of Slovenia.[29]

The sentences of the military court in Ljubljana were, as a result of the pressure of the general agitation in Slovenia, relatively mild: one and a half years in prison for Janša and Zavrl, five months for Tasić, but four years for Borštner. Under law, the defendants had to be released to the custody of the Slovenian judicial system, which was supposed to carry out the sentences. This the Slovenian judicial authorities passively did. Meanwhile, the defendants revealed that the military judges had been more interested in asking them about the internal dynamics within the Slovenian leadership than in probing the accusations as such.[30]

After the trial, the political situation in Slovenia changed significantly. Not only had the population and leadership now drawn closer on questions of democratization and the defense of national interests, but the notion of an independent Slovenia entered for the first time into the field of vision – in view of the danger emanating from Belgrade. In July 1988, an opinion poll found that 63 per cent of the population favored independence (this view being especially widespread among younger people), even if the course which might be charted to this goal was not yet clear.[31] The notion that Yugoslavia might be transformed into a loose confederation of independent states now emerged. Functionaries of the older generation, such as Jože Smole, continued to believe that Slovenia might one day succeed in obtaining a breakthrough for its ideas throughout the rest of Yugoslavia. Smole continued to see the path to democratization within the existing system; the party, in his view, should be converted into something along the lines of the Socialist Alliance, while the Socialist Alliance should be opened so wide that non-socialist groups and ideas could also find a place there.[32] These were the ideas behind the transition.

Sentiment in Slovenia during 1988 changed in connection with other major developments elsewhere in Yugoslavia. In Belgrade, Milošević had sounded the call for an attack on the autonomy of Kosovo and Vojvodina; in so doing, Milošević was calling into question the 1974 constitution and indeed the entire federal structure. The support which the LCY Presidium and the army gave Milošević in almost all questions must have seemed ominous to Slovenes. In autumn 1988, one could read in black and white even in Belgrade newspapers that there were "two concepts of Yugoslavia": a federalist, reformist, and liberal Yugoslavia, such as Slovenia wished to introduce, and a dogmatic-centralist Yugoslavia, which was closely linked with Greater Serbian hegemonism.[33] Slovenia saw itself constrained to resist centralist programs for constitutional reform. An important element in the development of public opinion in Slovenia was that, as a Central European people, Slovenes felt more and more cut off from Europe. The official foreign policy of Belgrade, which still clung to the dream of nonalignment and which slighted connections with Europe, contributed to this shift in Slovenian thinking. The dogmatic, anti-reformist, and as a result also completely unsuccessful economic policy of the Mikulić government, which caused living standards to sink even in Slovenia, had an even stronger effect. In a report of the Slovenian Ministry for Internal Affairs, it was confirmed that over a period of 10 years, the buying power of the average income in Slovenia had slid from 80 per cent of that in Austria to a mere 45 per cent.[34]

A joint conference of the extended state presidency of Yugoslavia and of the republic presidency of Slovenia on 13 September 1988 showed to what extent the leading figures in the central political organs of Yugoslavia, whether in the party or the state apparatus, stood on the side of the army.[35] Dizdarević, as chair of the Yugoslav state presidency, described the position taken by Kučan and Jože Smole *vis-à-vis* the military justice system as "unacceptable". Dolanc had to admonish Dizdarević that Slovenia was still a constituent part of Yugoslavia and not a foreign power. Šuvar was singing the same tune as Dizdarević and demanded that the Slovenian leadership "deal more effectively" with its opposition. Kadijević went so far as to accuse the Slovenian leadership of "espionage", because it had asked the army leadership to finally reveal what kind of document Sgt Borštner had been found guilty of having stolen. General Ljubičić, Serbia's representative in the Yugoslav state presidency, spoke of open separatism in Slovenia. Josip Vrhovec from Croatia was the only representative to express sympathy for the Slovenian position, at least to some extent. Kučan saw himself once more called upon to make a declaration that Slovenia was striving for a "free, modern, democratic, and sovereign development in a federal state founded on the principle of the equality of its constituent parts". Stanovnik, as Slovenian head of state, said that the army's behavior and the catastrophic economic policy were to blame for the direction in which public opinion in Slovenia was evolving.

At the second conference on 9 October,[36] Kadijević and Prime Minister Mikulić raised the question of the financing of the army. Within the framework of the anticipated constitutional reforms it had been proposed that the army, whose maintenance absorbed 70 per cent of the total Yugoslav budget, should in future be financed directly by subventions from the republics, thus without having to present its annual budget before the *Skupština* (the Federal Assembly). Mikulić revealed that, between 1976 and 1980, the army had received 6.17 per cent of the national income and that it was now receiving only 5.2 per cent. Because of the bad economic situation, it would only have received 4.94 per cent of the national income during 1987. Dizdarević and Mojsov (an adherent of the dogmatic wing of the party) mourned the high indebtedness of the army, estimated to have reached 555 billion dinars as of 1988. Now the Slovenes suddenly found themselves being wooed. In Ljubljana the word circulated that the army hated everything Slovenian except Slovenian money. It did not occur to any of the politicians present at this meeting to demand that the military cut expenses. Stanovnik stood alone in urging that the army could not ignore economic realities.

Kadijević said openly in his memoirs that the aforementioned first joint conference on 13 September 1988 was not so much an effort at "normalization" as an effort, on the contrary, by the army leadership to make a fresh attempt to prepare a broad political-military front against Slovenia. On 12 August, as he reports,[37] Kadijević took part in a session of the

Yugoslav state presidency, at which appropriate but unclear resolutions were adopted. Since the protocols of the sessions of the state presidency are not available, the progress of this meeting is difficult to reconstruct. Ostensibly the joint conference of 13 September should have confirmed any measures which might have been resolved on 12 August. But the proceedings of 13 September were, on the contrary, a big disappointment for Kadijević. First of all, the General remarked candidly that "no purely military measures can have political success unless their practitioners can also offer a remedy, inspired by an alternative policy".[38] But instead, the majority of the members of the Yugoslav presidency simply retreated before the "complete unity of the Slovenian leadership".

With these events in autumn 1988, the conflict between the army leadership and the Slovenian government became one of the prominent features of Yugoslav politics. The danger of intra-Yugoslav aggression now hovered over Slovenia. Could one expect Slovenes to accept this as a permanent condition? And Slovenia was even expected to continue to foot a large part of the army's budget, even as the army continued to threaten that republic.

Milošević stirs up a storm

As he took the reins of the party leadership in Kosovo in May 1987 – so said Azem Vllasi later in retrospect, the issue was not how to "normalize" the situation in Kosovo but how to defend the province's autonomy.[39] Milošević was determined to establish the "unity" of Serbia, without regard to the constitution or to public opinion in the rest of Yugoslavia. "He worked for the abolition of the autonomy of the province, while I worked for its retention," Vllasi would later say in defining the essence of his conflict with Milošević. The autonomy of Kosovo and Vojvodina was guaranteed by the Yugoslav constitution of 1974. One might have expected, thus, that federal authority, whether on the party level or on the level of the state apparatus, would have been brought to bear on the side of preserving the autonomy of the two regions. In reality, as will be shown, it was quite the opposite.

After his victory at the Eighth Plenum of the Central Committee of LC Serbia in autumn 1987, Milošević took time out to consolidate his power. It was winter and not a good time for public meetings. In February 1988, Kosovo was tense with anticipation. Vllasi seemed to have understood that nothing could be achieved through his earlier policy of supporting "differentiations" among the ranks of his own Albanian cadres, and that the real issues had nothing to do with the Serbian side's wildly exaggerated accusations of alleged "threats" to the Serbian population in Kosovo.[40] As a result of his change of heart, Vllasi had recovered some prestige among the Albanian population. For all that, the Albanians were already everywhere on the defensive. Insofar as Vllasi had accepted the thesis of "counter-revolution" in Kosovo in 1981, he had himself afforded the LCY Central Committee the possibility of now looking at things from this angle. Serbian agitation made full use of this.

When I spoke with the rector of the University of Priština, a Serb, in 1988, he was foaming at the mouth about further "differentiations".[41] The flag of the Albanian nation had to be changed and Serb emigrants who returned were so overwhelmed with privileges that many left only in order to return later. The so-called "federal intervention" of October 1987 seemed to Vllasi, for all that, to have somewhat strengthened his strategic position; he could drop some of the noisier Serb agitators from the party and even dared to take the side of the Albanians in Macedonia, who were at the time under severe threat and whose traditional walls, around houses and barns, were being torn down under the pretense of "urban planning".

However, the pressure for change to the Serbian constitution (in the sense of the "unification" of Serbia), and also for changes to the appropriate clauses in the federal constitution, had already begun. At the beginning of 1988 the aforementioned proposals (p. 84) for the revision of the federal constitution were publicized, and on 11 January the Serbian Assembly initiated the process of constitutional revision in Serbia. This pressure was intensified at the end of May with the nomination of Milošević's close associate, Borisav Jović, to serve as president of the constitutional commission of the Serbian parliament.[42]

In February 1988, all the Albanian politicians in Kosovo were reassuring me that there was a "general agreement" about a revision of the Serbian constitution but that this would "never" affect the autonomy of the province. One could, further, rely on the support of the other province in union with Serbia, Vojvodina. I was struck by the extent to which most of the Albanian politicians of Kosovo misunderstood Milošević's absolute intentions. They seemed to believe that Milošević might be satisfied with some formal concessions to "the unity of Serbia" and that the result of negotiations would be a compromise which would both confirm the province's autonomy and offer some satisfaction to the Serbian side. It seemed acceptable to many that some things connected with the constitutional position of Serbia should be revised.

In May 1988, Vllasi was relieved of his duties as chair of the party leadership in Kosovo and replaced by Kaqusha Jashari, a 42-year-old civil engineer and later trade union functionary. It was said at the time that her mother was a Montenegrin; this seemed to make her "acceptable" to the Serbian side.[43] Belgrade seems to have played a part in Vllasi's resignation, although it more or less followed established procedures of "rotation". At any rate, Vllasi remained a member of the party leadership and continued to hold the strings of power in his hands. Moreover, Jashari, as would soon become clear, defended the same viewpoints as Vllasi.

Shortly after taking office, Jashari had to acknowledge that the "winter vacation" was over. She saw herself now confronted by a suddenly ignited Serbian offensive, with which she concerned herself, visibly irritated, at a session of the federal party leadership.[44] The Serbs, so she said, were aiming at a "separate existence" in Kosovo, were organizing their own activities at the party level and in all social organizations of the province, and wanted to ignore the common organs, including those of the party, as much as possible. Jashari reported that signatures were being collected for countless petitions, in which it was alleged that nothing had changed since 1981. The base for these activities was furnished by the party organizations of Kosovo Polje, in which Serbs had a majority.

In the middle of 1988, this agitation came into the open. The communists among the Kosovo Serbs organized a counter-manifestation to the official party conference of the League of Communists of Kosovo and "rejected" the information which Jashari had presented at the conference. Among other things, Jashari had spoken about the unfavorable impact which the unfolding constitutional discussions in Serbia promised to have for the autonomy of Kosovo and Vojvodina. Only the rights and jurisdiction of the Republic were being defined, she noted, and these in a far-reaching way; nothing was being said about the rights or jurisdiction of the provinces.[45] The position of the autonomous provinces, as prescribed in the federal constitution of 1974, should not be changed, she argued. In the course of public meetings at Kosovo Polje and elsewhere, Kosovar Serbs were adopting ever more aggressive tones which betrayed the intention of bringing the tactics of such meetings to other regions as well as of offering themselves as a "phalanx" for Milošević in the whole of Yugoslavia. In Kosovo Polje, local Serbs demanded that punitive measures be adopted against a number of federal and former Serbian functionaries because of their support for the constitution of 1974 and their resistance to the "reunification" of Serbia.[46] A petition signed by about 50,000 Kosovar Serbs included the threat: "If the Yugoslav and republic leaderships are not prepared to fulfill their governmental or party duties, we demand at least that you do not prevent us from organizing our self-defense of our freedom, honor, and dignity."

On 11 June 1988, a draft of a new Serbian constitution was published.[47] The draft provided that all authoritative state functions, including defense, security, and international cooperation (which included, thus, cooperation with the Socialist Republic of Albania), would be concentrated in the hands of the Republic authorities. The work of the security forces, it said, should be "completely unified". It has never become known why Kosovo's deputies in the Serbian constitutional commission accepted this draft at all. Even the Serbian side seemed not to have anticipated this success, for *Politika* wrote at the time that it was expected that there would be three different drafts (one from Serbia and one from each of the two autonomous provinces) and not just one draft with some "variations" as proposed by the autonomous provinces. That it had developed as it had was, thus, a "great victory". This assessment by *Politika* made sense, because it was now going to be easier for the Serbian side to overcome the resistance of the two provinces to total "unity". The Serbs could now refer to this preliminary "agreement in principle" and, if need be, accuse the provinces of acting in contradiction to their own views.[48]

In July 1988, Milošević transformed his tactic of "anti-bureaucratic" meetings into a broader strategy. Šuvar now stood at the pinnacle of the federal party leadership. To the surprise of many, the first target of the new, almost violent offensive was not Kosovo, but Vojvodina. Its leadership was dominated by so-called "old settler" Serbs. It was not liberal in color, but it stood by the province's autonomy. On 7 July, several hundred Kosovar Serbs came to Novi Sad and conducted noisy rallies in front of the governmental and party buildings for two days, provoked clashes with the police, and displayed banners with slogans which accused the Vojvodina leadership of being "Traitors to Socialism" or a "Fifth Column".[49] Vojvodina's politicians were, allegedly, opposed to the changes in Serbia, because they were worried about their posts.

The leaders in Vojvodina, people like Krunić, former General Petar Matić, Djordje Stojšić, Milovan Šogorov, and others, now showed that they were not inclined to yield to pressure from the street and closeted themselves in a closed session of the province's Central Committee. Afterwards, they considered it correct to reveal the substance of their deliberations to the public. The result was a storm of agitation throughout all of Serbia. Some headlines appearing at the time in *Politika* will illustrate the point: "The masks have fallen", "Factional activity of a part of the leadership in Vojvodina", "Krunić, Matić and Stojšić are prepared to destroy Yugoslavia in order to hold onto their jobs", and "Encouragement for Irredentism".[50] Alongside Belgrade Television and the purged staff of *NIN*, *Politika* was now one of Milošević's main mouthpieces.

The events which had taken place in Novi Sad had a weight which militated that they be reviewed by federal authorities, as indeed they were. But to the consternation of many Yugoslavs, the LCY Presidium emerged on 30 July, after a lot of hemming and hawing, with a declaration to the public,[51] which endorsed not the besieged party leadership in Vojvodina, but Milošević and his cohorts.

The declaration did concede that such illegal assemblies, as had taken place in Novi Sad should be prevented, as far as possible. But once the assembly took place, the declaration continued, the Vojvodina leadership not only should have received a delegation from the demonstrators, but should also have conducted "a broad discussion with all the demonstrators". This assessment was tantamount to an endorsement by the federal party leadership of Milošević's whole strategy of public meetings. Second, it was judged that the publication of the stenographic record of ostensibly closed deliberations had led "to a further aggravation of the situation". The preservation of secrecy concerning views expressed in party organs seemed, to the federal party leadership, still an appropriate means for conflict resolution.

Third, the party presidium now expressly endorsed efforts aimed at the revision of the Serbian constitution. It did not go into details, but Milošević could chalk up the "principled" position taken by the Presidium as a success; indeed, he was able to use this document later to put pressure on the two provinces.

An indignant and irritated Krunić said, after this declaration was read in the LCY Central Committee, that he could have expected a clearer response from the party leadership if a member of the higher party organ had been denounced as a "traitor" to party and people. Šuvar responded that in the resolution there was also a statement against "coarse slander". The party leadership of Kosovo was attacked too, because allegedly it had not worked sufficiently hard for the adoption of CC decisions on the Kosovo question. Nowhere in the declaration could one find a direct criticism of Milošević and his policies.

The LCY Presidium under Krunić and later under Šuvar had always taken the army's side in the Slovenian question. Now the same body had sided with Milošević too, even endorsing his "direct" methods, which the Serbian leader would presently employ in the pursuit of his goals. The Presidium's declaration of late July 1988 may, thus, be seen as an important milestone in the death of Yugoslavia. One should also note that, at the same time, the Central Committee as a whole had an entirely different viewpoint from its own Presidium. Various speakers criticized Milošević's politics, among them Vrhovec.[52] Montenegrin Vidoje Žarković compared the style of the Serbian leader with that of the Chinese Cultural Revolution. Šuvar and his men, however, simply ignored the warning signs signalled by the Central Committee.

For the rest of 1988 and 1989, articles in the international press, those I wrote for the *Frankfurter Allgemeine* being no exception, went back and forth as to whether Milošević would achieve his goals or whether he would be stopped. The uncertainty derived to a great extent from the fact that it was difficult to be sure just what Milošević ultimately wanted. Did he want a strong Serbia or a Serb-dominated, centralistic Yugoslavia? Today one can see that he simultaneously pursued both goals as alternatives. He took what he could and worked toward both goals. If blocked on one front, he pushed in the other direction. Certainly a "strong Serbia" was closer to his heart than a "strong Yugoslavia"; but he still hoped that he could realize his "strong Serbia" within the framework of a "strong Yugoslavia" ruled by him.

One could then anticipate that Milošević would not allow himself to be delayed for long by the criticism in the Central Committee at the end of July 1988.[53] It is true that many functionaries confronted him from time to time, including some in the higher offices of the government and even the military. Where would it lead if one just "marched in" in the event one did not like one republic leadership or another? Milošević had also registered a demand, at the Central Committee session, for the convening of an extraordinary party congress. What he intended with such a congress was not clear, for one could calculate that he would remain in the minority there, unless he could succeed in the meantime in turning around a sufficient number of other republic leaderships. When he came close to this goal and when the Congress finally took place in January 1990, the Slovenes would frustrate him by walking out. The federal party collapsed rather than become Milošević's instrument.

Immediately after the CC session of late July 1988, the Kosovo Serbs established a committee for "meetings"; this signified the institutionalization and, at the same time, the broadening of the "anti-bureaucratic revolution". On 11 August, Kosovo's party leader, Jashari, announced in the LCY Presidium, in the face of Serbian agitation, that she had had just about enough of the whole thing; there were constantly demonstrations by Serbs in Kosovo. They wanted to have their own institutions everywhere; one could not work with them.[54] At that point, the liberal-oriented Montenegrin, Žarković, who had already taken a position against Milošević at the aforementioned CC session, delivered a long speech in which he condemned Milošević's agitation in all its aspects and asked why the party leadership did nothing to respect the will of the party itself, why it did not stop the baiting of the information media in Belgrade, why the party leadership allowed those who were defending the valid constitution of the land to be dragged before the court. In Kosovo, according to Žarković, a movement was being formed which did not merely concern itself with Kosovo but which wanted to impose its will on the entire Yugoslav public.

Žarković had a personal reason for this attack, because Milošević's adherents and the Kosovar Serbs had begun to stage demonstrations against the local leadership in Montenegro too, with slogans such as "We want weapons!" and "Montenegro is Serbia!"[55] These demonstrations were intensified after Žarković's speech, although it had not been shared with the public. The Central Committee of the Montenegrin communist party took Žarković under its protection in late August. It criticized, with all understanding for the situation of Serbs and Montenegrins in Kosovo, the extralegal gatherings and activities which aimed at disturbing the "good relations" between Slavs and Albanians in Montenegro. The fever pitch which Milošević's agitation at public rallies had reached could be discerned in a letter from Franc Šetinc, written at the end of September 1988 as he resigned as Slovenia's representative in the LCY Presidium. Šetinc, a somewhat idealistic socialist, wrote that he could no longer bear it that mass demonstrations in Serbia displayed slogans such as "Death to Albanians" or "Death for Vllasi". Such slogans could not be reconciled with the will of most Yugoslavs, that there be peace in Kosovo.[56]

None the less, Milošević continued his advance. He astutely understood that he needed to present his agitation as an expression of stipulations previously adopted by the LCY, interpreting them always in such a way as to bring him a step closer to his goals. When the Slovenian representatives in the LCY leadership tried, in September 1988, to strike the word "counter-revolutionary" from the draft of a party document about policy in Kosovo, Bogdan Trifunović, a close collaborator of Milošević's, could reproach them that they wanted "to revise party decisions".[57] The word "counter-revolutionary" had indeed been used in earlier documents but never in order to discredit the local leadership in Kosovo. As late as 1985, the LCY leadership had agreed, in a compromise formulation, that one had to avoid "the absolutization of the state question in Serbia"; on the other hand, the provinces should not negate the sovereignty of the republic "as a whole". Now it was said that it was exclusively up to the republic to organize its operations. The new position represented a relativization of the constitutional position of the autonomous provinces. The LCY leadership did not, of course, want to force Vojvodina and Kosovo to accept these charges unconditionally, but declared itself in favor of seeing the "basic state functions", thus also including the police, "uniformly regulated and led".[58] Jashari, as spokesperson for Kosovo, could only say that the common republic should, in that case, really be common for all who live there; it would be unfortunate, she thought, if this republic would continue to be designated as the state of only one nation, the Serbs.[59]

Slovenes followed the Serbian campaign to asphyxiate Kosovo with special concern, in that the hegemonistic and centralistic tendencies which underlay that campaign were also directed against Slovenia. For the Serbian press, the Slovenes were, at the time, regarded as state enemy no. 2, right after the Albanians. Kučan told me in summer 1994 that Slovenian policy-makers were always very aware of the problem of Kosovo and behaved accordingly.[60] The question remained, of course, whether Slovenia could not have done more politically. It is true that during all of 1988 Slovenia had its hands full just dealing with the escalating conflict with the army. On the other hand, people like Slovenia's representative in the Federal Presidency, Stane Dolanc, still adhered to conformist views.

According to Slovenian documents, early July 1988 was the first time that officials seriously considered extending cooperation and assistance of a so-to-speak party nature to party organs in Kosovo. The Serbian media had, by this point, begun to demand a comprehensive revision of the 1974 constitution, from the direction of greater centralism. The Slovenes countered this by introducing the concept of a Yugoslav "confederation" into the discussion, but in view of the threats from Belgrade, it seemed dangerous to allow oneself to enter into the constitutional discussions at all. There remained only the option of rejecting any and all proposals for revision along centralistic lines.

The use of public meetings to air viewpoints and exert pressure was explicitly endorsed by the army leadership at the end of September. Addressing an audience of army officers, Deputy Defense Minister Stane

Brovet said there were three kinds of meetings: first, hostile meetings, including those critical of the army; second, meetings having socio-economic roots, reflecting the difficult economic situation; and third, meetings in which people, especially Serbs and Montenegrins, tried to secure their rights within the system. One could not condemn meetings of this third kind. Other than that, Brovet called on the federal party leadership to finally take a "clear position" on the question of the Serbian constitution.

Since it was obvious that the two provinces were not going to be won over to a position of understanding for the Serbian constitutional reforms, Milošević decided, after such efforts had failed, simply to remove the respective leaders by whatever means available. On 5 October, 100,000 Serbs assembled in Novi Sad, most of them from Kosovo and adjacent parts of Serbia, but also including some local Milošević loyalists, while the Central Committee of the provincial party sat in session. After learning that the Serbian Central Committee, controlled by Milošević, wanted to hold the leaders of Vojvodina responsible for "the failed policy of autonomism", the party leadership in Novi Sad, confronted by double pressure from the street and from the Serbian leadership, submitted its collective resignation.[61] With this, Vojvodina ceased to exist as an autonomous province for all practical purposes. The federal party leadership did not consider it necessary to call a special session, so rapidly had things unfolded. The Vojvodina leadership, for its part, had neglected to look for allies in time. The leaders did not want to have anything to do with the Albanians because most of Vojvodina's leaders were Serbs; it did not make any alliance with the Slovenes because its members were, for the most part, dogmatics. At the end, the leaders of Vojvodina showed their personal weaknesses.

Only three days later, *Politika* could triumphantly announce that the obstacles which had stood in the way of Serbia's constitutional reform had been removed.[62] This was not entirely true, since, in spite of Serbian demonstrations in Priština, the Kosovo leadership was still holding on. Now Milošević tried to turn Montenegro around with a surprise coup. On 7 October 1988, crowds as large as those in Novi Sad gathered in front of governmental buildings in Titograd, to demand the resignation of the Montenegrin leadership. The Titograd leadership relied on force, dispersed the demonstrators, and even obtained support for this action from the LCY leadership, which was beginning to feel uncomfortable, after all.

However, things then turned around completely at the federal level – in both the LCY Presidium headed by Šuvar and the state presidency under Dizdarević – on the demand of Serbia. On 11 October, the LCY Presidium held a joint session with the party leadership of Kosovo; at this session, Šuvar orchestrated a vote holding the party leadership of Kosovo (i.e., the communists of Albanian nationality) primarily responsible for "the open emergence of counter-revolution" and for the seclusion of Kosovo from the rest of Serbia. The communists of Kosovo had "for years drawn closer to nationalist positions and had lost the ability to mount resistance against them".[63] With that, the fire was lit under the then-leading functionaries of Kosovo. Šuvar deferred the rest until the Seventeenth Plenum of the CC LCY, set to convene a week later.

Shortly before these events, on 9 October 1988, the chair of the state presidency, Raif Dizdarević, in a televised address to all Yugoslavs, had explained that the time of "real reforms" – economic, political, and such as were required within the LCY – had finally arrived. He raised the specter of a state of emergency throughout the whole of Yugoslavia and demanded that the reforms which had been prepared for the federal constitution be adopted as a "package". The Slovenes at once set themselves against him, not wanting to hear anything further about the primacy of federal law over the laws of the republics. Half an hour before Dizdarević's address, Belgrade Television broadcast that the proposed changes in the Serbian constitution would "of course" mean, too, that the provinces would act on the federal level only in agreement with the Republic.[64] Until now, almost everybody had insisted that the constitutional reforms in Serbia would not diminish the role of the provinces on the federal level.

The Seventeenth Plenary Session of the CC LCY, 17–20 October 1988, was, in and of itself, no capitulation before Milošević. On the contrary, Šuvar himself voiced his opposition to the marches and extralegal meetings because Milošević had threatened that he would, at the close of the CC session, bring a million people to Belgrade unless the CC did as he wished. Šuvar even fashioned an alliance of sorts against Milošević. Macedonian Vasil Tupurkovski spoke at the time of an "unprincipled alliance".[65] In a certain sense he was right. For Šuvar and others it was not a question of principles such as constitutionalism or national equality. Rather, they believed that, despite all their criticism of Milošević, if they allowed him to "gobble up" Kosovo and Vojvodina, he would give them some rest. As a result, in his report, Šuvar supported the changes proposed for the Serbian constitution; the party had already agreed on these, he noted.[66] Simultaneously, he demanded "personnel changes" to the leadership bodies in Priština. In this way, it suited his purposes to cooperate with Milošević in bringing "new and anti-bureaucratic forces" into the Central Committee.

The Slovenes saw this somewhat differently; only market economists should step forward, one of them said.[67] Milošević tried to make political gains in his own way. "Obviously" Jashari was among those whom the Central Committee had criticized and whose resignation had been demanded.[68] Entirely in the sense of the "unprincipled alliance", a working group was formed which was supposed to establish the "responsibility" of Vllasi, Shiroka, and the ostensibly Albanophile Serb, Svetislav Dolašević; a narrow majority of the Central Committee approved the formation of the working group. Šuvar expressed his expectation that the question of Kosovo would be resolved "as quickly as possible" and in a "comprehensive" way.[69] In the state presidency, Dizdarević held to his opportunistic standpoint, with even less political distance from Milošević than heretofore.

The alliance against Milošević was also "without principles" in the view of the party leaderships of the republics, who openly or secretly stood behind it. Only Slovenia's position was clear. Croatia and Bosnia-Herzegovina were worried that Milošević's agitation could also infect the Serbs living in their territories. They were therefore in favor of "solving" the problem in Kosovo as Milošević wished and earnestly hoped that this would calm Milošević down. The leadership in Montenegro was already fearful about its future.

In this way, in spite of the "alliance", the Albanians finally stood alone – except of course for the equally besieged Slovenes. The "alliance of the unprincipled" was not also an alliance for reforms, democratization, and progress; it was, in fact, heterogeneous. It was no match for Milošević.

The end in Kosovo was rapidly approaching. With the help of the Central Committee's concepts about the rotation of cadres and Šuvar's general critique of the leadership in Kosovo behind them, the Serbs pushed with all their power to obtain the resignation of Jashari and other adherents of Vllasi's course in Priština. The formula was simple and had already been put to the test: The Serbs refused to cooperate with them, held noisy demonstrations, and then asserted that the leadership was not in a position to guarantee normal relations in Kosovo. The federal party leadership guaranteed them, again in partial contradiction to the view which was prevalent in the Central Committee, further support. On 10 November 1988, a resumé of the previous day's plenary session of the LCY Presidium, prepared by one of the Presidium's "experts", appeared, in which it was stated that the leadership in Kosovo was not carrying out the decisions of the LCY and that, in its present composition, it could not ensure the successful execution of its tasks.[70]

This report did not satisfy Milošević. On 14 November, the Serbian party chief complained that his statements at the 9 November session had not been correctly reported.[71] He had demanded that Jashari relinquish her functions "immediately" because she was "incapable" of fulfilling them. Aside from that, he had also wondered why the party presidium did not allow the Serbs of Kosovo to organize a parallel but separate communist organization. In common party organizations, Kosovo's Serbs were permanently in the minority. In Serbia it was generally expected that, in executing the decisions of the LCY Central Committee concerning the rotation of cadres, the leadership of Kosovo would be removed immediately "without procrastination or playing for time".

Šuvar and the majority of the LCY leadership seemed to submit to this tone of command. So Milošević acted. First the Serbian members of the party presidium in Priština resigned, rendering the rump Presidium ethnically homogeneous and therefore incapable of functioning. Then some outspoken members of the circle around Vllasi and Jashari were induced to step down – among them, Ekrem Arifi. Finally, thanks to these initial resignations and to continued pressure from outside, the unnerved provincial party presidium was induced to remove Jashari and Vllasi. Jashari remained, to be sure, a member of the provincial party leadership. In the case of Vllasi, who was also a member of the LCY Central Committee, it was objected that he could not occupy two posts at once. But he was also rebuked for having criticized Milošević in "too militant" a way.[72]

Even today, people in Kosovo ask why the provincial party committee capitulated before Milošević's "salami tactics" on that occasion. Vllasi said in retrospect that the situation at the time looked almost completely hopeless to him, since the highest organs of the federal government had clearly taken Milošević's side. Most likely the Kosovo party hoped that by yielding on personnel questions, it might win support in the LCY leadership on the question of the province's autonomy.[73] One could clearly detect such notions on the part of Remzi Kolgezi, Jashari's provisional successor, who would later emphasize his "loyalty" to the League of Communists of Yugoslavia and who wanted to transform the dispute about Kosovo from a "Serbian question" into a "Yugoslav question". Given the circumstances, such hopes would seem to have been hopelessly naïve.[74]

Finally, when it was nearly too late, it occurred to the already half-purged leadership of Kosovo to have recourse to the methods of agitation which Milošević and his followers thought they had monopolized. The Kosovo leaderships mobilized the "Albanian masses", above all the workers at the large enterprises, such as Trepča, as well as the students at the university, and called on them to take part in demonstrations in Priština. The demonstrators demanded that the resignations be annulled. Vllasi and Jashari addressed them in the stadium and promised that the question of the resignations would be resolved without yielding to pressure.[75]

The Serbian leadership blew its top. It feared that its well-prepared scenario might, at the last moment, be torpedoed. Over the weekend of 19 November, Milošević called on a million Serbs to come to Belgrade. "You have no right to set yourselves against the federal party, because you are bound, under democratic centralism, to respect its decisions," a Serbian speaker in the party committee in Kosovo reproached the Albanian functionaries.[76] The Belgrade press was by then reporting about "good Albanians" such as the new district secretary of Priština, Husamedin Azemi, who should unseat the rebels. Shortly after the session of the district committee, Rahman Morina, who had been named police chief under Vllasi, took the Serbian side and fired a large number of Albanian policemen who were identified as Vllasi loyalists.

Now that the Albanians were also demonstrating, federal officials became aware of a feeling of "great danger for security" and sent Dizdarević, Tupurkovski, and LCY Presidium secretary Stefan Korošec (from Slovenia) to Priština. This "mediation" made it absolutely clear to the Albanians that the Yugoslav federal leadership had definitely taken a position against them. On 19 November in Belgrade, Milošević organized his mass meeting, the largest ever to take place in Yugoslavia, telling those assembled there, "No power can hold up this process (the unification of Serbia) in the future." Milošević complained that the other peoples of Yugoslavia were not showing enough solidarity with Serbia. "But," he said, "this is a moment not for sorrow, but for struggle." At the meeting, slides were shown which exposed members of the Yugoslav leadership, such as Tupurkovski, to ridicule.[77]

The demonstrations of Albanians in Kosovo lasted for several days, but they could no longer change anything. The new provincial party chief in Priština contradicted Milošević and his people on different occasions, but at the session of the party presidium a few days later, he promised that "differentiations", i.e., purges, would be continued in Kosovo.[78] In fact, Kolgezi hardly had any real power, since – with Morina's conversion – the police were, for all practical purposes, in Serbian hands.

Milošević changed direction once more. At the year's end, Montenegro seemed to him to be ripe for plucking. Since the economy was in desperate straits here, Milošević's followers did not find it difficult to organize, once again, massive demonstrations in Titograd in the first week of January 1989, in order to bring about the collapse of Montenegro's leadership, which was not especially popular in the republic anyway. On 11 January, the leading figures in Titograd, including the former Yugoslav Prime Minister Djuranović, now head of state of the republic, stepped down under the pressure of the demonstrations.[79] The demonstrators shouted slogans also against Šuvar, whose long indulgence of Milošević was in this way poorly rewarded and who, because of his "unprincipled alliance" was now promoted to the front row of "enemies of the people". After the resignations at the top, there followed an avalanche of resignations at all levels of party and state in Montenegro. Montenegro's two elected members in the LCY Presidium also found themselves branded as "enemies": Marko Orlandić, even though he had, almost to the end, always sided with Milošević, and Vidoje Žarković, who at the last minute had tried, without success, to switch horses.

The successful storming of Montenegro was received as a shock throughout all of non-Serb Yugoslavia. Montenegro did not belong to Serbia. The Montenegrins, although they felt culturally very close to Serbs, had always been very attached to their own political and national identity. Many of them had mourned the disappearance of their separate kingdom through its joining to Yugoslavia in 1918. Some of these "Greens", as Montenegrin autonomists were called, had seen their hour strike with the Italian occupation in 1941; there were relatively close connections with Italy and Italian King Vittorio Emanuele III had married a daughter of the last king of Montenegro, Nikola. The Montenegrin civil war in the

Second World War was, for a long time, a three-cornered contest pitting Chetniks, Partisans, and Autonomists against each other. After the war, Montenegrin intellectuals behaved in an especially dogmatic way, Djilas being no exception; in 1948, the proportion of Montenegrins among the "Cominformists" was comparatively high. In later years, a certain liberality gained ground in Montenegro, thanks to promotion by people such as Žarković. The leadership could not solve the difficult economic problems, to be sure; these had their origins above all in the so-called "political investments", such as the Nikšić Steelworks.

The "conquest" of Montenegro by Milošević's supporters, such as the new party chief and later president Momir Bulatović, showed, at a stroke, that something which had hardly occurred to anyone before could come to pass, viz., that Milošević, and with him Serbia, would some day dominate the institutions of Yugoslavia – and this from the top down, through the party presidium and state presidency, as well as through the parliament. Milošević could now count on the votes of Serbia, Vojvodina, Montenegro, and Kosovo in all federal bodies, even if the battle was not yet completely over in the last of these. Moreover, Macedonia was also supporting him at the time; the leadership there had needlessly entangled itself in a similar conflict against local Albanians, as had Serbia. In addition, the politicians in Bosnia-Herzegovina and even in Croatia had to worry about internal disturbances in the event that they resisted Serbian wishes. The army leadership stood on Milošević's side in all important questions. The principle of consensus functioned only on the state level and even here it was by no means impermeable.

The new situation set off alarm bells not only in Ljubljana but also in Zagreb and Sarajevo, and for that matter also in the central organs of the federation. The frail Dizdarević unexpectedly told the next session of the LCY Presidium where he was present that what had occurred in Montenegro was the collapse of the party; in view of the massive wave of resignations there, the question presented itself as to whether the party organs in Montenegro could still claim to have any legitimacy.[80] He further raised the question as to whether the complete breakdown of the system of public security in that republic did not call for federal measures. One had already experienced this phenomenon in Vojvodina and in Kosovo where something similar was happening. Thus, as Dizdarević pointed out, the party had, for all practical purposes, been dissolved through demonstrations, which is to say, through extra-institutional procedures, in three parts of the country. Could one put up with this?

Milošević at once tried to reassure the others. In Vojvodina everything was "solved" and in Montenegro one needed to replenish the party organs. If the LCY leadership had seriously considered withdrawing recognition of the legality of the highest party organs of Montenegro, it should have held an extraordinary party congress in that republic. That would have been extremely unfavorable for Milošević because it was one thing to drive exhausted leaderships to resign with a few thousand followers shouting on the street; it was quite another matter to win over the silent majority of party members.

Under the influence of such insights and, as well, out of concern for his own position, Šuvar looked, for a short moment, ready to fight.[81] One should send a delegation to Montenegro and then bring the matter before the Central Committee, he urged. Milošević contradicted him vigorously, arguing that the situation in Montenegro could only be judged by people from there. This riposte took the wind out of Šuvar's sails, and it was now decided to recognize the legitimacy of the Montenegrin party organs as they were now constituted. Kučan offered the comment that in his view meetings and demonstrations had nothing to do with either democracy or democratization. The last opportunity to stop Milošević had passed. Šuvar served out the remainder of his term as chair of the highest party organ in the spirit of opportunism, but his hope of appeasing Milošević with the surrender of the two autonomous provinces had foundered. With the successful *putsch* in Montenegro, the Serbian leader had, for the first time, struck outside the borders of Serbia.

The end of autonomy in Kosovo

Milošević had understood that, in order to accomplish the final liquidation of the autonomy of Kosovo, it was necessary above all that the highest federal authorities and other conceivable opponents, if they could not be rendered totally docile, should at least be intimidated. Immediately after the "case" of Montenegro, Milošević intensified his campaign against Šuvar, on the grounds that the latter had opposed Serbian street meetings and had characterized them as "undemocratic". The mood in the highest federal organs was now such that no one wanted any longer to tangle with Milošević. His opponents found themselves on the defensive on every front. To ensure that nothing could go wrong, Milošević fired fresh volleys at Slovenia, in order to isolate its leadership and prevent it from "interfering" in common Yugoslav affairs.

Nevertheless, one consequence of the events in Montenegro was that, on Dizdarević's proposal, the state presidium elected Ante Marković, rather than Jović, to become the new Prime Minister. In Zagreb and Sarajevo also, it was now understood that, as a result of Milošević's politics, the danger of the splitting of Yugoslavia had now arisen.[82] Among intellectuals in the western republics, the idea began to be articulated, more as a reflex to feelings of uneasiness, of a West Yugoslav state, consisting of the republics of Slovenia, Croatia, and Bosnia-Herzegovina. At the beginning of March 1989, the magazine *Mladina* in Ljubljana published a map of such a "state" with the skeptical caption, "Would you like to live in such a state?"[83]

At the end of January 1989, police chief Rahman Morina, who had come over to the Serbian side in the Vllasi era, was elected president of the Party presidium in Kosovo. The vote came, as the Zagreb magazine *Danas* wrote at the time, describing it in all its details, under pressure from the Serbian leadership after some Albanian functionaries had declared themselves for one or the other of the two other prominent pro-Serb exponents among the Albanians – Husamedin Azemi or Ali Shukrija.[84] Having a policeman at the head of the now almost completely disciplined leadership of Kosovo seemed a safer solution to Milošević.

On 30 January 1989, the LCY Central Committee convened. Milošević's followers now intensified the attack on Šuvar and demanded his discharge. Milošević could now send his "satellites" forth to do his bidding. The demands for Šuvar's discharge and for the summoning of an extraordinary party congress were formally presented by the District Committee of Vojvodina.[85] The Central Committee rejected the demand for Šuvar's dismissal on formal grounds, but the altered relations of power were reflected also in the (formally) highest party organ, which had been comparatively open before. Šuvar found himself pushed onto the defensive. Grasping the situation belatedly, Šuvar applied his energy against attempts to erect a "unified commando-party" and a "centralism without intra-party democracy". He mentioned the "fundamental conflict between pro-reform and anti-reform forces", and even warned of the danger of a "civil war". But he did not mention Milošević by name even once; he had tailored his talk to justify himself and it did not stimulate any kind of action against Milošević.

Milošević had made a special effort to draw the delegates of Macedonia into his camp; his publicists therefore emphasized, in their attacks on Šuvar, certain infelicitous remarks of his made earlier about Macedonia. But these efforts had the contrary effect because some Macedonian delegates complained later that they had been placed under "almost unbearable pressure".[86] The Central Committee allowed the demand for an extraordinary party congress, but wanted to consider it "extraordinary" only in terms of its timing, and not in terms of procedure. That meant that the party congress would be conducted according to the normal statutes and not according to procedures which the initiators of this event might lay down. The representatives of the army displayed a certain reserve; the idea that Yugoslavia could fall apart shocked some of them. On the other hand, in Croatia, the attacks on Šuvar convinced many that it was time to rethink some of the premises of the system; many Croats rallied to Šuvar in the face of Milošević's attacks. Croatia's second representative in the LCY leadership, the liberal Ivica Račan, told the Central Committee that he disagreed with Šuvar about many things, but that one had to defend him against immoderate attacks.

In Kosovo itself, however, Milošević now had a free hand. On 22 February 1989, the amendments to the Serbian constitution which had been prepared by the Serbian leadership were unanimously adopted by the constitutional commission of the Serbian parliament.[87] Only two days later, the Serbian parliament unanimously endorsed the amendment package in a plenary session. The intimidated deputies of Kosovo did not dare to oppose the bill, given that lists of "hostile separatists" were already being drawn up.

In his address to the Serbian parliament on this occasion, Jović rehearsed the well-known Serbian arguments in support of constitutional reform and even went a bit further. He claimed – the first time that it had been put this way – that Serbia had been stripped of its sovereignty by the federal constitution of 1974.[88] Now Serbia was "on the path to equality with the other republics". At the same time, Jović claimed that the Serbian constitutional reforms did not threaten the autonomy of either Kosovo or Vojvodina.

Moreover, to the great surprise of people throughout Yugoslavia, at the last minute parliamentary assent was also obtained to an amendment which stripped Kosovo and Vojvodina of any veto power over future constitutional changes in Serbia. This unanticipated *coup de main* signified in formal-legal terms a decisive step toward the liquidation of the autonomy of the two units. I was later told in Croatia that the abolition of the right of the provinces to veto constitutional changes in Serbia was adopted contrary to an understanding with other republics, Croatia included.

A new obstacle appeared at the last moment. "The people made themselves heard" in Kosovo – to use a formula dear to Milošević; only this time it was the *Albanian* people. There had already been demonstrations in Kosovo after 20 February, i.e., before the constitutional amendments had been adopted. Now in particular, the miners of the zinc and lead mines at Trepča near Kosovska Mitrovica went on strike. At the Stari Trg mine, 1,500 of them began a hunger strike deep below the pit; they demanded the resignations of the "traitorous leaders" Morina, Azemi, and Shukrija, as well as the retention of the constitution of 1974 and guarantees for the autonomy of Kosovo. The conditions under which they conducted their strike were dreadful. Poisonous lead vapors blew through the tunnels of the mine and ventilation was inadequate. It was the last important gesture of defiance by the Albanians of Kosovo for years to come.

The hunger strike of the Albanian miners concerned the communist regime in Yugoslavia as a whole. The Kosovo question suddenly obtained a social dimension; it was not intellectuals but ordinary workers who were stepping forward. At risk to their lives they were striking for the retention of the valid constitution of the land. Dizdarević and the head of state of Serbia, the former general and later federal Interior Minister Petar Gračanin, traveled to Kosovo, but avoided talking with the strikers. The leadership of the Socialist Alliance of Working People of Croatia said that the strike and the determination of the Albanian miners showed that "the appropriate methods of working with the Albanians of Kosovo had not been found".[89] In Slovenia, the manifestations of sympathy for the miners at Trepča offered a welcome political opportunity to express concern for the current political tendencies in the country as a whole. This was uncomfortable for Milošević.

On 24 February 1989, the day after the passage of the new Serbian constitution by the Serbian parliament, Šuvar and Milošević visited Kosovo together. Whoever might have believed that Šuvar might finally find his way, with the support which he was now obtaining from all parts of Yugoslavia outside Serbia, to a clear stand against Milošević, was once again disappointed. Šuvar told the party *aktiv* in Priština that the passage of the new Serbian constitution was a good thing. Already in 1985, the LCY had endorsed the position that while Kosovo and Vojvodina were constituent parts of the federation, Serbian sovereignty should be preserved. "Where did the Albanians get the erroneous impression that the region's autonomy was being abolished? Why are they shouting 'We won't give up the constitution of 1974!'?" It was just as difficult for Šuvar to understand the demands of Albanian intellectuals that the autonomy of Kosovo should, because of that province's specific national composition, be organized differently from that of Vojvodina.[90] Šuvar's talk made it easy for Milošević once again. The Serbian leader told the Albanians that they had nothing to fear. The provinces would not lose their autonomy as a result of constitutional changes in Serbia. "The constitutional changes do not threaten anyone," Milošević told them. The Albanians would lose neither the right to school instruction in their own language nor the right to their own cultural development. But Milošević also said that those who had sown "hatred and discord" in the region should leave politics and relinquish their social functions. The "differentiation" process had to continue in Kosovo.[91]

The discomfort in the Serbian camp in the face of this strike was genuine. Vllasi, Serbs claimed, was the puppeteer behind all these demonstrations; he had even visited the miners in Stari Trg.[92] Vllasi had never denied his political involvement. The hunt for the "puppeteer" behind the demonstrations of November 1988 had already been launched. A report of the federal Ministry of the Interior of 18 December 1988, which now lay before the LCY Presidium, named in the first place Vllasi and Ekrem Arifi.[93] There were rumors that Morina, Kosovo's new party secretary, had drawn up a list with the names of 90 "puppeteers" who were held responsible for all the agitation among the Albanians.[94] In Slovenia the witticism was going around that with the next revision of the Yugoslav constitution it would be explicitly indicated which peoples and nationalities of Yugoslavia enjoyed the right to stage public demonstrations and which did not.

Since the Albanian miners had shown themselves determined to continue their strike, Milošević mobilized all means at his disposal over the subsequent days to prepare to send police reinforcements to the region; for this he needed only the endorsement of the state presidency, where the advocates of extraordinary measures were not in the majority. But on 27 February 1989, Milošević's plans were overtaken by events, and not at all in the way he had planned.

First, in the early evening hours that same day nearly a thousand Slovenes had gathered in the Cankarjev Dom in Ljubljana, to express their solidarity with the miners of Stari Trg. The meeting had been organized by some 20 social organizations of Slovenia. Jože Smole, chair of the Socialist Alliance of Working People of Slovenia, declared his "highest respect" for the miners, and said they were engaged in a just struggle. Kučan also spoke. He mentioned the political as well as the humanitarian and social aspects. In Belgrade, the meeting and Kučan's appearance there were used to stir up a huge amount of commotion; students and other followers of Milošević immediately took to the streets in the vicinity of the *Skupština*. A permanent meeting now began, in which eventually about a million Serbs took part; this was the first time that Milošević's adherents would use street demonstrations to exert direct pressure on *federal* organs.[95]

In the early evening of that same 27 February 1989, the three "good Albanians" – Morina, Azemi, and Shukrija – resigned from their posts in Priština. Even today it is unclear just how this came about. The stage was an extraordinary session of the presidency of the party organization in Priština. It is possible that they simply could not endure the pressure from the Albanian environment; there continued to be the danger of fatality for the striking miners in the lead shafts, and the tradition of "blood revenge" was still alive in Kosovo. Now the miners could come out of the tunnels, Azemi said in his resignation speech.[96]

Milošević seemed not to have expected this to happen. The first Serbian reactions were nervous and perplexed. It would later be claimed that Milošević had organized these resignations himself, first in order to justify the declaration of a state of emergency, and second, in order to mislead the miners. Actually, the resignations were not accepted by the standing party organs in Kosovo, although this was said only after the arrival of intervention forces. But the affair does not seem to have been so simple. On the other hand, Milošević now had a passable argument in his hand for an immediate introduction of a state of emergency in Kosovo. Otherwise, he seems to have argued, there would be a "blood bath".

The state presidency under the chairmanship of Dizdarević immediately assembled on Milošević's demand, i.e., on the evening of 27 February. The meeting was arranged without consultation with the party presidium; the Slovenian representative was absent. The course of this meeting can only be partially reconstructed here. The Slovenian President Stanovnik told me later something of what happened there.[97] Since Slovenia's representative in the presidency, Stane Dolanc, was attending the funeral of the Emperor of Japan in Tokyo, Stanovnik was allowed, under established procedures, to take part in the deliberations of the state presidium, representing Slovenia. But when the meeting turned to a vote concerning a state of emergency, Stanovnik's right of participation was refused on a technicality; it was claimed that Dolanc's absence was not the kind of "impediment" which empowered the president of the republic to step in as a substitute with full powers of the office. This claim was, juridically speaking, not entirely false, but, at the same time, the meeting could have waited until Dolanc's return. But Milošević and his allies did not want this under any circumstances, since the principle of consensus was in force for a decision concerning the employment of the army.

Thus, late in the evening of 27 February 1989, the state presidency decided on "special measures" for Kosovo. This was an unrestricted state of emergency, Dizdarević told the LCY Presidium on the following day; it was only out of concern for the impression this would make abroad that the milder euphemism had been adopted.[98] The army units stationed in Priština immediately took up positions and 1,500 federal police under Serbian leadership, among them about 150 Slovenes, made their way to Kosovo. They brought anything but peace to the province, carrying out a campaign of physical repression of the Albanian people which was without precedent in post-war Europe. The absence of the Slovenian representative at the decision was dismissed as without great meaning since Dolanc, after his return home, said that he would in any case have voted for the measure, as the only chance of avoiding a "blood bath".[99]

Dolanc came under criticism in Slovenia because of this statement. He told the Slovenian presidency on 20 March 1989, somewhat cryptically, that all measures which had been adopted by the Yugoslav state presidency were "legal", if not exactly following the constitution. It is possible that he meant the measures were justified by the provisions of the law on national defense. On the other hand, the procedural guidelines of the state presidency explicitly required party approval for the declaration of a state of emergency. But the LCY Presidium met only the following afternoon, i.e., on 28 February. Kučan angrily remarked at the session that the state presidency had decided on "special measures", even though no one even knew what that meant.[100] To that, Dizdarević replied that it meant a state of emergency. In view of the somewhat precarious legal situation, parliamentary approval was now also sought, and as quickly as possible.

The session of the LCY Presidium of 28 February was stormy. Meanwhile, large numbers of people were camped in front of the *Skupština*, some distance from the party building in which the LCY Presidium was meeting. The declaration of a state of emergency in Kosovo was not enough for the Serbian demonstrators; they demanded, further, the cancellation of the resignations on the part of Morina, Azemi, and Shukrija. If these resignations had really come about, they would have been a setback for Milošević. The demonstrators loudly demanded the arrest or even execution of Vllasi, whom the Belgrade propaganda apparatus had described as the chief conspirator behind the events in Kosovo. Milošević demanded immediately, at the beginning of the session, that, because of the explosive situation in the capital city, the LCY Presidium had to decide two things and announce these to the demonstrators, before it could even discuss other matters. The two items were: first, that the LCY Presidium categorically rejected the resignations of Morina, Azemi, and Shukrija; and second, that it would demand "immediate measures" against the ringleaders of Albanian agitation in Priština.[101]

The situation remained fluid. The army's representative in the party presidium, Petar Simić, said in muddled sentences that there was "unrest in the whole country". The Slovenes, who contested that, affected "ignorance". Simić spoke of "unpostponable measures" which the state presidency should adopt; it could do this on the basis of the law on national defense. Simić was supported by the dogmatic party chief of Macedonia, Jakuv Lazaroski, who said that the situation was "bad in all of Yugoslavia" and that it was necessary to bring "tranquility" to the country. From such words one could infer that Simić and some dogmatic politicians were testing the waters to see if they might obtain a majority for the declaration of a state of emergency in all of Yugoslavia. But Milošević himself seemed to have no interest in this idea, as he had to concentrate on the situation created by the demonstrations in Belgrade and Kosovo, a situation which was now almost out of control.

The reaction of the Slovenes was sharp. One should not submit to pressure from the street, said Boris Mužević, Slovenia's representative in the party presidium; Morina and the others were "grown-ups" and knew themselves whether they wanted to resign or not. Ivica Račan of Croatia lent his support to the state of emergency in Kosovo, but did not want to yield to pressure from the streets. Kučan noted that when someone sends the people onto the street in order to exert pressure on political organs, this could be the start of a civil war. What did it mean to accuse the Slovenes of "ignorance"? The extraordinary measures had been adopted without Slovenia's consent, and one did not yet know the details. If the LCY Presidium was going to attack Slovenia constantly and to insinuate that Slovenia and Croatia were supporting "counter-revolution" in Kosovo, then the party presidium should adopt an appropriate resolution, publish it, and then convene the Central Committee. The others obviously did not want to do this.

In the meantime, Dizdarević, chair of the state presidency, had gone outside to the demonstrators and had begun to speak. "I know that your concern about Yugoslavia has brought you here," he said, continuing: "One must finally bring the constitutional changes in Serbia to fruition."[102] Dizdarević's appearance, expressly – as he put it – "in the name of the presidency of Yugoslavia", shocked non-Serbs throughout Yugoslavia. Nor did this appearance avail Dizdarević much, as Serb demonstrators hissed at him. But he provided Milošević's propaganda with a justification to declare this demonstration, which was the expression of extreme Serbian nationalist intolerance, a "meeting for Yugoslavia".

Scarcely back in the session of the federal party leadership, Dizdarević began, together with Milošević, to demand that something be done: "The demonstration is becoming too big. We must calm things." It was for this purpose that he had gone out to the demonstrators. Šuvar considered it necessary to say that the party leadership stood unwaveringly behind the constitutional changes in Serbia. After a pause during which a resolution was drawn up, Milošević renewed his pressure for an immediate answer to the demonstrators. Račan warned, "If we follow Milošević's advice, we will in future have to submit to every such mass demonstration." Kučan: "Is there any point at all in discussing this? I do not accept ultimatums". Milošević now resorted to outright blackmail: If the demonstrators were not given an answer, he would not take responsibility for what would happen in Belgrade. But with this challenge, the Serbian leader had gone too far. Račan: "I reject blackmail and pressure tactics". Šuvar tried to find a compromise: one could describe the resignations as a "moral act" which could be countermanded. But Milošević had only contempt for this proposal. "That sounds like a funeral peroration," he commented. Šuvar and Korošec set themselves against attempts to introduce a passage about the responsibility of the LCY Presidium. Milošević was making wild attacks on the Slovenes and said that he would go out to the rally. Kučan replied that if Milošević went out, he would too. The Slovenian leader repeated his demand that a resolution be formulated specifying the ostensible responsibility of the Slovenes, if this claim continued to be upheld.

The decision, which was finally passed by a majority, was less than Milošević had wanted. Thereupon, the Serbian leader himself obtained what he had been unable to obtain in the federal party presidium. Shortly after 9 p.m. he spoke to the demonstrators: "We will fight for the return of peace, order, justice, and unity in Kosovo and in every part of our country. There is no price too high, no force which can shake the leadership of Serbia and the citizens of Serbia in their fight for their just goals."[103] Then came the threats: "In a short while the names of the organizers of the demonstrators will be published, and I would like to say to you that those who have pursued anti-Yugoslav goals will be arrested and punished". The applause was colossal.

On 2 March, Vllasi and the two leading figures in the Trepča mines, Aziz Arbasi and Burhan Kavaja, together with other leading Albanian politicians and managers, were arrested. Vllasi was taken into custody in Bijeljina (Bosnia), the birthplace of his wife, and was transferred to Serbia by the local Serbian police there.[104] People now spoke of "arrest by acclamation". In the western part of Yugoslavia there were harsh reproaches made against Dizdarević and other leading federal authorities, for having permitted this to happen and for having capitulated to a crowd of demonstrators in Belgrade.[105]

The arrest of Vllasi had been prepared through a further manipulation of the federal leadership, executed by Macedonia's representative in the state presidency, Lazar Mojsov. As already mentioned, under Article 317 of the constitution, the federal *Skupština* was supposed to be allowed to approve the proposed "special measures" in Kosovo. Speaking before both houses of parliament on 2 March 1989, ostensibly in the name of the state presidency, Mojsov claimed that the presidency had in its possession a "document" which it had received on 25 February. According to this "document", Vllasi and other Albanian leaders in Kosovo had worked out a "three-phase plan", beginning with the strike at Trepča and ending with the outbreak of armed insurrection. Only the declaration of a state of emergency had hindered the execution of this plan. Mojsov also said that the Albanian secret service in Tirana had been implicated in this plan.[106] Doubts were immediately expressed throughout non-Serbian regions of Yugoslavia concerning the authenticity of this supposed "document"; people spoke contemptuously of a "Mojsov Plan".[107] It was later proven that Mojsov had fabricated the story. Dolanc told the Slovenian republic presidency on 20 March that what Mojsov had said before the *Skupština* in Belgrade was not the standpoint of the Yugoslav state presidency, but merely Mojsov's own personal initiative, ostensibly advanced with encouragement from Kadijević.[108]

The effect of these events in the rest of Yugoslavia was incisive. The Serbian bloc and its helpers at the federal level had pushed through the state of emergency and deployed armed forces using juridically dubious methods. "Federalism" as the fundamental principle of state had been decisively sabotaged and even criminalized, or at least that is the way things looked in Slovenia. The magazine *Danas* said then what most Western diplomats in Belgrade did not want to utter until summer 1991: either one defends Yugoslavia on the basis of federalism and national equality, or one does not defend it at all.[109]

In Kosovo, the Trepča strike lasted a few more days, but under political pressure, the presence of police and army, and the leadership vacuum after the arrests, the strike soon crumbled. The miners had been threatened with forced removal. The goal of Serbian policy was now to use the massive deployment of instruments of coercion to bring about the smooth endorsement of the Serbian constitutional changes by the Kosovo parliament. Then one would not need to rely on the federal organs any more. An army spokesperson said that the policy in Kosovo needed the support of all of Yugoslavia.[110] Serbian enterprises called for a boycott of Slovenian wares and for a withdrawal of deposits at Ljubljanska Banka. Milošević's wife, Mirjana Marković, a professor at the Economics Faculty in Belgrade, said that a revolution of the kind the Serbs were demanding, could not be accomplished with "protracted procedures".[111]

The vote in the Kosovo parliament concerning the constitutional changes in Serbia was set for 24 March. While the new Yugoslav Prime Minister, Marković, demanded a "new morality" for Yugoslavia, reports came from Kosovo that members of the provincial parliament who were expected to have an adverse attitude regarding the changes to the constitution had been summoned by the police and threatened. They were told that if they voted "no", they would be treated as "counter-revolutionaries". These reports reached the federal party leadership too, but there was no reaction. In Priština, there was no longer any talk about the resignations of Morina and the others. The work of the party leadership in Kosovo, so Morina argued, would be markedly "simpler" after the passage of the amendments.[112]

On 22 March, the government of Kosovo proposed acceptance of the new constitution to the provincial parliament, and on 24 March television cameras zoomed in on each Albanian deputy individually, in order to establish with precision who showed any signs of doubt. When some deputies still dared to ask questions, Serbian members of the provincial parliament such as Vukašin Jokanović shouted menacingly, "We are not dealing with questions here, but with something else". Outside, Albanian students who were demonstrating were beaten back by Serbian police with rubber truncheons and tear gas. Tanks were positioned on all the street corners; according to *Danas*, the army had stationed 15,000 men in Kosovo at the time of the vote.[113] The direct sorties were, nevertheless, left to the police, while the army provided logistical support. Of the total of 187 deputies in all three houses of the provincial parliament, only 10 dared to vote against the constitutional amendments. Some of them were later arrested.

The demonstrations only became more intense after the vote; they were crushed by special units of police with unusual brutality. The pictures which reached the world were shocking.[114] They reminded people in western Yugoslavia once again what could be expected within the framework of the common state. There was criticism in a session of the LCY Presidium on 28 March, but the Serbian bloc could reply that the problem of Kosovo was now a Serbian internal matter. The majority bloc in the presidium adopted a resolution condemning not the Serbian police, but the Albanian demonstrators.[115]

On the evening of 28 March 1989, while corpses lay on the streets of Priština, the new constitution of the Socialist Republic of Serbia was celebrated in the Belgrade Sava Center. The Serbian Assembly had earlier proposed that Milošević become the new Serbian President and Jović the next Serbian representative in the state presidency. Jović said in his speech that the federal constitution of 1974, which had strengthened the autonomy of the republics, had "destroyed" Serbia; the thesis "weak Serbia, strong Yugoslavia" had long guided policy in Yugoslavia. Serbia had thus taken up the struggle and in this "special war", had achieved victory, thanks to the entire people. Serbia was now "equal". This equality consisted in each republic having its own competence, knowing which powers lay in the jurisdiction of the Yugoslav government and which fell to the sovereignty of the republics. That was the condition for the "normalization" of relations in the country. There followed a demand to the federal authorities to keep out of Serbia's affairs from now on: "The time can never and shall never return when decisions about Serbia are taken outside Serbia."[116] Serbia had led a "fight for Europe", *NIN* wrote.[117] Numerous Western diplomats joined in the celebrations in the Sava Center. On the Serbian side, one could hear it said that Western diplomats in Belgrade supported Serbia's approach in Kosovo, because it strengthened Yugoslav "unity".

The victory in Kosovo, which had been won by force, stimulated feelings of intoxication among ordinary Serbs and Serbian leaders alike. Serbia had now received support for changes in all of Yugoslavia, wrote *Politika*.[118] The protocols of the sessions of the LCY Presidium for the following weeks reveal discussions about "comprehensive reforms" not only in the economic sector but also in the state and party apparatus – and all with a clear centralist tendency. The Serbian representatives turned savagely on proposals of the Slovenes to anchor the principle of consensus also in the party.[119] On 14 April, Šuvar presented a speech in which he took a position against "street democracy", as he tried, in somewhat confused terms, to tackle the question of political pluralism. The Central Committee confirmed the convocation of a qualified extraordinary party congress. Milošević seemed to want to exploit his newly strengthened position in the federal party organs, to spread his hegemonic and centralist program throughout the entire country.

In Kosovo itself, the Serbian apparatus of repression allowed the mask to fall.[120] Heavily armed police traveled in groups of four or five through Priština, followed by the stares, full of hate, of young Albanians. The police conducted themselves with unbelievable brutality, Albanians related. Many more young Albanians than officially acknowledged were shot or clubbed to death. In some towns, Albanian police tried to stop the violence against civilians. The ensuing confrontations between Serbian and Albanian police resulted eventually in the expulsion of all Albanians from the police force in Kosovo. The prisons were filled to the brim; some of them could be described as concentration camps. Police were constantly roaming the university area. Over Serbian Radio in Priština one heard the frenetic demand, in shrill tones, for further "differentiation" (purges). On the radio, lists of names of people who needed to "go" were read. Many police vehicles on the streets were, in fact, army vehicles, on which police identification numbers had been temporarily marked. In this way, the role of the army was supposed to be kept "in the background". In the Secretariat of Information, there were now only Serbs. "The Albanians of Kosovo believed that they had found their home in Yugoslavia on the basis of equality. Now this Yugoslavia has disappeared, and the Albanians see themselves vanquished and suppressed in a nationalist-ruled Serbia," as one Albanian put it to me at the time.[121]

There were Albanian reactions. More than 200 Albanian intellectuals, among them many professors at the University of Priština, who had been dismissed from their posts, protested against the *de facto* abrogation of the federal constitution of 1974; their appeal was insultingly described as a "pamphlet".[122] There were even faint admonitions from the Serbian side not to let matters get out of hand. The leading political figure in

Kosovo after the upheaval, Tomislav Sekulić (a Serb), the new secretary of the provincial party committee, told *Danas* that there was no need for any "drunken Serbism".[123] Sekulić was a representative of the Serbian old settlers and, in spite of everything, did not want to close off all communication lines with the Albanians. About a year later, Sekulić was pushed to the background as a result of his moderate behavior. However, even he impudently claimed in an interview that "not a single person" had been beaten in Kosovo. Party chairman Morina seemed to hope that he could now reap the reward for his change of orientation and be accepted as a "partner" and not merely as an instrument.[124] A few months later he died under circumstances which were not entirely clear.

The worst was yet to come, viz., revelations about the treatment of persons held in protective custody. This affair acquired political significance not only because of the brutality which had been meted out to those prisoners but also because of the questionable legal basis for this measure and, above all, because it had not been reported to federal organs. It was, none the less, Josip Vrhovec, the Croatian representative in the state presidency, who, on 11 May 1989, brought this to the attention of the public. In response, the Interior Secretary of Kosovo, Jusuf Karakushi, had to concede that 237 persons had been placed in confinement without proper legal procedures.[125] A short while later, it became known that most of those people had been taken to Serbia, where they had been severely beaten by police (above all in Leškovac). One of them was beaten almost to death merely because he was a cousin of Vllasi's. It was later stated, on the Serbian side, that some police had exceeded their authority, but the Serbian government further claimed that the proceedings had been entirely legal. This claim was contested on the grounds that protective confinement had been prescribed only for wartime.[126] The Serbs' intoxication with victory attracted notice even abroad. On 22 May, Milošević said in Vojvodina, "I would like to say to everyone in Serbia and outside that Serbia will not, intoxicated by its victories, rest on its laurels."[127]

On 28 June 1989, the commemoration of the 600th anniversary of the Battle of Kosovo took place. This festive event, which recalled the defeat of the Serbian army by the Turks, a defeat which initiated the decline and collapse of the medieval Serbian kingdom and ushered in a long period of Turkish overlordship, provided the setting for a dramatic increase in the Serbian sense of victory. The talk was of Serbia's "final return" to Kosovo. Milošević presented a speech which set off alarm bells everywhere in Yugoslavia, above all because of the following passage: "Six hundred years later, we find ourselves once more engaged in conflicts. There has been no recourse to arms as yet, although such recourse in the future cannot be ruled out".[128] Armed conflicts against whom? At that time, Slovenia was being incessantly and constantly attacked.

Not all Serbs approved of Milošević's policy. The venerable Najdan Pašić warned of the consequences of Serbia's setting itself against the ideas of liberalization and thereby against Europe, while for novelist Dobrica Ćosić, on the other hand, this policy did not go far enough. Serbia, as he put it, could find its own way.[129]

In August 1989, the state prosecutor's office in Kosovo completed the preparation of its case against former party secretary Vllasi and the other accused Albanian politicians and managers, charging them with activities of a "counter-revolutionary" character, in violation of Article 114 of the Yugoslav penal code. Again Serbia presented the rest of Yugoslavia with a dilemma: At the very moment when the countries of the Warsaw Pact announced liberalization measures, Serbia was organizing a manipulated political trial, Stalinist-style, against the dismissed leaders.

On 30 October 1989, the trial began in the courthouse in Kosovska Mitrovica. In front of the courthouse several hundred Albanians demonstrated and shouted "freedom" and "Vllasi". Immediately after the trial was opened, the defense attorneys, some of them from outside Kosovo, went on the offensive; they succeeded in presenting countless incidents and indices which allowed the court president and the state prosecutor to seem prejudiced. The political police played a role in the interrogations, and excluded the attorneys, who had only just received the indictment shortly before the trial. Then Vllasi read a prepared statement, portraying the proceedings as a "fixed political trial": the charges of "counter-revolution" and "deceitful claims" were groundless; since 1988, Milošević had sought Vllasi's political liquidation; at rallies organized by the Serbian party leader there had been demands for Vllasi's death; the then-chief of the Kosovo party organization, Morina, had promised his support for Vllasi's political annihilation; the state prosecutor's office had passed along the indictment to the Belgrade daily, *Politika*, before it had actually been filed. The protests of Vllasi and of his defense attorneys were convincing to people in the rest of Yugoslavia and abroad; at any rate, the trial was adjourned.[130]

Milošević could not realize his objective in this trial. True, a motion to suppress the proceedings foundered in the state presidency on an indecisive vote 4 to 4, pitting the Serbian bloc against the rest of the country.[131] But during the trial three interactive external processes grew ever stronger: the pressure of the changed relationships in Eastern Europe as a whole, the interventions from the rest of Yugoslavia and abroad, and as well, the attempts on the part of the Albanian population to seek new ways of organizing themselves after the abolition of the province's autonomy. On 24 April 1990, Vllasi and the others accused were acquitted. The Serbian reaction was sour, but Milošević did not dare set a fresh trial in motion.

One cannot reproach the Albanians in Kosovo with being unclear about their opposition to the abolition of the province's autonomy. There were larger or smaller demonstrations and incidents across Kosovo throughout the whole winter. The presence of police and army did not hinder them. Because of the way in which Serbian authorities had behaved, it was now also possible to present the Kosovo question, to both domestic and foreign audiences, as a human rights question. The western republics of Yugoslavia were thereby afforded new opportunities to refer to the impossible position *vis-à-vis* the world public to which Milošević's politics was bringing Yugoslavia. Only Prime Minister Marković went about his work as if the Kosovo question did not exist. After a visit to the United States, he boasted that he had "spoken his mind" to congressmen who asked him about the human rights situation in Yugoslavia.[132]

Of course, certain changes in Serbia had taken place towards the end of 1989, which had consequences for Kosovo. Opposition parties and groups had been granted permission to take part in the Serbian elections at the end of 1989; they were not capable of posing a threat to Milošević, but even so, they marked the achievement of a certain level of democratization in political life. Insofar as Kosovo was now considered merely a region in an indivisible Serbia and no longer had its own legal system, Albanian groups could also be organized. These were, to be sure, not registered as a rule by the Serbian power-holders, but, for better or worse, they had to be tolerated. Thus, the end of the year 1989/90 saw the establishment of the Democratic League of Kosovo, under the leadership of Ibrahim Rugova, president of the Union of Writers of Kosovo; Albanians soon joined this party in large numbers. Among those who took part in the founding of the League was Jusuf Buxhovi, a journalist and novelist who had been dismissed from the editorial board of the newspaper *Rilindja*, and his colleague, Veton Surroi (likewise dismissed), who would later call into life a socialist-oriented Association for Yugoslav Democracy. On the Serbian side, it was claimed that these groups had emerged as a result of inspiration from Albania,[133] but that was so absurd that even Serbian officialdom did not want to pursue this. The Albanian organizations invited the Serbian side to open dialogue but were brusquely turned down. In spring 1990, the brutal policy of repression was resumed and intensified; an uninvestigated affair concerning poisoned drinking water in Podujevo was used as a pretext to dismiss a large number of Albanian police who had remained in the force until now.[134] Serbia wanted, for the second time, to issue a new constitution; this new constitution was designed to further curtail the rights and status of the two provinces. The new constitution, which also strengthened the office of President of the Republic, was supposed to be approved through a referendum at the beginning of 1990.

The Albanian parliamentarians and politicians who remained in office had unified up to a point and put up some resistance. They asserted that the new Serbian constitution was in violation of the federal constitution, since it no longer made any acknowledgment of the position of Kosovo as a "constituent factor" of Yugoslavia, while the Serbian politicians had promised to respect that constitution just half a year before. In response, the Serbian parliament passed a decree on 27 June 1990, without the participation of the Albanian deputies, mandating the establishment of a

Serbian special administration over Kosovo; Momčilo Trajković, a close collaborator of Milošević's and deputy prime minister in the Serbian government, became "commissar" with unrestricted powers. In the Belgrade newspapers he was described as "governor"; on the occasion of the installation of his successor in early May 1991, *Borba* raised the question as to whether such a "governor" was at all necessary since, by then, the new constitution had introduced a unified administrative system for the entire republic.[135]

On 2 July 1990, the legally elected deputies to the provincial parliament of Kosovo found themselves locked out of the meeting room and the entrance blocked by Serbian police. In response, the parliamentary deputies, sitting on the steps outside the building, decided to proclaim Kosovo a "republic", as a sovereign unit within Yugoslavia. Against Serbian accusations, Albanian speakers explained that this was not an act of separation but only the execution of the same step which had been taken already by almost all the Yugoslav republics; even Bosnia-Herzegovina and Serbia had, in the meantime, declared themselves "sovereign". Kosovo, as a recognized "constituent factor" of Yugoslavia, had the right to do the same thing.[136]

The reaction of Serbia followed shortly. On 5 July 1990, the provincial parliament was declared dissolved – in any form. After the provincial government was likewise abolished, Kosovo ceased to enjoy the autonomy guaranteed it under the Yugoslav constitution of 1974. The 114 deputies were threatened by the Serbian Interior Minister with prosecution and, for the most part, had to go underground or emigrate, many of them choosing to go to Slovenia or Croatia. At the same time, the only newspaper in Albanian, *Rilindja*, was forbidden and the independent Albanian radio and television in Priština were suspended. In enterprises across Kosovo the last-remaining Albanian managers were dismissed, as were thousands of Albanian workers; the entire economy of Kosovo, including the banks, was Serbianized. At the University, as it was said to me officially, a ratio of 1 to 1 between Albanian and Serbian students would be maintained, even though more than 80 per cent of the population of Kosovo was Albanian.[137]

The abolition of the constitutionally-prescribed political organs of Kosovo created problems in the federal organs. Serbia thought that the prerogatives hitherto enjoyed by Kosovo and Vojvodina had now been transferred to the corresponding organs of the Republic of Serbia, though in May 1991 it was not at all clear even to Jović who, for example, should designate the representative of Kosovo in the Yugoslav state presidency.[138] Riza Sapunxhiu, who had still been elected by legal organs, was careful but, in the event, still represented his own opinion. His position is indicated in the following scene, described by Mesić on the basis of the protocol: In March 1991, Sapunxhiu said openly in the state presidency that what was going on in Kosovo had nothing to do with the constitution. Tanks had been sent against schools and schoolchildren. To that, General Adžić, not even a member, gave the retort, "Please watch out what you say!" There were, he claimed, no "tanks moving against schools" in Kosovo. To that, Sapunxhiu replied, "But there were armoured cars in Uroševac!" Adžić: "But armoured cars are not tanks".[139] Shortly after this exchange, the Serbian government had Sapunxhiu removed by parliament. Just in case there might be opposition to this illegal procedure in the state presidency, Sapunxhiu was prevented from coming to Belgrade.

The Serbian parliament, to which, under the Serbian constitution, allegedly all the prerogatives of the no-longer existing organs of Kosovo had fallen, appointed in May 1991 a certain "Albanian alibi" named Sajda Bajramović to serve as representative of the "province" in the Yugoslav state presidency. Now, there would have been an opportunity to weaken the Serbian bloc by contesting the legitimacy of this vote. This step would have had to succeed in the federal parliament, because the parliament was required to confirm the vote. Mesić conceded that the question would often be raised in Croatia later why the Croatian parliamentary delegation did not leave the chamber then. Mesić claimed that the Croats had in fact left the chamber together with the Slovenes and the Albanians.[140] But the President of the *Skupština*, a Serb, had explained, that only the Slovenes and Albanians had done this, and therefore the parliament would have lacked the necessary votes to postpone Bajramović's confirmation in office.

In the Yugoslav state presidency, the ratio now stood definitely at 4 to 4 between a monolithic Serbian bloc and the rest of the representatives. There was nothing that the state presidency could do any longer against the Serbian bloc. Only Prime Minister Marković still retained some freedom of action. He said in the last days of July 1991 that "the suspension of the entire constitutional system" was "questionable", but it was not his part, but that of the constitutional court, to pass judgment on this step of Serbia's.

In Kosovo itself, there was great fear, after the proclamation of the Republic of Kosovo, that Serbia could now feel free to suppress the Albanian organizations and unleash a bloodbath. To be sure, the arrests and other repressive measures continued, but the worst did not come to pass. Serbia felt secure now. The Albanians reacted to the suppression of the last vestiges of their autonomy with a one-day general strike. Describing the total "de-Albanianization" of the region, the Zagreb magazine *Danas* said that the repression in Kosovo was worse than that in South Africa. The magazine noted in particular the dismissal of Albanian physicians from the hospitals; the health services for the entire Albanian community now broke down.[141]

Elections were scheduled in Serbia for 9 December 1990 on the basis of the new constitution. Well-meaning Serbs tried to convince the Albanian organizations to take part in the elections, and in this way to insert themselves into the political life of Serbia. Meanwhile, events elsewhere in Yugoslavia had developed in such a way that Kosovo now seemed to be only a sideshow. Nevertheless, the events there affected federal relationships, for example with the question as to whether the Yugoslav federal parliament was still at all legitimate, since the delegates from Kosovo had been robbed of their legal authority and rights. The Albanian organizations of Kosovo decided to boycott the elections. Election Sunday was a decidedly cold winter's day; only Serbs went on the icy streets in Priština to vote.[142] It was clear that the regime had, from the beginning, assumed that the Albanian population would boycott the elections and probably would not have allowed the Albanians to vote anyway had they wanted to, lest they "spoil" the election result for Milošević.

The developments which now unfolded in Kosovo on the local level make for a sad epilogue. In autumn 1991, public education for Albanian schoolchildren came to an end when almost all Albanian teachers refused to follow the newly mandated standardized school plans for the Republic of Serbia, and continued to use the same curricula as before. Almost all of the teachers were then sacked.[143] In the following year, when the war in Yugoslavia was well under way, there were brutal acts of violence against the Albanological Institute, practically the last institution still left to the Albanians.

At the same time, the Albanian organizations built up a kind of parallel Albanian administration alongside a parallel private educational system. To maintain this parallel system, economically active Albanians were expected to contribute about 10 per cent of their income, while those working abroad were expected to contribute about 3 per cent. In Germany, a "government" of the Republic of Kosovo was established under physician Bujar Bukoshi, in order to represent the interests of the Kosovar Albanians abroad.

The radicalization of political life during the war years impacted on the situation in Kosovo negatively. Serbian authorities left the leadership of the parallel administration unmolested, but arrested sundry second-rank and third-rank members. The leadership of the Democratic League, with Rugova at the helm, held to a policy of nonviolence, which was more or less forced upon them anyway, because the Albanian population of Kosovo had almost no weapons and Albania showed little enthusiasm for allowing itself to be dragged into a conflict in Kosovo. The international community showed ever greater inclination to forget about Kosovo, conceptualizing the situation variously as an internal Serbian problem or as a humanitarian problem or perhaps as a minority question. But the Kosovo question cannot be reduced to any of these formulations: Kosovo's position, described in the Yugoslav constitution of 1974 as a constituent factor of Yugoslavia, included its independent participation in the sovereignty of the common state. Therein lay an element of Kosovo's own sovereignty. Any effort to resolve the Kosovo problem will have to proceed from this essential fact.

4 Western Yugoslavia reacts

From Mikulić to Marković

In early summer 1988, two years after his accession to office, Prime Minister Branko Mikulić was confronted with the fact that his administration's dogmatically-oriented policies had reached a dead end. The patience of the western republics of Slovenia and Croatia was exhausted. There were growing problems with the International Monetary Fund. The real situation in the economy showed not the slightest sign of improvement. Inflation was rising rapidly. And the country's external debt stood unchanged at around US $20 billion. None of the government's measures had been without controversy; by the same virtue, none of them had had any positive effect whatsoever.

As already mentioned (p. 43), Mikulić tried at first to stabilize the economy with administrative interventions. After half a year this effort was abandoned. There followed a period of drift. In the course of 1987, the balance-of-payments situation became critical. It seemed advisable to make contact with the IMF about concluding a new debt agreement. The idea was to conclude a long-term agreement which would reduce the annual expenditures for debt servicing from 45 per cent to 25 per cent of foreign currency earnings.[1]

The matter was not simple because in the first phase of his government Mikulić had unambiguously gone against the recommendations of the IMF. So he was immediately confronted, in new contacts with the IMF, with the demand that he finally present a serious program for fighting inflation. This could not be avoided, and Mikulić was forced to realize that it was better to work out such a program than to leave that to the IMF. He could hope, in this way, to retain at least state interventionist methods. For that purpose Mikulić now tried to build up the IMF as the scapegoat for the expected belt-tightening as well as for any possible further failure. One of his principal advisers, Jakov Sirotković (a Croat), the former Minister of Economics in Belgrade and one of the chief exponents of the so-called "contract economy", pinned the principal blame on the IMF for the fact that Yugoslavia had allegedly "lost ten years" and had "almost ruined" its system of self-management.[2]

When Mikulić announced his anti-inflation program in parliament on 19 October 1987, supported by Lazar Mojsov, then chair of the state presidency, it was apparent that this program did not in any way reduce the level of administrative intervention, and, on the contrary, included some 120 new government acts. Mikulić even conceded in his address that the long-term program of economic stabilization would not be carried out. He presented a number of reasons, omitting only to mention that he himself had been opposed to the aspirations of that program. He could not commit, as yet, to any relaxation of the central currency controls, but he said that work in that direction would continue. There were no provisions for a liberalization of prices. Mikulić, like Mojsov, linked the question of further economic reforms with the planned changes to the federal constitution. It was imperative, according to Mojsov, to strengthen the role of the federation.[3] The program envisaged a reduction of the share of the social sector in the social product from 35 per cent to 30 per cent. That this reduction would not be achieved was foreseeable due to the position of the army.

The "anti-inflation program" was badly received in the country. The Croatian parliament formally rejected it; in Slovenia the trade union council demanded the government's resignation, on the grounds of incompetence.[4] In essence, the program proposed measures which had already proven ineffectual once before. Instead of trusting to the market, the government proposed to rely on administrative decisions. Against the votes of the Slovenian deputies as well as of some of the Croatian deputies, the *Skupština* in Belgrade decided to accept the anti-inflation program "in principle", but mainly in order to facilitate the opening of negotiations with the IMF. The individual measures would be announced as decrees. Immediately thereupon strikes broke out not only in Slovenia and Croatia, but also in Skopje. The new year would begin without a parliamentary decision about the budget or the one-year indicative plan. Slovenia made its agreement to the budget conditional upon the revision of the law on hard currency earnings in its favor.[5]

At the beginning of April 1988 an accord was reached between Yugoslavia and the IMF, which promised to ease Yugoslavia's debt burden.[6] At the same time, Yugoslavia was placed again under the tougher controls for "stand-by" credits; aside from that, the IMF also asked for effective measures to combat inflation. As of early 1988, the annual rate of inflation stood at about 160 per cent.[7]

Incredibly, this accord almost met Mikulić halfway on a variety of points. It embodied the concept of "targeted" inflation, which came close to Mikulić's earlier idea of "planned" inflation. One axiom was that wages should only increase in proportion to growth in the social product. This was not unrealistic; since, however, the government did not have a differentiated instrument of inflation control at its disposal, the danger existed that this could open the door to a return to administrative interventions.

Moreover, this program of the IMF seemed to require centralistic measures. As a result, Ljubljana and Zagreb immediately issued warnings that they would not accept new centralized measures.[8] These warnings were directed also at the IMF.

Slovenia and Croatia abandoned the accord in May 1988 with the demand that the Yugoslav parliament take a vote of confidence concerning the work of the Mikulić government. In this they remained in the minority; but they did succeed in bringing it home to Mikulić that he should review his own basic approach *vis-à-vis* the western republics.[9]

Although it was rejected in parliament, the vote of no confidence shook the foundations of the Mikulić government. The accord with the IMF could not be put into force on 15 May 1988 as had been intended. Mikulić now had to be in command against the expressed wishes of the two economically most important republics. Because of low agricultural prices, Vojvodina also gave its partial support to Croatia and Slovenia. Even the LCY Central Committee criticized Mikulić without contributing any suggestions for economic policy on its own part.[10] The attitude of Croatia and especially Slovenia cannot be viewed except in conjunction with other developments, which were then unfolding in Yugoslavia, such as the army leadership's threats against Slovenia and the pressure to consent to centralize changes to the constitution. Before Milošević's coup, voices for economic reform had been relatively strong in Serbia. Even in April 1988, a reform proposal presented by the party leadership in Serbia demanded, *inter alia*, the repeal of the restrictive 1986 law on enterprises concerning "associated labor", one of the holy cows of the system.[11]

At the end of May 1988, shortly before a national party conference and under the double pressure from the IMF and internal factors, the Mikulić government finally decided to switch to a path of reform. The prime minister announced a series of almost surprising measures, which corresponded to the spirit of the demands of both the IMF and the western Yugoslav republics. Sixty per cent of all prices and 40 per cent of imports were liberalized; wages could fluctuate within a margin of 15 per cent of price hikes; the dinar was devalued and the currency law revised. To be sure, hard currency proceeds would still have to be surrendered, but now as a sale to a currency exchange; here, in future, the rate of exchange was supposed to be allowed to float.[12] After a period of transition, the system functioned – in the beginning through the interventions of the National Bank, later above all because the eastern parts of the country increasingly lacked money to buy hard currency.

This so-called macroeconomic reform was exclusively a matter for the government. The highest party organs hardly concerned themselves with it. Many commentators, nevertheless, held at the time that Yugoslavia was making its first serious effort at reform.[13] Skeptical questions, none the less, also emerged at the beginning. Would the government be in a position to withstand the social pressure which its measures would have to incite?

Would macroeconomic reforms, which would leave the system as such undisturbed, be sufficient?

Polemics ensued in the following months, especially in the eastern parts of the country; on the one hand, Yugoslavia wanted Western assistance, but on the other hand, some of its politicians condemned the West's interpretations and accused the West of conducting a "special war" against the country. Kučan had pinpointed this contradiction in March 1988 when he had protested against the idea of military intervention in Slovenia.[14] The tension had not been relieved when, in that same month, Dizdarević, to whom, as Jože Smole put it, Yugoslavia's observer status on the Islamic Conference was more important than relationships with Europe, had been succeeded as Foreign Minister by Croat Budimir Lončar. None the less, it was expected that he would take a greater interest in good relations with Europe.

The skepticism proved to be justified. The macroeconomic reforms were not sufficient, so there was always the temptation – possibly even the necessity – to return to administrative interventions. The prices climbed much more quickly than had been expected; thus the inflation was not stopped after all, and there were further problems with the IMF. Mikulić could not hold to a policy of keeping real interest above the level of inflation, as a result of which one of the principal authors of the long-term stabilization program, Belgrade Professor Oskar Kovač, resigned at the year's end. Already in mid-October 1988, one had the impression that certain possibly necessary interventions in the economy had, for all practical purposes, rendered the agreement with the IMF null and void. On the other hand, Kučan saw the danger that through the negative economic developments, especially in the eastern parts of the country, there would be ever greater burdens imposed on Slovenia, which would, in addition, come to be permanently treated as an enemy of the state.[15]

The most prominent Serbian representative in the government, Vice President Miloš Milošavljević, blamed the lethargic pace of the reforms on an inadequate constitutional groundwork. His remarks to this effect were made in autumn 1988, when it was already certain that all the proposed constitutional amendments with a specifically economic content had been adopted and would be put into effect on 29 November.[16] But he was referring not to these amendments, but rather to proposed amendments of a more political character which, because of their centralist inspiration, were unacceptable to Slovenia. The government made itself, in this way, an instrument of political pressure, which weighed down on Slovenia, and culminated in the demand that all the proposed constitutional amendments be accepted *in toto*.[17] The Slovenes, however, could prevent that, even if they did agree to the military budget as a concession.

It should be conceded, none the less, that the Mikulić government now held fast to the principle of reform and earnestly began work on the core of the reform, a new law on economic enterprises. This law would repeal

Kardelj's nonsensical atomization of the economy and create units capable of production. But in the meantime, the political landscape had changed. Milošević, who after his seizure of total power in Serbia in September 1987 hesitated for a while to engage himself in economic matters, now decisively took the side of the opponents of reform. He openly opposed Mikulić, just as the latter was undertaking earnest reforms.

Even today, it is hard to expunge the thesis which was, at the time, circulating among Western diplomats in Belgrade – that Milošević might be politically unacceptable, but he was all the same an economic "reformer". The very fact that Milošević came out against the Mikulić government just as it had decided on a reform course confutes this thesis. Milošević stood not for a market economy, but for state capitalism. The economic structure of Serbia, with its profusion of steelworks and arms industries, naturally led him to this position. In an interview with the magazine *NIN* in July 1988, he said that, in his view, private property would never play a large role in the Yugoslav economy.[18] A short while later, he personally introduced to the public a book written by Croatian economic manager and politician Ivo Perišin. Perišin was one of the leading figures in the Zagreb school of "contract economy", a late-Marxist alternative to the market economy. Only shortly before, Perišin had conducted a major campaign against real interest and, indeed, against any kind of interest under socialism. There could, thus, be no doubt as to where Milošević stood and it is no surprise that in December 1988 the pressure against the Mikulić government came primarily from Belgrade and less from the western republics.[19]

So it was almost unavoidable that on 30 December 1988, Mikulić and his government had to resign, after being handed a disastrous vote in the Yugoslav parliament. It was again not possible to pass the budget and indicative plan for the following year. Whereas Slovenia and Croatia felt that the reforms did not go far enough, the Serbian government considered that the reforms already went too far. Mikulić tried to defend his policy in parliament by noting that it was linked to the conditions of the IMF; but he had released himself from these conditions several times.[20] Added to this was the fact that Mikulić's prestige had been damaged by the financial scandal in Bosnia (pp. 41–2). It was true that he had had only a peripheral connection to the Agrokomerc scandal; but he had been implicated in the not entirely regular construction of summer houses in Neum, Bosnia's sole outlet to the sea.

I had a conversation with economist Marijan Korošić in Zagreb in October 1988. I wanted to find out what really underlay the Yugoslav economic catastrophe and why all attempts to extricate the country from this catastrophe up to then had failed. Korošić, who rejected the "contract economy" camp and was not affiliated to the self-managing utopianism of Branko Horvat either,[21] held that Yugoslavia needed an "open economy" in which free economic activity would be possible. This would not be possible without political democracy. The "tyranny of the status quo", to use Milton Friedman's expression, manifested itself in Yugoslavia in such a way that the communist party organization at all levels – also in the local communities and even in Slovenia – did not want to pull out of the economy, since that was the source of much of its power, not to mention its finance. Thus, reform efforts were always sacrificed to political expectations, according to Korošić. Mikulić had finally obtained some successes in exports, but the most important question was total economic volume. Without an increase in the social product, a recovery as such was inconceivable; but the social product was, on the contrary, falling from year to year by an annual rate of between 1 and 1.5 per cent. There was, thus, no reduction in the foreign debt, Yugoslavia's great crucifix. Korošić held that the time for economic reforms had probably passed, since the political conditions above all in the eastern parts of the country had now changed. There one found almost only deficit enterprises and with enterprises in such a condition, it would be difficult to build a market economy, even if one wanted to.

The job now was to find a successor for Mikulić. The polarization which had developed in the country in the meantime complicated the search, which was, moreover, overshadowed by the overthrow of the government in Montenegro, by the threat that Milošević might obtain effective control of the central institutions of Yugoslavia, and by the unfolding developments in Kosovo. Would Milošević try to take control even of the government itself? That Milošević might want to become Prime Minister himself seemed improbable, as the post entailed only economic responsibilities. It seemed more likely that Milošević would propose one of his cohorts for the post – which, in fact, was what he did.

As is evident from protocols of the sessions of the LCY Presidium, the initiative was left to the state presidency. General Kadijević, the Defense Minister at the time, writes in his memoirs that when, immediately after Mikulić's resignation, he had proposed Milošević as his successor, Raif Dizdarević, then chair of the state presidency, had asked him to contact the Serbian leader,[22] but Milošević had said that his first priority was to work for the unity of Serbia. That the army leadership tried everything to install an opponent of reform at the helm of the government sounds plausible.

The candidate of Slovenia and Croatia was the Croat Ante Marković, an experienced economic manager known as an advocate of reform and a member, at the time, of the Croatian state presidency. Slovenia had given up on its own candidate, since the next chair of the Yugoslav state presidency, according to the prescribed rotation system, was supposed to be a Slovene. Slovenes swore that their republic had had nothing to do with the removal of Mikulić who had, after all, recently changed his attitude about reform. It would not have been clever to have brought about Mikulić's fall over a law which was oriented in the right direction, viz., to the reduction of state expenses and the combating of inflation.

Milošević proposed as his candidate Borisav Jović, a loyal follower who, as President of the Serbian Constitutional Commission, had successfully led the fight for the "unification of Serbia". In the state presidency, opinions were divided. Only the representatives of Serbia and Macedonia supported Jović. Dizdarević's fear of Milošević now eclipsed his erstwhile desire to support him. So finally, on his proposal, Marković was endorsed by the state presidency. Behind closed doors this consensus in the state presidency was explained as follows: Marković convinced the presidency that he really wanted the job, while Jović comported himself as a "forced recruit".[23] But this decision could not be interpreted as an endorsement of reform by the highest organ of state; it figured, rather, as a political reaction to the coup in Montenegro. Milošević himself realized, at the time, that he needed to back off temporarily. His behavior in Vojvodina and Montenegro had awakened historical comparisons with the fascist "conquest" of Italy in 1922.[24]

Marković took office under an unlucky star, however. With the proclamation of a state of emergency at the end of February 1989, the battle over the autonomy of Kosovo went into its final phase; the now predominantly reactionary state presidency proved, under Dizdarević's leadership, to be little more than Milošević's executive assistant also in this last storm. Marković complained that in his conversations about the construction of a new government he found the politicians in the republics concerned with other matters.[25] The skepticism of the Serbian leadership *vis-à-vis* Marković was well known. The two Deputy Prime Ministers were Aleksandar Mitrović, a Serb from Croatia, and Živko Pregl, a Slovene. Lončar remained Foreign Minister and Kadijević stayed on as Defense Minister. The Ministry of Internal Affairs was headed by former General Petar Gračanin, a firm Milošević loyalist.

The existing political constellation inclined Marković to make a cautious beginning. He professed a solid reform policy under which the workers' collectives should make their decisions largely independently, but he avoided the expression "new socialism". Cautiously he tried in his accession speech to suggest to the army that its interests could best be secured through the success of economic reform. Aside from that, Marković demanded above all a "new morality". But for all that he said he would base his policy, including the establishment of an exchange rate, on "real values".

The rather general character of this program and the lack of clearly outlined measures at first met with understanding. One might suppose that the Prime Minister would need time to set forth a clear policy. The inflation in the early months of 1989 had so sharply increased that an annual inflation rate of 1000 per cent was expected.[26] Marković replied to his critics that there was no sense in decreeing anti-inflation measures unless they were linked to a total concept. In the vicinity of the Prime Minister's office one would hear, at the time, that the whole policy of the government was concentrated on fighting inflation. The strategy would have had to include a damming up of the disbursement of private credit by banks and enterprises as well as a reduction of state outlays, including those earmarked for the army.[27]

28 March 1989, the day of the solemn proclamation of the new Serbian constitution in the Belgrade Sava Center, found a smiling Marković cutting up a holiday cake between Milošević and Trifunović. Only a few non-Serb politicians took part in this triumphal celebration. Already in his programmatic speech, Marković had said that "the acceptance of the Serbian constitutional amendments [constitutes] the precondition for the stabilization of relations in Kosovo". His participation in the celebration of the Serbian constitution was a gaffe, according to Predrag Tašić, Marković's last press secretary in the federal Ministry of Information.[28] People in the western republics were taken aback and never forgot it. Marković seemed to think, however, that the train of events in Kosovo had run its course and that he could scarcely perform his job without good contact with Milošević. This may well be the case, but Marković should have been more careful about his behavior. While his relations with Kadijević remained tolerable for a long time, his relations with Milošević and the other Serbian leaders became shaky again in early summer 1989. This occurred at the moment when Marković, as a sign of his resolve to combat inflation, wanted to stop the uncontrolled increase of credits in clearing dollars for exports to the Soviet Union, above all from Serbia.[29]

People now no longer understood why Marković held back for so long from taking comprehensive measures while the situation in the country became steadily worse almost by the week. In mid-July Deputy Prime Minister Pregl (a Slovene) told me that the previous governments had collapsed in connection with their anti-inflation programs.[30] Pregl called for specific measures, all of which were suited to containing inflation. Prices and imports were liberalized by degrees; the duties were moderated, facilitating imports. The government took better control of the money supply, and tried to hold the increase in the money supply to 30 per cent less than the rate of inflation. Pregl notes also that the distorted structure of prices and wages remained an issue with which the government had to grapple. This had to be corrected, but this very correction would create a new round of inflation. Pregl also wanted to restrict the damaging influences of the local authorities on the work of "their" enterprises. The army had agreed to be content with a share of 4.5 per cent of the social product. Pregl conceded that the government's measures adopted up to then had encountered resistance, especially in Serbia, because people could not give up the idea that the market economy would work to the detriment of the less developed parts of the country. In Serbia, some measures had been adopted which put money into the hands of the state rather than into a free economy, as in the loan for the "rebuilding" of Serbia announced by Milošević.

Only on 18 December 1989 did Marković present his program for currency reform to the parliament, together with associated measures. A new dinar was to be established, with a stable exchange, pegged at seven dinars to the DM. It was anticipated that that would entail some hardships, especially for the eastern parts of the country. Some $150 million had been allocated to ease these hardships. Marković's program elicited some expressions of displeasure in Slovenia, because Marković had included in his program some new proposals for constitutional reform which were seen as "centralistic" in Ljubljana. Slovenia was, moreover, subject to a kind of Serbian economic boycott.[31]

The Serbian rejection was clear and total. "Serbia does not support the government's policies," a headline of the Belgrade daily *Politika* announced on 20 December 1989. The paper published the resolution of all three houses of the Serbian parliament. Serbian Deputy Prime Minister Miroslav Mišković provided some reasons for Serbian opposition, under the headline, "Why Serbia is Against it": The measures affected Serbia more than the other republics. The gravest consequence of galloping inflation, according to Mišković, was that investments had ceased, so that companies were concentrating exclusively on current activities. To the question whether the state should undertake the desired investments, Mišković said, one could "not sit down and watch how the economy exhausted itself in a hunt for money which would be spent immediately and exclusively on boosting the wages of workers".[32]

Marković's program reflected the influence of Harvard Professor Jeffrey Sachs who, on the invitation of the new Slovenian chair of the state presidium, Janez Drnovšek, had come to Yugoslavia. Drnovšek was the formal Yugoslav head of state since mid-May 1989. Across Eastern Europe communism was facing its imminent demise, while in Serbia, Milošević's communists, now calling themselves socialists and orienting themselves along nationalist lines, consolidated their hold on power. As is well known, in his advice for the transformation of communist systems, Sachs found the "lever" in the property question. But the Yugoslav phenomenon of "social property" evidently puzzled him. For the short to medium term, he urged authorities to get to work on monetary questions. This advice was scotched in Marković's policies.[33]

Professor Alexandar Bajt in Ljubljana had been active at the time as adviser to Marković, together with two other economic experts, Dragomir Vojnić and Kiro Gligorov. This trio had, in summer 1989, more or less completed work on a concept of economic reform; it would have been less radical, but none the less comprehensive. As early as September or October it had become clear, however, that Marković had decided for a "shock therapy" along the lines of Sachs' ideas. As a result, Bajt resigned at the end of November 1989, as Marković pushed forward with his own plans.[34] The reliance on Sachs contributed to the fact that Marković would later be treated as a hero by Western diplomats.

Had Marković come to office two years earlier, and had he been able to begin immediately with these reforms, one would have been able to speak of a victory for the western republics and for the progressive reforms which they had been championing. But Marković and his reform efforts came too late. His major reforms, introduced at the end of 1989, made some impact, but a lasting success was denied to him. Serbia had committed itself to a state-capitalist course, and the western republics, as a result of broader developments in the country, could not do anything but look out, in the first place, for their own interests.

Slovenia's answer: democracy and independence

The events which led to the snuffing out of Kosovo's autonomy induced deep consternation in Slovenia. With the support of the Yugoslav federal authorities, including both the state presidency and the LCY Presidium, the constitutionally guaranteed autonomy of a constituent unit of the Yugoslav federation had been extinguished. People who supported the valid constitution of the land were criminalized, threatened, arrested, ostracized, and manhandled. Had other members of the common state not every reason to fear that something similar would happen to them once the Kosovo question had been settled?

Reactions in Slovenia were not entirely coordinated. The meeting in Cankarjev Dom in Ljubljana (in February 1989) had sprung out of a genuine feeling of humanitarian and political solidarity. But then came the disagreements. In a session of the LCY Presidium on 28 February 1989, Kučan had still maintained that the state of emergency in Kosovo had been imposed without the participation of the Slovenes, because no Slovene representative had taken part in the state presidency's vote on this matter. But then, upon his return from Japan, Slovenia's representative on this body, Dolanc, said that he would have also voted for the "special measures".[35]

It was equally incomprehensible that Slovenia's deputies in the federal *Skupština* subsequently voted for the state of emergency and helped to approve it, even though one could be almost completely certain that Mojsov's story about Vllasi's conspiracy was a total fabrication. The deputies later explained that they had not received any instructions and did not know how they were supposed to vote.[36]

Kučan said later that the situation had not been easy. The confrontation found Slovenia unprepared; this extent of federal support for Milošević had not been expected. In addition, the events in the state presidency and in the parliament had shown that in spite of the principle of consensus, Slovenia could be outmaneuvered. The immoderate sorties from Milošević's camp could already be seen as a preparation for actions against Slovenia.[37]

Paradoxically, the events in Kosovo in connection with the state of emergency had, meantime, brought a kind of relief for Slovenia. Croatia seemed to have woken up; the leadership of this republic now saw itself threatened by Serbia. The hitherto close relationship between Serbia and Macedonia also began to melt away slowly; younger functionaries, who were beginning to replace the dogmatic politicians like Pančevski, Lazaroski, and Mojsov, began to recognize the danger with which Serbia presented Macedonia. The first visible conflict between these republics broke out in April 1989 over the so-called law on colonists.[38] The first Yugoslav state had settled Serbian colonists in "south Serbia", i.e., Macedonia and Kosovo, on properties confiscated from Muslims, Turks, and Albanians, under the rubric of agrarian reform. Most of these colonists had been Serbian veterans from the Balkan Wars or from the Salonika front. During the Second World War many of them had been driven away and in 1945, in order to avoid creating any new national complications, Tito had barred them from returning. Under Serbian pressure, the prohibition on their return was now to be lifted through a new federal law, much to the displeasure not only of the Albanians but also of the Macedonians. Only when it was too late did the Serbs realize their mistake and try to amend their draft law to apply only to Kosovo. But the damage had already been done. With Macedonia's gradual withdrawal from its alliance with Serbia, the danger of Slovenia's being isolated in the federal organs was reduced.

But many Slovenes thought that a more tangible improvement in Slovenia's position in Yugoslavia could only be accomplished by effecting certain changes within the republic itself: specifically, on the one hand, democratization and, on the other, the passage of legal instructions which would give the republic a stronger constitutional profile and give its officials clear handles as to its behavior *vis-à-vis* the federal government and other republics.

Kučan's theses about "another socialism" and the principled affirmation of a pluralism on the (West) European model demanded institutionalization. In fact, the democratic movement had already achieved a decisive breakthrough in the course of the fight against the threat of military intervention in 1988. A series of private associations had been established, which pursued political goals, among them a League of Peasants, which was established in autumn 1988 under the leadership of Ivan Oman; the League already displayed some characteristics of a political party. Since peasants comprise only 15 per cent of the population of Slovenia, its significance was limited. In January 1989, a Social Democratic Association was established under Franc Tomšič, but it failed to have any wide impact. Characteristic of both organizations was that they had been established outside the framework of the Socialist Alliance and thereby no longer followed the "channeled" concept of democracy represented by Jože Smole.[39] Within the Socialist Alliance, a Democratic League of Slovenia had been provisionally set up in January, which later became the Democratic Party. Moreover, the Association of Socialist Youth of Slovenia, with its chair, Jozef Školc, progressively took on more of the character of a political party with a liberal orientation.

One must constantly keep in mind that 1989 was the year of political upheavals in Eastern Europe and that Yugoslavia was clearly lagging behind in the process. That fact created a politically and psychologically difficult situation for Slovenia. In July 1989, the Yugoslav army leadership came out openly against political pluralism and criticized Hungary and Poland because of the "meltdown" of socialism taking place in those countries.[40]

The first institutional manifestation of the Slovenian process of democratization was the election of the new Slovenian representative in the Yugoslav state presidency in April 1989. The party had announced that it would present the candidacy of Dolanc's successor before a consultative referendum and respect the result. From the ranks of the party, the former President of the Slovenian Trade and Economic Chamber Marko Bulc was proposed; he was a technically oriented functionary with experience in Belgrade. From the ranks of the Socialist Alliance, the 39-year-old economic and finance specialist, Dr Janez Drnovšek, presented himself at the same time as a candidate; he had briefly served in the diplomatic service, and was later a Slovenian deputy in the federal *Skupština*, always with special responsibility for connections with the IMF; his Ph.D. dissertation had dealt with Yugoslav relations with that body.[41] In the consultative vote Drnovšek won with 56 per cent of the vote against 41 per cent for Bulc. This result reflected people's desire to see "new people" brought into positions of responsibility rather than seasoned functionaries, even where the latter enjoyed people's respect. The importance of this vote was magnified by the fact that the Slovenian representative on the Yugoslav state presidency was scheduled to assume the chairmanship of this body on 15 May 1989. Politically the situation was new insofar as Drnovšek, by virtue of his popular mandate, would enjoy considerable independence of action *vis-à-vis* the Slovenian governmental organs, while the Yugoslav constitution of 1974 had expected the occupants of federal appointive offices to behave in principle as the representative of the republic's authorities. The special position of the new Slovenian representative in the Yugoslav state presidency actually created some problems in the transition to Slovenian independence.

At a press conference in Ljubljana in mid-April, the future Yugoslav head of state sounded a note of caution. Yugoslavia needed a period of peace, in which it could concern itself more with its economy. The state of emergency in Kosovo should be handled "correctly", as should the trial of Vllasi. One could discuss a future "rationalization" of the army. The West's interest policy was partly to blame for Yugoslavia's debt problems, but Yugoslavia had to integrate itself into world trade. In contrast to his predecessor, Dizdarević, he would not present himself at any mass meetings.[42]

Drnovšek considered it a personal success that, practically in the first days of his term as Slovenia's representative in the state presidency a proposal to establish new procedures for the proclamation of a state of emergency was tabled. These procedures had, however, been hammered out earlier. The new guidelines introduced precise definitions and excluded the organs of the party from participation in the necessary decisions. That was an advance, since the party organs worked on the basis of "democratic centralism". The new precepts set forth clearly that the introduction of combat forces could be accomplished only after an explicit resolution by the Yugoslav state presidency and on the basis of Article 316 of the Yugoslav constitution, thus not on the basis of the law concerning people's defense.[43] Slovenia nonetheless remained skeptical about the proposal, which put too much emphasis on the rights of federal organs and too little on those of the republics.[44]

The following period can be described as that of a "Slovenia of two speeds". While Jože Smole tried to arrange a kind of round table for discussion within his Socialist Alliance, in which every group or organization which was so inclined might take part, alternative and opposition groups were becoming ever bolder with their independent demands, which went further than official policy in the direction of democratization and Slovenian independence. The opposition groups published a "May Declaration" in May 1989, with an intentional symbolic reference to that of 1918, in which they hardly bothered to disguise their demand for independence. The publication of this manifesto on 8 May 1989 coincided with the day on which Janša and his friends had to begin serving the sentences handed down by the military court.[45] In this matter, there had been pressure from Serbia, including threats of boycott; the Slovenian authorities did not want to allow themselves to be drawn into open confrontation at this point.

Slovenian officialdom, i.e., the circle around Smole, responded in June with a "Fundamental Charter of Slovenia", for which signatures were gathered among the public.[46] Of course, this charter was not entirely "official", since its originator was the organizing committee for the aforementioned meeting in Cankarjev Dom (p. 88); almost all political organizations of Slovenia had been represented in this committee. The camps began to blend; one had the impression that the difference between opposition and the "official" establishment was vanishing. It should, however, be taken into account that the leaders of Slovenia at that time were under permanent pressure from Belgrade, while the opposition found it sometimes convenient and safe to hide behind the skirts of the leaders.

The Fundamental Charter (*Temeljna listina*) announced in its first passage: "We want to live in a democratic state grounded on the sovereignty of the

Slovenian people, human rights, and the liberties of citizens". The Charter continued, "We will live only in such a Yugoslavia in which our sovereignty and our lasting and inalienable right to national self-determination are secured, together with the equality of all nationalities and minorities, in which the differences among peoples are protected and guaranteed, and in which the common tasks in the federal state are regulated on the basis of consensus". The Charter also registered an explicit demand for political pluralism, including freedom of association and free voting. There followed the request to all officeholders in the republic to keep the will of the people in mind as they engage in the work of constitutional reforms both in Slovenia and in Yugoslavia.[47]

The Charter was a great success, since it doubtless reflected the prevalent opinion in Slovenia. Janša criticized it for still being "Yugoslav-minded".[48] But the Charter linked any possible future affiliation with Yugoslavia with the realization of certain fundamental principles. If Serbia demanded to become "a state in which no outsiders can interfere", Slovenia was surely entitled to the same thing.

Only a few days after the publication of the Charter, Kučan embraced its essential demands in an important speech on 17 June 1989. For this purpose he had chosen a Partisan celebration in the vicinity of Ljubljana. Kučan could proceed from the fact that shortly beforehand Milošević had sharply rejected his offer to engage in talks; the Serbian leader had informed Kučan that no such talks were possible until Slovenia changed its viewpoints. Kučan replied that he would not make any further offers of talks to those who had spurned his invitation.[49] As regards the "May Declaration", Kučan underlined that "we can share in only such a Yugoslavia" as girds itself with a "successful concept of socialism" and guarantees the equality of its peoples. Only such a federation assures space for the realization of all human, political, and national rights. Slovenia was prepared to talk also in the future with people for whom Yugoslavia and socialism lay close to the heart. "Today, however, we say openly, that no one can scare us by calling us separatists and destroyers of Yugoslavia". Serbia was pulling a curtain over events in Kosovo and using Slovenia as an alibi for the failure of its policies. The relations between the peoples in Yugoslavia could be framed only in linkage with democracy. At the end of his speech, Kučan said that the Slovenian communists endorsed the Fundamental Charter. He demanded that, on the 200th anniversary of the French Revolution, all political prisoners in Yugoslavia be released, that the precepts governing the uses of armed forces and police and especially of the "state of emergency" be reviewed, that everything be eliminated from those precepts which was menacing to human rights, that the practice of protective confinement be terminated, that republic leaderships stop attacking each other and support the reform policies of Prime Minister Marković.

In the course of discussion, slogans emerged in Slovenia which would later become important. "If we cannot unite ourselves, then we should separate peacefully," said "official" socialist Viktor Žakelj. He could have been referring, with this, to a similar statement made in Titograd shortly before by Serbian novelist Dobrica Ćosić, who would later serve as president of rump Yugoslavia.[50]

But Milošević continued his march. He turned the celebrations of the 600th anniversary of the Battle of Kosovo on 28 June 1989 into a victory celebration. There was no word about reconciliation with the Albanians, no word about democracy or human rights, no word about a Yugoslavia of national equality. Serbia was in the grips of nationalist fever. In Belgrade, it was widely believed that Milošević would draw the entire area under his influence and away from federal authority. That meant a kind of separation. People also spoke of the establishment of Serbian "hegemony" throughout the rest of Yugoslavia. The image was of a kind of dual Yugoslavia consisting of an inner core under direct Serbian control and a periphery under indirect Serbian influence.

The revived state presidency with Drnovšek at the helm could apparently not succeed in moderating Serbia's open repression in Kosovo. Incidents in which Serbian police ruthlessly shot down Albanians in cold blood were not investigated. There was only one new development: At the triumphal celebration of the Battle on the Field of the Blackbirds, in contrast to the celebrations of the new Serbian constitution in Belgrade, no Western diplomats took part.[51]

After their invitation to talks had been declined by Milošević, the conflict with the Slovenians came into the open. The presidency of Slovenia declared on 2 June 1989 that a reply should be made to Serbia that Slovenia is a sovereign state, and has both the right and the duty to concern itself with general Yugoslav questions.[52] Almost at the same time, the President of the Slovenian parliament and specialist for constitutional questions, Miran Potrč, had received a uniquely insolent reply from the army leadership to his endeavor to sort out existing disputes between Slovenia and the army directly. The army's reply declared that Potrč's letter could have provided a basis for discussion, but in view of its "shortcomings, incompleteness, and one-sidedness" in respect to the anti-army sentiment in Slovenia, it could not do so.[53]

Furthermore, the announcements of the highest federal organs and of Serbia in regard to the question of political pluralism, to the fundamental questions of a new constitution, and to the guidelines for a reform of the party were one-sided and dogmatic, so that cooperation was not at all possible. Again there were Serbian demands for an "effective federation" while, on the other side, proposals to eliminate "democratic centralism" in the party had, from the beginning, come up against inflexible resistance.[54]

Could Slovenia still hope, under such conditions and after such answers, to play the role of "trailblazer of democracy" for the rest of Yugoslavia, as American Ambassador Zimmermann and individual Slovenian politicians of the older generation, such as Jože Smole, had imagined? That seemed not only hopeless but even dangerous. On the other hand, Slovenia was no longer expected to forego the normal achievements of a contemporary European nation. The result was the emergence of ideas concerning the transformation of Yugoslavia into an "asymmetric federation". Slovenia would, according to this idea, organize itself as it saw fit, while the other republics would organize themselves as they wanted; they could also arrange relations among themselves accordingly. If they wished to have closer relations with each other than Slovenia wished, they could freely decide on this.[55]

Out of these reflections came the draft of a new Slovenian constitution, or, rather, a series of constitutional amendments. Miran Potrč, who in addition to serving as president of the Slovenian Parliament also chaired the constitutional commission, played a large role in the rapid work on these amendments. In the new constitutional clauses there would be clearer definitions of some matters which had been expressed unclearly and in summary form in the Yugoslav constitution, relating above all to the statehood of Slovenia, including the right to dissolve its association with Yugoslavia. Slovenia rejected the thesis that its right of self-determination had been "consummated" through its accession to Yugoslavia. Further Slovenian constitutional amendments dealt with human rights, political freedoms, democratic procedures, economic freedom including the right to own property, the use of the Slovenian language in Slovenia including on the part of the federal organs, the financial obligations of Slovenia *vis-à-vis* the federation, and the rights of the army. A state of emergency could be proclaimed in Slovenia only with the consent of the republic's parliament.[56]

The first conflict over the Slovenian constitutional amendments broke out at the end of August 1989 in the LCY Presidium. Milan Pančevski, chair of the presidium, demanded an "explanation" of the surprised Kučan, since perhaps the Constitutional Court and the Yugoslav *Skupština* could be involved in these questions.[57] Kučan expressed amazement. Why an explanation? This was the first time that such a thing had been demanded of any Yugoslav republic. The proposals had been publicized long in advance. If the presidium wanted, he could furnish an authorized text and even a summary, but no "explanation".

A few days later the Yugoslav state presidency followed suit, over Drnovšek's negative vote. The presidency declared that some of the Slovenian constitutional amendments were contrary to the federal constitution. The Slovenian politicians and Slovenian public disagreed. Slovenia had merely filled in certain gaps in the federal constitution. The republics had the right to make their own determination concerning matters not conclusively regulated by the federal constitution. Clearly, there seemed suddenly to be a desire to lead a "concerted action" against Slovenia, orchestrated by Serbia and the army.

There were some problems inside Slovenia, too. The former Slovenian party chief France Popit protested against the republic's submission to "antisocialist" tendencies.[58] Kučan asked Popit to refrain from taking any greater steps and the feared "rebellion of the Old Guard" did not take place. Under the leadership of Potrč, the authorized committees of the Slovenian parliament took pains that the constitutional amendments would, as planned, be brought before the then still tricameral Slovenian parliament on 27 September.

In the meantime, the campaign from the eastern part of the country reached a new fury. Tempers in the east were inflamed not least by the clause requiring the organs of Slovenia "to take into consideration the material possibilities of the republic in regard to the acceptance of financial obligations connected with the realization of the functions of the federation".

If the Serbian media had seemed to be leading the campaign at first, it suddenly seemed, in the last week of September, that the army leadership was taking over this function. The army leaders were incensed above all by the new constitutional article which made the proclamation of a state of emergency in Slovenia conditional on the approval of the Slovenian parliament. They saw this as a curtailment of the army's freedom of movement. So one had to worry about the army once again. At the instigation of the army leadership, according to Kučan, the Central Committee of the LCY was hastily convened on the afternoon of 26 September 1989 for an extraordinary session with only one item of business: the Slovenian constitutional amendments. The session had been called so suddenly that the Slovenian members of the CC were unable to obtain any flights to Belgrade and had to be brought to Belgrade on an army transport plane.[59] There was barely time, before the flight's departure, to hold a session of the Slovenian Central Committee.

It was, according to all who took part, a memorable meeting. Yugoslavs could experience directly on television just how deep the differences had become and with what tone of voice the country's leaders spoke with one another. The Slovenian leaders set forth frankly, perhaps for the first time, everything which the Slovenes did for Yugoslavia, contrasting this with the accusations that they wanted to destroy Yugoslavia. With 8 per cent of the population, Slovenia accounted for 22 per cent of the national income, with a corresponding contribution to the federal budget. Slovenia further accounted for 30 per cent of Yugoslavia's exports to countries with convertible currency and 25 per cent of total exports. To that one had to add the contributions of Slovenian enterprises to the fund for the underdeveloped parts of the country.

The Slovenes could then see on their television screens with what antipathy and hatred the Serbs replied to the Slovenian representatives. Trifunović, a close collaborator of Milošević's, said he was proud that Kučan was his enemy. Many Slovenes told me that they finally realized, in the course of that night, that Yugoslavia had nothing more to offer Slovenia. This realization was mixed with satisfaction that the Slovenian leadership had resisted immense pressure. Late in the night, Kučan defended Slovenia's standpoint in detail once again, in a speech lasting nearly an hour; he made it clear, beyond any possibility of misunderstanding, that Slovenia would proceed with the adoption of its constitutional amendments.[60] The Central Committee decided then, by a vote of 97 to 40, to call on the Slovenes to delay parliamentary ratification of their constitutional amendments; there should be a chance, so the majority in the Central Committee argued, to discuss further the problems which had arisen, *inter alia*, within the framework of negotiations concerning a new reform of the federal constitution. That was a partial victory for the Slovenes. A motion to condemn the Slovenian constitutional amendments outright would probably not have found a majority.

Kučan and other participants in the session later spoke of the "menacing atmosphere" which they had encountered at the time in Belgrade. In an open threat, Admiral Petar Simić, the army spokesman, said it would not be "good" if Slovenia were to adopt its constitutional amendments. At any rate, after the end of the session in the early morning hours of 27 September 1989, the Slovenian delegates felt a pressing need to get out of Belgrade as quickly as possible; they were happy when the Director of the Slovenian Airline, Janez Kocijančič, himself a member of the CC LCY, succeeded in organizing a flight back at the time needed.

The collision with the army at the CC session would have come about in any case, but the intense emotional engagement of the Serbian leadership and the Serbian media can be explained not only in terms of Milošević's desire to demonstrate solidarity with the army at any cost. There were real Serbian interests at stake. The Slovenian constitutional amendments seriously threatened the creation of a Serb-dominated Yugoslavia, Milošević's first option. Slovenia, with its opposition and its principled federalist commitment, stood in his way; his goal was to isolate the Slovenian leadership and, if possible, to overthrow it. Kučan thought that Milošević still subscribed to the slogan, "a unified Serbia and a unified Yugoslavia". It had not been Serbia's aspiration from the beginning to push Slovenia out of Yugoslavia, Kučan thought.[61]

Kučan's thesis is supported by the fact that during the deliberations in the Slovenian parliament there were reactions in parts of the Serbian zone which seemed to lose all hold on rationality. In Titograd local party chief Bulatović demanded, at a "spontaneous" anti-Slovenian meeting, that the army be sent against Slovenia, even though economically bankrupt Montenegro was one of the chief beneficiaries of subsidies paid by Slovenia. "One should not take it amiss when we demand weapons," Bulatović shouted. "We have these weapons. They are in the hands of the Yugoslav People's army, for we are all its soldiers".[62] I remember the impression which the television transmission from Titograd made in the corridors of the Slovenian parliament, reinforcing the conviction that with the adoption of its constitutional amendments, Slovenia had finally found the means to combat such "impudence". Bulatović had gone too far; the army leadership let it be known that it did not want to let anyone lead it by the hand.[63]

The Slovenes, as a "successor nation" of the Central European Danubian monarchy, seemed to have great faith in the efficacy of legal norms even in Yugoslavia. Kučan says now that one always took care, even on later occasions, to ground one's own policy on existing law.[64] This approach was not entirely unrealistic for even in the case of Kadijević, who polemicized endlessly against the constitution of 1974, one finds the comment that in spite of everything the army wanted to hold onto this constitution, as this was preferable to "complete anarchy".[65]

Similar reflections may have induced Milošević to cancel a projected meeting in Belgrade set for the evening of 27 September, which would have been analogous to that in Titograd. It might have led to attacks on Slovenes or on Slovenian property and that might have provided the Slovenes with a pretext to challenge Belgrade's status as the capital of Yugoslavia. In August 1989 Serbian police beat up Slovenia's representative in the federal party presidium, Boris Mužević, after the latter committed a traffic violation. Contradicting the LCY Presidium, the Serbian Ministry of the Interior announced that nothing had happened, while the Belgrade city committee spoke of "brutal lies".[66]

The mood in the Slovenian parliament was calm but high-spirited as Miran Potrč announced the adoption of the constitutional amendments at 9.30 p.m. on 27 September 1989. In an introductory speech earlier, he had stated that the Slovenian parliament was the only organ authorized to decide about the republic's constitution, in the name of the Slovenian people. Any decision taken outside Slovenia would be neither legal nor possible. The Slovenian representative in the Yugoslav state presidency, Drnovšek, had hurried back from New York and found himself an honored guest in the assembly. A children's choir sang the new Slovenian national anthem, the patriotic drinking song, *Zdravljica*, with verses written by the nineteenth-century national poet, Franc Prešeren. As the Slovenian politicians left the parliament building, they were applauded.[67]

The adoption of the Slovenian constitutional amendments did not mean Slovenia's departure from Yugoslavia. But it signified an offer, if not in fact already the realization, of a model of "asymmetric federation"; in Slovenia, the law of the republic now took precedence over federal law. With its behavior in Kosovo and with the Serbian constitutional reform, Serbia had long been behaving in an "asymmetric" way. The Slovenian constitutional amendments were a prelude to democracy. Toward the end of the year, the law concerning political associations, i.e., parties, was passed, together with an election law. There were admonitions to the new Prime Minister, Marković, that he finally say openly who was blocking his policies.[68]

In mid-November 1989, the Slovenes learned that the famous Committee for Meetings set up by Kosovar Serbs had decided to hold a big meeting in Ljubljana, in order to "explain" Serbian views to the Slovenes and to tell them that the policy of their leadership was "false". The Serbs thereby revealed their intention of denouncing the new party program which the League of Communists of Slovenia had just issued, in anticipation of its congress in December.

This program was truly extraordinary in a communist context. It not only approved political pluralism in the sense of a multiparty system but also concretely demanded its immediate introduction, including free elections. To the question whether he had considered that the communists might lose these elections, Kučan said at the time that at least since their last congress the Slovenian communists had ceased to view themselves as a special force. Maybe there were older people who would find it difficult to part with a communist party of the traditional type, but the party was finally there for all its members.[69] For the new coat-of-arms the communists of Slovenia had adopted a blue field with three yellow stars; this was supposed to express both the party's and Slovenia's feeling of belonging to Europe.

The army leadership reacted to the new developments by becoming even more convinced that the army was the only clasp holding Yugoslavia together. On 18 October, Kadijević told a group of party *aktiv* of the army that the Yugoslav People's army respected only the constitution of Yugoslavia.[70] That was a questionable contention for, as was immediately emphasized from the Slovenian side, the constitutions of the republics also belonged to the constitutional order of Yugoslavia, which the army was obliged to protect; the generals were not entitled to pick which constitutions they liked and which they did not.[71] The officers' understanding of their mission could result in a *putsch* or something similar, as Kučan realized; Kučan replied that the Slovenes, for their part, had the right to express their opinion about the army, insofar as it was also *their* army.[72]

As for the meeting in Ljubljana, people disagree even today as to what Milošević actually intended with it. A popular conjecture in Slovenia held that the would-be demonstrators wanted to provoke unrest in Ljubljana, in order to create a pretext for proclaiming a state of emergency for Slovenia. The conviction with which the state presidency of Yugoslavia supported the meeting project was suspect. In its 21/22 November session, the majority of the state presidency had declared that the bad situation in the country demanded "direct consultations in a democratic spirit" between "interested Yugoslav citizens" and the organs of Slovenia.[73] After 1 December the state presidency became angry that the Slovenian authorities had not followed its advice.[74]

That the abandonment of the traditional communist emblems by the communists of Slovenia contributed to the resolve to hold a rally in Ljubljana is hardly likely. There were, of course, statements made in Serbia to the effect that one day "the red star will once more shine over Slovenia", together with similar statements, but this consideration could scarcely have preoccupied Milošević. He had just won the parliamentary elections in Serbia by a wide margin; these elections had been conducted in the "old style", and Milošević could expect to be elected President of Serbia by the new parliament on 5 December 1989. On this day he spoke in Belgrade of the decline in living standards, which was paving the way for "war in Yugoslavia". Serbia demanded that this "war" be terminated.[75] That seemed to suggest that Milošević wanted to hold the Slovenian leadership responsible for his own difficulties.

At any rate, the Slovenian authorities banned the demonstration on 1 December and committed a large contingent of police and police reserves to guard the borders of Slovenia, as well as Ljubljana. Some smaller incidents had no results. The Slovenian authorities always took care to make sure, as Kučan points out, of the legal foundation of their ban, since all the higher organs of the federation, which had never opposed any of Milošević's rallies, would now presumably take a position against Slovenia.

On 4 December, the Belgrade daily *Politika* carried a huge headline: "Serbia Breaks Relations with the Slovenian Regime". In an announcement the leadership of the Socialist Alliance of Working People of Serbia called on "all institutions and all enterprises of Serbia" to "break off all connections with Slovenia", since basic human rights and freedoms had allegedly been "suspended" in Slovenia.[76] This summons closed with an interesting clause, which had not appeared publicly in Serbian declarations before: "We recommend that no citizen of Serbia ask Slovenia to stay in Yugoslavia". The proclamation signified an economic boycott of Slovenia by Serbia. From Titograd there came threats: If the leadership of Yugoslavia was not in a position to restore order in Slovenia, then "the people will overthrow it".[77]

The Serbian economic blockade did not trouble Slovenia much. However, it should have upset Prime Minister Marković, who was standing up so much for the "unity of the Yugoslav market". Yet Marković said almost nothing about the boycott – a fact which provoked many people in Ljubljana to ask just what a common Yugoslav state was supposed to be. The question was put to the silent army leadership whether an economic boycott of one Yugoslav republic by another was not more dangerous for the stability of Yugoslavia than a few articles in the youth magazine, *Mladina*. As if nothing had happened, Marković, who had presented his economic program to parliament on 18 December 1989, proposed some constitutional changes a few days later, in order to better realize the "unity of the Yugoslav market".[78] A few days later, on 16 January 1990, the constitutional commission of the Yugoslav *Skupština* stipulated that prevailing conditions were not conducive to changes of the Yugoslav constitution.[79]

The proclamation of the boycott reflected the fact that Milošević had realized, after his plan to stage a rally in Ljubljana had miscarried, that he was not going to be able to bring Slovenia into line; his reaction was now openly to do his utmost to push Slovenia out of Yugoslavia. At least that was the impression in Ljubljana at the time. The Slovenian reaction, on the part of both leadership and opposition, was henceforth to consolidate Slovenian independence in earnest and to strive to reduce the maneuvering room for anti-Slovene forces within Yugoslavia. The Fourteenth Congress of the LCY, to be held in January 1990, would soon provide an opportunity to advance these goals. The Slovenes also found a reply to the Serbian economic boycott: on 26 February 1990, Slovenia discontinued remissions to the federal fund for the underdeveloped regions, as Serbia and its regions benefitted from that fund.[80]

Overdue political change in Croatia

On 11 May 1989, quite unexpectedly, the outgoing Croatian representative in the Yugoslav state presidency, Josip Vrhovec, took the microphone at the beginning of the evening news on Croatian television. He was somewhat perplexed to have to report grave events in Kosovo which had only just been made known to him as a member of the highest state organ of Yugoslavia. Some 245 Albanians, mostly intellectuals, had been placed in protective confinement in connection with developments in Kosovo concerning change in the Serbian constitution. Among them were 215 signatories of a petition in support of the Yugoslav constitution of 1974. Many of these people had been physically abused; most of them were taken to prisons outside Kosovo and were held incommunicado.

I was spending that day in Zagreb and remember very well the deflating impression which that announcement made. Vrhovec by no means qualified as a liberal politician; he had stepped into political life after the political debacle of the "Croatian Spring" at the end of 1971 and had long been one of the principal agents of the so-called "anti-Croatian policy in Croatia". But now, thanks to Milošević, things had changed. Some days before a Croatian musical group had won the Eurovision song contest, and the Zagreb daily *Vjesnik* had cited this as proof that even Yugoslavia was finally drawing closer to Europe. What Vrhovec had to report seemed to be a reversion to the darkest days of the Ottoman yoke.[81] Immediately people raised the question openly as to why Croatia, like Slovenia, had to put up with such things. At the same time, one was conscious that in Yugoslavia there was now a quarantined "Serbian zone" to which even the Croatian member of the highest state leadership had no political access.

Ever since the events in Montenegro of January 1989, the Croatian chair of the LCY leadership, Šuvar, was subjected to increasing Serbian attacks, which in time would have undermined his ability to function in office, if the Croatian parliament had not elected him in May 1989 as the new Croatian representative in the Yugoslav state presidency. The attacks on Šuvar had induced all the Croatian functionaries to rally behind him, even if they were not always in agreement with him.

With the exception of the weekly magazine *Danas*, it was still difficult in Croatia to find public evidence of a change in the game. However, the events in Kosovo at the end of February 1989 shocked Croats as well as Slovenes.

The danger that Milošević might obtain control of a majority of votes in the Yugoslav state and party leadership was perceived also in Zagreb. The Croatian leadership felt cheated, since it had tried to support the Republic of Serbia in the dispute concerning the Serbian constitution, but it could not accept repression on this scale or the open violation of the constitution of 1974. The agents of the hitherto "silent Croatia" policy, with the colorless Serb, Stanko Stojčević, at the head of the party were exposed. The era of "silent Croatia" was over, the weekly *Danas* wrote in April 1989.[82]

Šuvar had represented not the "silent Croatia" but something else – the so-called "Yugoslav synthesis". This "synthesis" had been reduced to practically just Šuvar himself. Nonetheless, it should be conceded that this complex functionary had acted, in all his dogmatism, from Yugoslav positions, and that his weak response to Milošević, even to the point of selling out the Yugoslav constitution, was motivated by the aspiration to thereby perhaps save Yugoslavia. Authoritative people in *Danas* remained loyal to Yugoslav positions too, but on a liberal and federalist basis. "Yugoslavia is not just Serbia – Yugoslavia is all of us," wrote Jelena Lovrić in the magazine, after the events of late February 1989.[83]

With Šuvar's transfer to the state presidency, efforts to save Yugoslavia under the banner of old-style party socialism came to an end. Šuvar was now a kind of "Croatian Ban" (ruler), who had belatedly converted to a notion of a "Croatian synthesis", according to *Danas*.[84] That may have been a play on words, but the fact was that, from this moment, Šuvar was tasked to protect *Croatian* interests. Croatian policy as a whole remained, to be sure, locked on a pro-Yugoslav course. That was logical; for all that, the republic had, in Marković, furnished the Prime Minister, whose goal was to promote reform in the common state.

But it seemed necessary also on other grounds to defend the interests of Croatia from Yugoslav positions. Croatia was disunified not only as a republic, but also in its communist party. Alongside the liberal elements, Croats and Serbs, there were nationalist elements on both sides; there were convinced Yugoslavists and unvarnished dogmatics, again among Croats as well as among Serbs. Šuvar had scarcely come over to the state presidency when Serbian commentaries interpreted his opposition to Milošević by characterizing him as a "Serb-hater".[85] The first incidents followed thereupon, in Knin on the occasion of the 600th anniversary of the Battle of Kosovo at the end of June 1989. These incidents were primarily the work of Serbian provocateurs from Vojvodina, who had come to Croatia in order to instill in local Serbs a greater "battle fever".[86] Shortly afterwards, the Belgrade magazine *NIN* published a lengthy discussion of the situation of the Serbs in Croatia. From today's perspective, one must say that this was already the foundation stone on which the construction of a "Greater Serbia" would later be assayed.[87]

These events happened, as must be stated explicitly, long before the first stirrings of a Croatian will to independence, when the communist regime was still firm in the saddle in Zagreb, and they were, to a large extent, instigated by Belgrade. At that time, the Serbs in Croatia still enjoyed their privileges in the party and police unchallenged. No one could accuse the Zagreb leadership at that time of "*Ustaše* tendencies"; the highest party chief Stojčević himself was a Serb. But the "Yugoslav synthesis" being promulgated by Zagreb obviously bothered Milošević because it did not aim at a Yugoslavia hegemonized by Serbia, but at one based on the principle of national equality. Milošević had been able to profit from Šuvar's politics and ambition; now in summer and autumn 1989, he no longer needed him. The Serbian "march" of which Milošević and his young adherents constantly spoke and which was supposedly "unstoppable" now set its sights on Knin and Banja Luka.

In Croatia in those weeks and months in autumn 1989 the old historical dilemmas, which had affected the relationship of Croats with the idea and praxis of the Yugoslav state since long ago, emerged again. One could even say that the Croats had invented the idea and concept of "Yugoslavism". The Croatian Bishop Josip Juraj Strossmayer (1815–1905), called to serve as Bishop of Djakovo in Slavonia in 1850 during the reign of Ban Jelačić, noted that, in his diocese, to which at the time almost all of today's Serbia belonged, Serbs and Croats lived together geographically intermingled. His conclusion was that under such conditions it made no sense and would even be dangerous if these two peoples of the same language, divided only by inherited religion, gave themselves over to national exclusivism. The national renewal movement of Serbs and Croats, so held Strossmayer, should therefore develop under a common "Yugoslav" name and, as much as possible in a "European" framework.[88] Strossmayer, a liberal and generous spirit, had great respect for the Orthodox Church. This he showed symbolically in the layout of the new cathedral he built in Djakovo, which united Western and Eastern architectural elements and which was dedicated to Saints Cyril and Methodius.[89] Strossmayer's "Yugoslavism" was, thus, completely different from Catholic proselytism. Ideally he could link up with the previously active Illyrist movement, which, in the years before 1848, had aspired to a kind of national unification of all south Slav peoples.

Communist historians tried to discredit Strossmayer's Yugoslavism as "Austro-Slavism".[90] It was so inasmuch as Strossmayer hoped that through the transformation of the Danube Monarchy into a union of equal peoples, it might have been possible to solve the "Oriental question" within a Western framework, rather than within an absolutist framework sponsored by Russia. Strossmayer said this more or less in a speech to the Croatian *Sabor* in 1861.[91] His train of thought was not unlike that which Czech historian František Palacký had followed in his answer to the Frankfurt Paulskirche in 1848.

In regard to today's occurrences one does not hesitate to concede that Strossmayer's fears as regards the coexistence of Serbs and Croats were well placed. But his idea of a Yugoslav nation was too intellectual and too ethereal for even the intellectuals of the following generation, let alone the broad strata of the population. Moreover, the dualist reorganization of the monarchy in 1867, which brought Croatia and Slavonia once more under Hungarian rule, but Dalmatia under Austrian rule, destroyed any political basis for a Yugoslav solution under the auspices of the House of Habsburg.

The nationalist Croatian reaction made its debut at the *Sabor* in 1861 in the person of deputy Dr Ante Starčević (1823–96). He had originally been an Illyrist, but his disappointment over developments after 1848 induced him to answer the question, "Vienna or Budapest?" with a decisive, "neither, nor".[92] He held to this exclusivist Croatian orientation with the uncompromising rigidity of his character. In opposition to Strossmayer's *Narodna Stranka* (People's Party), the governmental party, he founded his *Stranka Prava* (Party of Right). He never succeeded in garnering more than a quarter of the votes in the *Sabor*, though, in view of the prevailing system of suffrage, this cannot be taken as an adequate measure of his popularity.

Starčević's program was not politically realistic but rather, one may say, principled. His point of departure was Croatian state right. The Kingdom of Croatia was, he said, an independent state; it had, at the time of unification in 1102, elected the Hungarian king as King of Croatia of its own free will. This link had ended in 1848, when the right to independence was restored to Croatia.[93] However, Starčević did not rest with this. In the modern interpretation, he held, Croatian state right must extend to all areas where Croats in the sense of a "modern" Croatian nation were to be found. He conceptualized this nation in grandiose terms. The whole Balkans "between the sea and the Danube, between Carinthia and Bojana"[94] was either historically Croatian or inhabited by Croatian or Croatized inhabitants; a Croatian state had to be reconstituted. To Vuk Karadžić's solution, "Srbi svi i svuda" (Serbs, all and everywhere), Starčević replied in an even more exaggerated way with a "Hrvati svi i svuda" (Croats, all and everywhere); he wanted to make all the Serbs, Muslims, Slovenes, and even Albanians that he could find into Croats. In Starčević's favor it must be said that he later saw what was unrealistic in his program and made his political peace with Strossmayer. His ideas had a damaging effect, however, in that they brought Croats to a course of confrontation with their neighbors and gave more extreme persons than Starčević ideological weapons for a pernicious policy.

The first of these extremists was Dr Josua Frank, Starčević's political successor after 1895 who, in his Pure Party of Right, made anti-Serbian actions an everyday occurrence in Croatia. Frank had originally been a merchant in Osijek, paradoxically of German-Jewish stock, who entered politics out of sheer opportunism and found his platform in extreme Croatian nationalism.[95] Through his anti-Serbian orientation Frank gravitated automatically toward cooperation with the so-called "Greater

Austrian" circles in Vienna, such as that of Conrad von Hötzendorf, the Chief of the General Staff, or the *Reichspost*; Starčević would have avoided such an orientation.

It was the Hungarians and their governor in Croatia, Dragutin Count Khuen-Hedervary, who profited from Frank's policy and the resulting worsening of relations between Serbs and Croats. This Hungarian governor in Zagreb, who ruled from 1883 to 1903, was the instrument of the nationalist Hungarian regime then in office in Budapest; the Hungarian policy of the day aspired in a completely unrealistic way to a kind of "Magyarization" of Croats, at least to the extent of establishing Hungarian as the prevailing official language and as the language on the railways. Khuen-Hedervary courted the Serbs as allies for this policy and encountered no difficulties in this regard. The Serbs of the Krajina were dissatisfied with the lifting of their special status in the old military frontier; they did not want to be inducted into the "normal" Croatian state. Under Khuen-Hedervary, the Serbs won a position in Croatia similar to what they would later enjoy under the communists.

An overview of Croatian national ideological and political currents in the nineteenth century would be incomplete without reference to the situation in Bosnia-Herzegovina. It was there that politicized Catholicism entered the ideological arena of Croatian exclusivism. Starčević had been strongly laicized, while Frank represented the normal secular orientation of a bourgeois movement in the progressive nineteenth century. With the occupation of Bosnia-Herzegovina in 1878, religious lines of division came to play a transcendent role. In Turkish times, there had not been a Catholic hierarchy in Bosnia-Herzegovina; the Franciscans had enjoyed the exclusive right of pastoral care for Catholics living in the region. In the purely Croatian western Herzegovina, the Croats, together with the Franciscans there, were militant, much as they are today; in Bosnia, they were open to coexistence with the other nationalities.

All in all, interethnic relations in the Croatian area at the turn of the century were in hopeless disarray. Something new had to be ventured, especially with regard to interethnic relations; at the time, both Croats and Serbs had to recognize that all endeavors to find support in one or another direction within the Austro-Hungarian Monarchy had failed, while both Vienna and Budapest played on the nationalist differences between them. Efforts to make a new beginning came from two entirely different camps. In Croatia, the brothers Antun and Stjepan Radić established the Croatian Peasant Party in 1905; this party would later become the dominant political force in Croatia in the interwar period. The point of departure was the notion that a country in which peasants made up 80 per cent of the population could not find its national form without the emancipation of the peasantry. The party opposed both the Yugoslavist coalition and the Frankists. It did not display any anti-clerical tendencies, but it was immediately attacked by the clergy – a "typical reaction of the educated class", as its later leader Vladko Maček writes.[96] Archbishop Dr Ante Bauer banned polemics of this nature in 1911, but the Peasant Party remained secular.

Just as important was the impulse, which came out of Dalmatia, for a renewed national rapprochement between Croats and Serbs. There, under Austrian rule, conditions were different. If there was a national opponent it was the Italian element, who represented a common foe for both Croats and Serbs. At the same time, it was important to defend the interests of the region *vis-à-vis* Vienna. On this point as well Serbs and Croats stood on the same side. All that was necessary now was politicians who could turn these general notions into concrete policy. The most important of these was Frano Supilo (1870–1917), born in Cavtat, in the region of the earlier Republic of Dubrovnik, who edited the newspaper *Novi list* in Rijeka at the turn of the century and who was later a leading member of the Yugoslav Committee in London.

The Serbs and Croats of Dalmatia initiated cooperation in 1902. In the following year, the possibility opened up for them to extend their cooperative framework into Croatia proper. Khuen-Hedervary had given instructions to his official "Croatian" delegation in connection with the negotiations for a new Hungarian-Croatian financial agreement, which amounted to a Croatian renunciation. This affected Croats and Serbs equally and the possibility of letting differences between them play out was lost. Khuen-Hedervary was recalled. But the "damage" had already been done; the "new course" had been carried through, and flowed soon into political Yugoslavism. This happened already with attention being paid to Belgrade, where in 1903 the pro-Austrian line had come to an end with the murder of the last Obrenović and the accession to power of the national-Serb orientation.[97]

The official "establishment", so to speak, of the Croat-Serb coalition was the so-called "Rijeka resolution" of 1905. The content was comparatively trivial: it dealt with a declaration of solidarity *vis-à-vis* the new Hungarian Independence Party under Ferenc Kossuth (Lajos Kossuth's nephew), in the hope that Croatia could profit from its struggle for a revision of the 1867 *Ausgleich*. These hopes were neither realistic nor in correspondence with the true goals of the Serbian and Croatian parties. In Vienna, at any rate, the general view was that the political goals of the Croat-Serb coalition led away from the monarchy. The most important exponents of the coalition and its policy were, aside from Supilo, the mayor of Dubrovnik Pero Cingrija, the later Foreign Minister of the first Yugoslavia, Ante Trumbić from Split, and the leader of the Serbian unitarist-oriented "Independents", Svetozar Pribičević.

The monarchy countered the Yugoslav orientation in Croatia with two high treason trials – the first in Zagreb involving 55 Serbs, and then the so-called "Friedjung trial" of 1909, in which, as was said in jest in Vienna at the time, the actual truth was to be substantiated with falsified documents. The trials dashed the last hopes for "trialism". The idea of a unification of all South Slavs under the aegis of Serbia encountered scarcely any opposition thereafter. With the outbreak of war in 1914, Supilo, Trumbić, the sculptor Ivan Meštrović, and other leaders of the coalition left the country and established the "Yugoslav Committee" in London, while the remaining coalition politicians in Zagreb engaged in a semi-opportunistic, semi-representative "government spectacle", until they joined the Slovenes in founding the "Yugoslav Club" of 1917 in Vienna.

One can always ask, as already in the case of the Slovenes, why those South Slavs of the monarchy who were Catholics and who felt that they belonged to Central Europe should suddenly develop the will to unite with Serbs to the east in a state outside the monarchy. In the case of the Croats, the reasons were clear: The *Ausgleich* of 1867 had assigned Croatia to the jurisdiction of Hungary, whose politics became ever more nationalistic as the end of the century approached. Even the limited autonomy which Croatia enjoyed was respected less and less by the centralistic government in Budapest. So the Yugoslav orientation prevailed politically in Croatia, even before the so-called London Agreement of 1915, which promised Istria, Friulia, and Dalmatia to Italy as a reward for its entry into the war.

Concerning the form which the Yugoslav framework would take, there were soon profound differences of opinion within both the Yugoslav Committee in London and the Serbian regime under Nikola Pašić. The majority of the Committee, including above all Trumbić and Pribičević, subscribed to a unitarist concept of a "unified, tri-named people", while Pašić and his Serbs, as already noted, wanted to preserve the identity of Serbia and thought in terms of extending it to the "new provinces". Between these two sides Supilo defended a concept of a federal state which would reconcile the claims on behalf of Croatian state right with the Serbian desire for a protection of its identity. Supilo eventually resigned from the Yugoslav Committee in frustration over the Committee's rejection of his ideas but continued to be a negotiation partner for Pašić. In a memorandum to the British Foreign Secretary, Edward Grey,[98] Supilo contested the thesis that the new state could be diplomatically represented exclusively by the Kingdom of Serbia; there were, on the contrary – Supilo argued – two equal state factors: the Kingdom of Serbia and the historical tri-named Kingdom of Croatia-Slavonia-Dalmatia. In July 1917 he presented to Pašić in Korfu a concrete proposal which foresaw that the most important concerns of state, such as foreign policy, defense, and finance, would be centrally run, while everything else would be allocated to the autonomous constituent units of state. Corresponding to the developments which had taken place in the meantime, not least in Slovenia, this concept was no longer merely dualistic, but authentically federalistic.[99]

Maybe it was a tragedy that Supilo died in London in September 1917, so that the idea of a federative or at least mixed system was left without a strong advocate. There are signs that Pašić was by no means hostile to Supilo's ideas; Pašić's concern was, in the first place, to protect the identity and sovereignty of Serbia, not to subjugate Croatia and Slovenia. To be sure, Pašić had to hold his own against narrow-minded Serbian elements in his own neighborhood. But the fact is that at the time of actual unification, in late autumn 1918, the Serbian side encountered only the Yugoslav unitarism represented by Trumbić and other Committee politicians, which the Serbs tried to imbue with Serbian hegemonic strivings. Then there were the Slovenes, who did not yet feel comfortable in the new world they had entered. The as yet small Croatian Peasant Party remained politically isolated in its advocacy of Croatian state right.

Those events which took place after the establishment of the state, which were so disappointing for the Croats, resulted in the permanent oscillation of Croatia between a Yugoslav orientation and a position of Croatian exclusivism. The Croatian Peasant Party under the brothers Radić rejected the new state. The Croats' Serbian partners now sat in Belgrade, and relations with the Serbs in Croatia evolved on a secondary level. For the greater part, the Serbs of Croatia were united in Pribičević's unitarist party and resisted, with all available means, every Croatian exertion in the direction of autonomy. When in 1925 Pašić concluded his agreement with Stjepan Radić and accepted some ministers of the Croatian Peasant Party into his cabinet, he excluded Pribičević's party from the government.[100] On the other hand, the Serbs of Croatia made themselves available, all too easily, to be misused as accomplices of the central government in the repression of Croatian aspirations, whenever extreme centralism prevailed in Belgrade.

What was life like for the Croats of Yugoslavia in the interwar era? Certainly the Croats were subjected to a stronger impact from the Belgrade central government than were the Slovenes. But in actuality, Croatia had experienced Hungarian, not Austrian, government before the First World War; so the change was not all that drastic. Croats felt culturally superior to the Serbs and resented the latters' political dominance in the new state. At that time, there was no trace within the Catholic Church of a mystical feeling of a special role of Croatiandom as an *"antimurale christianitatis"* directed against Orthodox, so-called "Byzantine", Serbs. These tendencies came later.

To be sure, the agreement between Pašić and Radić did not long survive the death of Prime Minister Pašić (in 1926), but the Croatian Peasant Party had found a path to realistic cooperation in the new state. Then came an event on 20 June 1928 which once more changed the mood of the country – the assassination in the Yugoslav *Skupština*. A Montenegrin deputy (Puniša Račić) shot to death two Croatian deputies in the hall of the Assembly, one of them Stjepan Radić's nephew; in addition, Radić himself was so severely wounded that he died a few months later. Against the advice of Vladko Maček, Stjepan Radić's successor as head of the Peasant Party, that when one had buttoned up one's waistcoat in the wrong way one had to unbutton it and button it up from scratch,[101] King Alexander rejected the proposed federalization of the country and introduced a nominally "Yugoslav", in actuality Serbian, dictatorship on 6 January 1929. Croatian and Slovenian politicians were interned, and in Croatia there were instances of police infringements of human rights amounting to national repression.

The double blow against Croatdom was more than the Yugoslav state concept could bear. One must understand how the situation was understood in Croatia at the time. The Yugoslav state initially had signified emancipation from Hungarian repression. But now Croats were faced with a repression harsher than anything they had known in Hungarian times, and this as a consequence of an act of terror by a Serb. The entire thing seemed utterly contrary to logic, as it certainly was. One did not have to wait long for consequences. After the assassination in the *Skupština*, deputy Dr Ante Pavelić, representative of the nationalistic "Croatian bloc", traveled that same evening, or so it is reported, to Sofia, in order to discuss terrorist actions with the Macedonian IMRO. On 4 September 1928 Pavelić raised the demand, for the first time, for an independent Croatian state. On 7 January 1929, one day after the proclamation of the royal dictatorship, he established the *Ustaše* (Insurrectionary) movement and went abroad. He was sentenced to death in absentia.[102] On 9 October 1934, King Aleksandar fell victim to an assassination, which had the earmarks of a collaboration between the *Ustaše* and the Macedonian IMRO.

In *Ustaše* ideology, one finds that mystical linkage of nation and religion which one otherwise finds only in extreme nationalist movements in Orthodox countries. In those countries this ideological mix is the result of the close association of state and autocephalous Church, as of national renewal movements and Churches. Now, after the events of 1928 and 1929, such ideas obtained a certain weight in parts of Croatia. Many of the first *Ustaše* came from Herzegovina or from the Dalmatian Zagorje, where these ideas were, so to speak, endemic. Students from these parts brought these ideas into the Zagreb student community. The *Ustaše* wanted a "Greater Croatia" which would reach as far as the Drina and even to the gates of Belgrade. In their blind fanaticism, they claimed that the Muslims living in Bosnia were actually Croats and that the Serbs living in Croatia were generally "Slavicized Vlachs", an "impure" race.

To be sure, one cannot find confirmation in any source of a remark attributed to novelist-turned-*Ustaše* minister Mile Budak, who would later serve as Croatia's ambassador in Berlin, that one third of Croatia's Serbs should be killed, one third expelled, and the remaining third rebaptized as Catholics, thus as "Croats". But there is no doubt but that the *Ustaše* thought along such lines and wanted to behave accordingly. There are enough other declarations by prominent *Ustaše* to prove that; besides, their deeds reflected their intentions all too clearly.[103]

A Catholic Croatian publicist of some rank told me at one time that the Croats were, in the final analysis, not a Central European nation at all, but, so to speak, an Orthodox nation in Catholic garb. The actual dividing line in Yugoslavia lay on the Sutla between Slovenia and the rest of Yugoslavia.[104] That may be true of that portion of the Croatian spectrum which considers itself obligated to uphold the religiously oriented "anti-Byzantine" national mythos, but is scarcely true of the Zagreb citizenry or the Zagorje, let alone of Dalmatia and Istria. There, in the Mediterranean parts of Croatia, Yugoslav tradition was noticeable even during the war years, alongside elements of traditional rationality. At this point, it would be useful, if space permitted, to provide a detailed assessment of the old Republic of Dubrovnik and its *raison d'être*. Even then, when the old cosmopolitan tradition was waning in most of Dalmatia's coastal cities, as a result of immigration from the interior of the country, myths of all kinds did not find much acceptance there. The *Ustaše* found little support in Dalmatia and by no means only because Pavelić had agreed to turn over a large portion of Dalmatia to fascist Italy as the price of power.

In today's independent Croatia of Franjo Tudjman, the historical myths do not enter the picture as forcefully as they did in *Ustaše* times, but they are, nonetheless, more strongly expressed than in any of the Croatian political movements prior to the Second World War. They resulted, *inter alia*, in some damage to relations with Istria and Dalmatia. The often penetratingly expressed ideas of Tudjman and his adherents concerning the special role of Croatia and of its "western" Christianity in history may be traced, on the one hand, back to Tudjman's personality and, on the other hand, to the special circumstances in which Croatian independence had to develop. The communist regime in Yugoslavia was, as a matter of principle, hostile to Croatian national consciousness, being inspired by a mixture of communist, Yugoslav, and Greater Serbian tendencies. The anti-national policy in Croatia after 1971, already described (p. 17), worked especial mischief. It was the time when the Catholic Church stepped forward as the only refuge for Croatian national feeling. One could reproach the Church, if one wished, that it played on this to build up its strength. The great convocations, which the Church organized in the late 1970s and early 1980s, sometimes conveyed the impression that the direct activity of the hand of God in Croatian history had to be revealed.[105] But one must consider that the posture of political-spiritual combat had been forced on the Church and that it made use of such weapons as it had at hand. I cannot remember any religious manifestations from that time which were directed against another people, for example Serbs. That the Catholic Church of Croatia was by no means the tabernacle of all the wild ideas about the role of Croatia as *"antimurale christianitatis"* was shown in the clarity with which Zagreb Archbishop Kuharić criticized Tudjman's Bosnian policy.

Certainly, the so-called forced conversions were a sad chapter in Croatia's history. Here, especially during the persecutions by the *Ustaše* in

1941–42, many Serbs in the Krajina and other parts of the country, including Bosnia, were forced to convert to Catholicism. On this point, one should say that the marked disunity which characterizes Croatia in geographic, historical, and political terms also made itself evident within the Church. That was Archbishop Stepinac's big problem. A second historical point was the difficulty of demarcating the Church from an ideology which, by contrast with German national-socialism or Italian fascism, inserted religion into the national mythos. The correct interpretation is probably that at the beginning the upper clergy of the Church in Croatia, Stepinac included, were rather taken by the idea of spreading Catholicism eastward.[106] The Vatican had to underline that only voluntary conversions could be accepted.[107] The same sources mention, however, that the *Ustaše* state had treated the question of conversions from the start as an affair of state.[108] When the first persecutions of Serbs became public, the problem took on yet another dimension for the Church. Now conversions often seemed to afford the only possibility of saving the lives of Serbs, as Maček also writes,[109] while, on the other hand – and here, once more, the old differences were observable – especially in Bosnia-Herzegovina, one still found a primitive missionary zeal.

Neither the events in the Second World War nor certain attributes of the Tudjman regime as it was shaped by the war for independence can obscure the fact that, in the final analysis, the Croatian people, in their entire modern political history – in spite of certain lapses – had always found its way back to moderation. In the 1930s, this moderation was represented by Maček's Peasant Party. The *Ustaše* and the other extremists were a small minority. Maček immediately took up offers of compromise which were offered to him first, hesitantly, by Stojadinović, and then openly and concretely by Prince-Regent Paul. Certainly, one must proceed from the fact that after the *Skupština* murder and the proclamation of the royal dictatorship, the majority of Croats saw their future in state independence. Even Maček is not entirely clear as to whether he saw his contacts with Italian emissaries as a tactical means of exerting pressure on Belgrade or as a way of sounding out alternatives to Yugoslavia.[110] The *Sporazum* (Agreement) of 1939 was, in the eyes of most Croats, only a first step; they noted, too, how hesitantly the Serbian side, especially the military, yielded its control to the newly-created semi-autonomous Banovina of Croatia. The *putsch* of 27 March 1941, undertaken by Serbian officers without any consultation with Croats, was, in Croatian eyes, irresponsible in view of the international situation, and indirectly also aimed at the *Sporazum*.

Thus, the *putsch* of 27 March 1941 provoked ill temper among Croats, in spite of Maček's somewhat controversial participation in the new government of General Simović. When, on 10 April 1941, immediately after the entry of German troops, the nationalist-oriented Slavko Kvaternik called for an independent Croatian state, without saying anything as to its political coloration, he had the sympathy of most Croats. The Germans tried at least once to persuade Maček to take over the leadership of this state, as Maček writes in his memoirs.[111] The Peasant Party leader declined because he did not want to serve as head-of-state under the auspices of an occupation regime. Thus, the scepter was passed to Mussolini's proteges, the *Ustaše*. What, in the eyes of many nationally-oriented Croats, should have been a well-ordered successor to the Danube Monarchy became, instead, a criminal state. One cannot absolve the German Nazis of responsibility, of course, in spite of Italy's role as midwife, since the German emissary in Zagreb, Siegfried Kasche, a Nazi party functionary, was constantly defending this regime and was mostly effective in representing its interest to Hitler.[112] Certainly it is true that German military authorities watched the *Ustaše* persecutions of Serbs without any satisfaction, because they drove the Serbian population first into the ranks of the Chetniks, and then, beginning in mid-1942, into the ranks of the communist Partisans.

The murderous actions of the *Ustaše* against the Serbian population in Lika, in Banija, and in Bosnia began around June 1941, around Glina, where the *Ustaše* Minister of Justice, Marko Puk, had his political base. The *Ustaše* had the crazy idea that they would move their capital to Banja Luka, where the majority of the local population was Serbian; they had in mind to expel the Serbs living there.[113] In the Italian occupation zone where, paradoxically, the *Ustaše* were hindered in their activities, the Serbs established a foothold, especially around Knin, for the most part as Chetniks. With the arrival of Tito's Partisans in autumn 1942, they switched over to the Partisans and, in this way, laid the foundation of their future strong position in the administration and political apparatus of communist-era Croatia.

The *Ustaše*'s murderous actions against the Serbs have been happily cited to the international public up to today in order to win understanding for the secession of the Serbs in Croatia. Without a doubt the earlier events still have their importance. But to derive from that the claim that Tudjman's Croatia had threatened the Serbs in equal measure and had justified the Serbs' actions in 1991 is simply nonsense.

It should not be forgotten either that the Chetniks of Knin, before they became Partisans, had also committed massacres against Croats during 1941/42. Moreover, the Serbs of the Krajina opposed the *Sporazum* and wanted to be left outside the Banovina Hrvatska. The Serbs during the Second World War were as much under the influence of mystic and religio-national movements as the Croats; the Chetniks and the Ljotić movement were both likewise inspired by such mystical ideas. Today very little is said about the annihilation of Muslims by Chetniks in eastern Bosnia or the Sandžak, although they began about the same time as *Ustaše* actions against the Serbs. When I visited Novi Pazar at one time, I was told how this city, the capital of the Sandžak, was saved from a massacre by Chetniks in the winter of 1941/42 only by the arrival of some 2,000 nationalist Albanians from Kosovo.[114]

The Partisans operating in the region of Croatia were by no means merely an affair of the Serbs. Many Croats likewise joined. Djilas describes how, on the occasion of a visit to Partisan main headquarters in Croatia, under the command of Andrija Hebrang, he found the atmosphere "very Croatian".[115] As in Slovenia, the conflicts in Croatia had many of the earmarks of a civil war. At the end of the war, the British turned over many Croatian *Ustaše* and *Domobranci* (members of the regular Croatian army), together with Slovenian *Domobranci*, to the Partisans, who proceeded to slaughter them.[116]

Today's Croatia has a much greater connection with the movement of 1970/71 than with the state of the Second World War, even though the leading personalities of the "Croatian Spring" – Savka Dabčević-Kučar and Miko Tripalo – were denied a political "comeback". One should rather think, in connection with the condemnation of certain features of the Zagreb government today, that in Croatia's difficult fight for independence, patriotism frequently had to substitute for adequate weaponry. Still, some of Tudjman's utterances, both before and after his accession to power would have been better left unspoken. Even Karadžić, the Serbian leader in Bosnia, himself conceded in early 1991 that Tudjman's Croatia was not the *Ustaše*.[117] The number of national symbols which a nation has at its disposal is limited. The *Ustaše* had adopted a lot of the old Croatian tradition or folklore; it would have been unusual if these symbols had not been endorsed also by today's Croatian state. Even in Germany, today's national anthem and the name of the currency were used by the Nazis, but no one has ever suggested that this signified that the Federal Republic was associating itself with Nazi tradition. Even Tudjman's book about genocide in history,[118] which has often been viewed as somewhat dubious, aspires to no more than highlighting the evil of genocide in general and freeing Croats from the polemical reproach which has been pressed by the Serbian side that Croats are, by nature, inclined to genocide. The most important original leaders of the Croatian Democratic Community (HDZ), the current ruling party of Tudjman, including Tudjman himself, as well as the earlier prime ministers Josip Manolić and Stipe Mesić and the former Interior Minister Josip Boljkovac, came from the "Partisan wing" of the party.

In May 1989, I had a conversation in Zagreb with CC Secretary Dragutin Dimitrović, a realistically-oriented member of the Croatian party leadership of that time.[119] From his answers, it was clear that separatism was the furthest thing from his mind; he kept returning to the theme of how Croatia could make a contribution to the stabilization of Yugoslavia, above all by putting its economic strength in the scale. In the effort to avoid provoking conflicts, the Croatian leaders had perhaps kept silent about certain things for too long. Croatia wanted to be part of Europe and that would involve democracy. Here Croatia found itself admittedly lagging behind. Everything was happening too quickly for the Croatian leadership. Dimitrović emphasized the need for caution: "In Serbian Belgrade certain people are waiting for us to put our Croatian heads on the chopping block, so that they can whack them off". On one point, Dimitrović was unambiguous: Milošević would not be allowed to gain control of the majority of the vote in either the state presidency or in the party presidium. A hegemonized Yugoslavia would be unacceptable for Croatia, and without Croatia there could be no Yugoslavia.

Dimitrović's answers reflected an awareness that Croatia stood at the gateway between a Yugoslav and an independent orientation. The maneuvering room had become quite narrow within only a short time. A stronger defense of the interests of the republic and democratization would provoke an intensification of Serbian attacks and that, in turn, would automatically strengthen the Croatian wish for independence.

Two noncommunist organizations presented themselves for registration at that time: the "Democratic League" of former General Franjo Tudjman and the "League of the Yugoslav Democratic Initiative" under Professors Branko Horvat and Predrag Matvejević. The authorities could not put them off. But there was not yet any legal basis for registering political associations except under the auspices of the Socialist Alliance. The Social-Liberal Alliance initiated by Slavko Goldštajn had established itself within the framework of the Socialist Alliance. It must have hurt Croatian pride to have to acknowledge the Slovenes as tutors for democratization, but many eyes in Zagreb were fixed on Ljubljana.

The change began, much as in Macedonia, with Milošević's speech on the 600th anniversary of the Battle on the Field of the Blackbirds on 28 June 1389, in which the Serbian leader spoke of "struggles" which might also be "armed". Shortly thereafter came Kadijević's speech; Kadijević spoke out against all efforts toward democratization. In response to a reference to developments across Eastern Europe and China, Kadijević said that Yugoslavia had never adopted "foreign models".[120]

Since there was nothing constructive in sight and the party was difficult to manage already because of its composition (30 per cent Serbs), the leadership in Zagreb continued to promote some sort of "Yugoslav synthesis". This signified above all support for the policies of Prime Minister Marković. Internally, Croatian authorities could decide neither for a clear democratization nor for a return to the old course. There remained only the option of a more or less sloppy "*laissez-faire*".

In the noteworthy session of the Central Committee of the LCY orchestrated by the army on the night of 26/27 September 1989 – to deal with the constitutional reforms in Slovenia – all the CC members from Croatia voted against resolutions which would have condemned those reforms. This determination was not least the work of Račan who, in contrast to Šuvar, represented the liberal, federalist orientation in the party. The reactions among the Croatian public were even clearer: It was impermissible, so wrote *Danas*,[121] that the army, which had not reacted in the least to Milošević's speech at Kosovo polje, now tried to interfere with force in the affairs of other republics.

The transfiguration of politics in Croatia came rather suddenly with the Eleventh Congress of the League of Communists of Croatia on 12 and 13 December 1989, convened among a series of republic party congresses in preparation for the Fourteenth Congress of the LCY set for January 1990. It was at this congress that Račan was elected chair of the Croatian party, taking the place of Stojčević, who was stepping down; at the same time, the party assumed the supplementary name, "Party (*Stranka*) of Democratic Changes".

For Račan, the success of his candidacy came as a surprise.[122] It worked in his favor not only that the vote was taken on the basis of a secret ballot but also that it followed a vote taken among all ordinary members. Račan had calculated that the candidate of the "center", Ivo Družić, would be elected and this result would have been assured, had the delegates to the congress not been bound to respect the preliminary vote of the membership. One had to keep the heterogeneous character of the Croatian party always before one's eyes. Račan's friend in the party, Zdravko Tomac, told me that the departing entourage around Stojčević would have liked, ideally, to have installed the retired Admiral Mamula as Croatian party chair.[123]

So internal democratization came to Croatia rather suddenly. The new, de facto existing groups could now be formally constituted as parties and the first free elections were scheduled for 22 April 1990. In contrast to the rather compact reformed-communist party in Slovenia, the unity of the reformed Croatian party under Račan's leadership remained problematic. It must be emphasized that the party functionaries of Serbian nationality did not present any special problem for Račan at this time; as Račan told me in 1994, there were just as many dogmatic politicians among Croatian party members as among Serbian party members.[124]

The first great test for the reformed Croatian communist party was the Fourteenth – and last – LCY Congress in January 1990, from which the Slovenes withdrew. In Račan's view, this congress was being held under inopportune conditions. Although, in the meantime, all of Eastern Europe had been democratized, the majority of the LCY, under the influence of the "Serbian bloc" and the army, had held fast to anti-pluralist and dogmatic views. Račan had declared, 12 hours before the beginning of the congress, that in the event that the Slovenes left, the Croats would do likewise.

Milošević, according to Račan, had clearly miscalculated the situation. The collapse of the congress was a defeat for him and deprived him of the party as a potent political instrument. Milošević had known that the Slovenes would walk out, but he had hoped to be able to continue the congress without them. Milošević had not expected that Račan would be able to keep the Croatian delegates united. After the Slovenes left, Račan took the Croatian delegates into an adjacent room to discuss the situation; the overwhelming majority of the Croatian delegation stood behind Račan. Only three Croatian delegates favored remaining at the congress.

As Račan told me, his surprise "coup" immediately after the departure of the Slovenes played an important role. At the moment when Slovenian party chair Čiril Ribičič announced the Slovenes' decision to withdraw, Račan hurried to the microphone, ahead of Milošević and Milošević's ally, party chairman Pančevski, and proposed that the work of the congress be interrupted. A majority of the delegates voted in favor of this.[125]

Ivica Račan had changed a lot over the years. In 1971, when Tito liquidated the "Croatian Spring", Račan had allied himself with the new power-holders, not, to be sure, as an agent of repression but in the role of ideologist. I remember a rather useless conversation with him shortly after Tito's intervention. But then Račan started to have doubts and he was soon shunted off to serve as director of the party's training school in Kumrovec, where Tito had been born. By the time Račan returned to active politics in the 1980s, he had adopted relatively liberal views, which he defended, within the federal party leadership, against his more dogmatic countryman, Šuvar.

5 Irreconcilable positions

Serbia and the army insist on hegemonism and socialism

The Fourteenth and last party congress of the Yugoslav communists, held in the second half of January 1990, took place a good half month after the fall of the last communist regime in Eastern Europe aside from Albania. The erstwhile Executive Secretary of the LCY Presidium, the otherwise neutral Stefan Korošec, had given expression to the pressure exerted by international developments: "As Yugoslav communists we must know that we do not constitute an isolated oasis, whether in Europe or in the world."[1] Under the management of Pančevski, the dogmatic Macedonian behind whom the Serbian bloc stood in close ranks, the only concession which the congress wanted to make to the spirit of the times was the renunciation of the leading role of the party. A Slovenian delegate remarked at the time that this had actually already been decided at the Sixth Party Congress of 1952.[2]

Noteworthy were the motions, mostly presented by the Slovenes, which were rejected: the transformation of the federal party into an association of independent parties of the republics, the ending of all prosecution on the basis of Article 114 of the penal code (counter-revolution) as well as all other political trials throughout Yugoslavia, a ban on torture, and an anchoring of the right of disassociation "within the framework of the constitution". The Slovenian motion to condemn Serbia's economic blockade was blocked to especially strong applause.[3] The new Slovenian party chief, Čiril Ribičič, said that with this action congress had declined to do the bare minimum which the Slovenian communists considered necessary, given developments in Yugoslavia and in the world. Neither the principles of federalism nor the principles of human rights and democracy nor the proposals for reform and for the transformation of the League of Communists, which had been demanded by the Slovenian party congress, had received even minimal attention.[4] After Ribičič's declaration to this effect, the Slovenes walked out.

One may grant Račan[5] that it was, however, not the departure of the Slovenes but the behavior of the Croatian delegation, i.e., its decision to follow the Slovenes, which constituted the decisive moment for the end of the congress and, thus, of the LCY as well. Some attempts to reconstitute the congress and thereby to save the federal party collapsed because it was utterly impossible to speak of a Yugoslav party in the absence of both the Slovenes and the Croats. Even the Macedonians and the Bosnians did not want to have anything to do with a "rump structure" which would have been under Serbian control and under the "whip" of the army leadership.[6]

The decision for democracy, multi-party system, and free elections was now irreversible not only in Ljubljana but also in Zagreb. The Slovenian elections had been set for 8 April, those in Croatia for 22 April 1990. Račan says that some people in his party had wanted, after the transfer of power in December 1989, to hold elections "immediately", after the model of what Milošević had done in Serbia. This would have reduced the elections to a mere formality, assuring the communists of victory. But Račan rejected such a maneuver; he stood for authentic and "fair" elections.[7]

As to the question of the election law, Račan says that the majority system seemed to be the only conceivable option in Croatia because of the complicated nature of the parliaments at the time. In the federation as well as in the republics, the parliament always consisted of three houses. One could have introduced a proportional system for the first chamber, but that solution would have led to new discussions and delays. Račan says that his party concerned itself rather little with the elections – perhaps too little – since at that time there was a lot going on in Yugoslavia generally. The electoral system was worked out by Professor Smiljko Sokol, an expert hired by the party; it was assumed that he would create a system which, at the least, would not be disadvantageous for the communist party. But it was later shown that the majority system worked to the advantage of the Croatian Democratic Community (HDZ), rather than to that of the communists, and gave the HDZ a disproportionate majority in the houses of the parliament.[8]

Preparations for the elections did not proceed entirely smoothly; Račan said that high officers in the army approached him several times and asked him to cancel the free elections; the army would then assume power in Croatia and would install him, Račan, as political leader, in Croatia. Račan rejected these proposals.[9] He did not want to say which officers had contacted him, but Manolić claims that Kadijević and Brovet at least were involved.[10]

The end of the LCY actually hit the army harder than Milošević. The Serbian leader had been served a defeat, to be sure, but he could always shift the offensive to another front, as he had done before, for example to the state presidency. For the army leadership, the end of the LCY and of its central organs signified a tangible constriction of its political field of action. The army leadership had been represented in the federal party organs – in the presidium and in the Central Committee alike; it was not represented in the state presidency. Moreover, "democratic centralism" did not apply in the organs of state.

The army leadership seemed, in those spring days of 1990, to have nurtured new intentions of intervening in all of Yugoslavia; the offer to Račan was ostensibly part of a larger scenario. These intentions were given a lift through the decision taken in the state presidency on 20 February concerning the deployment of the army in Kosovo. From Jović's memoirs,[11] however, two further points emerge. First, the army leadership was not entirely overjoyed with Serbian politics. General Blagoje Adžić openly reproached the Serbian leadership for behaving in an arrogant way toward the other peoples of Yugoslavia and for having ignored the possibilities for political solutions.[12] Second, the timidity of the army leadership in acting outside the framework of the constitution was clearly shown in this period; the Serbian leadership, or at least Jović, would have been pleased had the army been less timid in this regard. Certainly General Kadijević presented a four-point program on 3 April 1990, five days before the Slovenian elections.[13] The program aimed at the "restoration of constitu-tionality" and the achievement of certain "reforms", but after he failed to win backing for his plans in the state presidency, he distanced himself once more from any notion of undertaking "measures". Kadijević blames Marković and his ministers above all for this result. But Jović instead accuses Kadijević of "fatal indecisiveness".[14]

Actually, I remember that, at the time of the Slovenian elections in Ljubljana, there was talk of plans for a *putsch*, though with the comment that such things could no longer make any impression. The army's efforts to influence the Slovenian electoral battle were limited to the complaint, registered shortly before election day, that opposition leader Jože Pučnik had allegedly "insulted" the army. The authorized state attorney rejected the charge as "trivial".[15]

The question as to what kind of "constitutionality" the army leadership wanted to "restore" with an intervention before the Slovenian and Croatian elections and which "reforms" the army hoped to realize in the state and society was never clearly answered. That this involved at the same time an endeavor to obstruct the elections in Slovenia and Croatia seemed quite certain. On the other hand, several responsible reform-communist leaders in Ljubljana told me then that the army leadership had evidently realized that after the collapse of the communist system throughout Eastern Europe the country could proceed forward only on the basis of a certain pluralism and even a certain confederalization. Manolić told me in November 1994 that the army had possibly been prepared to allow a degree of pluralism, approximately on the constricted model which Milošević had chosen for his elections in Serbia in December 1989.

There were definitely differences of opinion within the army leadership. This emerges from both Kadijević's public speeches and his memoirs; he also feels the need to justify himself publicly *vis-à-vis* Milošević today.

Against Kadijević's account, Admiral Mamula, now living on a pension in Croatia, allegedly harbored somewhat different views. Many people in Zagreb told me that Mamula's view (in 1989–90) was that it would have been good for Yugoslavia if Milošević and Kučan had both disappeared from the scene. Misha Glenny claims that Mamula was the great "*éminence grise*" of the army establishment and was even consulted by Kadijević on a regular basis.[16] There seems to be little evidence for this interpretation. Certainly among all the high generals at the time, Mamula was still the most intelligent. He was a primarily Yugoslav-oriented Serb from Croatia; he had political ambitions and certainly he was often consulted. Later, at the beginning of 1991, he also played a role in the establishment of the so-called army party. He was a political partner for dogmatic and Yugoslav-oriented elements in the Croatian party. But for the Slovenes, after the events of 1988 in which he had been implicated, he was no longer a partner. His possibilities for action were limited.

In contrast to the army leadership, Prime Minister Marković accepted the collapse of the LCY with composure. The state did not need the party, he said in a commentary.[17] For Marković, the collapse of the LCY could only result in a strengthening of his position. An important center of power in the federation had disappeared; that could only work to the benefit of the remaining institutions. The Prime Minister seemed for the first time to be confident that he could play a role beyond the economic sphere. Western diplomats in Belgrade allowed themselves to be influenced by this expectation; their *idée fixe*, that Marković was a prime minister as in other countries, with corresponding powers, was formed at this point in time.

On the other hand, Marković seemed to hope that he could now make himself indispensable to the army, because he was practically the only person who could guarantee the financing of the combat forces. This actually placed Marković in the position to oppose *putsch* attempts or similar adventures on the part of the generals; this is what had made Kadijević so bitter at the beginning of April 1990. This "halo" stayed over Marković until the end of June 1991, when he himself provided the army leadership with the political cover for its attack in Slovenia. The relationship of Marković to the army remained conflicted, however. Besides, Marković remained true to his inclination to meddle in delicate political matters as little as possible. He called on the leaderships of Serbia and Slovenia to settle their differences in direct talks.[18]

In the end no one could interfere in the electoral contests in Slovenia and Croatia, in which the victory of non-communist forces was ever more clearly indicated. The "Demos" coalition in Slovenia included, under the chairmanship of Social-Democratic leader Dr Pučnik, the right-of-center Christian Democrats (under Lojze Peterle), the Peasant Party (under its popular leader, Ivan Oman), the Democratic League of Slovenia which was primarily made up of intellectuals (under the chairmanship of the later Foreign Minister Dr Dimitrij Rupel), as well as the Greens, a party of manual laborers, and an Association of Retirees. The Liberals (later to be called Liberal Democrats), under Jozef Školc, remained outside the "Demos" coalition; this party had been constructed on the foundation of the old Youth Association. Other parties contesting the 1990 elections included the Socialist Party (which had evolved out of the old Socialist Alliance of Working People of Slovenia and was led by Jože Smole and Viktor Žakelj), the reformed communists whose unofficial leader, Kučan, was also running for president, and several right-wing groups, among whom the most colorful personality was Zmago Jelinčič, who was beginning to verbally attack non-Slovene residents of Slovenia.

According to the account of its chairman, Pučnik, the political coalition "Demos" emerged in October 1989.[19] At that time, he had met with the representatives of the Peasant Party and the Democratic League on a farm and had agreed on political cooperation. The Christian Democrats were, at the time, just being formed. This meeting had been preceded by an effort by Jože Smole and his Socialist Alliance to contain the democratization process within the framework of the Socialist Alliance and, in this way, to preserve the "system". In October 1989, Pučnik broke off talks with Smole, because it had become clear that this route could lead, at best, to a circumscribed democratization. The first official session of "Demos" took place on 1 and 2 November 1989, this time with the participation of Peterle's Christian Democrats. On 4 December 1989, the coalition presented its program at a press conference, announcing its aspiration to assume governmental responsibility in Slovenia.

All of the conversations I had with Kučan and other reformed communist leaders indicated the firm commitment of the communists not to influence the electoral outcome, to respect the result, and, in the event of a defeat, to surrender power. At the most, the reformed communists betrayed a certain bitterness that many people did not acknowledge their good faith and wanted to vote "anti-communist" at any cost. Kučan, who distanced himself from his own party, did not doubt that he personally would be re-elected, even though, given that the vote would be split among four candidates, he might not win the necessary 50 per cent of the votes in the first round. In the event, he obtained "only" 44 per cent of the vote on 8 April 1990. According to the constitution, Kučan was not yet "President" of Slovenia, but only "President of the Presidency", i.e., chairman of a collective board consisting of five members. This collective presidency, especially in its expanded composition, remained the most important organ of political leadership in Slovenia also during the struggle for independence.

The future relationship of Slovenia to Yugoslavia constituted the principal theme of Slovenia's electoral contest. The two camps drew noticeably close in standpoint, under the buzzword "confederation". The proposals for a new constitution along more centralist lines, which had been revived in the Yugoslav *Skupština* on the initiative of the state presidency and in which Marković had a hand, were rejected; the time for centralist solutions was definitely over now. The Slovenian presidency stated at the beginning of 1990 that one could not discuss a new constitutional text without first clarifying the fundamental principles of union, and this had to be in the direction of democracy and equality, "in accord with the level of development reached in Europe".[20]

On 18 January 1990, the Slovenian state presidency adopted a position in opposition to the Yugoslav state presidency's formulation that the crisis was only a matter of ethnic conflicts. In reality, what was at stake were "different views concerning political, social, and economic problems". The repressive regime in Kosovo had damaged Yugoslavia's reputation in the world; it even threatened to bar the path into Europe for Slovenia. In the aforementioned session of the Slovenian presidency, the representative of Slovenia in the Yugoslav state presidency was even criticized for not having defended Slovenian positions strongly enough. Drnovšek replied that this reflected the nature of the state presidency as a collective body.[21] Later, it would be shown that Jović did not feel similarly encumbered when he (a Serb) sat at the helm of the state presidency.

What the Slovenian population thought about the future position of the republic and its relationship to Yugoslavia was shown in mid-1990 in a poll conducted by the newspaper *Delo*.[22] According to *Delo*, 52 per cent of Slovenian respondents supported the transformation of Yugoslavia into a confederation, 28 per cent preferred Slovenia's immediate secession, and only 8 per cent favored the continuation of the federation as it had existed. Demos conducted its election campaign under the slogan of independence (*samostalnost*) for Slovenia.[23] However, by this term even the opposition leaders at that time understood by no means primarily secession, but rather, still, a confederation.[24]

The result of the election of 8 April 1990 corresponded more or less to the forecasts: The "Demos" coalition garnered about 55 per cent of the votes, against 17.2 per cent for the reform communists. Within Demos, the strongest party, rather surprisingly, was the Christian Democratic Party, with 13.3 per cent, followed by the Peasant Party with 12.3 per cent, and the Democrats with 10 per cent. The Liberals (later Liberal Democrats), who had entered the race on their own, won 15.1 per cent. Kučan won the presidency in the second round of voting on 22 April with 58.6 per cent of the vote – a clear absolute majority.[25] The results obtained by the individual Demos parties gave the Christian Democrats, by previous agreement, the right to name the Prime Minister. Accordingly, Peterle became the Prime Minister of the first non-communist government within Yugoslavia.

I remember that at the time many in Ljubljana would have rather seen the politically prominent Pučnik at the helm of the government. Pučnik had spent time in prison for his convictions and had subsequently spent long years in exile in Germany. The Christian Democrats, who were politically the furthest removed from the communists, were visibly lacking in political experience; they were, in particular, completely unfamiliar with the situation in Belgrade. Moreover, while the Christian Democrats wanted to build a modern party, something of the legacy of old clericalism continued to hang over them.

Another matter which was talked about after the formation of the new cabinet was the appointment of Janez Janša, who had been condemned by the military court two years earlier, to serve as Minister of Defense. The army could have seen the appointment as an open provocation. But nothing happened and Janša later successfully fulfilled his responsibilities in the struggle for independence.

In Croatia, things were more complicated. The drafting of the law on parties and elections had cost some time; the electoral campaign could start only in the first week of February 1990. The new party landscape emerged only rather tepidly out of anonymity, and for a long time it was difficult to come to a realistic appraisal of the relative strengths of the chief parties. On the left was the reformist League of Communists of Croatia–Party of Democratic Changes, led by Račan. A number of parties of a left-bourgeois or liberal orientation united in a Coalition of National Understanding; among its affiliate parties was the Social Liberal Party, led by Dražen Budiša, a former student leader during 1970/71, and the Croatian People's Party, in which the reform communist leaders of 1970/71, Miko Tripalo and Savka Dabčević-Kučar, were involved. Certain prominent Zagreb intellectuals, who had also in part played a role in the events of 1970/71, such as Slavko Goldštajn, Vlado Gotovac, and Ivan Zvonimir Čičak, also tried to make their political presence felt within some smaller parties. Finally, there was the Democratic League of Istria and the Serbian Democratic Party under psychologist Jovan Rašković, which was largely based in Knin. At the time, however, the Serbs were still over-whelmingly backing the reformed communists. Among these communist Serbs, some of them, such as Boro Mikelić, the director of the Gavrilović Salami Factory in Petrinja, were gravitating in the direction of Milošević. At the extreme right wing stood the newly created Party of Right under the leadership of Dobroslav Paraga.

The main interest was soon concentrated on the party of Dr Franjo Tudjman, which had now constituted itself as the Croatian Democratic Community (*Hrvatska Demokratska Zajednica*, or HDZ) and which, together with some smaller groups such as the Christian Democrats, entered the race under the rubric of the "Croatian Democratic Bloc".

According to Manolić, the HDZ organization was formally established at a meeting in the House of the Association of Writers on 28 February 1989; this had been preceded by some preliminary meetings and organizational probes.[26] The HDZ, according to Manolić, was already at that time characterized by a diversity of currents. The core of the party was the "Partisan wing", consisting of people like Tudjman, Mesić, Manolić, and General Janko Bobetko – all of them "victims" of the purge at the end of the Croatian Spring in 1971. Only a few *Ustaša*-oriented elements had joined the HDZ; those inclined to extreme-right views generally joined the Party of Right or other splinter groups. Manolić himself had served as the police chief of Zagreb 1960–65, but was responsible only for general police actions. Then he happily relinquished that post and took a seat in the Croatian parliament, the *Sabor;* he worked there, above all in the constitutional commission, until he was forced from this position in 1971.

Manolić and Mesić told me in November 1994 that, from the very beginning, the HDZ had in mind to realize Croatian state independence. One could not fix a deadline for this aim, according to Mesić, or say whether it would become reality immediately or only in 10 years. The eventual goal, however, was fixed. Mesić himself had reckoned that the HDZ would collect about half of the votes and that it might possibly share power with the reform communists.

Tudjman conducted his electoral campaign from explicit nationalist positions, offering an economic program colored by state-capitalist views. I remember his appearance on Croatian Television at the beginning of April 1990.[27] It seemed to me at the time that Tudjman hardly had Yugoslavia in mind at all, not even as a confederation. He spoke exclusively of Croatia and its sovereignty; Croatia had to retain its "natural and historic borders". A glance at the map, showing Croatia as a half-moon around Bosnia, allowed the suspicion to arise that he aspired to the inclusion of at least the Croatian parts of Bosnia. Tudjman was for a market economy, but with the preservation of "national values". The electoral meetings which Tudjman held drew large crowds of up to 30,000 persons.

It seemed that the Croats had not yet registered the fact that they could actually vote freely. So the groundswell of support for the HDZ emerged largely in the last two weeks of the campaign. The first round on 22 April brought the big surprise. The HDZ won 41.4 per cent of the vote for the lower house and 44 per cent of the vote in the Council of Communities; after the second round of voting on 29 April, it was calculated that the party had obtained between 60 and 70 per cent of the seats in all houses of the *Sabor*, thus an absolute majority.[28]

The reform communists received 23.7 per cent of the votes in the two main chambers in the first round of voting. The clear defeat of the liberal Coalition of National Understanding was surprising. The Coalition garnered only between 13 and 15 per cent of the votes for the two main houses in the first round and, in accordance with the majority system, only a few mandates. The electoral law, as the Slovenian daily *Delo* pointed out, had helped the HDZ.[29] To that one should add that the HDZ did not draft the law. The Belgrade *Politika* wrote at the time that Croatia was openly sliding from one one-party system to another.[30] The Serbian Democratic Party won a few mandates in the Knin area. As concerns regional divisions, Tudjman won an overwhelming victory in Zagreb but was less successful in Osijek, or in Split and other Dalmatian cities. Rijeka, with its strongly mixed population, voted predominantly reform-communist, and in Istria, the regionalists were victorious.

Tudjman came across as very self-confident in a conversation we had shortly after his victory, but in the decisive questions he was nonetheless realistic.[31] Indirectly he admitted that he had not expected his electoral victory or his ascent to exclusive power in Croatia. He wanted to explain some of his statements in the campaign, especially as regards Bosnia, in terms of his need to tap nationalist votes. He said that the "almost plebiscitary decision of the Croatian people for complete national freedom of decision" must be respected also on the international plane. Those circles in the West who still dreamt of a centralized Yugoslavia should finally bow to reality. Tudjman adopted the demand for the transformation of Yugoslavia into a confederation. There could be, in the future, a kind of "Europe in miniature", i.e., a unified market-oriented economic space founded on national states exercising their own sovereignty. He would not lay any obstacles in the path of Marković, but the Prime Minister had to divorce himself from his centralist fantasies. The division of labor and the division of currency earnings had to be reorganized under new regulations. Tudjman, a bit prematurely, did not expect any major actions on the part of the army; the will of the people had manifested itself too clearly for that. That Croatia laid claim to some prerogatives in foreign policy was clear; as a Central European land it aspired above all to a close relationship with Germany. It was thanks to Milošević, Tudjman said, that events in Yugoslavia had taken this route; one could only be distrustful of a leadership which organized the armed overthrow of the leaderships in other republics and provinces.

Tudjman was aware that the Serbs, who constituted about 14 per cent of the population, would present the greatest problem in Croatia. He seemed prepared to grant Rašković, the leader of the Serbian Democratic Party, a post in the government. The Serbs (of Croatia), he said, were in general taking a realistic and cooperative approach. The population of Bosnia-Herzegovina should vote in a referendum about its status as a republic, but geographic considerations would already dictate a close cooperation with Croatia.

The Central Committee secretary of the reform-communists, Boris Malada, said in a conversation[32] that the 25 per cent of the vote was the best that a communist party could do, at the time, in free elections in the eastern part of Europe. The party readily acknowledged that the democratic mechanisms had to be fully respected. Malada conceded that his party owed its relative strength in part to the strong support it had won among local Serbs; only one-third of the Serbs had voted for Rašković's party.

It is often said that Tudjman was Croatia's answer to Milošević. That may be, but Tudjman was likewise Croatia's answer to the suppression of the "Croatian Spring" at the end of 1971 and to the "anti-Croatian course" in Croatia which the victors of Karadjordjevo had pursued in Zagreb after 1971 and in which the Serb communist element had played a disproportionate role.

The victory of non-communist forces first in Slovenia and then in Croatia created a new political situation in Yugoslavia. This fact alone should have convinced all those concerned that Yugoslavia could have a future only on a confederal foundation and that the only alternative to confederation was disassociation. This concept of "disassociation" (*razdruživanje*, in Serbo-Croatian) became a characteristic component of everyday political vocabulary in Yugoslavia in those days. It signified among those using the term, who could be found not merely in Slovenia and Croatia but also elsewhere in the country, not the secession of individual republics but the dissolution of the common state on the basis of mutual understanding.

Only a short time after the second round of voting in Croatia, before 10 May 1990, Ljubljana and Zagreb presented their mutually agreed declarations of intent to reconstruct Yugoslavia as a confederation. Kučan said that Slovenia wanted, in any event, a "confederative status" in Yugoslavia. That signified that the Slovenian proposal for an "asymmetrical" form for the state remained on the table. Then Kučan said, "If other peoples of Yugoslavia also have such vital interests, which they would like to realize in a community of equal peoples and their republics, then it is realistic to expect that we agree on a new structure for common existence or, if that is not possible, disassociate peacefully."[33] Tudjman confirmed these ideas in his own declaration and appended the proposal that in a future Yugoslav confederation the army should consist of "integral" contingents of the republics, much like NATO. Constitutional obstacles to this restructuring, alleged by the army leadership, did not actually exist, because the constitution could at any point be altered.[34]

Whoever now believed that Milošević and the army would show the least respect for the new relationships in parts of Yugoslavia could only be described as naïve. On the contrary, there now began immediately a series of flagrant breaches of the constitution and open attacks, including military actions, as Borisav Jović, the Serbian representative in the state presidency, took office as chair of the state presidency from Drnovšek on 15 May 1990. On 14 May he had already appeared in *Borba* in an interview which discussed the adoption of unconcealed measures against the two newly democratic republics. Kučan once noted in conversation that even if Milošević was no longer interested in Slovenia, he had to admit to himself that the army still was.[35]

Jović said in *Borba* that there were no provisions in the constitution for political pluralism, as a result of which the elections in Slovenia and Croatia could only throttle the country with "new difficulties and uncertainties". As for the demands to transform Yugoslavia into a confederation, such a solution would require the assent of all the republics and provinces, and he doubted that such a consensus could be obtained. Then he explained that the state presidency had the advantage that it did not operate on the basis of consensus but decided by majority vote, with the result that certain measures for the protection of the constitutional order could be handled "more effectively".[36]

These statements of Jović's, which were repeated rather exactly a day later in his inauguration speech, provoked indignation. First, as was noted by Slovenian and Croatian spokespersons, the constitution did not prohibit political pluralism.[37] As for the voting method of the state presidency, Article 330 explicitly required that this be on the basis of compromise or consensus. The procedures of the state presidency did not stand higher than the constitution. One could thus fear that Jović was preparing the ground, with his ideas, for a state of emergency or for annulling the elections in the two western republics.

Jović did not waste any time and immediately launched his term of office with a coup. On 16 May 1990, thus practically in the first session, he brought before the presidency a report which he had written earlier in his capacity as chair of the Council for the Protection of the Constitutional Order, in which he had characterized the security situation in Yugoslavia as "alarming" and demanded "measures" of an unspecified nature. Drnovšek reported this a day later to the republic presidency of Slovenia.[38] In March, according to Drnovšek, no decision was possible, but now Jović was able to put together a majority vote in favor of his initiative. These proposals had now to be set before the parliament. Drnovšek had opposed this decision, but he had been alone in his opposition; even Šuvar, as Croatia's representative, had sided with Jović.

On 17 May the Slovenian republic presidency characterized the decision of the Yugoslav state presidency as unacceptable. This concerned an attempt to abort democratization and to prepare repressive measures. From Jović's action one knew now what to expect from the federal presidency in the future. One would have to mobilize the public and provide for good coordination between the different organs of the republic.

The army had meanwhile already taken action. In the same session of the Slovenian republic presidency, Kučan had to reveal that he had received disquieting reports that the army had confiscated the weapons of the Slovenian Territorial Defense forces in several districts and deposited them in army depots. He hoped to obtain more information and to speak about this the next day. The new Defense Minister, Janša, confirmed later[39] that he had likewise heard such reports from various districts on the afternoon of 17 May. It was the day on which the parliament was to swear in the new Slovenian government. Up to this point, thus, Janša had not yet assumed the responsibilities of office. In an informal talk, Kučan confirmed the state of affairs to him and said that the Commander of the Slovenian Territorial Defense (TO, from the Slovenian *Teritorialna Obramba*), the former Yugoslav Air Force General Ivan Hočevar, had not informed him about the action, even though he had been required by law to do so.

On the following day, 18 May 1990, the Slovenian republic presidency met once more, this time in the presence of Janša and General Hočevar.[40] Kučan said that Hočevar had told him the day before that it was only a technical question. But something was going on. Hočevar replied that the TO was part of the combat forces of Yugoslavia and not a Slovenian Army. It was of course legal for Slovenia to purchase weapons for its Territorial Defense forces, but one would have to secure them. To Kučan's question as to what the ostensible order from Belgrade signified, Hočevar tried to evade the issue; he said that the order was secret and that it signified only that the weapons had to be "physically secured". With that, the Slovenian presidency adopted a decision not to give up any more weapons. As Janša reports,[41] this decision was relayed to the districts by confidential telegram the following day, 19 May, and was carried out. In spite of that, 70 per cent of TO weaponry was, by then, in the hands of the army, including that which had already been in army storehouses.

It soon became clear that this was a prepared operation which had been planned the previous month[42] and which, while formally extending throughout the entire country, in effect was carried out only in the three "unreliable" republics – Slovenia, Croatia, and Bosnia-Herzegovina – and here, exclusive of Serb-inhabited regions. Moreover, in none of these republics had the civil authorities been informed in advance. In Croatia, Tudjman was not yet formally in office and was completely taken by surprise. Later he told me that the Croatian Territorial Defense forces had, in any case, been under Serbian control; there had been no possibility of making use of this organization in any way. Mesić disagrees and insists that Tudjman and the HDZ could very well have done something;[43] if the removal of weaponry from some Croatian districts in Herzegovina could be prevented, then the same thing could have been done in the purely Croatian districts of Croatia. Tudjman was already showing his inclination to bask in undiluted triumphalism while neglecting practical measures needed for the security of Croatia. On the other side, Račan told me later that he too, although still in a politically responsible position, was not able to do anything, because the army would have viewed any resistance as a provocation and would possibly have taken it as a pretext for certain actions.

All in all, as Janša writes,[44] the army leadership could be pleased with the results of its actions. The Croats and Bosnian Muslims stood largely weaponless; the new government in Croatia, which at first exercised only partial authority over the police and which had to contend with Tudjman's inclination to give highest priority to decking out his presidential office with ceremonial majesty, was thereby compelled to build up Croatia's armed forces via the police, which would prove rather ineffective upon the outbreak of the war.

In Slovenia, people certainly knew what to do. The then Information Minister, later Defense Minister, Jelko Kacin believes, to be sure, that

Kučan could have reacted somewhat more quickly to the measures taken by the army, but it is also true that Slovenia could not yet risk an open conflict with the army.[45] A Slovenian military force would now have to be built up, according to plan. For this purpose, the new Slovenian authorities were able to make use of a special institution known as *Narodna Zaščita* (National Protection) which dated from Partisan times and which had been anchored in the Slovenian constitution. In this way, it was possible to cover defense preparations with a mantle of constitutionality; after all, in 1985, the then Chief-of-Staff of the army, Serbian General Petar Gračanin, who would later serve as Minister of the Interior, had explicitly advised the Slovenian leadership, in a letter, that Slovenian "National Protection" was "not contrary to the constitution".[46] Janša notes that the political police in Slovenia had neglected to inform the authorities of their observations; this was taken as a cause for appropriate measures. The uniformed police had, meanwhile, been completely loyal to the new Minister of the Interior, Igor Bavčar, from the beginning.[47]

Kadijević mentions in his memoirs that he was content with the results of the army's operation and admits that its goal was to "paralyze" the territorial defenses in those parts of the country where "separatist forces" might have wanted to use them as the foundation on which to construct separate armies. At the same time, he said, the authorities were able to rely on some of the officers in the Territorial Defense forces in order to keep these organizations "out of the control" of ostensible separatists.[48] This remark of Kadijević is interesting because it confirms information according to which in Serb-inhabited districts of Croatia, especially in Knin, as well as in the Serb-inhabited districts of Bosnia, the Territorial Defense forces were directly used to provide rebel Serbs with a military structure and weaponry and this long before the outbreak of open conflict.

The session of the Yugoslav parliament at which Jović presented his proposals, characterizing them as the collaborative work of the state presidency, took place on 28 May 1990. Jović, who had been characterized as impertinent but no genius by many politicians who had to work with him, recited the entire catalogue of "serious threats to public order" but he had to realize that he had overextended himself.[49] The state presidency did not intend, he said, to proclaim a state of emergency or to declare the elections in Slovenia and Croatia null and void. But he claimed that some of the new political parties had close links with "extremist émigré circles" and might distribute weapons without proper authorization. He spoke of a "threat", of "attacks on everything that has been achieved", and so forth. His proposals consisted in the demand that both political pluralism and the right of disassociation had to be regulated by law. The centralistic constitutional changes already proposed by Marković should be accepted, and the allegedly "unconstitutional" provisions of individual republic constitutions should be repealed. Jović failed to obtain any resolution, however, because the delegates of Slovenia had strict instructions to block any such vote.

The big sensation that day was not so much Jović's speech as the announcement by Prime Minister Marković that he had in mind to establish a political party of his own shortly, as a "coalition on the basis of the government's program".[50] He linked this with an announcement that his government wanted to hold general, multi-party elections throughout Yugoslavia as a whole. These twin announcements met immediately with a furious reaction in Serbia. The Belgrade daily *Politika ekspres* spoke of a "great betrayal" and a "stab in the back of democracy".[51] The Prime Minister should consider the fact that it was the League of Communists which had put him in power.

It was clear that Marković's action was very inconvenient for Milošević, who would thus have to share his claim to represent the Yugoslav system with Marković. In general Milošević was having problems once more, in that the opposition in Serbia would organize large anti-communist rallies a short while later, in the first half of June 1990. In his response, Milošević announced that he was founding a "Socialist Party" which would work above all for a "united Serbia" and an "efficacious federation".[52] In Zagreb and Ljubljana, it seemed that the Serbian opposition was, if anything, even more nationalist than Milošević, but one hoped that, at the very least, Serbia would now be forced to hold multi-party elections, which might perhaps reduce the pressure on Croatia and Slovenia.[53]

These hopes were not fulfilled. With his keen political instinct, Milošević had realized that he could no longer rely on the exhausted framework of socialism; on this point he was a step ahead of the army leadership. He understood quite well that he could succeed in Serbia in future only by playing the nationalist card. Milošević did not want people like Šešelj or Drašković to pull the rug from under him. In summer 1990, the main objective of the Serbian regime was to complete the subjugation of Kosovo.

Milošević considered that a new Serbian constitution had to be drafted which would cement the "unity" of Serbia and entrench his personal position as leader and president. New elections could serve this purpose, as those of 1989 no longer provided any kind of legitimation, in the light of intervening developments. Since, meanwhile, the danger existed that after the general elections, at which the Serbian opposition and the Albanians might achieve a certain strength, the intended goals of constitutional reform might be threatened, Milošević had the Serbs vote on 1–2 July 1990 in a referendum to accept the constitution *before* the new elections. The new constitution effected not only the complete liquidation of the autonomy of the provinces and their organs, but also the complete framing of the "statehood" of Serbia and the position of its president. In Article 72, there is reference to the "sovereignty, independence, and territorial integrity of Serbia"; the "defense" of this republic lay entirely within the jurisdiction of Serbian authorities, without any limitation or qualification. According to Article 83, the President of the Republic of Serbia "commands" the combat forces in peace and in war. Adoption by the parliament followed on 28 September 1990. What the Republic of Serbia granted itself in this new constitution as regards sovereignty and independence went far beyond what Slovenia had claimed for itself in its constitutional amendments of autumn 1989. Nonetheless, the army leadership did not, at any point, issue even the most modest protest.

In early August, Prime Minister Marković, true to his word, announced the formation of his League of Reform Forces in the Kožara Mountains, a former Partisan stronghold. The League found some resonance only in Bosnia, Vojvodina, and Macedonia. The attempt was coming too late, and besides, Marković still wanted to avoid taking a position on the decisive political questions of the country, such as Kosovo. Slovenes and Croats thought that if Marković had the ambition to be "Yugoslavia's savior", he would possibly make further concessions to Milošević. They had had enough of this policy, which had only brought disadvantages to the western republics.[54]

Within Slovenia, there were nuances of opinion as regards independence. Kučan and other representatives of the reformed communist camp still nurtured hopes of transforming Yugoslavia into a confederation, while the politicians of "Demos" hardly thought in Yugoslav terms any more. They had never been involved in Yugoslav politics, and even Drnovšek's maneuvering in the state presidency was too much for them. The internal problems of Slovenia lay closer to their hearts – for example, the so-called "national reconciliation", i.e., coming to terms with the civil war during the Second World War, together with the liquidation of the *Domobranci* who had been turned over to Tito by the British. Kučan played his part in this process in a commemoration at Kočevje while Prime Minister Peterle repeatedly spoke of the renunciation of revenge.[55]

The later Information Minister Kacin said in October 1994 that the careful maneuvers after the elections and the measured reaction to Jović's provocations gave Slovenia time to prepare for independence.[56] According to the custom of the land, the Slovenes paid a lot of attention to laying the legal foundations. On 2 July 1990, the Slovenian parliament issued a declaration of principle concerning independence and adopted constitutional amendments which would lead to that result.

In Croatia, the consolidation of the new system proved more difficult. In contrast to Slovenian teamwork, authoritarian tendencies soon showed themselves in Tudjman's behavior. He changed even his closest collaborators repeatedly. This had particularly fatal results in the foreign ministry. Whereas Slovenian Foreign Minister Rupel could systematically build a network of relations, Croatia's foreign relations lacked continuity. In addition, Tudjman's personal style of argumentation was not always well suited to evoke understanding for the Croatian cause.

One of the few convincing departmental appointments on Tudjman's part came in August 1990 with the nomination of the retired former commander of the Fifth Army District in Zagreb, General Martin Špegelj, to Croatian Defense Minister. Špegelj was largely left alone by Tudjman. He would later have very negative things to say about the first period of Tudjman's term of office. The patriotic celebrations lasted for months; there was no danger, everything could be achieved through negotiations – that was the atmosphere.[57] Špegelj won a lot of credit for improvizing the resistance to the *putsch* attempts in autumn and winter 1990/91. Then, during the Slovenian war in summer 1991, Tudjman rejected Špegelj's proposals for an active strategy so that the general stepped down at the beginning of July 1991, probably very much to the detriment of Croatia during the coming months of war.

The question as to why Jović provoked confrontations with Slovenia and even more with Croatia immediately after assuming office as formal head of state was answered as early as July 1990. Scarcely had Milošević held the founding congress of his new Socialist Party of Serbia on 16 July 1990 than he began a massive propaganda against Croatia, playing with the Serbian minority there. "It is difficult to live as a Serb in Croatia," said a headline in *Politika* in those days. At that time, the Serbs in Croatia still had all their jobs, and the Tudjman regime was making an effort to win them over.

All indices confirmed that the rebellion of the Serbs in Croatia did not only arise out of their own ranks but was incited and even organized by Milošević. But it was not alleviated by Tudjman's errors. Of course, the Serbs in Croatia, about 600,000 in all, had scarcely been enthusiastic about the HDZ victory, since they had never, since the abolition of the Military Frontier, reconciled themselves to being governed by Croatian civil authorities and, besides, the memories of the Second World War were still vivid. In the Krajina around Knin, however, where the rebellion began, and in Banija, only 26 per cent of Croatia's Serbs were to be found.[58] Besides, at first the confrontations, even there, took place within a political-parliamentary framework. The leader of the largely Knin-based Serbian Democratic Party demanded a vaguely defined autonomy but was, at the same time, prepared to recognize the Croatian state and cooperate with it.[59]

Mesić, at that time Croatian prime minister, told me in October 1994 that one of the greatest mistakes of the new Croatian leadership had been that it had not immediately undertaken to make an "alliance" with Rašković's Serbian party. Certainly, in the initial phase of his government, Tudjman had signalled his readiness to make concessions, but he never clearly defined just how far he was willing to go.

In a conversation with Rašković, Tudjman promised cultural autonomy – a promise he later confirmed in conversations we had.[60] The problem was that Tudjman's whole rhetoric and symbology displayed what Rašković called "Croatocentrism". Rašković was even prepared to accept that. What he was not prepared to accept was a downgrading of the constitutional position of the Serbs of Croatia under the new constitution. The old constitution had defined Croatia, in Article 1, as "the national state of the Croats, the state of the Serbian people in Croatia, and the state of nationalities who live there". In the draft of the new constitution, which was later adopted, the Serbs were mentioned only as a minority together with all the others.

In the entire aforementioned conversation, Rašković made no secret of the fact that he had come under severe attack from Serbia because of his loyal disposition to the Croatian state, and that, in his locale, there were people who wanted to follow Belgrade's line. Actually, one gets the clear impression that Rašković wanted to offer Tudjman the support he needed, and to obtain the necessary reciprocation, in order to be able to continue his relatively moderate line. But Tudjman foolishly had the entire text of this conversation published, word for word, in *Danas*. This move discredited Rašković and the moderate line no longer had any chance in the Serbian Democratic Party.

There was unrest and agitation in Knin and other largely Serb-inhabited districts throughout the summer. At the end of June 1990, Milošević said for the first time that in the event of the transformation of Yugoslavia into a confederation, the borders of Serbia would be an "open question".[61] One did not assign too great a significance to this statement at the time. Serbia, which in its new constitution had represented itself practically as an independent state, was nonetheless, through the words of its leader, making clear for the first time what the Greater Serbian alternative to the Yugoslav federation would signify.

The "Serbian question" in Croatia became acute as a result of the referendum conducted by the Serbian organizations among Serbian inhabitants of Croatia on 18 August 1990. At this time, the propaganda from Belgrade reached new heights: the *Ustaše* were ruling, according to Belgrade, whose news organs were only too happy to elaborate on this theme. The referendum referred to "autonomy"; naturally nearly everyone who took part in this referendum endorsed autonomy. The Croatian authorities declared the referendum "illegal", even though they were unable to prevent it. Tudjman repeated to me, in those days, that he was ready to assure full "cultural autonomy" but never political or territorial autonomy. As for the content of such "cultural autonomy", Tudjman said it would relate to school curricula and cultural activities.

Only then did Tudjman open a first school for his new Croatian police and induct 1,500 volunteers into special units. The situation with the Serbs was still by no means bad for Croatia at the time. Interior Minister Josip Boljkovac summoned the administrative chiefs of the districts with majority-Serb populations and told them they should seek a solution to their problems within, rather than outside, Croatia. The district chiefs agreed with him, or so I was told, and spoke out, in principle, for loyal cooperation with the Croatian state; at the same time, they complained that they were being hindered by agitation from "outside".[62]

The first attempted uprising came on the day of the referendum, on 18 August 1990, in and around Knin. Armed civilians suddenly emerged and set up barricades in the roads; even the Dalmatian coastal road was cut in places, and tourists fled in panic. Four districts were affected: Knin, Obrovac, Gračac, and Benkovac. Rašković seemed to have disappeared; a new leader of the district administrators in Knin, Milan Babić, a dentist by profession, was setting the tone. To be sure, the barricades disappeared soon, but, as Mesić told me at the time, on that Sunday a part of Croatia had ceased to be under the control of the government. The local police, consisting of Serbs, adopted an ambiguous attitude, and where it was possible, passed along weapons to local civilians.

The strongest warning that Croatia had to heed, came, for all that, from the army, which prevented three helicopters of the Croatian Ministry of the Interior carrying police reinforcements from continuing toward Knin. When Mesić, then Prime Minister of Croatia, phoned the Chief-of-Staff, General Adžić, a convinced Serb, and protested, the latter threatened that the army would intervene if even a single Serb died. Mesić replied that in this case Croatia would declare its independence immediately. A few minutes later the chair of the state presidency, Jović, called back and told Mesić to ignore what Adžić had said.[63]

The view in Zagreb, that one could have won in a test of strength, was mistaken. In reality, what was involved was a voluntarily interrupted dress rehearsal and a victory for Milošević's infiltrators among the Croatian Serbs.

At the end of September 1990, the smouldering unrest in and around Knin once more flared up; a Serbian National Council was established and "autonomy" was proclaimed. The Croatian government said that individual officers of the army corps stationed in Knin, commanded at the time by Ratko Mladić, were helping the insurgents and that weapons were pouring into the area.[64] This time the unrest also touched the region of Banija, lying to the north. It was also clear that a similar movement was developing in the largely Serb districts of western Bosnia, even if the Bosnian Serbs still pretended to respect the unity of Bosnia. For the first time, one encountered the concept "western Serbia".[65] Traffic routes and railway lines were closed by the rebels. Since tree trunks were usually used to block the roads, the rebellion came to be called "the tree-trunk rebellion". The Serbian districts in eastern Slavonia remained peaceful at that time.

The insurgent movement of Serbs in Croatia reflected the fact that Milošević had not succeeded in realizing his primary concept of a Serb-ruled Yugoslavia. In demanding autonomy for the Krajina, Serbia was seeking respect for a principle which, in the context of Kosovo, it did not itself honor. All in all, it should be emphasized that there were no concrete acts on the part of the Croatian authorities which could be said to have instigated or justified the unrest. There were only errors and acts of sheer incompetence, not least in connection with the new constitution. It should be mentioned also that the Serbs in Croatia, mostly previously linked with the communist regime, were affected by the developments on two levels – as Serbs and as privileged communists.

The idea that wherever Serbs lived was Serbia, including districts where they were in a minority, was unprecedented nationalist arrogance. The idea, as played out in Croatia and later in Bosnia, entailed the expulsion or outright liquidation of the Croatian or Muslim populations. Sometimes, the Serbian side employed the argument that if the Croatian people laid claim to self-determination, they had to concede the same right to local Serbs. This argument was dubious, because the Yugoslav constitution itself recognized the statehood of the Republic of Croatia, on the basis of which it could claim sovereignty; there was no constitutional basis for a corresponding claim to "statehood" or "sovereignty" for Croatia's Serbs. Croatia could define its right within fixed borders, as would later be conceded by the international community.

As for the proportions of populations of those parts of Croatia now contested by Serbia, the following figures (according to the census of 1981) relate to the proportions of Serbs in each district: Knin 79 per cent, Gračac 72 per cent, Donji Lapac 91 per cent, but Benkovac only 53 per cent, and even Obrovac only 60 per cent. For Banija, the following data were provided: Glina 57 per cent, Kostajnica 56 per cent, and Dvor na Uni 81 per cent; Petrinja, on the other hand, had a slight Croatian majority. In west Slavonia, one could tally 38 per cent Serbs in Pakrac and 30 per cent in Daruvar.[66] Across from the Croatian Krajina in Bosnia there was a nearly compact Muslim enclave around the town of Bihać; Muslims accounted for 61 per cent of the population of the community of Bihać, 88 per cent of that of Velika Kladuša, 97 per cent in Cazin, and 68 per cent in Bosanska Krupa.[67] Bosanska Krupa would later be claimed by the Serbs, as if the legitimacy of their title were beyond question.

In spite of the now definitive and successful uprising of the Serbs in and around Knin, there would still have been some maneuvering room for Croatian policy in the Serbian question, even now. This fact was borne out in the course of my visit to Dvor na Uni, in Banija, at the beginning of February 1991.[68] Some time earlier Croatian special police had restored order there; moreover, the highest Croatian court had declared illegal the institutional form of communal associations which had been common under the old regime and which the Serbs had used as their vehicle for declaring autonomy. There was a lot of uncertainty among the Serbian district authorities, the more so because the situation on the other side of the border in Bosnia was still unclear; even the army was apparently not yet ready to get involved. The local Serbian representatives based themselves above all on the new, previously ratified Croatian constitution, and said that they wanted to be a "constituent factor" of the Croatian state and not a minority. They were not ruling out a compromise. I relayed this to President Tudjman the following day, together with the inference that the Serbs in those districts certainly could not all be won over by some merely formal concessions, but at least they could be divided. Mesić, who was also present for this conversation, shared such thoughts. But

Tudjman rejected all these considerations and would only repeat in a strained voice that the Serbs should finally comprehend that they were a minority.

Slovenia and Croatia choose independence

Since, after the free votes in early 1990, Slovenia and Croatia were exposed to the same barbed attacks from Serbia's state leadership and the army, it was logical that they would try to engage in close cooperation. The leaderships of both republics had spoken out in favor of the transformation of Yugoslavia into a confederation of independent states. After intensive discussions they presented a common proposal to this effect at the beginning of October 1990.

According to this proposal,[69] which offered a variety of solutions, the Yugoslav republics were the subjects of international law; there would not be a central government or even a capital city. There would, on the other hand, be a common market and a kind of monetary union. Slovenia and Croatia took for their model the example of the European Community; the preamble referred directly to this. The two republics submitted their proposal to the other republics and to the state presidency. In formal terms they based their step on the announcement by the Yugoslav state presidency in June that it wished to undertake a dialogue concerning a new political order for Yugoslavia.

In spite of common interests, some distance developed in the relationship between Slovenia and Croatia. In Ljubljana, there was no desire for a lasting link with Croatia; if Yugoslavia collapsed, then Slovenia wanted to be an independent state.[70] Slovenes did not want anything more to do with the Balkans, to which Croatia, with its many tangled issues, still very much belonged. Croatia, on the other hand, calculated that it could not escape as easily as Slovenia from those "Balkan entanglements".[71] There had never been warm feelings for Slovenia in Croatia. There were differences in mentality. While Croatian politicians immersed themselves in symbolic politics, unveiling monuments to historical figures and celebrating the role of Croatia in Europe, Slovenian politicians were absorbed with more practical concerns. In Croatia, where preparations for independence were deferred to the last minute, the break between the old and the new regime was abrupt; in Slovenia, on the other hand, thanks not least to Kučan, the transition was smooth. Slovenia was compact as a state and as a nation, while Croatia was often divided in various ways.

The Slovenian-Croatian proposal for a confederation, instead of being accepted as at least a basis for discussion, ended up as grist for the mill in Jović's machinations. On 10 October 1990, Jović set before the state presidency a Serbian counterproposal for an "efficacious federation" (*efikasna federacija*). That was his right, but then he allowed the state presidency to decide by majority vote that only the Serbian proposal would be presented to the Yugoslav *Skupština*, and not the previously drafted Slovenian-Croatian proposal. This excited energetic protests in the two affected republics. In addition to all that, Jović wanted, through various manipulations, to prevent the installation of Stipe Mesić as Šuvar's replacement in the state presidency; Mesić had been elected to this post by the Croatian *Sabor*. Here Jović stood on weak ground, for according to Article 321 the members of the highest organ of state were "elected" exclusively in the republics they were to represent and only "announced" by the federal parliament. On the occasion of Mesić's election to serve as chair of the state presidency seven months later, the situation was somewhat different.

Both the sessions of the state presidency in regard to constitutional reform and those in the *Skupština* were fruitless; officials in Zagreb and Ljubljana reacted by declaring that now even the chance of saving Yugoslavia by means of a confederal solution had been squandered. Prime Minister Marković tried to rescue the day by suggesting that a vote concerning both proposals be taken only when unified and free elections were held throughout the country (i.e., not merely on a republic basis).[72] The western republics retorted that such elections did not enter into consideration. All of this was played out against the background of the uprising of Serbs in Croatia and the events in Kosovo.

What the army did next by way of an additional provocation seems almost absurd. With a decision of the republic's presidential council on 17 July 1990,[73] Slovenia had decided to place the TO almost entirely under its own authority. This de facto situation was given a legal basis at the end of September, at which time Commander Hočevar, who was loyal to the JNA, was formally relieved of his duties and Reserve Major Janez Slapar was placed in charge of the Slovenian TO. As a result of the new constitutional amendments the Territorial Defense was now officially the armed defense force of the Republic of Slovenia. This provoked angry protests from the army, which claimed that the Slovenian TO was still subordinated to the Fifth Army District in Zagreb. The Slovenian presidential council reacted by taking certain precautions.[74] Then during the night of 4/5 October 1990, sixteen military police took control of the old headquarters building of the Slovenian TO in downtown Ljubljana in a "surprise attack"; but the Slovenian command structure had moved out the day before and was now ensconced in the neighboring Defense Ministry. Meanwhile, outraged citizens gathered in front of the building and began to demonstrate, but Defense Minister Janša told the crowd that the building belonged to the army anyway and that the military police could stay there as long as they liked.[75]

In November 1990, it seemed to dawn on the generals that they could lose their hides if they did not regain a place in the political structures of Yugoslavia. With the disintegration of the LCY, they had lost their institutional base within the power structure. To that one should add the events in the Soviet Union which completely confused the generals and even awakened messianic impulses in some of them. Around the middle of November 1990, Kadijević called the most important generals to two conferences – the first in Belgrade, the second in Niš[76] – and explained to them that the Yugoslav Army was, at the time, the only force in the eastern part of Europe which still defended socialism. Gorbachev was a traitor; he had turned Eastern Europe over to NATO. It was the duty of the Yugoslav Army to defend not merely Yugoslavia, but socialism itself. At the second conference in Niš, the question was discussed as to which circles in Slovenia and Croatia one could turn in order to reverse the process of democratization.

As these conferences were taking place, the army leadership had already laid the foundation stone for its return to politics. On 4 November 1990, an "army party" was established in Belgrade's Sava Center, under the name "League of Communists–Movement for Yugoslavia".[77] Among the prominent founding members were both active and retired officers, such as former Defense Minister Mamula as well as many politicians who operated on the basis of dogmatic positions. The earlier Chief-of-Staff Stevan Mirković, former Chief-of-Staff and then Interior Minister Gračanin, and Admiral Brovet could be seen alongside Kadijević himself. From the ranks of politicians one found, among others, Lazar Mojsov, Raif Dizdarević, and Momir Bulatović. The most prominent participant was Milošević's wife, Mirjana Marković. Milošević wanted thereby to demonstrate his affinity for the army once again.

Politically emboldened by their conferences, the generals moved once more to attack. The target of attack would be those armed units which had been removed from the control of the army – in Slovenia taking the form of the Territorial Defense, and in Croatia primarily taking the form of the new police force, for which Croatian authorities were procuring weapons abroad, after the army had denied them access to their own arms factories.[78] Around mid-November 1990, the Commander of the Fifth Army District in Zagreb sent a letter to the Slovenian presidency, demanding that all weapons of the TO be surrendered to the army by 28 November. This demand was immediately rejected, with the comment that such questions did not lie within the competence of the Fifth Army Corps, but within that of the Yugoslav state presidency.[79] Yet for all that, there was a certain concern in Slovenia. The Slovenian government made contact with its counterpart in Zagreb and the republic presidency decided on 5 December 1990 to have the police carefully monitor all troop movements and to counter any attempts to disturb the building-up of the TO.[80] Apprehension grew as a result of reports about Soviet measures in Lithuania.

In reality, as Ante Marković's press secretary believably reports in his book,[81] in autumn 1990 weapons began to be delivered to Slovenia and Croatia, at first by ship and then, in abundance, across Hungary, until Hungarian Prime Minister Antall forbade the shipments. The army could monitor these transports, above all in Croatia, whose authorities, by contrast with those in Slovenia, allowed agents of the army's intelligence service, the KOS, considerable freedom of movement. On 11 December 1990, according to Kadijević's account,[82] the Yugoslav Defense Ministry submitted for the state presidency's attention a report concerning the allegedly "unauthorized establishment of armed formations". By this expression only the Slovenian TO and the supplementary Croatian police forces were meant, and not those armed groups whom the Croatian media called "Chetniks", which were active in the insurgent Serbian districts.

With these political machinations in autumn 1990, the army became a direct party to the conflict. Since noncommunist forces had been elected in democratic elections in two republics of the land, the army would have had to depoliticize itself in order to maintain its claim to be the guarantor of the unity of Yugoslavia. A demand to this effect was emphatically pressed on the army by Slovenia and Croatia; in the case of Slovenia, the republic presidency undertook this step at the beginning of December 1990. It was not appropriate for the army to engage itself against the proposal for the confederalization of Yugoslavia, it argued. The army leadership posed as the protector of socialism and interpreted this role not in a democratic but in a "Soviet" sense. Kadijević had exceeded his authority; the danger had arisen that the army would now interfere in civil affairs.[83] As a result, as I was told in Ljubljana by Slovenian politicians, the Republic of Slovenia was released from any obligation to regard the Yugoslav army as being any longer a constitutional institution.

In autumn the noncommunist government of Slovenia advanced the idea of organizing a referendum in which the citizens of Slovenia would be asked if they wanted a truly independent state or not; this decision was not taken in direct connection with the army's behavior, but it was not completely unrelated either. There were some considerations, including on Kučan's part,[84] which suggested that this step should not be taken. There had already been plenty of declarations, it was argued; it was therefore possible that many citizens would not bother to show up at the ballot boxes and that the notion of Slovenian independence would thereby be discredited.

In the course of the discussion, it became clear that the overwhelming majority of Slovenes felt strongly about cutting the umbilical cord to the rest of Yugoslavia. So the plebiscite was organized relatively quickly on 23 December 1990 with the question, "Should the Republic of Slovenia become a self-sufficient and independent state?" Certainly, as was expressly indicated in the law concerning the plebiscite, concrete measures should be deferred for six months, i.e., until 23 June 1991, in order to wait for the Yugoslav state presidency to take up anew its already announced discussions concerning a new political order for Yugoslavia. Most Slovenes viewed the plebiscite, none the less, as a binding decision for leaving Yugoslavia, since it was not to be expected that Serbia would change its behavior.[85] In Serbia, elections had been set for December, but it was not expected that these would change anything.

This assumption proved correct. The Serbian elections of 9 December 1990 brought a considerable victory for Milošević and his Socialist Party. Milošević garnered 64 per cent of the popular vote in the presidential race, against 17 per cent for Vuk Drašković and only 8 per cent for the candidate of Ante Marković's party. The Albanians had boycotted the elections. The Socialists as a party obtained only 50 per cent of the votes, but this result brought them a strong majority of the seats. In Montenegro, Bulatović was able to notch his victory only in the second round of voting; one could see already that Montenegrins were not prepared to follow Milošević unconditionally.[86] One may conclude that Serbia proper, influenced by the Kosovo problem, stood almost completely behind Milošević.

The Slovenian referendum, with a turnout of approximately 85 per cent, yielded a majority of 88 per cent "yes" votes. In Ljubljana there were spontaneous celebrations. A day earlier, on 22 December, the Croatian parliament, the *Sabor*, had adopted the new constitution for the republic, which, after a somewhat pompous preamble about the history of Croatia, endowed the republic with complete sovereignty. The Yugoslav state presidency had condemned the Slovenian referendum in a majority vote, and had proposed to the government and parliament that "measures" be taken to prevent it from being conducted in the first place. Jović, who as head of the Serbian "bloc" had control of four votes, could still often rely on support from either Macedonia or Bosnia to constitute a majority. And this, despite the fact that on 12 December 1990, Macedonia too had held democratic elections. The problem was, however, usually with the often undecided Bosnian representative, Bogić Bogićević. The first house of the Yugoslav parliament assembled on 18 December, to find the motion from the state presidency against the referendum in Slovenia. Although in Article 294 of the constitution it had been explicitly set forth that matters of "special interest" for one republic had to be decided on the basis of consensus, the Serbian majority held that this qualification was not valid, whereupon the Slovenian deputies left the chamber.[87]

Milošević's electoral victory led at the end of December 1990 to that grave development which has become known as "the intrusion into the monetary system of Yugoslavia" and which, for all practical purposes, brought to an end the efforts of Prime Minister Marković to consolidate the unity of the country through economic and monetary reforms. His press secretary, Predrag Tašić, describes this event, which hastened the country's fragmentation, as follows.[88] After some secret meetings arranged by Milošević, in which the Serbian representative of the Yugoslav National Bank also took part, the possibility was discussed of making available supplementary financial assistance to the severely plagued Serbian economy with its bankrupt macro-enterprises. The Serbian representative of the National Bank told Milošević that some banks in Yugoslavia had provided for some supplementary issue of currency before. But because a larger amount was involved this time, it was decided to give the issuance a legal grounding by recording it as a loan to the Republic of Serbia on the part of the National Bank. The Serbian parliament approved his arrangement in a secret vote on 28 December 1990; the loan was for 28 billion dinars or about 2 billion DM. The money was used in part for the purchase of hard currency and in part for the liquidation of the debts of Serbian enterprises.

The reaction to this Serbian action, as soon as it became known, was prompt and massive. In the first days of January 1991, representatives of Slovenia and Croatia met and announced that from 28 December 1990 they would no longer recognize any new financial obligations of the federation, including foreign loans.[89] Slovenia decided, in addition, to discontinue transfers of hard currency to Belgrade and began to consider the creation of its own currency. The collaboration of the Yugoslav National Bank in the Serbian action was considered especially grave. Slovenia would continue normal payments in dinars to the federal treasury, but customs income would in the future be withheld, i.e., balanced with financial contributions which the republic owed to the federation from its own sources, including the contributions to financing the army.[90] From Slovenia there came reproaches against Prime Minister Marković, because he did not immediately sound the alarm upon learning of the Serbian action. Tašić writes that the Prime Minister had gotten wind of the matter from an "anonymous" source on 4 January 1991. At the same time, Tašić blames the Slovenes, however, for using the affair as a pretext to open a "new front", not only against Serbia but also against the government of Prime Minister Marković.

The events of the winter of 1990/91 had effected some important changes. No one could ever nurture any hopes any longer that Yugoslavia would in future exist, if at all, as a union of six independent and equal republics. The talks concerning this new system for the country, which had been arranged by the state presidency, could not continue within the framework of this organ now; negotiations could henceforth continue only on the basis of direct contacts between the responsible leaders of the republics. At first, this was arranged by holding sessions of the state presidency in a so-called "expanded framework", i.e., in the presence of the presidents of the republics and usually also of an army representative. From March 1991, the presidents of the republics began meeting outside and independently of the state presidency; the meeting place rotated from republic to republic.[91]

The second change consisted in the fact that after his success in the elections, Milošević definitely shifted from a hegemonist Yugoslav line to a Greater Serbian line. Outwardly one could not see this at once, but it was, so to speak, on record at a Slovenian-Serbian meeting on 24 January 1991 in Belgrade, between delegations led by Kučan and Milošević. The Serbian leader showed some understanding for Slovenia's path but he said at once that Serbia continued to consider the creation of an "efficacious Yugoslav federation" feasible and, indeed, the best solution. Already with any confederative solution, Serbia would have to open the question of border changes, since otherwise Serbs would be left behind as minorities in other republics. In the published communiqué, both sides stated qualified understanding for each other's own national path, which, however, should not be pursued at the expense of third parties. The significance of this meeting has been overemphasized by certain authors, such as Laura Silber and Allan Little, who construed it as a Serbian green light to Slovenia to leave Yugoslavia. But it was not any such thing, since Milošević still had to take other important factors into account, above all the army.[92] The Croats were alarmed when Kučan briefed them during his flight back. To the question as to why these verbal concessions to the Serbian viewpoint had even been necessary, Kučan told me that he needed to take as much pressure off Slovenia as he could. In mid-February 1991 Slovenian politicians in Ljubljana repeatedly told me that there was a "new situation" in the country. Milošević was proclaiming everywhere, including in internal discussions, that he was not going to allow any Serbs to live as "minorities" in any "other state"; everywhere where Serbs lived had to be Serbia. The other nationalities were at most "welcome". Milošević seemed to take aim especially at the Muslims in Bosnia, though also at those in the Sandžak, and to want to intimidate them so that they would not lay claim to their own state. According to Slovenian information, Milošević had told Izetbegović shortly before that the Muslims could neither leave Yugoslavia nor escape from Serbian dominion; it would, hence, be better if they came to an arrangement with the Serbs and recognized their authority. Again according to Slovenian sources, Serbia wanted to try to gain as much ground as possible by 15 May, when it would lose the advantage of controlling the chairmanship of the Yugoslav state presidency. Milošević needed the army if he was going to create a Greater Serbia. On the other hand, even if they still thought primarily in Yugoslav terms, the generals had no choice in the new constellation but to recognize Milošević as the sole remaining "strong man" in Yugoslavia. More and more they allowed themselves to be harnessed for his goals, especially because Milošević could supply them also with money, as he had already shown. Jović tried, as he attests in his diary, to accelerate this shift by all available means – which was more dangerous for the Croats than for the Slovenes.

On 9 January 1991, Jović and the generals were able to extract a majority of votes in the state presidency, calling on the so-called paramilitary forces, whose disarmament had been ordered the previous November, to be "de-activated".[93] Bosnian representative Bogićević provided the Serbian bloc with the necessary "fifth vote", though he later retracted his vote, when he saw the consequences of his action.[94] The decision was targeted almost exclusively at the Croatian police reserves. On 22 January, on the basis of the same majority, the state presidency issued a supplementary admonition, in case the original order should not be obeyed. The following day, as Kadijević confirms, the headquarters of

the army commandoes threatened to mobilize its troops in the event that
Croatia did not disband these units; aside from that, those persons who
were "responsible" for these units, above all General Špegelj, were to be
brought to account through military justice.[95]

The situation was ominous. On 22 January Kučan and Tudjman met
for talks; two days earlier the defense ministers and interior ministers of
Slovenia and Croatia had also met. In case of an intervention on the part
of the army, the two republics would take the following three steps: First,
both republics would immediately declare independence. Second, there
would be no further financial contributions to the federation. Third, they
would jointly contact the UN Security Council.[96] The first threat was
particularly telling, because it would have immediately signified war, and
it is open to question whether the army, which at the time consisted
predominantly of recruits stationed in barracks, would have been able to
deal with such a situation.

The decisive confrontation was played out on the night of Friday
25 January and Saturday 26 January. Tudjman had come to Belgrade,
even though this was not without some danger for him. While participants in the expanded state presidency tried, in the course of stormy
sessions, to reach some agreement, the army prepared plans for a *coup
d'état* in Croatia.[97] At 8 p.m. Belgrade Television broadcast film in which
General Špegelj, the Croatian Minister of Defense, was "unmasked" as an
arms smuggler; then he was shown in conversation, threatening army
officers and their families with dreadful consequences in the event that
the army moved against Croatia. Špegelj later claimed that he knew he
was being taped and filmed, which was why he spoke in this way. Some
doubts, however, remained. But Bogićević refused to support the Serbian
bloc on this point and Kadijević's plans for a crackdown in Croatia died
on the table. The British and American ambassadors had also intervened.
Tudjman cleverly agreed to formally demobilize some formations of the
Republic of Croatia, and the Croatian police reserves were "deactivated".
The weapons, however, remained under Croatian control. Unflinching,
Zagreb Television showed pictures that night of petrol tankers, their tanks
full of petrol, in front of the entrances to the barracks. Špegelj was doing
what was possible.

Tudjman interpreted the result as a victory for himself, because the
verbal statement of the army leadership and the state presidency held that
Croatia had the exclusive right to attend to security on its territory.[98] On
this point, Tudjman erred. In token of the now unambiguously Greater
Serbian politics in Belgrade there were now disturbances and uprisings
not just in Knin and adjoining districts, but everywhere in Croatia where
Serbs lived, including in eastern Slavonia and western Slavonia. As the
Serbs began disturbances in Pakrac in early March, Jović entrusted
the army with the task of "mediating" between the sides. This was an
open breach of the constitution, first, because Jović was not authorized to

issue orders to the army without a formal decision by the state presidency, and second, because the army was not allowed to take action within a given republic without the approval of that republic's authorities.[99]

The worst was yet to come. On 9 March 1991, there were large-scale demonstrations against Milošević in Belgrade, in protest of the complete exclusion of the opposition from politics after the Socialist electoral victory in December. Jović contacted members of the state presidency by phone and proposed that the army be sent in against the demonstrators. He later claimed that the representatives of Macedonia and Bosnia had assented to the army intervention.[100] The army was now sent into Belgrade; instead of Albanians, Slovenes, and Croats, some ten thousand Serbs were, for a change, playing the role of enemies of the state.

The Slovenian presidential council responded with a declaration alleging that Jović had once more violated the constitution. Instead of becoming depoliticized, the army was being turned into a factor in the confrontations even within the republics.

These events flowed directly into that remarkable coup in mid-March 1991. Mesić claims that Jović and Defense Minister Kadijević had already demanded, on the occasion of the army's ostensible "mediation" in Pakrac in early March, that a state of emergency be declared, in response to the deterioration in interethnic relations throughout the country, and that Jović be granted "full powers of war".[101] Jović had come to an agreement with Admiral Brovet, who said that the Defense Ministry's proposal was grounded on the "constitutional task of the army". In the 5 March 1991 session, Jović demanded that the army be authorized to take necessary steps, at which point Mesić left the meeting, since Jović refused to offer any explanations to the Croatian representative. Drnovšek remarked that, in this way, all chances for a peaceful solution in the country would soon be lost.

After the events in Belgrade, there was a session of the state presidency on 12, 14, and 15 March 1991, at which members of the presidency were pressured to agree to a proclamation of a state of emergency and to the transfer of authority to the army. Evidently, or so one must conclude, Milošević felt sure of the army's loyalty and certain that, with the concurrence of a majority in the state presidency, he could enlist the army for his own purposes. Once again, Jović engaged in unbelievable manipulations. Mesić reports how the members of the higher state organ were, upon their arrival at the federal building in Belgrade, asked to step into army buses, so that they might be taken to the headquarters of the General Staff, where the facts could be discussed more conveniently.[102] Mesić considered this an attempt to imply a physical threat; when he asked if this signified the arrest of the state presidency, he was told that such a conjecture was utterly without foundation. Mesić was of the opinion that this entire theatrical production was being staged above all to put pressure on the Bosnian representative, Bogićević, whose vote was needed in order to obtain a majority. But as they entered, Bogićević assured Mesić that he would remain firm. Drnovšek refused to attend the session at all, under such conditions.

Kadijević's proposals were: to proclaim a state of emergency in the entire country, to place the army in a state of combat readiness, to concede all police powers to the army, and to abolish all legislative acts which were incompatible with the federal constitution.[103] According to Mesić, this was a demand for a free hand for a comprehensive attack on at least Croatia. In spite of all endeavors to exert pressure on other members of the presidency, the Serbian bloc stood alone in supporting this proposal, which failed, thus, for lack of a majority.

There had been no session arranged for the following day – which puzzled Mesić. Only later did he learn that Kadijević had flown to Moscow on that day for consultations with Minister of War Dimitry Yazov – perhaps, as Mesić speculated, to coordinate the two planned *putsches*.[104] Later, in the BBC television series broadcast in 1995, Jović revealed for the first time that he had accompanied Kadijević on the flight to Moscow. Kadijević and Jović returned to Belgrade quickly, in time for the next session, scheduled for the following day, i.e., 14 March. This session saw a sharp exchange between Kadijević and Drnovšek, who was now present. There were open threats. Now everything depended, General Adžić asserted, on satisfying the generals, as to "whether the state presidency is capable of functioning at all".[105] Jović, enraged because of the miscarriage of his plans, accused Slovenia and Croatia of promoting the "collapse of the army". Serbia would oppose this, Jović continued, and would protect Serbs living in other republics. Croatia, he claimed, was behaving contrary to constitutional principles. To that the representative of Kosovo, who had been elected by the old authorities and who would soon be removed by the Serbian parliament, said that what had been happening in Kosovo had nothing to do with the constitution either. On hearing these words, Jović, the other Serbs present, and the generals all together pounced on the Albanian. The session ended with a new threat from Kadijević, who promised that command headquarters would, in spite of the state presidency's decision, draw "conclusions" on the basis of which the army would act.[106] This threat was received as a piece of unabashed impudence. The Slovenian Republic presidency, meeting two days later, laid down that the threat was unconstitutional and that there could not be a command headquarters in peacetime.[107]

The setback in the state presidency clearly induced a temporary panic on Milošević's part. Immediately after the dispersion of the state presidency on 15 March 1991, he ordered his adherent Jović to resign as chair and member of the state presidency. On the following day, Milošević announced on Belgrade Television that in the future Serbia "would no longer recognize" the state presidency of Yugoslavia; since it had set itself on a course leading to the "disintegration of Yugoslavia" it was, according to Milošević, "for all practical purposes incapable of functioning".[108] With that, a new situation had been created. Mesić, as vice president, had not succeeded the day before in convening a new session, since Jović explained, until his resignation was accepted by the Serbian parliament, he was still the chairman and he alone was authorized to convene sessions. After Milošević's speech, however, the situation had changed once again. Five members of the state presidency could meet, and declared that there was "no institutional vacuum" in the country. Among those in attendance was the representative from Kosovo. The fact that Jović had not been able to obtain a majority for his proposals did not mean that the highest organ of state was incapable of functioning. Marković supported Mesić by declaring that the ministers of the government were at their posts and performing their duties.[109]

Even today, it is puzzling as to what impelled Milošević to take this step, which he soon had to retract. One interpretation is that Milošević simply lost his nerve because the state presidency had prevented him from employing the army at this stage for the creation of a Greater Serbia. Now he seemed to believe that he would give the army freedom of action by bringing about an "institutional vacuum".[110] Events showed, however, once again, that the army leadership was not ready to take action without a political cover. Kadijević himself writes that it would have looked like an ordinary military *putsch*, even to the outside world, and would have destroyed any legitimacy still invested in the Yugoslav federation, on which the army too depended.[111] There were no troop movements anywhere in the country that weekend. Only in Knin did local Serbs react by declaring their "independence".

Milošević had been dealt a setback. But then Tudjman suddenly showed an interest in meeting with him personally, in order to stake out the Serb-Croat relationship. Mesić reports how he had a foreboding of Tudjman's mission around mid-March and then promptly came the report from Jović that Milošević would meet with Tudjman in about 10 to 14 days.[112] From Tudjman's standpoint, the time had not been badly chosen; it depended now under which star this "historical" meeting would take place.

The two men met on 25 March 1991 in the state estate of Karadjordjevo in Serbian Vojvodina. That Tudjman had chosen this location is itself noteworthy, for it was here that, in 1971, Tito had effected the political liquidation of the "Croatian Spring". Jović had encouraged Tudjman's hopes in advance when, in response to a question by Mesić as to why the conflicts with the Serbs of the Krajina could not be resolved peacefully, he had declared that Serbia had interests in Bosnia, but not in Croatia.[113] Milošević immediately pursued this same line in Karadjordjevo. Serbia, he is reported to have said, claimed 66 per cent of the territory of Bosnia; one should not entertain any illusions on this subject. In Croatia, on the other hand, Serbia had no territorial pretensions. This was music for Tudjman's ears, insofar as he had been hoping for a partition of Bosnia so as to grant Croatia borders corresponding more or less to those of the 1939 Banovina of Croatia, and seemed now to have found, in Milošević, his "historical" partner. The two of them proceeded to agree on a partition of Bosnia, at the expense of the Muslims.[114] Actually, according to Mesić, this was tantamount to a betrayal of the Muslims, for Tudjman had, up to now, always loudly declared his desire for partnership with the Muslims of Bosnia-Herzegovina.

Mesić said that the whole business was rather dubious, because one could not assume that Milošević would collaborate in the creation of a Greater Croatia; besides he, Mesić, had been in favor of cooperation with the Muslims and against the partition of Bosnia. This was the source of Mesić's differences with Tudjman. Tudjman, for his part, returned from Karadjordjevo almost exultant; he made statements such as "I shall build such a Croatia as has never before existed." A second meeting between Tudjman and Milošević at the end of April 1991 in Tikves failed to produce any concrete result.

The basic plan and progress of the meeting at Karadjordjevo, as well as the conclusions which Tudjman drew from it, stirred early doubts about the political abilities of the Croatian president. In essence, many of the political errors which Tudjman committed later could be traced back to the "spirit of Karadjordjevo". Tudjman visibly believed Milošević's assurance that Serbia had "no interests" in the Croatian Krajina or in eastern Slavonia; this belief caused him to underestimate the threat to Croatia. Even after the conflict in Slovenia, Tudjman was saying that there would be at most a short war on Croatian territory. Karadjordjevo also laid the groundwork for Tudjman's unsuccessful policy in Bosnia. To this very day, Tudjman has not relinquished the idea of a division of Bosnia; hence, instead of allying Croatia with the Muslims, he turned against them. Of the Croats of Bosnia-Herzegovina, he accepted only the Herzegovinans, who were in fact interested neither in a unified Bosnian state nor in cooperation with the Muslims. Tudjman's opinion that at Karadjordjevo he had solved not only the problem of the integrity of Croatia but also the problem of the 750,000 Croats living in Bosnia-Herzegovina is a piece of arrant nonsense.

As concerns Marković, it should have been clear in Western capitals by this point at the latest that the Prime Minister was for all practical purposes merely being tolerated now. But as has been shown, the Western and especially the American reaction was precisely inverted. Since autumn 1990 the subventions from the republics to the federal treasury were becoming steadily more meager. Not only Slovenia but also Serbia refused any further payments. This affected also returns from the turnover tax, which, on the basis of constitutional changes in 1988, were supposed to flow directly into the army's purse. In order to prevent his prestige with the generals from sinking to the point of nullity, Marković financed the army on a makeshift basis by simply printing the money he needed. That automatically meant inflation, since the army budget comprised 90 per cent of the federal budget at the time. In order to upset Marković, Jović formed a special expert group for economic questions, reporting to the state presidency, in October 1990, which presented its report for the first time in December, making it public at the end of March 1991.[115] In this report there was nothing which Marković could not have endorsed; and besides, on many questions, the experts were themselves divided. Even so, this maneuver of Jović's constituted an affront to Marković and, de facto, a Serbian vote of "no confidence" in the Prime Minister.

In spite of his precarious position Marković registered the demand, in his "minimal program", for a revision of certain constitutional articles, in a centralist spirit. His plans were abruptly aborted. The Serbian "theft" in the monetary system did not admit of a correction. Croatia raised the demand for placing the National Bank under the control of the IMF, while Slovenia wanted to move it out of Belgrade.[116] There was no longer any point in thinking about a reform of the banking system, as Marković had had in mind. The government in Belgrade itself came under the pressure of strike actions which Milošević had contrived. In February 1991, Marković seriously considered moving the government to another city, possibly to Bled or Ohrid.[117] Over the federal police Marković exercised no control; control was in the hands of Interior Minister Gračanin, a retired general and protégé of Milošević.

Weapons deliveries from abroad to individual republics, which in the first half of 1991 were becoming more or less routine, were a special problem. Marković claimed he would not be active here, because the army refused to furnish him with the information he needed. The army leadership in turn replied that customs control was the concern of the federal government.[118] Besides, the army was likewise equipping itself with weapons under dubious conditions. Kadijević's aforementioned blitz visit to Moscow on 13 March, sandwiched between two sessions of the state presidency, resulted in the conclusion of an agreement for the delivery of $2 billion worth of weaponry, including combat helicopters, missile launchers, and tanks. Misha Glenny believes that these weapons were never actually sent, because of the failure of Yazov's *putsch* in Moscow.[119] But that is by no means certain. That the Yugoslav Army equipped itself with modern Soviet weapons in 1991 and later seems to be well-documented; as Croatian Chief-of-Staff General Anton Tus told me on several occasions,[120] new weapons and weapons systems which he, as commander of the Yugoslav Air Force, had never seen in stock before, kept appearing in battle zones. Tašić at any rate confirms weapons supplies from the Soviet Union, but claims that Marković knew nothing about it; Deputy Prime Minister Aleksandar Mitrović, who was sympathetic to Milošević, probably organized everything.[121] Earlier, Marković had concluded an agreement with the Soviets concerning the settlement of Soviet debts to Yugoslavia; the agreement, as far as is known, included a provision for weapons supplies.

Marković may have assured himself of direct access to the Yugoslav public through the establishment of his own party and through the federal television station "Jutel", at least in some areas, but in reality his influence was steadily diminishing. The Slovenian and Croatian leaders granted that he had on several occasions opposed the adventurism of the generals, even when he had had to hear from them and from Jović that the army answered to the state presidency and not to the prime minister or the government.[122] As late as May 1991, Marković tried, ostensibly relying on Western support, to launch a final centralist program, with even a proposal for general federal elections. This latest proposal of his was likewise rejected.[123]

What happened now to the "round-table talks" which the state presidency had prescribed more or less formally in January 1991 in response to the Serbian proposal for a more "efficacious federation" and to the counter-proposal from Slovenia and Croatia for Yugoslavia's transformation into a confederation? For Slovenia, it was important to sound out the opinions of the other republics; Kučan spoke about this before the Yugoslav state presidency on several occasions between 27 December 1990 and 8 February 1991. After the aforementioned meeting with Milošević (p. 162), the Slovenes conducted talks also with appropriate representatives of all the other republics. On 18 February those commissioned for this purpose by the Slovenian republic presidency presented their report, which confirmed that outside Croatia no one else was really thinking of a confederal structure and that Slovenia therefore had to think in terms of establishing a separate state existence.[124] Efforts to fashion a new Yugoslavia were pointless, the report affirmed; one could already see that the joint state had been thoroughly destabilized by Serbian behavior, while, on the other hand, the army leadership continued to espouse a centralist solution on the basis of revivified socialist concepts. In addition, practically all of the republics, Serbia among them, had declared themselves states; if there were going to be negotiations, they could only be held on the basis of this reality.

Serbia, the report continued, was uncompromisingly committed to the concept of a tight federation. Bosnia-Herzegovina still wanted in principle to hold on to a federal state, though under certain conditions: the army should be depoliticized and all human rights and the rights of the republics should be guaranteed. Bosnia would be happy to remain in such a state, even if Slovenia should leave. Macedonia, for its part – the report concluded – would gladly stay in Yugoslavia, whether it be federal or confederal. But unless all the republics stayed in the new Yugoslavia, the inter-republic balance would be destroyed and Macedonia would be forced to choose the path of independence.

Kučan summarized things at the beginning of the session, when he said that there did not exist "any real possibilities for the transformation of Yugoslavia along confederal lines, except between Croatia and Slovenia". So the only option for Slovenia was the dissolution (*razdruživanje*) of

Yugoslavia. Two days later, on 20 February 1991, the Slovenian parliament endorsed this approach.

The problem was still how one could carry out this decision. The "summit" meeting of Yugoslav presidents held in Sarajevo on 23 February 1991, within the framework of an expanded session of the state presidency, brought only an agreement that Prime Minister Marković should be allowed, after the collapse of his legislative proposals, to continue to muddle through by a pilot light. Other than that – and this was a first concession to the ineluctability of the dissolution of the joint state – an assessment should be made about the resources of the Yugoslav state. Nothing would ever come of this. Jović commented, not wrongly, that in regard to concepts for the future of Yugoslavia, the republics remained aligned according to the formula 2 : 2 : 2.[125]

For Milošević, it remained decisive to maintain the nexus with the army leadership so that the army would remain at his service. For that purpose, the army had to be given political as well as financial guarantees, and also freedom of action. Croatia and Slovenia, as also Izetbegović later in Bosnia, were quite right in believing that the officers were trying to take care of their salaries and pensions, but Milošević soon had more to offer even here. The disproportionate representation of Serbian cadres in the officer corps gave the army a pro-Serbian disposition, but, as the campaign against Slovenia would show, it had not yet made a thorough-going renunciation of Yugoslavism in favor of a purely Serbian national state. But towards Croatia, the Serbs and the army coalesced around some shared views. It was difficult for President Tudjman to comprehend this. The illusions of Karadjordjevo continued to have their effect; for example, Croatian defense preparations proceeded rather slowly. Tudjman was unable to decide on a professional military orientation; for him the war was still a matter for the police or for the party. Soon the army began to establish its field of action even without authorization from the state presidency, at first on a local basis. On 2 April 1991, the army authorities handed the Croatian security forces in Plitvice, in the middle of Croatia, an ultimatum and demanded their withdrawal.[126]

Once again, there was at least a ray of hope for a peaceful resolution of the confrontation. At the end of March 1991, there was, for the first time, a meeting in Split of the six Yugoslav presidents, only this time no longer within the framework of the state presidency. Now the real representatives of the peoples and republics spoke with each other directly and on an equal basis. On 4 April 1991, there was a further meeting in Belgrade. One could entertain objectively hopes that this new framework for negotiation might produce results. In Belgrade, there even seemed to be an agreement that there would remain some kind of "common roof", even if of a very loose form.[127] That was important, because otherwise one could not count on the voluntary consent of Serbia to the general dissolution of the state. The timing was favorable, for Milošević had not yet recovered from the demonstrations in Belgrade and his failed endeavor to proclaim a state of emergency.

What was particularly memorable about the Belgrade meeting was that it took place at the same time as a troika of EC foreign ministers visited the Yugoslav capital city for the first time. Nonetheless, they declined altogether to meet with the six presidents; they talked only with Marković, whom the presidents had already marginalized, and with Foreign Minister Budimir Lončar, who had practically no more authority left.[128]

The newly awakened hopes soon faded once more. After a further meeting in Ohrid on 18 April 1991, the Slovenian president told me, in a tone of disappointment, that Milošević had returned to the very beginning, withdrawing the concessions he had ostensibly granted earlier. Serbia and Montenegro now held that in the so-called "Yugoslav space" there could be no other sovereign state than the joint state; they therefore had no interest in discussing a "common roof". The decision to hold a general Yugoslav referendum was still honored; this decision had been taken by the presidents a week earlier in the Slovenian town of Brdo and Marković was banking on it. Kučan expressed his misgivings, in Ohrid, that the behavior of the West, which only wanted to deal with the Yugoslav federal authorities, had encouraged Milošević's return to inflexibility.[129] The Slovenes were now more or less decided on independence. Any new conditions which might be erected would have to come afterwards.

Before it reached the point of a Slovenian declaration of independence, there were the dramatic events of mid-May 1991. According to Jović's account,[130] Kadijević registered a new demand on 6 May for full freedom of action for the army, on the grounds of the events in Croatia, in response to which Jović immediately convened a session of the state presidency, at which he gave his full support to the army leadership's demand. The session began on 7 May and ended only at early dawn on 9 May. This session did not give the army and Jović entirely what they wanted, but it did entrust the army with the assignment of placing itself between the two warring sides in Croatia and affirmed the army's exclusive rights to move across the front lines; this decision would shortly prove to have serious consequences for Croatia. In this way, regions in which the Serbian insurgency had gained a foothold were secured. The decision was reached because the Bosnian representative, Bogićević, went along with it.

Encouraged by this, Kadijević presented a new plan for the proclamation of a state of emergency throughout the whole country on the same day, though Jović argues that the decision already taken by the state presidency already provided for the "military option" and that it was only a matter of putting it into effect.[131]

The question was whether the army wanted to act in this one-sided way. Here there were some differences between Milošević and the army leadership. This may have inclined Jović to make a fresh attempt to cripple the state presidency, which could possibly still have watered down the decision of 9 May. This time he was in a better position. In agreement with Milošević and the entire Serbian bloc of four votes, he hindered the legally prescribed transfer of the chairmanship to the Croatian representative, Stipe Mesić.[132]

Actually, Article 327 of the Yugoslav constitution said that the state presidency should "elect" its chairman, not just "announce" him, as was the case with ordinary new members. The Serbs justified their behavior with the argument that since Croatia wanted to become independent, it did not make any sense to elect the representative of that republic as the Head-of-State of Yugoslavia. In reality, the Croatian voters would endorse independence by a 94 per cent vote of approval only on 19 May. Tudjman said at the time that if Slovenia declared its independence, Croatia would follow. But already at this point he added the reservation that such a declaration would only initiate, not yet finalize, the process of establishing Croatia's independence.[133]

The immobilization of the state presidency encouraged the Serbian insurgency in Croatia and the activity of the army on behalf of the Serbs. Now the unrest spread in force to eastern Slavonia, where local Serbs, evidently according to plan, were immediately supported by Chetnik formations of Šešelj or Arkan; then the army intervened. There, also according to plan, abominable massacres were carried out from the beginning. It was no longer a rebellion of local Serbs, but an offensive war against the Republic of Croatia, with the clear goal of changing its borders.

One might ask oneself whether the state presidency, even if it had still functioned as of May 1991, could have provided any kind of guarantee against the aggressiveness of Serbia and the army leadership. Already in mid-March 1991, thanks to Jović's manipulations, the army could openly threaten to set itself above the civil authorities. It was hardly probable that the army would have accorded much respect to a state presidency under the leadership of Mesić, against whose republic it already considered itself at war. Those Western politicians and diplomats who, after the war in Slovenia, invested such great hopes in seeing the army once more subordinated to a "functioning civilian authority", were living in the past.

Even aside from this, the state presidency had meantime become a precarious affair. Most of the time, things depended on the uncertain vote of the Bosnian representative, Bogićević. Early in the year, Izetbegović had promised to replace this young and inexperienced Bosnian Serb who, although a man of integrity, had difficulty coping with the enormous pressure under which he was placed, with a Muslim, but the Bosnian President never acted on this intention. Moreover, from mid-May, the Serbian bloc was completely monolithic, as Milošević and Jović succeeded in removing the Kosovar delegate who had been elected by the old leadership, replacing him with a Serbian marionette, Sajda Bajramović, whose selection was ratified by the Serbian parliament. A legal action against this dubious procedure was no longer even considered. From this point in time, Croatia and Slovenia had no further chance to see any proposal of theirs approved by the state presidency. That meant, among other things, that all decisions which had been taken up to then, such as that concerning the disarming of "illegal" formations, remained in force, and the Serbs or the army could cite these decisions in self-justification.

On 6 June 1991, the presidents of Bosnia-Herzegovina and Macedonia, Izetbegović and Gligorov, presented a compromise proposal for a new arrangement in Yugoslavia, at the last "summit" meeting in Sarajevo. It was a counter-proposal to the Slovenian-Croatian confederative plan. The Bosnian-Macedonian proposal foresaw that the new Yugoslav association, like its member states, would be a legal subject – the latter naturally dependent on external recognition. Other than that, Yugoslavia should constitute a unified economic, customs and currency zone; likewise, foreign policy should be common, though the member states would enjoy the right to take independent initiatives in foreign policy. This plan was stillborn, because it offered the Serbs too little, while it went too far for the Slovenes and Croats. Probably, as Gligorov later reflected, it had been formulated too late.[134]

Marković tried to tie his ship to the mast of the Bosnian-Macedonian compromise proposal. As late as 21 June 1991, he presented an exposé in the Belgrade parliament about the "new Yugoslavia", which he now wanted to see as a community of sovereign states. He also said, to be sure, that the "realization of the constitutional right of self-determination" should be a "democratic process", not a "one-sided act".[135] Privatization occupied a prominent place in Marković's program; the Prime Minister probably wanted to make points abroad with this. The final acts of the Marković government in regard to the privatization of self-managing enterprises provided the Serbs with a mechanism for seizing all Slovenian property within their territories.

The protocols of the Slovenian republic presidency from March 1991 onward hardly speak of anything other than practical preparations for independence. The Slovenian schedule was fixed; precisely half a year after the plebiscite, independence should become a reality. On 15 May 1991, the appropriate guidelines were adopted in the republic's presidium; now, as a resolution of the presidency put it, Slovenes would "have to work intensely in all areas".[136] Future relations to the other republics would even now still be accepted in principle, but first complete independence would have to be achieved. The Slovenian parliament explicitly confirmed this in a resolution of 20 May 1991.[137] The struggle over the state presidency hardly concerned Slovenia any longer; it had significance in practical terms only for Croatia.

The Slovenian leadership was conscious that its aspirations for independence faced the resistance and even opposition of the West. In his book, Foreign Minister Rupel reported at length concerning Slovenia's efforts to win some understanding abroad for its point of view.[138] Occasionally, Rupel and Prime Minister Peterle got in each other's way; the latter often thought that he could accomplish as much through his Christian Democratic party contacts. It is superfluous to point out that the Slovenian efforts were combatted both by the Foreign Ministry in Belgrade in general, and by Yugoslav diplomats of Serbian nationality more specifically. Rupel told me how people from Belgrade tried to make his life difficult when he was in Paris in November 1990 to take part in the CSCE conference as a member of the Yugoslav delegation. When a similar formula was chosen for the CSCE conference in Berlin on 20 June 1991, a few days before independence, the Slovenian foreign minister found himself confronted with an energetic plea, on the part of Budimir Lončar, for the preservation of Yugoslavia, which he tried to rebut as far as possible in informal talks.[139] The Slovenian presidency adopted a resolution denying that Slovenia bore any responsibility for the breakup of Yugoslavia and declared that stability in the Yugoslav region could only be achieved if one "radically altered" the relations between the Yugoslav republics.[140]

Slovenia was faced with a large number of practical problems which needed to be resolved prior to independence. Since one could not count on immediate recognition, one needed to assure, at a minimum, that Slovenia's declaration of independence would not meet with outright hostility. As Slovenian politicians told me at the time, some countries had promised a "benevolent" reception, above all Austria, but also Germany and Switzerland. Others, such as Italy and the United States, held back. The confiscation of Slovenia's hard-currency assets had to be prevented; similarly, credit lines had to be kept open. It would have been highly undesirable had Western creditors decided to make Slovenia liable for the entire Yugoslav foreign debt. Slovenia let it be known that it fully acknowledged the roughly $1.7 billion in foreign debts which had been contracted in its own name; of the roughly $5 billion of general Yugoslav debts, Slovenia was prepared to accept a proportion corresponding to its share of the Yugoslav social product. That would have come to about 20 per cent or $1 billion.[141]

People in Ljubljana knew exactly from which quarters Slovenia faced the most concrete dangers, viz., from the army and from Marković. In mid-May, Slovenia stopped sending recruits to the army, inducting them instead into its Territorial Defense forces.[142] Shortly afterwards, the army in Maribor provoked the first violent incidents at the installations of the Slovenian TO, which showed quite clearly how the army leadership felt about Slovenia and its aspirations toward independence. Kučan warned at the time, in the Slovenian presidency, of the "extreme anti-Slovenian temper" in the army.[143] In contrast to Milošević, who was above all interested in Croatia and Bosnia, the army remained absolutely unprepared to allow Slovenia to go its own way.

Marković was likewise interested in the preservation of Yugoslavia; for him, the borders and above all the customs borders stood in the foreground;

he, or rather the government, had jurisdiction over these. The Slovenes, in their legalistic way of working, had early on made the question of duties a symbol of sovereignty. Discussion went back and forth on this question. The fact is that already in May there was talk of a plan to take control of Slovenia's borders with the West, with the help of the army, and to cut the republic off from all external connections.[144] Marković succeeded in placing the question of borders and customs in the foreground also in the eyes of the West. Kučan told me in summer 1991 about the conversation which he had had with the American Secretary of State James Baker on 21 June 1991.[145] Baker's press secretary Margaret Tutwiler was holding a notepad in front of him, on which were written the words "Ask him about customs." Finally, Baker took up this point and asked Kučan how he imagined the question of customs might be resolved after the proclamation of Slovenian independence. Kučan replied that naturally Slovenia would take border controls and customs into its own hands. To this Baker shouted, "This is impossible!" Kučan asked him how he, the American Secretary of State, imagined state independence. Indeed, even American independence had begun with the question of customs. Besides, Kučan assured him, nothing much would change at the borders; up to now, the Slovenian police had monitored the borders, albeit under federal authority.

There remained the problem of the synchronization of Slovenia's declaration of independence with Croatia. There had always been contacts on the highest level. In March or April 1991, the defense and interior ministers of the two republics met for the purpose of coordinating preparations for defense. Croatian Defense Minister Špegelj says that common plans were developed; Špegelj even worked on plans for a common defense of Slovenia, Croatia, and Bosnia-Herzegovina.[146] For "well-known reasons", according to Špegelj, a common defense did not come about. By these "well-known reasons", Špegelj means the decisions, or lack of decisions, by Tudjman.

On 15 June 1991, the leading politicians of Slovenia and Croatia met in order to set down common political and military procedures. The Slovenes heard Tudjman tell them that Croatia would depart Yugoslavia "simultaneously" with Slovenia, but they had to recognize that the Croats had done very little by way of real preparations.[147] Kučan later said that the Slovenian representatives returned from Zagreb in a state of uneasiness, though they were of one mind that the plans should not be changed any more. But it was clear to them that Tudjman could neither take control of Croatia's borders nor break away militarily.

The situation was also bad in terms of the passage of necessary laws. Tudjman had said that Croatia would issue the necessary ordinances, but then Croatian Prime Minister Gregurić had corrected him, by pointing out that these laws were largely "in the freezer". The Slovenian representative stared in disbelief, as Rupel reports.[148] For Tudjman, the declaration of independence, which was planned for 25 June 1991, figured above all as a "declarative act". Besides, Tudjman was not pleased that the legalistically-oriented Slovenes wanted to set up customs stations also along the border with Croatia.

On Saturday 22 June 1991, Kučan and Tudjman had another meeting, but there was nothing new to report. Tudjman's marked reluctance to commit himself to the defense pact with Slovenia signified moreover that the Slovenes would also have to reckon with three army corps standing just beyond their borders, in Varaždin, Zagreb, and Rijeka. Later, some Croats would say that the Slovenes wanted to proceed too hastily. But the Slovenes' timetable had been fixed for a long time; they just refused to change it.

Almost exactly six months after the plebiscite, on the evening of 25 June 1991, the Slovenian parliament convened in a joint session to adopt a "declaration of independence" and two accompanying documents. The newspaper *Delo* published the resolutions the next day under the headline, "After 1,000 Years of German Overlordship and 73 Years in Yugoslavia, Slovenia is Independent."[149] Likewise on the evening of 25 June, the Croatian *Sabor* adopted its "declaration concerning the establishment of a sovereign and independent Republic of Croatia", together with corresponding constitutional documents.[150] It has been debated frequently as to whether this Croatian declaration actually was tantamount to a declaration of independence in legal terms, or whether it signified merely an empowerment for that purpose; this question was even discussed in the Slovenian presidency.[151] Events would show that it was in fact an irretrievable declaration of independence.

The next evening, on 26 June 1991, there was a great celebration in Ljubljana, first in the parliament and then on the main square. The next morning brought war. This has been described in detail in many places.[152] The preprepared defense plans clearly proved themselves. The four young ministers – Janša for defense, Bavčar for the interior, Kacin for information, and Rupel for foreign policy – proved themselves, as did also the entire government under Peterle's leadership. Their activities were energetically and purposefully coordinated by Kučan. Rupel, who later fell out with Kučan, admits that without Kučan's "energy and steady coordinative work", things might not have been so easy,[153] while Janša concedes at least that there was a "common exertion".[154] Parliamentary president France Bučar also played a significant role, alongside others.

The military operations followed the same plan everywhere. On the first day the army formations marched in the direction of the frontier, on the second day they became enmeshed in the net of the Slovenian Territorial Defense forces, and on the third day they had to give up for the most part, while most of their barracks remained blocked. There was only one moment during the whole confrontation when the Slovenian leadership felt a certain nervousness. That was on 1/2 July, when the army began to conduct aerial attacks against Slovenian targets, such as television stations and communications centers. The Slovenes possessed no weapons with which to defend themselves against high-flying aircraft. Moreover, the passivity of the Croats became noticeable.[155]

How did the army intervention come about? Without question, it had its origin with Prime Minister Marković who, as his press chief Tašić writes, wanted to "discipline" Slovenia, to set a precedent for other "disobedient" republics.[156] This seems highhanded, for Marković could not dare to try anything similar with the other republics, least of all with Serbia. But Marković really thought of himself now as the saviour of Yugoslavia.

During the night of 25/26 June the government adopted two decisions on Marković's initiative, the first of which was a declaration characterizing the independence of Slovenia and Croatia as "illegal" and "contrary to the constitution"; the government, it declared, had taken "measures" to restore the "normal functioning of the state" and to make possible the "security of the existing state and internal borders", as well as the "fulfillment of the international obligations of the state". In a second "decision", the government spelled out what was entailed in the aforementioned "measures". Here one finds the following sentence at the end: "The federal Ministry of the Interior and the federal Ministry of Defense will carry out this decree."[157]

This was clearly and incontestably an order to the army to secure the borders. The army leadership had often claimed before that it stood under the state presidency and not under the Prime Minister or his government. But now the army was quite happy to act on the basis of a warrant from Marković's government.

The army's actions were, in reality, directed largely against the border crossings. This included also Brnik airport at Ljubljana. It was against this target that the only truly dangerous army unit in Slovenia (which had been stationed in Vrhnika) was sent; it consisted almost entirely of professional Serbian soldiers from the tank brigade. Later, this unit would be transported through Croatia to Banja Luka, on a Croatian train, and it took part shortly thereafter in the attack on Croatian western Slavonia.

Kučan told me at the time that while the army wanted to take control of the borders, it was not motivated in this operation by any desire to restore the "normal functioning of the border crossings", as Marković's decree had prescribed. According to army orders which were intercepted, all border crossings were to be closed, with eight exceptions. Then the army had planned to push forward against Ljubljana from all sides, to remove the Slovenian leadership, to arrest the originators of the independent course, and to install a new leadership which would have allowed itself to be incorporated into a Serb-led Yugoslavia which would be socialist according to the army's concept.

Marković would later often claim that he had authorized a military response, but not in the form it took. The Slovenian politicians, including Kučan, were always of the opinion that while it was true that Marković had authorized the start of the shooting, the army had later taken this "assignment" into its own hands. But it is hard to determine just where Marković's plan, to occupy the borders, ended and where the army's own plan began. In the view of both Kučan and Kacin, the army leadership appeared to believe that it could intimidate the Slovenes with a mere show of power. Then the Slovenes would no doubt free themselves of their "disloyal" leadership. It is difficult to comprehend how the army could have subscribed to so utterly false an assessment of the situation in Slovenia, since it had the resources of its intelligence service, the KOS, at its disposal.[158] Tasić thinks that the army may have been in a state of frenzy, seized by an obsession with exacting revenge against Slovenia.[159] This frenzy would prove expensive.

One keeps hearing the argument, above all in the West, that the army could "easily" have defeated Slovenia, had it found the will and waged war "correctly". Laura Silber and Allan Little speak of a "phoney war" and even claim that the Slovenes declared war on the army, rather than the other way around.[160] This stance can be traced to the already cited misinterpretation of the Kučan-Milošević meeting of January 1991. Warren Zimmermann, the last American ambassador in Yugoslavia, claims that the army committed only 2,000 troops to the campaign in Slovenia.[161] A similar figure can be found in Silber and Little's book, although there the figure relates to a single operation.[162] In general, one finds several rather incomprehensible political judgments in Zimmermann's memoirs, in regard to both Slovenia and the rest of Yugoslavia. For example, he characterizes Slovenia's behavior as "selfish",[163] without specifying the reasons which led the Slovenes to despair of Yugoslavia. Slovenian Defense Minister Janša says that the army had 22,000 men stationed in Slovenia "on the day of aggression". Of this number, 2,000 retreated across the border with their equipment, 8,000 were captured, and 12,000 remained at large, until their departure by agreement.[164]

The army's defeat in Slovenia is easy to explain: viz., as long as it wanted to comport itself as a *Yugoslav* army, it had to respect the laws of the federation and had no possibility of waging war "properly". Indicative of the army's attitude is the fact that until the collapse of the SFRY, it avoided acting without a political cover. Its units consisted, with few exceptions, of recruits of all nationalities. General Špegelj writes that in 1990, when he led the Fifth Army District, 30 per cent of his soldiers were Albanians, 20 per cent were Croats, 8 per cent Slovenes, and 10 per cent Muslims; Serbs and Montenegrins comprised only 15 to 20 per cent of recruits stationed in his area of command.[165] It was not possible for the army to mobilize Serbian reserves in greater numbers prior to the outbreak of fighting; it is also questionable whether they could have been transferred to Slovenia. The then-Information Minister Kacin, later Slovenian Defense Minister, told me in April 1991 that Slovenia would prevent the transfer of any new troops into the republic. The army leadership would have had to risk an open conflict over this question, and was not able to take the political risk. Špegelj's successor was the Slovenian General Konrad Kolšek, whose bark was – probably quite deliberately – worse than his bite. A few days after the commencement of hostilities the army leadership replaced Kolšek with Serbian General Života Avramović, who was regarded as "tough". But, as time would tell, this had little effect.

The tactic of the Slovenian Territorial Defense was suited to the army's situation and therefore successful. The Slovenes too did not bring to bear their entire available military strength. Had the army leadership augmented its troop strength by drawing in units stationed in western Croatia, that part of Croatia would have been largely stripped of JNA troops, and, in that case, Tudjman's cautious reserve might have given way to Špegelj's offensive strategy. Kadijević himself writes that in order to have defeated Slovenia, he would have needed two new infantry brigades, a parachute brigade, and significant aerial forces.[166] He does not say, however, where he could have obtained these. On the contrary, he writes that even after such a "victory" it would have been impossible to keep Slovenia in Yugoslavia for long.

The different points of departure of the army leadership and the Serbian leadership played a role throughout the short Slovenian war. Jović provides a sharp account of how he wanted to divert the army's attention away from Slovenia and focus it in Croatia's direction. But the generals were "intoxicated by Yugoslav unity", he says, and Kadijević told everyone, completely in earnest, that he could save Yugoslavia, together with Marković. The army was "vanquished and beaten" in Slovenia. But in spite of the unpopularity of the Slovenian campaign among most Serbs and its irrelevance for Serbia's political goals, it was only after the army's defeat there that Milošević could intervene and provide political cover for the army's withdrawal.

6 Unwanted independence – the fate of Macedonia and Bosnia-Herzegovina

Macedonia

The Tenth Congress of the League of Communists of Macedonia took place in Skopje, 26–28 November 1989. The old dogmatic party leadership, which had held to a largely pro-Serbian course, was voted out of office at this congress. The new Macedonian party chief was Petar Gošev, a younger man trained in economics, who had served as a functionary in the trade union movement. Even if some of the old functionaries continued in office, especially in the federal organs, the dominance of the old Lazar Koliševski and his people was, with this outcome, at an end. With this, Macedonia joined the reformist camp in Yugoslavia; indeed, Macedonia would soon find itself on a confrontation course with Milošević.

In Skopje one could hear opinions to the effect that the changeover, especially as regards the attitude toward Milošević, had already been in preparation earlier, under the old leadership. An earlier member of the Macedonian CC Secretariat,[1] for example, holds that after the first skirmishes over the return of Serbian colonists, the next most provocative inducement to a change of course in Macedonia was Milošević's speech on the Field of the Blackbirds on 28 June 1989. Milošević's expostulations on certain aspects of Serbian history in regard to the southern regions of the then-Yugoslav state and in regard to the necessity of further "battles", including armed combat, provoked alarm in Skopje. The Macedonians demanded an "explanation". A few days later, Milošević came to Skopje for a visit, heading a Serbian delegation. The talks with him proved disappointing for the Macedonians. The Serbian leader behaved arrogantly and did not want to talk at all about certain Macedonian desiderata, such as a return of the Monastery of Prohor Pčinski, which was important for modern Macedonian national consciousness but which, as a result of an inadvertent decision taken after the Second World War, when the inter-republican borders were being drawn, had been assigned to Serbia. His behavior awakened the suspicion that Milošević also wanted to include Macedonia, which Serbs had called "south Serbia" in the interwar period, among "Serbian" territories.

In any case, it was largely fear of Milošević's aggressiveness which pushed Macedonia in the direction of democracy and independence in autumn 1989. Even before the end of the year, alternative political associations were given the green light to organize in Macedonia; as early as spring 1990, these "associations" constituted themselves as parties. On 24 September 1990, the parliament in Skopje, the *Sobranje*, decided to hold free elections, which took place on 11 November 1990. The leading forces united behind a reform-oriented leadership, in which the oft-recalled Kiro Gligorov was now summoned to serve as head of state. He was elected president by a large majority in the parliament on 17 January 1991. This was followed by the installation of the first freely elected government, under Professor of Economics Nikola Kljušev. Shortly thereafter, it was decided to strike the word "socialist" from the official name of the republic. The former communist party, which had already begun to refer to itself as the "Party of Democratic Transformation", changed its name to the "Social Democratic Union of Macedonia" on 20 April 1991, still under Gošev's leadership. This was followed, on 8 September, by a referendum on the establishment of "a sovereign and independent state of Macedonia, with the right to adhere to a league of sovereign states of Yugoslavia". On 20 November 1991, the new constitution was proclaimed; in practical terms, the proclamation was equivalent to a declaration of independence.

Macedonia has about two million inhabitants, of whom Albanians comprise 22.9 per cent, according to official statistics from 1994. Macedonia has experienced dramatic changes in the course of its history and the "Macedonian question" has often been the focus of European politics. Even today the Macedonian conflict continues to simmer. All the sides involved exploit historical myths, beginning with Philip of Macedonia and Alexander the Great.

That the Macedonians of antiquity were related to the Greeks, even if with an intermixture of Illyrian elements, is hardly disputed. But that this Hellenic relationship was not entirely unproblematic is shown in the Third Philippic of Demosthenes, where he writes that Philip of Macedonia " . . . is not only not a Greek but has nothing to do with Greeks, not even a barbarian from a country one can name with respect, but a scoundrel from Macedonia, where one earlier could not even buy a usable slave".[2] This citation shows, at a minimum, that in their exclusive claim to the Macedonian name, the Greeks could not base their assertions terribly strictly on documents from antiquity.

Shortly before 600 CE, the Slavs began to stream into the southern Balkans and, in most of Macedonia, displaced the culture of antiquity. The Slavic Macedonians of today claim that the Slavic apostles Cyril and Methodius used their language, the "Macedonian" language, to bring Christianity to the Slavs. What is correct is that both of the apostles, who were Greeks from Salonika, used the Slavic dialect found in the vicinity of their city and created from that basis a new written language, later known as Old Church Slavonic. The script which they used was Glagolitic, which was largely the invention of the two brothers. Only later, in the first Bulgarian Empire, was it transformed into the more comprehensible Cyrillic alphabet, which is closer to Greek. Some disciples of Methodius fled after being expelled from Moravia to the Bulgarian Empire, and established a significant cultural center in Ohrid, which today is claimed both by the Bulgarians and by the Macedonians in whose land it lies.

The character of the short-lived empire of Tsar Samuil *c.* 1000 is contested. One will probably be inclined to agree with Georg Ostrogorsky,[3] that this was a west Bulgarian rump-state, which was able to survive for a time after the Byzantines had smashed the first Bulgarian Empire. As if to make the confusion complete, it is also mentioned that the Byzantine emperor who wiped out Samuil's empire, known as Basileios II "the Bulgarian-slayer", came from a Byzantine dynasty which was called "Macedonian" at the time.[4]

In spite of all the ambiguity, until most recent times the whole history of the Slavic Macedonians was treated as nothing other than a part of Bulgarian history. Observers considered contemporary Macedonia to be "western Bulgaria" and its neighbors, above all the Greeks, spoke of the people living there as "Bulgarians". One can conclude that the label and assignment were taken over by those concerned. The short period of Serbian rule left few traces. The archbishopric of Ohrid figured, throughout the late Byzantine period and also in Turkish times, for the most part, not as a center of a specific local culture, but as a center of Byzantinization, and later of Greek ecclesiastical authority. The Turks were relatively unconcerned with the ethnic or linguistic characteristics of their subjects, placing their emphasis on religion. Most Christians in the Balkans were, as far as possible, subordinated to the Greek patriarch in Constantinople, whom the Turks held under tight control. As a result, the Orthodox Christians in Turkish times were subordinated to the Ottomans in secular affairs and to the Greeks in ecclesiastical and cultural affairs.

Most authors who concern themselves with the Macedonian question have obvious difficulties specifying the exact point in time when one can speak of the emergence of a truly "Macedonian" identity. One has to keep in mind that, in most cases, nation-building is a protracted process and that the concept of nation is multifarious. Political and constitutional elements, above all elements of consciousness, have as much relevance for nationhood as do language or ethnicity. The three-volume work, *History of the Macedonian People,*[5] which was published in Skopje at the end of the 1960s and tried to construct a "Macedonian" line of development practically from the time of antiquity, is today characterized by Macedonian intellectuals themselves as an "enthusiastic exaggeration". In autumn 1994, I had conversations with Macedonian intellectuals in Skopje, in which I tried again to collect some impressions about the emergence of Macedonian identity and, more particularly, of a national consciousness, but I received the answer that this question was "complex" and obscured by the fact that the Macedonian liberation movements, in their beginnings and even later, had all been socialist; consequently the national character of the Macedonian emancipation movement was long in the shadows.

Even the attempt by Elisabeth Barker[6] to locate the beginning of the Macedonian national movement in the struggle over the establishment of an autocephalous Bulgarian Exarchate during the years 1860–70 is not very convincing. This struggle was conducted exclusively in the Bulgarian name and aimed at the abolition of the Greek "ecclesiastical yoke". Macedonian historians and intellectuals often try to claim that this struggle was conducted in the name of Bulgaria only because no other name was at their disposal. But if the people of Macedonia had really felt a need for another name than the Bulgarian, they would surely have found one.

What one can say is that the struggle concerning the Bulgarian Exarchate marked the beginning of political activity in the Slav-inhabited part of Macedonia. One must then date the inception of a separate Macedonian identity to 1878, when the Congress of Berlin ordained that the area of Macedonia, including the so-called Pirin Macedonia, would remain part of the Ottoman Empire and that its Slavic inhabitants would not be allowed to conjoin their lands with either (or both) of the two Bulgarian states created by that Congress. The Congress of Berlin did prescribe certain "reforms" for Macedonia, out of which there developed a specific political fate, specific interests, and, finally, a political identity. All the inhabitants of Macedonia, with the exception of the Turks, wanted autonomy at least.

The entire area which was called "Macedonia" after the Congress of Berlin and which entered European political and diplomatic history under this name, was defined in purely geographic terms. It embraced all districts which were left to Turkey, and which could be described as Salonika's greater drainage area. It included, in any event, the entire region of today's Republic of Macedonia, with its capital at Skopje. The Macedonian area had a multiethnic composition. The purely geographic concept of Macedonia would be championed by the Greek side after the Second World War and the efforts of the Yugoslav republic of Macedonia and of its Slavic population to constitute itself as a state and as a nation under the Macedonian name were opposed by the Greek government.

In the 1960s, Greece made only sparing use of the Macedonian name in referring to its northern territories; for the most part, reference was made to "northern Greece" or to "the Greek North". The Greek side seemed to fear even the appearance of a Macedonian *regional* identity. Today, on the other hand, everything north of Mt Olympus is called "Macedonia" or "Macedonian" by the Greeks. The Greeks insist nowadays that they have an exclusive right to the name "Macedonia", in defiance of the historical record. History shows, however, that the contemporary Republic of Macedonia can, at the very minimum, lay claim to an equal "joint ownership" of that Macedonian identity.

Two things characterized the situation created by the continued
Ottoman rule in the Macedonian area between 1878 and the Balkan Wars
of 1912–13. First, the "reforms" promised by the Great Powers were never
carried out, and second, the Macedonian area was subjected to intense
cultural and political propaganda from all three neighboring states, i.e.,
Bulgaria, Greece, and Serbia. In 1883, a movement was formed in Salonika
in reaction to both of these factors, a movement about which a great deal
of fuss has been made: the VMRO or, as it is better known, the IMRO,
as an acronym for "Internal Macedonian Revolutionary Organization".
This organization did not want to be dependent on any of the neighboring
states and declared as its goal the autonomy or even self-determination of
the entire area known as Macedonia. Its slogan was "Macedonia for the
Macedonians". Its politically most capable leader was Goče Delčev, who
was murdered in 1903; today both Macedonians and Bulgarians claim
Delčev as their own.

This is not the place to trace the story of this organization, which
frequently split only to reunite, which sometimes had its headquarters in
the region and sometimes in Bulgaria or even elsewhere, and which
engaged in often purely terroristic activities. For my purposes, what is
essential is to identify its program. In the first place, IMRO was against
Turkish rule. Second, it tried to hold back Serbian and Greek influence.
Third, it constituted above all Slavic Macedonians. IMRO's attitude vis-
à-vis Bulgaria was more ambiguous, as was its attitude concerning which
other nationalities it still wanted to attract. Bulgaria provided armed
support, but there was a fraction of IMRO which did not want anything
to do with an annexation to Bulgaria. IMRO did not have a clear national
point of view; one therefore cannot say that Macedonian national feeling
was created in the Ilinden Uprising of 1903, which was the work of that
organization.

As for the Balkan Wars of 1912–13, IMRO's attitude was "Macedonian"
from the beginning, in the sense that its adherents viewed the wars not
as "liberation" for them but as entailing the partition of Macedonia. The
champions of the new Macedonian nationalism retain this interpretation
down to today and repeat it at every opportunity, as they did also at
jubilee celebrations under the Yugoslav communist regime. Even the
Albanians of Macedonia adhere to this "rejection front", claiming, not
entirely incorrectly, that with each earlier "liberation", they were merely
thrown out of the frying pan and into the fire.[7]

Of the three parts of Macedonia carved up in the course of the Balkan
Wars, that part annexed by Greece was to experience the most radical
ethnic changes. Immediately after the annexation of the new northern
districts, the Greeks began trying to either hellenize the local inhabitants
or drive them to emigrate. This effort was directed not only against the
Slavs but also, and above all, against the Turks and, in Epirus, against
the Muslim Albanians. The population movements in the Bulgarian-Greek-

Turkish corner began in 1913 and 1914.[8] The Peace Treaty of Neuilly called for a "voluntary" population exchange. The expulsion of about a million Greeks from Asia Minor to Greece followed in 1923; of this number, about half settled in Macedonia and Thrace. After 1923, another 53,000 "Bulgarians" left Greece, this time principally from the area east of Vardar. Stephen Ladas reports, none the less, stiff resistance to the forced emigration of the Slavic population of Macedonia to Bulgaria, above all in the districts west of Vardar.[9]

In 1924 this west Macedonian Slavic population in Greece paradoxically received support from Yugoslavia for its desire to remain there. After an agreement signed between Bulgaria and Greece, the so-called Kalvov-Politis protocol, all the Slavs in Greece were supposed to be defined as "Bulgarians", no doubt with an eye to further population exchanges. Yugoslavia's foreign minister at the time declared that his country could not accept that the same people could be defined as "Bulgarians" south of the border, while they were "Serbs" in Yugoslavia. Nothing came of the protocol,[10] and the Slavic population was able to remain in western Macedonia. At the census of 1928, the only Greek census in which the number of Slav inhabitants was openly reported, some 82,000 "Bulgarians" were still counted.[11]

It seems that open stirrings of Macedonian nationalism in the interwar period took place above all in the Yugoslav portion of Macedonia, Vardar Macedonia. The Macedonians were being classified there as "Serbs" – which pleased them a lot less than being classified as Bulgarians. In interwar Yugoslavia, direct pressure was exerted on the Macedonian population.

The communists had a following among the young intellectuals of Macedonia. That had some significance for the later development of the Macedonian question. A group of Macedonian communists and IMRO people began to publish the journal *Féderation Balcanique* in Vienna, in 1924, with Comintern support; the journal advocated an independent Macedonia as part of a greater Balkan federation. The notion of neutralizing national confrontations, which inspired this concept of a Balkan federation, had been advocated already by Serbian socialist Svetozar Marković. For the Comintern strategists, such conceptions were also, at the same time, ways to avoid conflicts in their own house. The most important Macedonian leftist politician who figured as an exponent of the "federalist" line was Dimitar Vlahov, who had begun his career as a deputy in the Turkish parliament.[12]

That the notion of a politically independent Macedonia emerged in this way for the first time within the framework of the Comintern has been exploited especially by the Greek side as a justification for characterizing the Macedonian nation as an "invention" of the Comintern. This is naturally nonsense. In reality, what happened in the Comintern reflected only the discussions among Macedonian communists and other leftist forces at home. The Macedonian communists already made a clear distinction between Macedonians and Bulgarians in the interwar period, becoming very militant about this during the Second World War, while the population itself only showed a growing disinterest in this particular question.

After the overthrow of peasant leader Alexander Stamboliski in 1923, IMRO developed, in its Bulgarian exile, into an extreme, right-oriented, terrorist conspiracy whose attacks not only in Macedonia but also in Bulgaria itself stirred up fear. Within Bulgaria at the time, IMRO figured as a state within the state. At the end of the 1920s, a certain Vance Mihajlov launched brutal attacks on his "federally" attuned rivals within IMRO, in order to seize control of this organization.[13] When, in 1934, the left-wing group of officers called "Zveno" took power in Bulgaria, it immediately banned IMRO. The fact that Bulgaria had been ruled by right-conservative and nationalist elements during the greater part of the interwar period, while the Macedonian movements supported by young intellectuals had been overwhelmingly left-oriented, undoubtedly played a role in cutting the umbilical cord. Even the right-oriented pro-Bulgarian IMRO could not shut its eyes to political reality. At certain times it embraced the concept of an autonomous Macedonia linked with Bulgaria.

Bulgaria did not take part in the April 1941 campaign against Yugoslavia, but it was nonetheless awarded Vardar Macedonia and the Thracian districts of Greece to occupy and administer. A certain Methodi Šatarov (Šarlo), probably on assignment from the Communist Party of Bulgaria, had used the confused situation to seize control of the communist organization in Skopje and pull it in a pro-Bulgarian direction. Tito and the other leaders of the CPY refused to acquiesce in this, as they had decided to preserve the state unity of Yugoslavia. They turned to the Comintern and at the end of August 1941 received a provisional decision, which provided that "Macedonia should be with Yugoslavia, for practical and general reasons".[14] With this, Tito had won an important victory.

But the problem was by no means solved thereby. The pro-Bulgarian current among the Macedonian communists remained strong and the Bulgarian party did not desist for long from its attempts to build its influence in those quarters. The Bulgarians sent a "delegate" by the name of Bojan Bulgaranov to Skopje; he would later become a leading functionary in communist Bulgaria. Shortly after his arrival, rather curiously, the leader of the Yugoslav-oriented Macedonian communists, Lazar Koliševski, was captured by the police and thrown in prison for the remainder of the war.[15] Complete disunity and chaos among the Macedonian communists lasted essentially until the beginning of 1943, when Svetozar Vukmanović-Tempo arrived in Skopje on assignment from Tito to create a new party organization and to fuel a Partisan uprising also in Macedonia. Vukmanović-Tempo has described his mission at length in his memoirs;[16] his mission embraced not only Vardar Macedonia but also Kosovo and Greece and was intended to prepare the way for a broader cooperation, if not for a federation of all communist Balkan countries.

As of summer 1943 and especially after the Italian capitulation in September of that year, one could already see the light at the end of the tunnel. Although there remained some skepticism in Macedonia concerning the reestablishment of Yugoslavia, it was none the less clear that there was nothing to be gained from a pro-Bulgarian orientation. Even the Albanians in west Macedonia were forced to realize that the now German-sponsored Greater Albania had no future. There were certain tendencies among Macedonian intellectuals who still hoped for an independent Macedonia, possibly even a "Greater Macedonia". Ideas of this sort appeared even in the ranks of the communists; it is said, for example, that today's President Gligorov had at least some contacts with such persons at the time. In the official Macedonian historical literature, memories of those times of doubt are by preference swept under the carpet.

A solution was finally offered at Jajce in November 1943 with the program for a new, federative Yugoslavia, articulated by Tito's communist leadership. Broad circles in Macedonia were won over to this concept. It even had something to offer the advocates of independence, for, thanks to Vukmanović-Tempo's preparatory work, they had come to believe that a "Greater Macedonia" could be realized one day within the framework of Yugoslavia.[17]

On 2 August 1944, this reorientation was formalized. Some 120 delegates assembled in the Monastery of the Blessed Prohor Pčinski, which today lies on the Serbian side of the border, to establish the Anti-Fascist Council for the People's Liberation of Macedonia, or ASNOM (acronym derived from the Macedonian) and to proclaim the People's Republic of Macedonia as an equal member of "Democratic Federative Yugoslavia". At the same time, it was decided to create an official Macedonian literary language on the basis of one of the central Macedonian dialects. This did not yet signify the formal act of establishing a Macedonian nation, let alone the culmination of "nation-building", but it was an important milestone in this process.

In a summons directed to the Macedonian people, the CP Macedonia included in its declaration the portentous sentence asserting that the Macedonians would achieve "also the unification of all parts of Macedonia" which had been divided by "Balkan imperialists" in 1913 and 1919.[18] This was directed against both Bulgaria and Greece and showed that Tito clearly planned to create a communist-led Balkan Federation in the future, which would include Albania as well as a communist Greece, and in which all the "national questions" of the region, including those of Kosovo and Macedonia, would be "solved" in the communist style. Tito found a willing partner in Georgi Dimitrov, the former Comintern secretary who had returned to Bulgaria in 1944. The cooperation between the two men provided grist both then and later for charges that they were effecting a revival of the old Comintern thesis about Macedonia.

The Greek side even today takes that abovementioned sentence in the party resolution for the establishment of ASNOM as a basis for the thesis that Macedonian statehood entailed, from the beginning, an "aggressive intention" *vis-à-vis* its neighbors, an intention against which these states must protect themselves. It is uncontested that grave acts followed on these words on the part of Macedonian communist leaders, but that was all more than 50 years ago.

The Greek communists had understood as much as the Yugoslav communists did the importance of gaining control of the "liberation struggle" and excluding democratic or nationalistic rivals. In December 1944, the Greek communists had practically the whole country in their hands, with the exception of Athens; but they were contained by energetic British intervention and by the effective reestablishment of the nationalist camp.

Already, during the Second World War Bulgarian elements of both the right and the left had tried, with only limited success, to obtain a foothold in Greek western Macedonia. The "Slavophone" population of the region had been subjected to a forcible hellenization campaign introduced in 1936 by the Greek dictator, Ioannis Metaxas,[19] but in spite of the hostility which this aroused toward Athens, local Macedonians still did not want to have anything to do with Bulgaria. They were more friendly toward the Greek communists, and responded positively to efforts on the part of the People's Liberation Army (ELAS) to call to life Slavic-Macedonian units or political groups. After the visit of Vukmanović-Tempo in northern Greece a "Slavic-Macedonian National Liberation Front" (SNOF) was organized, which began to introduce some Yugoslav influences toward the end of the war and which, on that account, became entangled in a nasty row with ELAS.[20] The Greek communists showed, even at that time, no inclination to support spontaneous movements of Slavs in the northern part of the country, let alone to change the borders of Greece.

The second phase of the Greek Civil War, beginning in 1947, was primarily characterized by the complete dependence of the insurgent communists on assistance from neighboring communist states to the north, principally Yugoslavia. The military leader of the insurgency, Marko Vaphiades, understood this. Tito and Dimitrov had by now embraced the concept of a Balkan federation in earnest, agreeing in principle, in the course of talks at Bled in August 1947, to a "step-by-step" unification. This concept foresaw the inclusion of a "Greater Macedonia" as a constituent unit. Tito himself acknowledged his aspiration to achieve the "unification of all Macedonians in one country" in a speech in Skopje on 11 October 1945.[21] Dimitrov's Bulgaria, a conquered country, allowed itself to be converted rather easily to this concept of a united Macedonia within a Balkan federation, and even allowed corresponding activities to be organized in the Pirin region, which it promptly annulled after 1948. I heard later, from the Bulgarian side, that Dimitrov agreed to the creation of a "Greater Macedonia" only because he expected that it would draw closer to Bulgaria than to Yugoslavia; thus "two Bulgarian states" would have been represented in the federation. This was important for Bulgaria because the Yugoslavs, as Kardelj explained in Sofia in November 1944, were not considering a federation on an equal basis, but wanted rather to conjoin Bulgaria to Yugoslavia as its seventh republic.[22]

It is not clear whether Tito, by embracing the aggressive theses of Macedonian nationalism, just wanted to reward the Macedonian communists for coming over, after their initial hesitations in 1943/44, to the Yugoslav line, or whether his primary intention was to use this aggressive nationalism as a spearhead for the realization of his imperial schemes in the Balkans. Maybe both factors played a role. In that event, however, why had the Greek communists initiated a rebellion which could only be premissed on support from the new communist regime in Yugoslavia? Possibly they thought in terms of purely communist-motivated solidarity and were afraid to lose all further opportunities for successful action.

In the wake of the Greek Civil War, some 68,000 persons, overwhelmingly "Slavophones", left Greece, according to official Greek statistics. Around 1955, the Republic of Macedonia undertook to collect these Slavic-speaking people, who had been strewn across several communist countries, in its own territory. A secret report of the Greek government in 1951 established that there were still 51,000 "Slavophones" in Greek western Macedonia,[23] whose numbers subsequently declined through emigration, above all to Australia and Canada.

Greece viewed the concentration of "Slavophone" refugees in Macedonia as a hostile act. For decades, the Greek government denied these people even the right to visit Greece, not to mention to return. In the 1970s and 1980s, when, as a result of the *numerus clausus* and other inadequacies at the Greek universities, many young Greeks were studying in Skopje, Macedonian authorities constantly tried to separate the "Slavophones" from Greece from the other Greeks and to form them into special groups. Greece countered that a diploma earned in a "language not used internationally" could not be recognized.[24] Even aside from this, there was still a subliminal irredentism in Macedonia, not least in academic circles. Greece had reasons to mistrust Skopje and to make Belgrade its exclusive point of entry for relations with Yugoslavia. Even President Gligorov admitted openly, in a talk in 1991, that Macedonia had to pay today for certain acts in the past.

Of course, Greece's behavior toward the Slavic minority on its territory is quite another matter. The problem of the linguistic minorities in Greece is a complex one. There are groups in this country who speak languages other than Greek, the most important of these being the Albanian-speakers, of whom there are still many in Attica as well as on individual islands such as Hydra, and then the Vlachs on Pindos Mountain. They both consider themselves Greeks. The only officially recognized minority in Greece is the Turks (together with some Pomaks) in Eastern Thrace. They were defined as "Muslims" in the Treaty of Lausanne in 1923. The problem of the Slavs is, again, different.

I visited the districts in question here on several occasions and was thereby able to establish that the majority of those perhaps 20,000 to 30,000 Slavic-speakers in the Florina-Edesse-Kastoria triangle today declare themselves "Macedonians", especially if one addresses them in their own language. They have their folklore and would like to see their particularity recognized, but they do not speak of being annexed to Macedonia. The times when gendarmes wanted to ban the use of their language and when they were not allowed to sing their own songs at weddings or other festivities are long gone. But their situation is still unsatisfactory.

The question is therefore of interest, because Greece grounded its boycott against the Republic of Macedonia *inter alia* on the argument that the Macedonian constitution of 1991 constitutes in Article 49, which obliges the Macedonian state to "care" for the Macedonians living in neighboring states and for emigrants, interference in the affairs of other states. However, quite apart from the fact that other states, including Greece, have such articles in their constitutions, Macedonia explicitly declared, in a constitutional amendment adopted at the insistence of West European states, that it did not intend to engage in any "interference" in the sovereign rights of the states affected or in their internal affairs. In a similar spirit, a further amendment affirmed that Macedonia did not nurture any territorial claims against its neighbors.

There are also problems *vis-à-vis* Bulgaria. In spite of the post-1948 repression, the Macedonian impulses in the Pirin district were not completely eradicated. I visited the Pirin district once, in the late 1970s, and established that the entire northern and central portions of the district, including the city of Blagoevgrad (since then once more Gornja Djumaja), had been totally "Bulgarianized", but that in the south, in the area of Melnik-Petrić, one could find many people who claimed that they were "Macedonians" and who complained that they were not officially allowed to be so. To the question of what proportion of the local population felt this way, I was regularly told about half. After the democratization of Bulgaria an association was formed in the Pirin district under the name "Ilinden", which assumed a Macedonian national orientation. The attitude of the Bulgarian authorities *vis-à-vis* these currents was ambiguous. "At least they no longer lock them up," people in Skopje said.[25] When I spoke with then-Prime Minister Filip Dimitrov in Sofia in autumn 1992, he held that the people in Macedonia could call themselves and their state whatever they wanted, but he declined to say anything about Macedonian currents within the borders of his own country.[26] The behavior of Bulgaria in regard to the Macedonian question seems all in all somewhat unclear and unstable according to the attitudes of the respective governments. In January 1992, Bulgaria extended diplomatic recognition to Macedonia; it was among the first states to recognize the new republic under its constitutional name. But Bulgaria declines to acknowledge the existence of a Macedonian nation. When Macedonian President Gligorov paid a visit to

Sofia in April 1994, the Bulgarian side was prepared to sign the final declaration also in a Macedonian version; it declined only to acknowledge that the language used could be called Macedonian.[27] Maybe one can describe the Bulgarian attitude more or less in these terms, that Sofia recognizes the Republic of Macedonia but wants to avoid anything which might encourage in any way "Macedonian" reflexes in its own territory.

Last but not least, it was the uncertain situation of Macedonia *vis-à-vis* its neighbors which prompted Macedonian leaders including Gligorov to proceed carefully and with reserve regarding independence. In summer 1990, it was clear enough that most Macedonians preferred to maintain the Yugoslav federation, assuming that this would be on an acceptable basis, so that the federation could represent Macedonia's interests in relations with unfriendly neighbors. If that was not successful, then confederation was acceptable to Macedonia as a second-best solution. Only if this solution also fell through were the Macedonians prepared to go it alone.[28]

The cautious course, which was also based on an appreciation of their strong economic dependence on the rest of Yugoslavia and above all on Serbia, was finally undermined by Serbian policy. As also elsewhere, the Milošević leadership reacted to Macedonia's "defection" from the Serbian bloc with hostility, threats, and attempts to exert pressure on Skopje. Immediately after the referendum on independence in September 1991, a Serbian deputy prime minister claimed that 300,000 Serbs were living in Macedonia and were being "repressed". President Gligorov told me in November 1991 that the 1991 census recorded the presence of only 43,000 Serbs in Macedonia and that 15,000 of these were either in the army or customs officials.[29] About 10,000 Serbs lived in Skopje. In Kumanovo the Serbian population accounted for 12 per cent of the local population – less than the Albanian contingent. There were compact groups of Serbs only in some villages northeast of Skopje. Parliamentary President Stojan Andov told me at that time that an army general in Skopje had boasted to him, in a threatening tone, that 150 of "his people" would be enough to arrest the entire "Macedonian baggage" and bring the republic back "in line".[30] At the same time, one could detect the first attempts at exerting economic pressure. For all that, leading personalities in Macedonia both then and later, including Petar Gošev and later Prime Minister Branko Crvenkovski, felt that Macedonia's most "natural" partner, especially in economic terms, was still Serbia.

Macedonian caution was expressed in the aforementioned last-ditch effort to save Yugoslavia (p. 174), which took the form of the plan jointly drafted by presidents Gligorov and Izetbegović and presented to the presidents of the other republics at the June 1991 "summit" meeting in Sarajevo.

In February and March 1992, President Gligorov conducted successful negotiations with the JNA with regard to its withdrawal from Macedonia; his accomplishment in bringing these negotiations to a successful conclusion was a great political achievement. On 27 March 1992, an appropriate agreement was signed with Yugoslav General Nikola Uzelac. Gligorov would often complain later that international recognition came ostensibly only to those Yugoslav successor states which had established their independence through war. The withdrawal of the army was certainly achieved, as Gligorov has noted, by no means without mental reservations, and one had the feeling that certain Serbian and army circles regretted the withdrawal later. The army leadership probably expected that Macedonia would be unable to safeguard its stability – Gligorov speculated in conversation – and that perhaps the Albanians would revolt and that the leadership in Skopje would then be forced to recall the army and to join the Serb-ruled new "Yugoslavia".[31]

One may note that, soon after the JNA withdrawal, Milošević contacted Greek Prime Minister Mitsotakis with a proposal to divide Macedonia between Serbia and Greece. Mitsotakis explicitly confirmed this proposal to me during a conversation we had in June 1992, indicating that it had been proffered about six months earlier, i.e., almost at the end of 1991. But Mitsotakis had rejected the proposal, and instead, had informed the European Union.[32] When the news hit the Belgrade press, Mitsotakis toned down his version somewhat,[33] but it was confirmed by Western embassies in Athens and also by Gligorov.

It would be unjust to judge today's Macedonia on the basis of its past under communist Yugoslavia. The dogmatic people installed in office under Tito's adherent Koliševski, who, with the exception of the short "liberal" period under Krste Crvenkovski (which ended with his removal from office in 1972), held Macedonia in their hands from 1945 until autumn 1989, bear the responsibility not only for the aggressiveness in the country's foreign policy but also for the internal repression and consequently for the bad relations with the Albanian minority. Since the transition to new relationships in Macedonia has gone smoothly, the old way of thinking has disappeared step by step. The past parliamentary president Andov, leader of the liberal party who had earlier been put in the "cooler" together with Gligorov because of his reformist tendencies, held that the old regime in Skopje had to share responsibility also for the collapse of Yugoslavia. He cites a remark made by Koliševski some time after Tito's death according to which, in contrast to the Marshal's evident opinion, he felt that a strong Serbia was conducive to a strong Yugoslavia. With this, Andov held, Koliševski had brought Macedonia into its ruinous alliance with Serbia. Milan Pančevski's entry as a member of the LCY Presidium was also problematic. Then one should recall also Lazar Mojsov's shameful behavior in March 1989, when he, as Macedonia's representative in the state presidency, made his accusations against Vllasi. Finally, Tupurkovski saddled the incipient resistance to Milošević with the unfortunate epithet, the "unprincipled alliance".[34]

At the elections of November 1990, it was not the reform communists, reorganized as the Social Democratic League of Macedonia, but the new nationalist-oriented party, "IMRO–Democratic Party for Macedonian National Unity", which emerged as the biggest vote-getter. But that ultimately did not count for much. Of the 120 seats in the parliament, IMRO obtained only 38 seats, against 31 for the reform communists, 11 for the liberals, and 17 for the strongest Albanian party, the Party for Democratic Prosperity. The latter three now formed a coalition, leaving the nationalists in the opposition. At the next elections, four years later, in October 1994, this party, together with Gošev's newly created Democratic Party, were so far behind in the first round of voting that they decided against participating in the second round and instead announced a "boycott". The result of the first four years of democratic government under President Gligorov was an unmistakable strengthening of the moderate left, as well as a confirmation of Gligorov's leadership. In spite of the attempted assassination of Gligorov, Macedonia may be characterized now, as before, as under presidential rule.

Gligorov's main service is certainly that, from the beginning of his term of office, he made a clear renunciation of Macedonian nationalism and came out in favor of having the constitution formulate Macedonia as a "citizens' state" (Article 2) rather than as the "national state" of the Macedonian people.

Of course, that alone could scarcely solve Macedonia's problems. On the right there remains the relatively strong nationalist party (IMRO) under the leadership of novelist Ljubčo Georgijevski, who wants a Macedonian national state and who accused Gligorov of having made too many concessions to the Albanians. Certainly Macedonia's nationalists have changed in some regards. Georgijevski told me once that his party was realistic; it had achieved its most important goal, the attainment of an independent Macedonian state, even if its borders did not correspond to the wishes of Macedonian patriots. Macedonian irredentism in today's conditions would be out of place; it was necessary to confine oneself to efforts on behalf of the recognition of the rights of minorities.[35] Later, after his election victory in 1998, Georgijevski even revised his attitude towards the Albanians and invited one of their party into his coalition government.

Georgijevski admitted rather frankly that one could afford to agitate against neighboring states earlier because one could always hide under Belgrade's skirt, as it were; but now Macedonia was an independent member of the family of nations and had to take responsibility for its own politics. Georgijevski's party seems, in this regard, to have some problems with Bulgaria. People keep appearing from time to time in the ranks of his party who want to link Macedonian national feeling with Bulgarian identity.

The relationship to the Albanians is difficult. Many Macedonians do not like the proximity to the Albanians; they view them with distrust. Now that the educational system is improving, and the number of Albanian cadres in the police and military is gradually increasing, some serious political conflicts could be finally resolved. The Albanian parties say that if Macedonia were to become a true "citizens' state", they would give up their demand to have the Albanian element established as a "second constituent factor" of Macedonia. But insofar as Macedonia must yet be seen as a Macedonian "national state", Gligorov's concept must be replaced by that of a binational state.[36] Much will depend in this regard on what will happen to Kosovo.

All in all, the Macedonia of today has left its past behind it, and has made the "European option", as Gligorov has formulated it, its own. That signifies a renunciation of every hostility toward neighboring states, and efforts toward compromise internally, together with the incremental linkage into European and international institutions. In the meantime, this constructive attitude has been noted not only by the international community but also, finally, by Greece. Under the new socialist government in Athens, relations with that country have, in part contrary to expectations, significantly improved.

There was – and still is – plenty of reason to question whether Macedonia can even survive. But to that one may respond that virtually any state which wants to survive can survive.[37] In the case of Macedonia, there seemed to be two basic presuppositions: First, that its independence not be threatened from outside and that its economic survival not be imperilled through boycott. Macedonia absorbed the worst pressure economically by reverting to a bazaar-economy, but that was purely a strategy of survival, and not a developmental policy. The deployment of some 500 US soldiers, undertaken under the Bush administration and under the umbrella of the UN, was one of the few acts of Western policy which had a positive prophylactic effect in the former Yugoslavia and worked in the direction of stability. The second precondition for the existence of Macedonia would be that the relationship with the Albanians be fashioned along constructive lines. The ties between the Albanians of Macedonia and those in Kosovo are close.

Bosnia-Herzegovina

One could foresee, from the beginning, that the process of the dissolution of Yugoslavia would be toughest in Bosnia-Herzegovina. Three peoples lived in this republic – Muslims, Serbs, and Croats – not only together, but intermixed in most of the republic's districts. According to the last census of 1991,[38] the Muslims comprised 43.7 per cent of the 4.36 million inhabitants of the republic, the Serbs 31.4 per cent, and the Croats 17.3 per cent. Some 5.5 per cent declared themselves ethnic "Yugoslavs". Self-declared Muslims could be found also in other parts of Yugoslavia, for example in the Sandžak, in Kosovo, and in Montenegro. But of the 2.28 million Yugoslav "ethnic" Muslims, 1.91 million lived in Bosnia-Herzegovina. Beginning with the census of 1971, they had been able to register as "Muslims" in an ethnic sense; after that, the growth of the Muslim population in Bosnia-Herzegovina was generally stronger than that of either the Serbs or, in particular, the Croats.

Two questions would have a determinative impact on the fate of Bosnia-Herzegovina: First, whether the consciousness of belonging to a common Bosnia-Herzegovina would be strong enough among all three peoples to guarantee the continued existence of this community after the end of Yugoslavia; and second, whether the Muslims could serve as the principal agents of a (new) state community. As is well known, the first question was answered in a most tragic way with a "no", while the answer to the second question was a conditional "yes".

The Muslim population clearly had the strongest feeling of Bosnianness among the three groups, even if, until the 1950s, many of them were not always completely committed to living in Bosnia and looked often in the direction of Turkey. The Serbs had, just as unmistakably, the weakest Bosnian identity; their whole national movement was directed toward the unification of all Serbs; it was in the name of this idea of unification that Serbs carried out the assassination of Archduke Franz Ferdinand in Sarajevo in 1914. In Yugoslavia, the Serbs were able to realize this unity. Coexistence with non-Serbs was partly accepted, especially in the cities, where people in general often thought in terms of a Bosnian condominium. The Croats in Bosnia proper traditionally had more of a Bosnian orientation, while those living in western Herzegovina, who had never lived with Muslims, were and are convinced Croats, who would rather be united with Croatia.

One thing was nonetheless absolutely clear, where Bosnia-Herzegovina was concerned, whether in olden times or in the days of united Yugoslavia or now, viz., that no one in the region felt like a "minority". One belonged, in each case and at any time, to a "nation" and it was a "constituent factor" of the larger community. It would be a complete misunderstanding of the relations in Bosnia-Herzegovina if well-meaning Western representatives wanted to operate here within the framework of "minority protection", as the Badinter Commission did at least once.

The communist regime in Bosnia-Herzegovina was, through all the years under Tito and after, especially repressive. When one asked representatives of the government about the reasons for this, one received the answer that the relations between the peoples were sensitive here, so that any disturbance could at once escalate. At the time of the so-called "Croatian Spring" of 1970/71, measures were even taken against people who sympathized with the Zagreb soccer team "Dinamo". The apparatus of repression in this republic was xenophobic and anti-Western in orientation, which was entirely out of keeping with the fact that it was precisely from this republic that an especially large number of *Gastarbeiter* were active in the West.

The Partisan war had indeed ravaged all parts of Bosnia, but it found only a limited echo among the population there. So there were only portions of each of the three peoples who joined the Partisans. There were hardly any representatives of the national elites. The Serb Djuro Pucar, one of those primitive power-wielders whom Tito preferred to install as governors in his provinces, held power in Sarajevo for many years. Sometime in the course of the 1960s he ceased to be bearable. Among the Bosnian Croats, people like Mikulić and Herljević came to the fore; the latter attempted to carry over his police methods into the federation. Among the Muslims, the Pozderac and Dizdarević clans were prominent.

The republic's economic development contrasted sharply with this picture of a "dark vilayet". Building on the natural resources of Bosnia, in the first place iron ore and coal, a strong raw-materials industry arose in the post-Second World War period; for strategic considerations, arms factories were soon attached to them. The relationship between the Bosnian raw-materials concerns and the refining industries in the other republics was often difficult, above all for reasons of price-fixing. In the 1960s, other large factories and enterprises, geared to the civilian market, also appeared in Bosnia. They all operated on a state-capitalist foundation, but often successfully, even abroad. Notable managers, such as Emerik Blum from the "Energoinvest" company, occasionally became too much for the communist functionaries. In Sarajevo, a Volkswagen spin-off was established under the name TAS. In the 1980s, the Agrokomerc agrarian concern, located in the west Bosnian town of Velika Kladuša and managed by Fikret Abdić, earned renown; this firm was notorious for its habit of creating a smokescreen around its debts.

The process of political democratization began relatively late in Bosnia, for the reasons outlined, and even then rather lethargically. In January 1990, the parliament did decide on a new constitution and introduced, in principle, a multi-party system. Immediately there was concern, however, that this would lead to the organization of party life along purely national lines; as a result, in April 1990, the establishment of parties under national names was forbidden. The Muslim party under the leadership of Alija Izetbegović had to call itself "the Party of Democratic Action". The fear of ethnic polarization was indeed only too justified, but the chosen solution was unserviceable, and the ban had to be lifted later. In the cities, above all in Sarajevo but also in Tuzla, many people, especially younger people, managers, and intellectuals, wanted to escape the national obsessions and their dangers, and the privileged supranational groups. The communists now subscribed to an (ethnically neutral) reform course. The new, all-Yugoslav party, the "League of Reform Forces", established by Prime Minister Marković in early August 1990, also entered the race.[39]

The first free elections in Bosnia-Herzegovina were set for 18 November 1990, a week after the elections in Macedonia. Visiting Bosnia three weeks before the elections, I found the atmosphere tense and highly-strung; there had been no "political spring" in Bosnia and no enthusiasm for democracy. In fact, the politicians and populations of all three nationalities would have preferred it if there had still been a modestly authoritarian but "liveable" Yugoslavia, which would cover up national antagonisms and render difficult decisions unnecessary.

The reason for the bad prospects for stability must be sought primarily in the orientation of the Serbian Democratic Party and its leader, Radovan Karadžić, a psychiatrist from Montenegro who had moved to Bosnia. As Karadžić told me on the eve of the elections,[40] his party would not accept Bosnian secession from the Yugoslav federation under any circumstances. Even a confederal Yugoslavia was unacceptable for Karadžić, let alone an independent Bosnia-Herzegovina. The Serbs would be a "minority" in such a state, and this was absolutely unbearable for them. If his concept did not prevail, Karadžić said, the Serbian people in Bosnia-Herzegovina would declare themselves "sovereign" and proceed to establish autonomous Serbian areas.

The other nationalities of Bosnia viewed the Serbian attitude as nothing less than blackmail, noting that the Serbs were openly threatening to stage an uprising and that, in the Serbian view, all districts in which Serbs lived, even where they were in the minority, had to be "Serbia". At that time, this was still considered to mean that the Serbs would have the authority in those areas, but not that they would resort to expelling or murdering the non-Serbs. This Serbian blackmail had operated in Bosnian politics already from 1988 on. Many members of the LCY Central Committee or parliamentary deputies from the republic, above all Muslims and Croats, would have regularly voted with the Slovenes and Croats in the appropriate federal forums, but they could not do so, because the Serbian delegates from Bosnia wanted to support Milošević, and they thought it best to give in to them in order to safeguard the cohesion of the republic.

The Muslim party under Izetbegović held the view that a federation such as that advocated by Serbia, would, after the withdrawal of Slovenia and Croatia, necessarily assume the form of a Serb-dominated structure. But it could not be demanded of Muslims and Croats that they live in a Serbian dependency. Thus, in Izetbegović's view,[41] a "Bosnian consensus" was essential. This state community would be neither Muslim-ruled nor would it simply remain within a rump of the former Yugoslav state. Whether Bosnia would be connected with other republics within the framework of a confederation or in some other way would depend on the situation.

The new Bosnian entity, which was being forced to take shape, should be organized as a unified state system, according to the concepts of Izetbegović's party, with the three peoples acknowledged as "constituent factors". The peoples of Bosnia would be assured of proportional representation in the organs of state. The organization of the state into regions or districts with some autonomy could be accepted, though in this event economic and logistical factors should play a role alongside national factors. The "primacy" of the respective "majority-nation" in each of these units could be accepted, though it should not be permitted to evolve into some kind of *national* autonomy. His party did not aspire to build an Islamic state, Izetbegović insisted, but a modern, democratic *Rechtsstaat* (nomocracy), and following the Western model. He himself had understood his 1976 "Islamic Declaration" not as a manifesto for a Bosnian state, but as a general endeavor to bring the principles of Islam into harmony with modern civilization. He nonetheless conceded that the Muslims viewed Bosnia as their homeland. They had earlier often played with the idea of migrating somewhere, above all Turkey, if Bosnia should no longer be able to offer them a homeland. Now, however, as Yugoslavia dissolved, they wanted to found their state here, a republic in which they could live, and they were determined to defend this state.

The party of the Croats, a kind of branch of the Croatian Democratic Community, under the leadership of Stjepan Kljuić, a Croat from central Bosnia, was in a difficult situation. The Croats stood closer to the Muslims than to the Serbs and, especially those in central and northern Bosnia, had a vested interest in keeping Bosnia-Herzegovina from reaching a catastrophic end. On the other side stood the Croats of Herzegovina, who would eagerly have been conjoined with an independent, non-communist Croatia, just as the majority of Serbs wanted annexation to Serbia. For the Croats of Herzegovina, the affirmation of the Bosnian state entailed a victim. Kljuić considered the Serbian drive to keep Bosnia-Herzegovina, by employing blackmail, within a Serb-dominated Yugoslavia, completely unacceptable.[42] In that eventuality, the Croats would have to decide their own fate. There was talk, at that time, that Zagreb should provide a "guarantee" that it would respect an independent Bosnian state, in order to obtain a similar concession from the Serbian side.

Many people thought at the time that, in view of the great dangers, something like a "Bosnian consensus" would be found. One advocate of this view was Adil Zulfikarpašić, the son of a Muslim landowner, who had just arrived from Switzerland, where he had been living. He had been a co-founder of the Party of Democratic Action, but he had quarreled with Izetbegović about relations with the Serbs, and tried his luck at the polls, with a liberal and secular platform. His electoral campaign had been unsuccessful.[43]

The elections of 18 November were conducted in a notably correct way, as all sides concede. This allowed certain hopes to be born. On the day after the elections, Karadžić said that the conditions had now been established for the three national parties, as the legitimate representatives of their respective peoples, to reach an agreement better and more effectively than the previous authorities could.[44] The apportionment of mandates rather closely followed the corresponding "national key". There were cities where the Reform Communists and the League of Reform Forces worked together especially closely, such as Prijedor and Tuzla.[45] In both of the houses of parliament, the "Party of Democratic Action" received 86 mandates, while the Serbian Democratic Party obtained 72 mandates, the Croatian Democratic Community 44, the Reform Communists and their affiliates 14, and Marković's party 12.[46]

Almost more interesting were the ad personam elections in the seven-member republic presidium. In the general elections, two representatives were elected to this body by each of the three nations, with a seventh member being chosen to represent all "others". Among the Muslim candidates, Fikret Abdić had received 48 per cent of the popular vote, well ahead of Izetbegović, who had to be satisfied with 40 per cent. It was nonetheless agreed that Abdić would remain in his "Agrokomerc" and that Izetbegović would become president of the presidium. Among the Croatian candidates, Kljuić had received more than 21 per cent of the votes, somewhat more than the proportion of Croats in Bosnia. It is noteworthy that the candidates of the Serbs received fewer votes than would have corresponded to the Serbian share of the population. Biljana Plavšić, a radical, a biologist by profession, received 26 per cent of the vote, while Nikola Koljević, a jurist, received 25 per cent. Could it be that not all Serbs supported the radical line of their leaders? The answer is not known for sure even today. Muslim Ejup Ganić competed as a "Yugoslav" representing "other nationalities", and received 32 per cent of the vote. He later served as vice president of the Republic of Bosnia-Herzegovina.[47]

One could also read the regional divisions in the electoral results. Bihać, Sarajevo, Zenica, and Tuzla presented themselves unambiguously as Muslim centers, Banja Luka and the area around Doboj as Serbian strongholds, and Mostar and western Herzegovina as the Croatian center of gravity in the new state. The formation of the government unfolded without complications, even if it was clear that the government in Sarajevo, together with the state presidium, would operate as a coalition of national representatives, rather than as an efficient and supranational body. Even then, there was concern that the national representatives in each province were behaving rather independently. That was true not only for the Serbs in Banja Luka but also for the Croats of western Herzegovina and even for the Muslims in their bastions.

Some authors reproached all the Bosnian politicians, including Izetbegović, for having established their politics on an ethnic/national foundation, rather than on a democratic basis representing political or economic interests. By this, they had allegedly brought about the "death of Bosnia".[48] This argument is unrealistic. During the entire history of Bosnia-Herzegovina, it was always the nation, even if understood on a religious basis, which constituted the most decisive category of differentiation. The electoral result merely confirmed the primacy of the national. One can at most say that in Bosnia-Herzegovina there had always been peace, to some extent, in national questions, when the political power relations were clear. Now the former regime was to be replaced, under the new democratic conditions, by a "proportional" state of three constituent peoples; this solution could have achieved its goal, even if it had produced only a weak, "neutralized" state with unclarified relations to the two most important neighbor-states. In any event, that would have been better than mutual slaughter. It came to that, however, because one of the three nations, the Serbs, did not want to have anything to do even with such a state and ruthlessly put its own interests above those of the other peoples of Bosnia-Herzegovina.

How did one arrive at such complicated, almost inextricable national and religious relationships in Bosnia and Herzegovina? It began in the first centuries after the Slavic immigration, when those in the western parts began to develop a Croatian identity while those in the east developed a Serbian political identity; there was an amorphous zone lying between these two centers. In this zone, on the coast, the Neretlians, a people living off piracy, made their home. Further inland, a duchy appeared in the tenth century, which slowly consolidated itself and later took the name "Bosna".

Some Serbian ideologues make an argument from this that in the first written documents from Byzantium, the name "Bosna" was used to describe this land as a portion of Serbia; the documents which have come down from this state were written in Cyrillic. But to want to assert a Serbian "primacy" in Bosnia on this foundation is as unrealistic as similar claims from the Croats.

A certain Ban Kulin of the Bosnian Duchy could establish a somewhat independent position around 1180 between Hungary, which already held Croatia and Dalmatia in its hand, and the Serbian dynasty in the east.[49] It was during the reign of Ban Kulin that those Manichaean sects, which have come to be known in Bosnia as the Bogomils, came into the country. Having originally appeared in the Byzantine Empire, the sect had gathered its adherents in the first Bulgarian Empire. Its worldview was distinctly dualist (light vs. darkness, good vs. evil, etc.). In his history of Bosnia, Noel Malcolm declines to use the term "Bogomils" in the Bosnian context, since this was a Bulgarian term. Still, this dispute seems unnecessary insofar as it was essentially the same phenomenon in both places.[50] Not only did this teaching win conversions among the people in Bosnia, but it was above all accepted by the ruling class and was soon declared the official state religion. Bogomilism became, one might say, an expression of the will to remain independent of Serbia and Croatia (now Hungary), and to claim a place between East and West.

The Bosnians did not have much luck with their Church, insofar as it provided Hungary, which encircled three-quarters of the country, with a standing pretext for crusades against Bosnia. The Bosnians therefore had to allow the Roman Catholic Church some influence; that Church's Franciscan monks won a following, especially among simple peasants, so that the Bosnian Church became steadily more and more of a "high Church". This did not prevent Bosnia from consolidating itself as a state, however. The reign of Ban, or King, Tvrtko I (1353–91) may be seen as the high point of this state. He succeeded in extending Bosnian rule to portions of Dalmatia and Croatia, forcing the Hungarians back.

Decline followed shortly thereafter, however. Not only did Hungary once more take up the banner of a "crusader war" but, in the east, the

Turks made their appearance, having beaten the Serbs on the Field of the Blackbirds in 1389. The poorly connected Bosnian state could not hope for Western assistance; the influence of Bogomilism was reason enough for the West to sit on the sidelines. It was able to rise one last time in the first half of the fifteenth century. Then, under its last rulers, it was forced to succumb to Hungarian pressure. But there was little enthusiasm to fight the Turks only to remain subordinated to Hungary. After a long period of going backwards and forwards, including attempts to negotiate with the Turks, the latter occupied the greater part of the country in 1481.

The preceding developments had consequences. The Bosnian upper crust had little loyalty to Western Christian notions, after their experiences with the Hungarians, and some of them were all too ready to convert to Islam. The desire to retain their hard-earned privileges was not the only motivation here. After some members of the noble class had set the example, the other social classes thought nothing of following their example. The conversions continued until well into the eighteenth century. In this way, there arose in Bosnia – in contrast to other regions in the Balkans where sections of the population had converted to Islam – a differentiated and perfected Muslim society, which developed its own economic and cultural life, embracing a comprehensive identity.

Around 1700, the borders between the Ottoman Empire and the Habsburg Empire were stabilized. Bosnia constituted a large Turkish administrative province, usually called the Pašaluk of Bosnia, because it was headed by a pasha.[51] The area known today as the Sandžak of Novi Pazar belonged to the Pašaluk; it was separated from Bosnia in 1878 and left under Turkish sovereignty. In this Sandžak, which is today divided between Serbia and Montenegro, there are a further 200,000 to 250,000 Muslims. The Party of Democratic Action, which at first conceived of itself as a general Muslim party in Yugoslavia, obtained a foothold there too and became the agent of an autonomy movement which is today repressed by Serbia. The region around Bihać and some other areas in the northwest of today's Bosnia did not belong to the medieval Bosnian state, and for a long time after its conquest the region was known as "Turkish Croatia". The Turks settled Muslims from other parts of the Pašaluk there to take the place of the original population, which had fled; this accounts for the rather compact Muslim population which one finds in the area.

The more the Ottoman Empire found itself limited to the defense of its borders, in the so-called period of decadence, the more functions and burdens it transferred to the domestic Muslim class, which in this way strengthened its position. This, in turn, made the Muslim class conservative and hostile to reform. Earlier, when the Turks were still thinking offensively, Banja Luka served as the capital of the Pašaluk; the Turks liked to spend the winter here, before they once more turned their eyes westward. The Ferhad Pasha mosque dating from 1580, which the Serbs blew up in 1993, was a unique cultural treasure from this epoch. Then Sarajevo became the capital, and along the way also for a time, Travnik. The stability of the borders was of a degree which allowed heroes to relax and to cultivate a refined life. But this stability was, on the other hand, not so secure as to banish all uncertainties. This mixture had its impact on all Muslim culture in Bosnia, and contributed to binding the entire society to the authorities, from the family up. The greatest modern novelist of the Bosnian Muslims, Meša Selimović, observes that the Muslim ballads and love songs, the "sevtalinke", were always dominated by this tension between the individual and the family as the most important social institution.[52] He also thinks that the Bosnian Muslims had, as the ruling class, always been a bit frivolous about economic matters. But that is perhaps a character trait of every landowning ruling class.

This way of life came to an end with the Austro-Hungarian occupation in 1878. After a time the new regime introduced the principle of proportional representation, along lines similar to those attempted in independent Bosnia-Herzegovina in 1991. For the Muslims, the new state of affairs meant that they had lost their political dominance. They also had to confront the modern concepts of nation and national identity. Serbs and Croats alike wanted to claim Muslims as "their own"; among the Serbs, it was precisely the socialists, such as Svetozar Marković, who proved to be the most energetic champions of such ideas. In his view, Bosnia was a country "in which the Serbs are divided into three religions".[53]

In order to create a local identity and take the edge off irredentism, the Austrians insisted on the terms "Bosnian" and "Bosniak". Catholics, Orthodox, and Muslims were all, thus, "Bosniaks". But this concept was accepted only to a limited degree; in the end, only the Muslims really took to it. There were attempts in 1990 to revive this concept among the Muslims. Adil Zulfikarpašić urged this identity, in the conviction that it was necessary to get away from the primarily religious designation "Muslim".[54] Izetbegović and other leaders of the Muslim party argued at the time that it would not do, because it would alienate Croats and Serbs from the Bosnian state idea. Today the Muslims reach back for the aforementioned designation, ostensibly in the endeavor to lend the Muslim-dominated regime in Sarajevo legitimacy for the common state.

That the Muslims in Bosnia have not merely a religious but also a cultural and political identity was clear to the Austrians and was not contested by the Serbs who, in 1918, extended their dominion over Bosnia. During the interwar years, 1918–41, the Muslims had their political party, the Yugoslav Muslim Organization, under the leadership of Mehmed Spaho; this party enjoyed especial acceptance under Stojadinović, because it fitted well with his concept of representative national parties in a unified Yugoslavia. Things took a turn for the worse, for the Muslims, with the "Sporazum" of 1939, which drew the boundaries of the partially autonomous Banovina of Croatia without regard to the existence of a strong

Muslim component in the area. This had some delayed consequences when, beginning in 1991, Tudjman aspired unflinchingly to a new partition of Bosnia more or less along the lines of the 1939 Banovina of Croatia. Tudjman was able to make this idea appealing to mediators Cyrus Vance and Lord Owen so that they readily assigned to Croatia predominantly Muslim towns such as Travnik, in the partition plan, only because these had belonged to "Croatia" in 1939. With this, they ensured that the Croats were the first to agree to the plan, indeed with enthusiasm, but the others did not do likewise; the consequent attempts of the Croats to save from the plan what could be saved led directly to open hostilities with the Muslims.[55]

The events in the Second World War brought death and suffering to all three peoples of the region. Pavelić's comment that the Muslims were "the flower of the Croatian nation" gave those affected little and left them cool.[56] The basic attitude of the Muslims, who had learned their lesson from history, was to wait until it was clear which side would emerge victorious and then ally themselves with that side. Where the Serbs were concerned, they felt very much attracted by the Chetniks, until that ceased to be a viable option. That the Serbs in Bosnia basically leaned toward the Chetnik ideology seems to have figured as a subliminal source of the conflict between Karadžić and Milošević in 1994. There were Muslims, during the Second World War, who hoped for the victory of the Axis powers – for example, the organization Young Muslims (*Mladi Muslimani*) or those who joined the Waffen-SS division "Handshar". These, however, were oriented not to the *Ustaše* but to the Germans, whom they viewed as "neutral" protectors and with whom, in their difficult situation, they sought a direct relationship. One must mention, in this connection, that the behavior of the Partisans toward the "neutral" Muslims was anything but positive.

After the war, the communist regime did not know exactly how it should view the Muslims in national terms. At Jajce in 1943, Bosnia-Herzegovina was declared a sovereign republic, but this was less for the sake of the Muslims than to neutralize the region between the Serbs and the Croats. For all that, even the communists began, as early as 1941, to distinguish between "Muslimani" (as a nation) and "muslimani" (as those adhering to Islam), using capitalization to distinguish the one from the other.[57] The decisions at Jajce spoke only of "the peoples of Bosnia-Herzegovina". Under communism, the Muslims found themselves at first designated "persons without ethnic orientation";[58] they had little alternative at census-time but to declare themselves "undecided", since the designation "Yugoslav" was still prohibited. The authorities took a dim view of any national impulses, particularly on their part. The negative description was more than merely unsatisfactory. At the end of 1959, Tito concluded that his ideologues had had their way for too long; "those things connected with the nationality of the Muslims should be gradually liquidated," he said.[59] Four years later, in Belgrade, he declared that it was nonsensical to discuss whether the Muslims were a nation. "Everyone can be what he wants to be."[60] That applied above all to the question whether it was permissible to declare oneself a "Yugoslav", but it could be understood more generally as well. In 1963, the Muslims were described as a "people" in the new Bosnian constitution.

The Muslims of Bosnia in fact felt that they were a nation. I have already indicated in the section dealing with Macedonia that the concept of nationhood is multifarious and that consciousness is just as important as ostensibly "objective" indicators. So the Muslims pressed to have their nation once more acknowledged as it had been before under other auspices. The census of 1971 was the first time that they were free to declare their nationality as they saw fit. The economic boom of the 1960s, from which Bosnia had profited along with other parts of the country, had given the Muslims, after all their misfortunes, some status, self-confidence, and prospects. So they wanted to see themselves as a constituent factor in their country, on a par with the other peoples of Yugoslavia. Their ancestral name had national roots; in the Turkish empire, nation and religion had always been identical. It is therefore false to say that the Muslim nation was "created" in the 1960s; it was always in the consciousness of the people and had now merely found its modern form. "Muslim – whether one is comfortable with the name or not, there is no other designation," a Professor of Orientalism in Sarajevo wrote in 1987.[61]

While the question about how the Croats came to be in Bosnia-Herzegovina may be answered rather easily – the Croatian enclaves in central Bosnia may be traced back to the Franciscan missions, while those in western Herzegovina were directly connected with Dalmatia – the question as to how the Serbs came to the area is more complicated. It is hardly probable that the Byzantine influences in the early Bosnian state had opened the doors for a Serbian Church structure. More important was the fact that the expanding Bosnian state annexed important Serbian areas after 1300. At that time, the Church relationships were firmer. No one demanded that the Serbian Orthodox believers convert. Even territorially, they did not cross paths with the Bogomils and Catholics, since they were in the eastern and southeastern parts of Bosnia, while the Bogomils and Catholics were represented in the central and western parts.[62] The Serbs, to the extent that one can call them that at that time, retained their Churches and their monasteries. King Tvrtko I even nurtured Greater Serbian ambitions and used these institutions in support of those ambitions.

More important for the religio-ethnic picture of Bosnia today than these relationships from pre-Ottoman times were the migrations which took place under the Ottomans. The Serbian Orthodox inhabitants, or at least those who lived in the highlands and were therefore not included in the Turkish feudal system, were much more involved in these migrations than were the other peoples. Without wanting to wear out the thesis of these Serbs being Slavicized Vlachs, it is none the less certain that there were many such elements among those migrants. We know little about the migrations in Turkish times; but we know that they took place and that they were generally in the direction of east to west. Sometimes these were demanded by the Turks, for example, when there were empty stretches of land in western or northern Bosnia to be resettled, after wars with Austria. These westward migrations on the part of the Serbs continued into the years after the Second World War. Often there were also migrations from the villages to the cities. In Turkish times only a few Serbs lived in Banja Luka; as of 1991, they constituted 56 per cent of the city's inhabitants.[63]

At the end of 1990, as Bosnia's past was confronted with the exigencies of the present, the three nations were one reality in Bosnia, and none of them could base any special claims on past history. The proportional role of each people in the community was accepted; it was contested only how this should be realized. There was also disagreement as to the status which the state of Bosnia-Herzegovina should have under international law in the event of the evident collapse of Yugoslavia.

In 1991 one could still cherish hopes in Bosnia-Herzegovina that the new institutional context could be invested with normative value. The republic did succeed in holding free and democratic elections and in forming a government. In general, the population wanted to safeguard peace on this foundation. On the other hand, one could not ignore the fact that, in the context of the collapse of Yugoslavia, a Greater Serbian program had gradually emerged as an alternative. Nonetheless, hopes were still alive that with time realities would induce a "Bosnian consensus" even under conditions of independence.

Such hopes were expressed through the fact that internal Bosnian debates during this entire period focused less on the external status of the republic than on its internal organization. Here, nonetheless, there were huge differences of opinion. On the occasion of a visit to Sarajevo at the end of May 1991,[64] I found that the Serbian party was pressing for a regionalization of the republic according to primarily national criteria. Since the division of Bosnia into regions would result in the reappearance of "minorities", ethnic proportionality was supposed to be employed also on the level of regions and communities.

Against this, Muslim politicians continued to cling to their concept of a "unified" state and said they would "oppose" any true regionalization. But neither then nor later did they possess any means of compelling the Serbian center in Banja Luka or the Croatian center in western Herzegovina to accept this. There was a heavy use of demagogic slogans at the time; the Serbs said they did not want to come under "Turkish rule" a second time. The Muslim politicians did not completely reject the concept of the "cantonization" of their republic, but they wanted to limit the competence of these units to the bare minimum. In addition, all three political camps were thinking earnestly about relations with the neighboring republics, in which the Serbs and Croats had particular interest. Here the

Muslim politicians spoke more positively than in the question of region-alization; open borders and double citizenship, under certain conditions, seemed to them worth considering.

In 1991, it was above all events in the vicinity of the republic which cast shadows on the chances of a common state. Certainly, Milošević and Tudjman did not explicitly agree on a partition of Bosnia-Herzegovina at their meeting in Karadjordjevo in March 1991, but the mere thought of a Serb-Croat "compromise" had to entail something of this order. It would have helped had Tudjman and Milošević been prepared to accept an inde-pendent Bosnian state. But neither of them wanted to do so. At the time, the notion of a "confederation" was once more revived as a last chance to save Yugoslavia. In this situation, Izetbegović and Gligorov presented their proposal in May 1991 for a new Yugoslav community.

Izetbegović and other Muslim politicians made a decisive error in their strategy for Bosnia's survival, viz., they believed that the Yugoslav Army would behave differently in Bosnia-Herzegovina from the way it was behaving in Croatia. In view of the extraordinarily strong presence of the army in the republic, one frequently heard Muslim politicians say that the army would try to hold onto Bosnia as a strong base and rather try to protect the peace here, in the interest also of their numerous family members living in Bosnia. Izetbegović even made statements according to which, in the case of unrest which, for example, might be stirred up by the Serbs, he would call on the army to help.[65] This attitude has been taken as an expression of political *naïveté*; the *naïveté* contributed to the fact that the Muslim side neglected its defense needs. Even if the army truly had been interested in the preservation of peace in Bosnia-Herzegovina, nothing had been said about the political content of the peace which the army might want to preserve.

When I was once more in Sarajevo at the beginning of December 1991, the situation was entirely different. The army, which had provided massive assistance to the Serbs in the Croatian Krajina, was enlarging its position in Bosnia, entirely contrary to Izetbegović's expectations, without any coor-dination with republic authorities, in evident agreement with the Serbs, and with an unmistakably hostile intent toward the non-Serb population. Heavy weapons were being brought into position around the cities of Sarajevo, Mostar, Bihać, and Tuzla, so that these cities could be bombarded at any time and kept under control.[66] "We are occupied," Croatian party leader Kljuić told me at the time. Other persons with whom I spoke felt that they had tried to break free of communism and instead of that, had come under army control. Izetbegović still would not give up hope as to the army's attitude and the willingness of the Serbs to make a compro-mise, but I was also told then that, as a result of events in Croatia, all three nations in Bosnia were experiencing a radicalization.

It was clear that the entire disposition of the army was directed to preventing Bosnia-Herzegovina from pursuing a path to independence and to keeping the republic within a truncated rump Yugoslavia. This did not mean absolutely that the army was working directly to create a Serbian protectorate, but in practice, this is all that Bosnia's fate in any truncated Yugoslavia could have been. Izetbegović spoke emphatically against such a solution; the Muslims also had some claim, according to the principles of a right of self-determination, to live in their own state, even if in association with equal partners.[67] The Croats had just as little desire to live in a Serbian protectorate.

I had the impression in December 1991 that Izetbegović was by then trying only to postpone the outbreak of hostilities for as long as possible. The Muslims must have known that the Serbs had, for a long time, been arming themselves for a civil war and that it was high time to make up for their past neglect in establishing their own armed militias. That was difficult because the army had already confiscated the weapons of the Bosnian Territorial Defense forces earlier, as it had done in Slovenia and Croatia. I spoke at the time with Ejup Ganić, member of the state presidency and later vice president of the republic. He openly conceded that Bosnia was far behind in weaponry and thought, with resignation, that perhaps the only option by then, in the event of military action by the army and the Serbs, was to declare Bosnia-Herzegovina an "occupied country" and call upon the international community for assistance. When I asked him if he really believed that the international community would do anything for Bosnia in this eventuality, he shook his head. Moreover, the procurement of the necessary weapons was now blocked as a result of the international embargo.[68] As if that were not enough, the UN refused to send any "blue helmets" to Bosnia, on the grounds that there was no conflict there. At almost the same time, the UN had declined to send peacekeeping troops to Croatia, on the argument that there was a conflict there, which should first be ended.

In Croatia, there was at the time a hostile feeling toward Izetbegović, because the army had operated against Croatia from positions in Bosnia, and Izetbegović and the Muslims had allegedly not done anything to stop this. The reproaches were unjustified, however, because Izetbegović had not been in a position to do anything to oppose the movements of the army; in the Serbian districts of western Bosnia, he and his people no longer exercised effective jurisdiction. Besides, in late June and early July 1991, when the army had attacked Slovenia in part from bases in Croatia, Croatia had been equally passive.

The hard-fighting Croats in western Herzegovina played an important role in the Croatian independence struggle of summer and autumn 1991. They ranged over all of central Dalmatia, including Split, and on several occasions prevented army units with tanks from moving from positions around Mostar southward against the coast. Later, in April and May 1992, the army unleashed its fury by bombarding Capljina and Mostar; its goal was to establish the Neretva as the boundary between Serbian territory and territory held by others. But it was not successful.

One must concede that the Croats, and above all those in Herzegovina, had no illusions in regard to their relations with the Serbs and the army. In contrast to the Muslims, they armed themselves in good time, enabling them later to save the lives of many Muslims. Nonetheless, Tudjman allowed himself to be seduced by the useful relationship which he had with the Croats of Herzegovina and secured for them the leadership of the Bosnian branch of the HDZ, even though the Herzegovinan Croats comprised only 40 per cent of Croats in the republic as a whole. At the beginning of February 1992, the erstwhile chair of the HDZ in Bosnia-Herzegovina, Stjepan Kljuić, had to step down in order to make room for Mate Boban, a Herzegovinan. Tudjman began to talk more intensely about a partition of Bosnia-Herzegovina about that time, not the least, or so one may suppose, because he was under the spell of the so-called "Herzegovinan lobby" in Zagreb.

At the end of February 1992, Kljuić told me about some unbelievable but revealing statements made by Tudjman when he was not yet president and was only preparing for the first elections. Evidently Tudjman had told Klujić at that time that he would garner 70 per cent of all the votes in Bosnia-Herzegovina for the HDZ. To Klujić's objection that the Croats comprised only 17 per cent of the population of the republic, not 70 per cent, Tudjman answered that that was not true; all the Muslims felt as Croats and would vote for the Croatian party.

One cannot, to be sure, reproach Tudjman that he would like to conduct a Greater Croatia policy *vis-à-vis* Bosnia-Herzegovina and try to obtain the Drina as the border for Croatia. As president, Tudjman behaved relatively moderately; as already mentioned, he had not reckoned with his electoral victory himself. He could nonetheless not refrain from doubtful statements. Indeed, it is possible that Tudjman's attitude, which was well known everywhere, may have encouraged the Serbs on their part not to accept the newly emergent Bosnian state. The leadership of the Bosnian Serbs was sooner prepared to respect the positions of the Croats than those of the Muslims. The Croatian member of the Bosnian state presidency, Miro Lasić, told me in March 1993 how Karadžić had at one point offered to cooperate with the Croats, with the remark that together they would "hurl the Muslims into the sea".

Croatia's undertaking, after the outbreak of hostilities in Bosnia in 1992, to protect its countrymen there, is another matter. Croatia was effective in this undertaking only in Herzegovina. Opposition politician Zdravko Tomac told me in September 1992 that Tudjman had said the previous May that the Posavina in northern Bosnia, i.e., the Sava plain, could not be held by Croatia. But some 300,000 Croats lived there, albeit not Herzegovinans. It occurred to many people in Zagreb in summer 1992 that Tudjman had not made any serious efforts to hold the Posavina, even though this was the crucially important corridor which connected Serbia with the Krajina and western Bosnia. Only a few bridgeheads were held, of which one, Bosanski Brod, would later be sacrificed under not entirely clear circumstances.

Tudjman and other representatives of the Croatian establishment took care to mention, as a justification, first, that Croatia was under strong international pressure and second, that a serious engagement in the Posavina would make too strong a claim on Croatian forces. In fact, the Western states were at the time threatening Croatia with sanctions, if it continued to maintain its presence on Bosnian territory. The argument ran that if one was going to cover Serbia with sanctions because it was supporting the Bosnian Serbs, then one had to do the same to Croatia in the analogous case.

Against this simplistic argumentation, Tudjman could have offered diplomatic resistance and could also mobilize support. In reality, Tudjman seemed to have viewed the Posavina as a barter object to trade for a Serbian-Montenegrin withdrawal from the area south of Dubrovnik. The "offer" was nonetheless only taken up when Bosanski Brod was thrown into the bargain. A former close collaborator of Tudjman's told me in November 1994 that the Croatian president had always said that as long as one left the Serbian corridor in peace, one could "talk" with the Serbs. Tudjman seems, accordingly, to have seen his passivity in northern Bosnia as a prepayment for an imagined, desired dialogue with Milošević. He often spoke about the dangers of Islam and of an Islamic state in Europe, even in moments when a firm alliance between Croats and Muslims was especially necessary.

The referendum with which Bosnia-Herzegovina was supposed to decide about its independence took place on 1 March 1992. It had been suggested by the so-called Badinter Commission of the EC, as a precondition so to speak for the recognition of the republic as an independent state. Through this intrusion of foreign factors, the Bosnian question seemed to be on the way to internationalization. This process was initiated as a result of a meeting, held in Lisbon during February under American and European pressure, of the leaders of the three Bosnian peoples concerning the future configuration of the common state. The meeting brought about something approximating a "fundamental agreement". On the one hand, or so it was thought in all three camps, there was an agreement on preserving the "integrity" of Bosnia-Herzegovina; on the other hand, there was a consensus about a "regionalization". A document was signed, even if each party subsequently made of the "agreement" what it wanted. But it is not at all the case, as Laura Silber and Allan Little have written,[69] that Izetbegović "retracted" his assent after his return. What was important was what the Serbian side was then preparing, openly or in secret: On 9 January 1992, the Bosnian Serbs had proclaimed their own "republic" and at approximately the same time, Milošević, Karadžić, and Kadijević decided to station in Bosnia, as far as possible, troops of Bosnian Serb extraction, who were thus planted in support of the Serbian leadership there for use in the coming conflict.

The referendum, as the Muslim and Croatian leaderships stressed, should make international recognition of Bosnia's independence possible; with this international backing, Izetbegović and his team hoped it would then be easier to establish the final internal configuration of the republic.[70]

The question posed in the referendum read: "Are you in favor of a sovereign, independent Bosnia-Herzegovina, a state of equal citizens and of the peoples of Bosnia-Herzegovina – Muslims, Serbs, Croats, and others who live in it?" The Serbs boycotted the referendum; they had already conducted their own plebiscite. But it seemed to politicians and observers alike, on that beautiful sunny Sunday, that in view of the unavoidability of the collapse of Yugoslavia and now thanks to Western support, the concept of independence would be realized. Already in the midday hours, pennants and automobile decals appeared everywhere, with the republic's new coat of arms, six lilies on a divided field. People in Sarajevo wanted to revive the medieval tradition of an independent and ethnically neutral Bosnian state and believed that they were already over the worst.

President Izetbegović, who strolled around in the vicinity of his office building in Sarajevo in a relaxed way, told me that day that the international community would now have to make good its promise and recognize Bosnia-Herzegovina immediately and unconditionally; otherwise the Serbs would break out of the established framework once again and try for "other solutions". That the Serbian politicians found themselves in a difficult situation one could see; no rational person could in fact understand why they would not agree to independence, since there was now hardly any other possibility.

A few hours later, early in the afternoon of 1 March 1992, having taken my lunch, I was waiting for the streetcar in the old Muslim quarter, so that I could return to my hotel. On a parking lot across the street, a wedding party arrived, bearing a Serbian flag, as was customary in weddings. Suddenly there was a double explosion. At first, it seemed to be a detonator, but then I saw people in a frenzy; I heard cries and saw someone run to the nearest telephone and saw the terrified faces of passers-by. Someone – as it later turned out, a criminal of Muslim nationality – had shot at this group and had killed a man. One could see the concern at the press center later, but there were also official promises that the crime would be explained as quickly as possible and the guilty party punished. This did not help. Even before midnight, Serbs were erecting barricades in the suburbs which they controlled. The police could not do anything; otherwise, as would often be said, the army would immediately intervene on the side of the Serbs. On the following Monday morning, a "crisis headquarters" of the Serbian party demanded, as a condition for the removal of the barricades, that the entire process of moving toward independence be reversed.[71] Karadžić and his deputy Koljević had hurried to Belgrade. In fact, the barricades were later removed; they had figured only as a general "testing of the waters". The impression was that neither Milošević nor the army supported a Serbian insurgency at that time.

There followed almost a month of tense uncertainty with many incidents across the republic. Under the not inept leadership of Portuguese Foreign Minister João D. Pinheiro, insofar as Portugal chaired the EC Council during the given half-year, negotiations produced a new agreement among the Bosnian parties on a package involving independence and simultaneous cantonization, but all three parties avoided signing this "agreement". At first Karadžić was demanding 62 per cent of the territory of the republic for the Serbian cantons – a demand which the Portuguese mediator rejected as a piece of shameless impudence. His counter-proposal was that the Muslims and Serbs should be assigned 44 per cent of the territory each, with the remaining 12 per cent to fall to the Croats. An economics professor in Banja Luka calculated, however, that this proposal would have left 50 per cent of all Serbs and 60 per cent of all Croats outside "their" cantons.[72] Here the handicap of the Portuguese showed itself: They could be trusted, thanks to their colonial experience, to understand certain mentalities, but they lacked the necessary knowledge of the concrete relationships in this case.

There was lacking also the most important precondition for a peaceful solution: Western recognition of the Republic of Bosnia-Herzegovina and active involvement on the part of the West in the search for a peaceful solution. The fear which Izetbegović had voiced on the day of the referendum was now being proven to have been justified. Although the referendum had been considered a precondition for recognition and had obtained the necessary majority, the expected recognition from the EC and the United States did not arrive. Even today it is not clear what were the reasons for the delay. From the memoirs of U.S. Secretary of State James Baker one obtains the impression that he was not in the least aware of the connection between the referendum and the expected speed of recognition or of the urgency of the situation.[73]

Now one could argue that, in a case which depended so much on a real consensus, a referendum which produced only a numerical majority was not the height of wisdom. The result of the referendum corresponded, at any rate, to what had been expected. Voter participation amounted to about 60 per cent, which meant that most of the Muslims and Croats went to the polls, while the vast majority of Serbs stayed away. In the West, within the EC as well as in Washington, officials had none the less placed great importance on the referendum and had made the appropriate statements; but recognition came only on 6 April 1992, when the war in Bosnia was already in motion.

I later had several conversations, including with Serbs, in an effort to clarify just why the leadership of the Bosnian Serbs, contrary to all appearances of the weeks prior, had taken up weapons even though it had every prospect of realizing its goals in a thoroughly acceptable way through negotiations.

After the outbreak of war, it was no longer possible to speak with Karadžić and Koljević; the two of them would also not have given honorable answers. Two years later, Karadžić would tell *The Washington Post* that the Serbs would have been willing to live in a common state in Bosnia-Herzegovina if the Muslims had honored "the promises of Lisbon".[74] The American Ambassador Zimmermann had allegedly persuaded them not to do so, as recognition was about to be granted. This statement of Karadžić's seems senseless, since both the cantonization and the character of Bosnia-Herzegovina as a state formed the basis of that "agreement".

The explanations of Serbian behavior generally cited different factors. First, the Muslims were militarily so badly prepared and organized as to provide, as it were, an invitation to the Serbs to take what they wanted by force, and when the EC mediation did not grant the Serbs the fulfill-ment of their maximum demands, the recourse to war once more looked attractive. The Serbs wanted, thereby, to create a *fait accompli*. Second, the West's hesitation with recognition gave the impression that neither the EC nor Washington had a firm policy on Bosnia or the will to carry it through. Third, Milošević had not only approved of war at that point in time, but had directly agitated for war; moreover, the army had indicated its preparedness to support the Serbian leadership in Bosnia. The Serbs began their war in the first days of April 1992.

In the Croatian Krajina, the transformation of the army from a "Yugoslav" institution to a purely Serbian one was completed in winter/spring 1991/92. In Bosnia, this transformation came somewhat later; the "Yugoslav"-oriented officers in the higher echelons were removed only some weeks after the outbreak of hostilities, to be replaced by extreme Serb nationalists such as Ratko Mladić. One ought, however, not over-estimate the contrast between "Yugoslav" and "Serb" oriented officers. Among those who were "Yugoslav"-oriented, most of the higher ranks were for a Serb-dominated Yugoslavia and wanted to keep Bosnia-Herzegovina within such a framework. Besides, at that time, after Macedonia's declaration of independence, the difference between a rump Yugoslavia and a Greater Serbia had been reduced to a minimum. It all hinged on the subjugation of the Muslims. The difference was, at most, that the "Yugoslav" officers still had the old image of the army as a state within the state before their eyes, and did not want to subordinate them-selves to Milošević, much less to Karadžić.

There were some preconditions for an "independent" role for the army in Bosnia. For all that, the units stationed there were estimated at more than 100,000 men (with families), and the huge amount of money being printed in Belgrade and given to the army threatened to flood the Bosnian economy even before the war.[75] The "Yugoslav"-oriented higher officers let themselves be easily pushed to the side; they evidently lacked any partic-ular political or intellectual abilities. The already oft-cited memoirs of General Kadijević show this transformation of the army quite clearly. At the end of April 1992, after the proclamation of his "Federal Republic of Yugoslavia", Milošević tried to distance himself politically as well as militarily from the events in Bosnia, but the army always remained a logistical unit, and troops from Serbia took part in operations, according to need, especially in eastern Bosnia. Only in autumn 1994 did the separation become clearer.

7   From the Yugoslav tragedy to the tragedy of the West

The collapse of efforts to restore Yugoslavia

The question suggests itself whether Marković, in his resolve to "discipline" Slovenia with the help of the army, did not feel emboldened by the behavior of the Western states, i.e., to what extent Western policy bears the blame for the outbreak of violence in Yugoslavia. It is generally accepted that Marković felt he was politically justified by the behavior of the West, of the United States as well as of the European Community, in standing up for the ostensible unity and integrity of Yugoslavia and in opposing the declarations of independence on the part of Slovenia and Croatia. Witnesses report that Marković was going around Belgrade in those days telling people that he had "more than just one mandate". Even at the talks with the European troika on 7 July 1991 in Brioni, he still tried to bring the army to the border, until he was dissuaded by the troika.[1]

On the other hand, there are no indications anywhere that either the U.S. government or the EC and its members had openly encouraged the employment of force for the purpose of preserving unified Yugoslavia. Baker's visit to Belgrade on 21 June 1991 was directed against "unilateral actions", i.e., against any attempt at disassociation, as well as against "the use of force", as then-American Ambassador Warren Zimmermann has noted.[2] A close adviser of Baker's, Robert B. Zoellick, who was, however, not on hand in Belgrade, reports that Baker had made it very clear to the Serbian side that the United States, in a choice between democracy and unity, would decide for democracy.[3]

Nevertheless, Kučan seems not to have heard any such position, whether from Baker or from European representatives. Baker had approximately ten conversations in Belgrade on that day and evidently wanted to be done with Yugoslavia's sundry problems. The Slovenian ambassador in Washington after recognition, Ernest Petrič, said in spring 1994 that he was still confronted by American officials with the rebuke that Kučan had "promised" Baker that Slovenia would put off any "unilateral actions".[4] Kučan disputes this. He had explicitly said that the Slovenian efforts to transform Yugoslavia had not produced any results, that the Slovenian blueprint, based on the plebiscite and on parliamentary decisions, remained firm, and that only the Slovenian parliament was authorized to make changes.[5] Scarcely before his departure, Baker shouted once more, "Negotiations! Negotiations!" But with whom and concerning what the Slovenes were supposed to negotiate, he did not say.[6] Petrič is of the opinion that Baker may well have believed that when the representative of the United States makes clear his views, those concerned will automatically accept these views.

Baker's account of this meeting conveys the impression that the Secretary of State had familiarized himself with Yugoslav problems rather superficially and that he was inadequately informed. Besides, he gave out that the preservation of Yugoslavia was his only goal, without indicating any practical recipes for its realization. That the United States would, at a pinch, give preference to democracy over Yugoslav unity was evidently something which he said only to Marković, and, even here, Baker paired this caution with a decisive rejection of "unilateral separation".[7] Zimmermann feels that Baker had, at bottom, given no green light, but no red light either, for the use of force to preserve Yugoslavia. Speaking with Marković, Baker had even said, "It might be logical to use the army to prevent the Slovenes" from taking over the border posts; such an action would, however, ignite an explosion, he conceded.[8] It is interesting what Baker says about Tudjman's view here. The Croatian president did not expect a war in Yugoslavia. He knew the mentality of the officers – as Baker quoted him – and they would never march against Croatia and Slovenia.[9]

It was quite clear to the Slovenes, from their talks with Baker, that the United States would not recognize any "unilateral actions", as Baker put it, and that the U.S. was of the opinion that the federation had to function until the republics had reached an accord among themselves.[10] With this rather simple position, Baker took his leave of the Yugoslav scene for many months. The American demand, which basically coincided with that of the EC, was unrealistic for Slovenia and Croatia, insofar as it did not at all take into account the entire intra-Yugoslav course of events which had driven Slovenia and Croatia to decide on independence. It also ignored the perils which any further delay might occasion for the two republics, given the attitude of the army. Nor did anyone think of extending security guarantees of any kind to Slovenia and Croatia at that time.

The strong, often almost mindless support which the United States above all, but also the states of the European Community, had given Marković up to now, together with the ambiguity of Baker's statements, made it possible to think that the Prime Minister would feel at least indirectly encouraged to use force in the effort to preserve Yugoslav integrity. At the time, there was some fuss about the fact that the American military attaché was in Slovenia as the fighting started. Even if one does not want to attach too much significance to this fact, there was nonetheless a contradiction in the Western, and especially the American, position. One could not at the same time demand that Yugoslav unity be preserved and insist that the use of force to achieve this end be renounced. Even Marković must have seen this. Slovenia proceeded "nonviolently", of course, but its goal was clear. The Slovenian parliamentary president, Bučar, said, on the evening of 25 June 1991, i.e., after the Slovenian declaration of independence, that with this act, Yugoslavia together with its organs had ceased to exist.[11]

The suspicion arises that the Western states and perhaps also Marković simply did not take the intentions of Slovenia and Croatia seriously. Marković, or so one can surmise from the available evidence, seemed to want, especially *vis-à-vis* Western diplomats, to reduce the entire conflict with Slovenia to a dispute over customs borders. Already on 5 June 1991, after Marković had undertaken an attempt to solve the "customs war" and had traveled to Ljubljana, Prime Minister Peterle indicated in the Slovenian parliament that "the federal government still (did) not understand the full dimensions of the Slovenian plebiscitary decision".[12]

That Marković was inclined, by character, to superficial optimism is undisputed. The Western diplomats in Belgrade, most of whom went beyond the city limits of the capital only with great reluctance and whose usual conversation partners were above all Marković, Lončar, and their entourage, seemed, practically without exception in the last two years of Yugoslavia's existence, to have misunderstood the realities of this country. In the last six months of Yugoslavia, their hostility to reality assumed grotesque dimensions. I must admit that the views which I heard from the circle of Western diplomats at this time made an almost traumatic impression and that I had never before encountered such a colossal jumble of political error, lazy thinking, and superficiality as I encountered then among the Western diplomatic corps in Belgrade. These people bear their share of responsibility for the catastrophic errors of the West's policy in Yugoslavia. Among these, the most important were Warren Zimmermann (USA), Sergio Vento (Italy), Hansjörg von Eiff (Germany), Michel Châtelais (France), and Peter Hall (Great Britain).

One may object that these ambassadors stood "under instructions" to work for the continuance of Yugoslavia. But in that case, one could have demanded of them, at a minimum, that they separate their analyses from their politics. In reality, it was quite the opposite. For a long time, practically until the last months before the final collapse of Yugoslavia, Western foreign ministers and politicians were paying almost no attention to the country's realities. This was the time of great transformations in Eastern Europe, of German reunification, of the Gulf War, and of earthshaking events in the Soviet Union. The former German Foreign Minister Hans-Dietrich Genscher told me that until the spring of 1991, the so-called 2 plus 4 negotiations occupied the center of attention for his foreign ministry; this treaty was ratified only in March 1991. Until then, Germany had to take care not to cause any annoyance to the Soviet Union or to other Western powers. The German foreign ministry had taken cognizance of the Yugoslav problem, but wanted to be reserved; only later did Bonn pay full attention to this question.[13] In view of the higher priority being accorded to other concerns in the Western foreign ministries, the ambassadors in Belgrade enjoyed considerable influence and considerable freedom of action. Only in Washington did one find any particular interest in Yugoslav affairs, in the persons of then-Deputy Secretary of State Lawrence Eagleburger and National Security Adviser Bent Scowcroft. Both of them had a "Yugoslav past" – the former as ambassador in Belgrade, the latter as military attaché. Eagleburger was pro-Yugoslav, Zimmermann said of his supervisor at the time, but not necessarily pro-Serbian.[14] He had private commercial interests in Yugoslavia, but one should not place too much stress on this point.

One of Zimmermann's American diplomatic colleagues told me at one time that when the ambassador filed his reports following trips to other republics, his reports were often quite realistic, but as soon as he was back in Belgrade, the unavoidable Belgrade viewpoints, together with the obsession with Marković, once more took hold of him. As for Milošević, as already mentioned, Zimmermann had arrived with the assignment to break with the pro-Milošević disposition associated with his predecessor, John Scanlan, and to be more critical of the Serbian leader. But Zimmermann himself admitted to me later that criticism was not enough; it was necessary to take decisive steps.

Even Zimmermann concedes today that the Kosovo question sounded the death-knell for Yugoslavia.[15] An "active" stance would have entailed exerting pressure in the first place in 1989, in combination with the problem of granting Western assistance. That was, nonetheless, something for which the Western states were not prepared. Zimmermann admits that the Slovenes had good reason for their behavior, but he believes that they did not make sufficient use of the possibilities for negotiation. In Zimmermann's view, the Slovenes should have stepped forward as the champions of democracy in Yugoslavia. Zimmermann does not explain how they could have done so, given the constant political and military threats. Like Eagleburger, he seemed to place great hope in the Serbian opposition, as regards the problem of Milošević. In April 1991, after President Bush, acting on the advice of Zimmermann and Eagleburger, had sent a letter to Belgrade expressing support for Marković and his reforms, I asked Zimmermann why he thought this was a good idea. His answer was that the reforms were the most important thing, and he did not believe that Slovenia and Croatia took that sufficiently into account.

The majority of EC ambassadors showed an arrogant rejection of and even open hostility toward the two Western republics. Kučan reports that Slovenia tried, in April 1991, to invite all the ambassadors of EC states stationed in Belgrade to Ljubljana in order to acquaint them with the Slovenian viewpoint. To the query which was presented through the German ambassador, who was still the most open to contacts, came the answer that, with one or two exceptions, none of them had any interest.[16] The then-German ambassador in Belgrade adopted exactly the same attitude of rejection of the aspirations of Slovenia as did his EC colleagues; there is, therefore, no evidence whatsoever that Germany supported the Slovenian and Croatian aspirations toward independence in any form. The French ambassador even engaged himself in a silly dispute over protocol with Slovenian Foreign Minister Rupel, only because he did not want to meet with him.[17]

The EC ministers shared their "concerns" about developments in Yugoslavia with Marković and Lončar on 4 April 1991 and called on the Yugoslavs to settle their disputes "peacefully". They would have done better to have said this directly to Milošević. Then the European ministers said that the "disassociating" republics would never have any prospects of joining the EC. One wondered even at the time in whose name they made this pronouncement. There were no prospects for a unified Yugoslavia to enter the EC either.[18] Moreover, Slovenes were quick to point out that the warnings of the EC ministers were directed almost exclusively at Slovenia and Croatia. Where was the recognition that the behavior of Serbia in Kosovo and in Croatia, as well as the attitude of the army, had made the common state unviable, for all practical purposes, for the non-Serbian peoples?

EC Chairman and Luxemburg Prime Minister Jacques Santer and EC Commission president Jacques Delors attained a new height in solipsism on the occasion of their visit to Belgrade, on behalf of the European Community, on 29–30 May 1991. In the meantime, yet another important event had taken place: the refusal of Serbia to confirm Croat Mesić as the new chair of the state presidency. To be sure, the EC guests deigned, this time, to speak also with the presidents of the Yugoslav republics, but their proposals were completely one-sided in Marković's favor. The EC delegates offered Marković financial assistance, to the tune of about a billion dollars, as well as the cancellation of part of Yugoslavia's foreign debt. Here there were, of course, difficulties, because the Paris Club of Yugoslavia's creditors did not want to go along with this; moreover, two days later, the EC ministers withdrew the offer of assistance which had evidently been extended somewhat hastily by Delors and Santer.[19] The offer had not been unconditional: it would have required that "human rights" and minority rights be respected, including in Kosovo, and that "constitutional conditions" be restored, that is to say, that the obstructed state presidency be restored to good working order. Jović tried to use the European interest in the revival of the state presidency to argue that, in this case, the best thing would be to simply skip over Croatia in the order of rotation.[20] At any rate, while in Belgrade, Santer and Delors, in accord with the official policy of the EC at the time, endorsed an "integral", if also democratic, Yugoslavia, without breathing a word to Yugoslav representatives as to how this might be accomplished. The offer of financial assistance to Marković was already unrealistic insofar as Slovenia and Croatia had explicitly declared, in the wake of the Serbian incursion into the monetary system of the federation, that they would not recognize any new debts on the part of the federal government.

An easy, if scarcely noteworthy, modification in Balkan policy was realized at the CSCE Conference on 19–20 June 1991, in Berlin, according to a close collaborator of Genscher's.[21] Here, with the assent of the Soviet Union and of the Yugoslav representative himself, European interest in the unity and integrity of Yugoslavia, on a democratic foundation, was confirmed, but for the first time it was stated that "it is incumbent on the peoples of Yugoslavia alone to decide about the future of the country". The previously discussed declaration (p. 215) of U.S. Secretary of State Baker on the following day showed, however, that this formulation was by no means a "breakthrough". But it is true that the unrealistic and inflexible attitude of the EC had met with discomfort here and there in Europe.

As for the reasons for the West's rejectionist attitude, these were rather diverse, quite apart from the fact that diplomats in general love the status quo, and even more, the status quo ante. There were so-called "sentimental" motives: France and Britain in particular viewed Yugoslavia up to a point as "their" political creation, even though that was only partly true; the United States, again, had found in Tito's Yugoslavia a support in the Cold War, and a whole series of American diplomats felt that their personal prestige was bound up with this pro-Yugoslav policy. Then there was the fact that the collapse of Yugoslavia might serve as a "model" for the collapse of the Soviet Union. In Germany, there were inhibitions, in the sense that the country had just achieved its own reunification and therefore could not allow itself to take part in the dissolution of another state. Finally, the principle of the unchangeability of borders (except by peaceful negotiations), anchored in the Helsinki Charter, also came into play; the explicitly stipulated exception, according to which borders might be changed by mutual agreement, was taken into account by the constantly repeated demand that the individual Yugoslav republics should realize their independence through negotiations. Then there were countries such as Spain and Italy, who feared that the fragmentation of Yugoslavia could excite parallel ideas among the minorities living within their own borders. In some politically confused minds, another argument took hold: one had to preserve Yugoslavia because Croatia and Slovenia would otherwise fall into a "German sphere of influence".

If, in the Western state community, a manifestly strong feeling of this sort was present, that Yugoslavia should be preserved at almost any price, it then seems justified to ask why the politicians and diplomats of the West had not worked harder toward this goal, when there was still time. There had been an opportunity when the foundations of the federal Yugoslav state had been destroyed in Kosovo and through the threats of an army *putsch* in Slovenia. It is a platitude to assert that a federal state can only exist as long as all of its peoples feel at home in it. To the question why the advocates of Yugoslavia had not done anything at that time, one usually receives the answer from Western diplomats that they did not want to interfere in the internal affairs of a sovereign state. Later, Western politicians felt quite free to interfere unabashedly in the internal affairs of the Yugoslav successor states.

The employment of force against Slovenia immediately after its declaration of independence sparked a first change in Western policy. The first to sound the alarm was Slovenia's neighbor, Austria, and above all, its foreign minister, Alois Mock.[22] Then alarm bells went off also in other capitals in the European Community. Genscher learned the news during a visit to Rome; he and his Italian counterpart, Gianni de Michelis, addressed Yugoslav Foreign Minister Lončar and warned him against the further use of force. The use of force now became the standard argument which Genscher would apply in his policy toward the former Yugoslavia; the Slovenes and Croats, he held, had acted without recourse to arms; they therefore could claim a right that force not be employed against them.[23] At the end of a session of the Council of Europe on 29 June 1991, Chancellor Kohl underlined this point, declaring that the unity of Yugoslavia could not be maintained through armed force. On 5 July 1991, in view of the continuing hostilities, Foreign Minister Genscher broached for the first time, in the council of EC foreign ministers, the possibility of recognition of the two new states.[24]

It is correct that Genscher was the most prominent in warning of further resort to violence. He spoke of a "new situation" which had been created by the violence; this – Genscher thought – could require "a new approach, which would include recognition".[25] This declaration has frequently been interpreted, especially by Anglo-Saxon authors,[26] as signifying that Germany had taken the side of Slovenia and Croatia from the beginning. This was, however, by no means the case, as we have already seen. Naturally, geographic proximity and the Central European character of Croatia and Slovenia were broadly conducive to a closer relationship, but that was also the case for Austria, Italy, and even Switzerland. In addition, for the two previous years, there had been a steady stream of vile defamation of Germany's good name percolating out of Serbia; the newspaper *Politika* was an especially serious offender in this regard. Kadijević's memoirs are also replete with such defamatory language.[27] Usually it was occasioned by the fact that the German media expressed disapproval of Serbian behavior in Kosovo.

The intervention of the EC in the Slovenian conflict, at first with the talks conducted by the troika of Poos, Van den Broek, and de Michelis in Belgrade and Zagreb on 29 June 1991, as well as the later visit of the EC troika in Brioni on 7 July 1991, was directed entirely against the aspirations of Slovenia and Croatia toward independence, and had the goal of reestablishing Yugoslavia as a state. The fact that it did not occur to the three EC foreign ministers even to come to Ljubljana, even though Slovenia was a combatant, was in itself a bad sign. As a result of this, Slovenian President Kučan and Foreign Minister Rupel had to travel to Zagreb taking irregular by-ways, and at risk to their lives. People in Ljubljana knew that the two of them would be placed under severe pressure. Janša describes in his book the concern among Slovenes as to whether the two men would be able to withstand the pressure.[28]

The goal of the troika was to achieve a truce on the basis of the following three points: first, withdrawal of the army to its barracks; second, a three-month moratorium on the activation of the declarations of independence; and third, the "observance of the constitution" through the installation of Mesić as president of the state presidency. These points contained some absurdities. Kučan told the Europeans quite clearly, and repeated this in his report to the Slovenian republic presidency,[29] that there could be no question of a "suspension" of the declaration of independence or of the associated constitutional acts and laws. Rupel writes that he had told the EC representatives that the renunciation of an "activation" of the declarations of independence for three months could not be allowed to become a "step backwards".[30] But this was precisely what Marković and the Serbs in Belgrade had proposed, viz., that the state of affairs of before 25 June had to be restored. This would have meant that the border would once again have become "Yugoslav".[31]

The "return of the army to the barracks" created, in any case, problems for the Slovenes. The Yugoslav Army had had to swallow a nasty beating; many of their columns had been surrounded and isolated. A "return to the barracks" would have allowed them to regroup. Besides, some of the units had been brought into Slovenia from Croatia. The European troika also breathed not a word about the discontinuation of aerial operations or about the reopening of the Slovenian airports.[32]

Rupel describes how the European troika considered it almost their greatest success that they had succeeded in winning Serbian assent to the installation of Mesić as chair of the state presidency, thereby making that body once more "capable of functioning". The Slovenes, including Drnovšek, puzzled over this.[33] The EC troika apparently thought that this would restore "civilian authority" in Yugoslavia and that the army, which now seemed to be operating entirely independently, would once more be subordinated to the "constitutionally designated commander-in-chief". That was not only naïve, but a new admission that Van den Broek and his troika cared exclusively about the restoration of Yugoslavia; in their minds, everything else was secondary. At least that was the impression among Slovenian politicians at the time.[34]

The question suggests itself as to how far Van den Broek, who was responsible here, behaved in accordance with the views of the collectivity of EC states. De Michelis had already said, on the occasion of his first visit to Slovenia, that the Slovenes should "wait" for three months, and then they could do as they pleased.[35] That was apparently not what Van den Broek had in mind. Rupel describes Van den Broek's attitude, also later during the negotiations on Brioni, as "harsh" and hostile to the Slovenes,[36] while Poos from Luxemburg had, after some initial closed-mindedness, opened up to Slovenian viewpoints, to a certain degree.[37]

The Slovenian position in Zagreb was made more difficult, in addition, by the behavior of Croatian President Tudjman, who not only refused to provide any military support for Slovenia but also seemed to share the views of the EC troika against the Slovenes. Thus, for example, Tudjman construed the passage about the "suspension" of declarations of independence as Van den Broek did. This was understandable, since Croatia had even now done practically nothing to prepare to assume independence.[38]

As regards the installation of Mesić, Tudjman attached great importance to this, probably in the belief that he could apply the brakes to the ever more menacing activities of the army in Croatia. In spite of Serbian dilatory maneuvers, the election of Mesić was finalized in Belgrade on 30 June, in the presence of the troika.[39] I had asked Tudjman sometime in summer 1991, why he was pressing for the revitalization of the state presidency although he knew that Croatia could never put together a majority in that body, that perhaps Slovenia would soon cease to take part in it, and that Mesić's powers as chair would be limited, especially in relation to operational directives to the army. Tudjman's answer was that one had to have "some kind of framework" within which to negotiate.

On 1 and 2 July, the German foreign minister paid a visit to Belgrade; this visit was not connected in any way with the work of the EC troika or with any assignment from the EC. In connection with this, a visit to Ljubljana had also been planned. Even the German ambassador in Belgrade, who accompanied Genscher, for the first time no longer spoke of the "integrity" of Yugoslavia.[40] Genscher's goal was to put a damper on the violence and to search for a "political solution". At the same time, he still spent a lot of time with old confidants, such as Foreign Minister Lončar; but they were for all practical purposes irrelevant by now. Nothing came of the visit to Slovenia; instead, he met with Kučan and Rupel in the Austrian town of Klagenfurt.

Genscher says that he cancelled the trip to Slovenia because the Slovenes wanted to hold the talks somewhere other than Ljubljana.[41] Indeed, there were overflights by Serbian military aircraft above Ljubljana at the time. But Slovenian sources say nothing about any Slovenian desire to hold the talks anywhere but in Ljubljana.[42] For that matter, I never heard any other version from my own Slovenian contacts. Rupel reports that the two diplomats accompanying Genscher – the German ambasssador in Belgrade, von Eiff, and the German consul-general in Zagreb – had had a negative disposition toward the idea of a visit to Slovenia.[43] It is thus not excluded that Genscher was influenced by his diplomats in Yugoslavia, in that the visit to Slovenia could possibly have been construed as a kind of recognition of the equal claim of this embattled republic *vis-à-vis* Belgrade. But the renunciation of violence figured now also in relation to the activity of the army in Croatia. Genscher gave this enlarged assessment to the session of EC ministers in The Hague on 5 July.

When Luxemburg's Foreign Minister Poos set out for Yugoslavia on 29 June at the head of the first EC troika, he uttered grand words: "This is the hour of Europe." His Italian colleague, de Michelis, added, "When a situation becomes delicate, the community can act as a political unit. From our standpoint, that is a good sign for the future of the political union."[44] Today such words provoke bitter disdain.

On 7/8 July, the EC troika under Van den Broek's leadership met on the island of Brioni with representatives of the Yugoslav presidency, with the leaders of the republics of Croatia and Slovenia, and with Jović as Serbia's representative. The European Community tried to dictate a "final" peace pact to the conflicting Yugoslav republics at this time. Van den Broek's arrogance, especially toward Slovenia, knew almost no bounds, as various eye-witnesses have confirmed. He announced that in regard to borders and other questions of statehood, the relationships prior to the declaration of independence had to be restored. It was more a diktat than any kind of negotiation, Kučan told me later. The declaration had the form of an ultimatum. It did allow that the peoples of Yugoslavia had the right to decide about their own future, but in connection with the three-month moratorium it was stated, in an annex concerning borders, that "The situation which prevailed before 25 June 1991 will be restored."[45]

The stipulations in the Brioni declaration concerning the meaning and importance of the state presidency, as unrealistic as they were, could be supported by reference to the 5 July declaration of the EC Council of Ministers in The Hague. The passages concerning the authority at the borders and in the skies appear to have been specifically Van den Broek's personal ideas. The Slovenes were of the opinion that, in spite of its scarcely acceptable prejudices, the Brioni declaration accomplished the "internationalization" of the conflict, including the dispatch of observers, providing, all in all, greater security for Slovenia and the inception of the process of recognition. Of course, neither Slovenia nor Croatia received any guarantees against new attacks. But for Kučan, there was, in spite of that, no doubt but that the declaration should be accepted.

The Slovenian assessment proved correct, although there had been some annoyances especially with the EC military observers from Italy and the Netherlands. These viewed the Yugoslav Army as a professional institution and not as a political force which had no interest in a correct relationship with the Republic of Slovenia, above all not where it concerned the reciprocal return of property and weapons.[46]

But a subsequent development was soon to render large portions of the Brioni diktat unworkable. Even on Brioni, Drnovšek had taken Jović, his colleague from the state presidency, aside and carefully tried to draw him to the idea of a withdrawal of the army from Slovenia. To Drnovšek's surprise, Jović's reaction was not at all negative.[47] On 11 July, the Serbian leadership suggested to Kadijević that the army should be overhauled and should henceforth concentrate on the defense of what remained of Yugoslavia. That meant withdrawal from Slovenia.[48] On 12 July, Jović and Kadijević raised this question in the state presidency. If the Slovenes considered the army an enemy force, then the best thing was to pull out, Kadijević said.[49]

Mesić resisted: The Brioni Declaration, which was being discussed, foresaw the army's return to the barracks also in Croatia or even a total withdrawal from Croatia. The Serbian bloc raised a strong objection against this, holding that any such withdrawal would mean "bloodletting up to the knees" and civil war. The article in Annex I did not mention any republic expressly, they said; on the other hand, it could in no case be assumed that all of Yugoslavia was necessarily meant. The presidency was thus free to stipulate within which territory and jurisdiction the declaration applied. Drnovšek, consulted by telephone, was, of course, in favor of the withdrawal from Slovenia. So it was decided to pull the army out of Slovenia. Mesić cast the sole vote against this. In Slovenia, his attitude was given the most negative interpretation and was taken as a new sign of Croatia's lack of loyalty. Some of the generals also had objections, above all Chief of the General Staff Adžić, who only a short while earlier had announced the total defeat of Slovenia. Milošević could now concentrate his attention fully on Croatia and Bosnia. Kadijević had helped him to succeed in overcoming the resistance in the army, although for the generals, the withdrawal was a source of disgrace.

The decision concerning the withdrawal of the army from Slovenia was finally adopted on 15 July and publicly announced on 18 July;[50] it came as a surprise not only to most Slovenes but also to Marković and the EC states, or at least those who had hoped to restore Yugoslav unity. With the withdrawal of the army, Van den Broek's attempt to restore the Yugoslav state borders evaporated. After all, with this decision to withdraw the army, it had become difficult to claim that Slovenia was not a state and that recognition could come only after a "democratic negotiation process". The three-month moratorium on the activation of independence no longer made any sense where Slovenia was concerned. Marković was now completely out of the game; he showed some displeasure over the decision. The Slovenes, who had never relaxed their vigilance, could even dictate to the army, to a considerable extent, the conditions of its withdrawal and take the greater part of the heavy weaponry for themselves.

It struck observers, including Croatian politicians, at the time how completely differently Van den Broek reacted to the rejection of his peace plan for Croatia, now that the rejection came from Serbia. Van den Broek had presented Slovenia and Croatia with an ultimatum and had threatened them with consequences if they did not agree. Now, however, on 4 August, he received an unadorned "no" from the Serbian side in Belgrade when he presented a similar plan for Croatia, including the dispatch of EC observers. The Serbs, who in the interim had largely harnessed the army for their goals and who had tallied one success after the other against the poorly armed and disorganized Croats, considered a "solution" on the Brioni model unnecessary.

The Serbs achieved exactly what they wanted. Immediately after the Serbian rejection, Van den Broek stopped making any effort. "We cannot do anything more," he said. "Our efforts have remained barren."[51] Van den Broek did not even want to name the one person who was responsible for this failure – Milošević. He accepted that Serbia would not be interested in an internationalization of its conflict with Croatia, at least as long as it remained successful, and showed that, in his view, the protection of Croatia against attacks by the army and Serbia did not lie within the EC's sphere of interests.

The behavior on the part of Van den Broek and his EC troika was questionable, because it was by no means certain whether this still represented a majority opinion inside the EC.[52] In principle, after the Serbian refusal, the question of the recognition of Croatia and Slovenia should have been considered open. Slovenia was already a functioning state; Croatia was, to be sure, embroiled in conflict, but it was holding its own as a state, and Milošević's Serbia had egregiously snubbed the EC. Genscher's early warning of a "stiff reaction" against whichever party initiated hostilities should now have been made good.[53]

It was, in fact, at this time that Genscher first considered sanctions, and on 24 August 1991, he declared, "If the blood-letting continues and if the policy of using violence to create *faits accomplis* with the support of the Yugoslav Army is not immediately halted, the federal government will have to review in earnest the possibility of recognizing Croatia and Slovenia within their established borders. Our government will also press for a corresponding review within the EC."[54] Genscher could also refer to the fact that the monitoring commission of the EC had established, beyond any doubt, the fact of Serbian advances on the territory of the Republic of Croatia as well as the army's support for them. With this, the question of recognition had been put to public discussion for the first time. The idea behind it was that, in the case of recognition by the U.S. and the EC, Croatia and Slovenia could reckon on the protection of the international community.

Instead of this, the EC continued in quite the opposite direction, as advocated by Van den Broek, and this led directly to the conference at The Hague and to the recall of Britain's former Foreign Secretary Lord Carrington to serve as EC agent for Yugoslavia. The conference in The Hague was France's idea and was accepted by the EC foreign ministers on 27 August 1991. Carrington worked for an end to hostilities even as he worked toward a political solution.

The Dutch diplomat, Henry Wynaendts, called by Van den Broek in mid-July 1991 to lead the existing and planned European mediation missions in Yugoslavia, had exposed something about the premises from which he and those who stood behind him were proceeding. He thought that Tudjman's Croatia was usefully characterized as having allegedly taken over the checkerboard coat of arms from Ante Pavelić's state, as if the checkerboard had not always been the Croatian coat of arms, since long before the *Ustaše* or the communists had come on the scene.[55] Wynaendts' hopes were unmistakably bound up with Kadijević, whom he saw as an ally for his policy of trying to restore Yugoslav unity in some form or other; he went so far as to insinuate that his goals were threatened at the time not only by advocates of Greater Serbia but also by the "aggressive Croats" and their "attacks".[56] A similar trust in the army as the last guardian of Yugoslavia runs through Zimmermann's memoirs; Kadijević even prints a thank-you letter to him from Zimmermann at the end of his book.

The agreements among all the Yugoslav presidents on 1 September, which had as their goal the introduction of EC observers, were seen by Wynaendts in the first place as signifying that Tudjman's hopes for a "common EC action against Serbia" were thereby destroyed – a corollary which pleased him.[57] He showed prejudice toward Slovenia; the Slovenes had agreed at Brioni, he said, to "demobilize" their militias[58] – which was not the case. The principal threat to his mission, in his eyes, came from Genscher, with his suggestions that Slovenia and Croatia be recognized; in his view, this had given Tudjman hope that the EC might, in collaboration with him, undertake "measures against the Serbs".[59]

All in all, the role played in the former Yugoslavia by the Dutch under Van den Broek and his people at that time was negative. As of mid-September, one could not identify any positive results, either on the basis of the conference at The Hague or on the basis of local agreements in Yugoslavia. It seemed justified already then to speak of an EC débâcle, whereby the partiality and, in part, *naïveté* with which the Dutch politicians, diplomats, and military observers had worked, figured as a catalyst.[60] The fraternization of the military observers with the army was not overlooked either in Slovenia or in Croatia. The Dutch General Johan Kosters protested against the pillaging by Croats of military transports leaving Slovenia, even though the matériel transported thus would be turned against Croatian security forces only a few days later. Dutch representatives demanded that Croatia supply the army and even Serbia with petroleum and gasoline. They demanded of the Slovenes that they once more hoist the Yugoslav flag on their borders. The Dutch diplomats, supported by diplomats from other EC states, worked with all their might to extend the moratorium, even though de Michelis had promised the Slovenes and Croats full freedom of action at its expiration. I remember that the word was going around Slovenia that now that they had freed themselves from the Serbs, they still had to free themselves from the Dutch.

The appointment of Lord Carrington as European "commissar" for Yugoslavia should have further secured the control of the EC's policy in Yugoslavia by those states and forces which stood for a restoration of Yugoslavia. The first phase of talks produced no results since the European ministers rejected, on 19 September, Van den Broek's idea of sending "lightly armed" European peacekeeping troops into the combat zone.[61] This outcome signified, *inter alia*, the definite end of efforts on the part of the EC as regards so-called "peacekeeping". The EC now turned to the UN. France, which at that time was chairing the Security Council, proposed the dispatch of an "emergency force" under Article 7 of the UN Charter. At the same time, France also proposed that the UN Security Council impose an arms embargo on the entire Yugoslav area. This was adopted in principle on 25 September 1991.

This embargo was to have enormous consequences for the subsequent course of the war, in Croatia and especially in Bosnia. It may have sprung from the notion that weapons deliveries could only inflame or prolong the conflict, but it did not take into account the fact that, in practice, it was a one-sided embargo aimed against those parties to the conflict who did not have (adequate) weaponry. The Serbian side had succeeded in taking control of most of the Yugoslav Army's weapons arsenal, especially tanks, artillery, and mortars, as well as practically the entire air force and the greater part of the navy. The weapons embargo robbed first Croatia and later the Bosnian Muslims, as the legal government of UN-member state Bosnia-Herzegovina, of the right to self-defense guaranteed in Article 51 of the UN Charter!

On 18 October, the conference in The Hague met once again under the joint chairmanship of Lord Carrington and Van den Broek; the presidents of the Yugoslav republics, the entire state presidency, Prime Minister Marković, and Foreign Minister Lončar were also invited. An armistice was proposed but nothing came of this or of Carrington's comprehensive plan for a new order for Yugoslavia.[62] In essence, he had prescribed a "loose association" of republics, approximately along the lines of what Presidents Izetbegović and Gligorov had proposed at the end of May 1991, whereby both the association and the individual republics would have the status of subjects under international law. The former Yugoslavia should constitute a customs union and a unified market, and share a common currency. There was a lot of space in this plan devoted to human rights and minority rights. In the section concerning the right of autonomy, Kosovo was not mentioned by name even once, in contrast to the Serbs in Croatia.

Mesić asked himself at the time,[63] whether it could be expected of Lord Carrington that he might have the necessary distance from the narrow foreign policy pursued by Foreign Secretary Douglas Hurd, which was oriented solely to British national interests. The answer is largely negative, as could already be seen in the complete disregard of many events which had occurred between the first and second session of the conference at The Hague. Kučan says that Lord Carrington had never made a secret of the fact that he was friends with Prince Karadjordje in London.[64] In his first draft of 18 October 1991, he had overlooked the arguments which Slovenia had registered in the discussion, as if they did not exist. Later he realized that it would be impossible to execute a simple restoration of Yugoslavia and then adopted a more realistic attitude.

The most important events which Lord Carrington tried to overlook in his draft of 18 October were as follows:

First: On 1 October 1991, the vice president of the Yugoslav state presidency, the especially controversial Branko Kostić, had convened a "session", even though, as vice president, he did not have the constitutional authority to do so; aside from the Serbian bloc, only Bogićević (from Bosnia) and Tupurkovski (from Macedonia) took part. According to established procedures, which Milošević himself had confirmed on the occasion of Jović's "resignation", the vice president was not authorized to convene a session of that body. After protests from Mesić, Bogićević and Tupurkovski understood the situation for what it was, and on the following day, the Serbian bloc members found themselves alone with the generals in the Belgrade meeting room.[65] This body sent an "ultimatum" as "the state presidency" to the leadership of Croatia and, in the event of its rejection, threatened a "general attack" on Croatia. On 4 October 1991, the army, asserting its control of the skies, prevented a session of the state presidency, which Mesić had called to take place on Brioni, from taking place, by the simple device of closing the airport at Pula. This was – and one can hardly describe it any other way – a *coup d'état*; the presidency of Yugoslavia had, from this moment on, ceased to exist. Even today, it remains unclear why Van den Broek, Lord Carrington, and those who stood behind them, nonetheless invited the members of the state presidency to The Hague.

Second: On 7 October 1991 the moratorium, which the EC had imposed on Slovenia and Croatia as regards their independence, expired. Slovenia had made it crystal clear to Lord Carrington that it remained committed to full independence and did not want to hear anything about a new Yugoslav association.[66] Only the Croatian leadership still tried to maneuver. The Yugoslav Army was on the verge of completing the withdrawal of its last units from Slovenia; as foreseen, the last soldiers left Koper by ship on 23 October and the commander of the Slovenia TO, General Janez Slapar, could report to his president, in a short ceremony, that Slovenia was "free of the enemy".[67]

Third: The army and the Serbian insurgents had, in association with the events connected with the state presidency, escalated their attacks on Croatia in early October; as a result, one had to speak of a completely new situation. The army under Kadijević now showed itself quite openly, as Kadijević claims in his book – to his own credit – to be the agent of

Greater Serbian politics.[68] Osijek, Dubrovnik, Vukovar, Šibenik, Zadar, and other Croatian cities came under heavy artillery bombardment; valuable Croatian cultural treasures were threatened with destruction. The attack on Dubrovnik was flanked by a Montenegrin move to plunder the area south of Dubrovnik, the Konavlje.

The siege of Dubrovnik was also a particular provocation to the European Community. Today many people say that the EC should have intervened at this point. These attacks effected the long-overdue reversal in Tudjman's policy; now the Croatian president finally realized that his republic was confronted with a war and that he had to behave accordingly. He could set aside the hopes he had pinned on the international state community. Already at the end of September 1991, Croatia had begun to move against those army garrisons which lay within unoccupied territory, i.e., within territory under the *de facto* control of the Croatian government. This strategy was now intensified. This was the so-called "war for the barracks", i.e., the systematic attempts on the part of the Croatian combat forces to isolate the barracks and other installations of the army, in order to compel army units to surrender; in this way, Croatia could finally arm itself suitably. Events proved what Špegelj had suspected from the beginning, viz., that some commanders, for example the commander in Varaždin, had no will to resist. It seemed that this new strategy had to be wrung out of Croatia's wavering president.

The EC and UN mediators naturally found Croatia's new strategy of defense extremely inconvenient and dangerous. The UN inserted itself into the conflict with a direct reprimand of Croatian defense efforts. The then-Secretary General of the UN, Javier Perez de Cuellar, was approaching the end of his term of office and was visibly unwilling to assume this new burden. He therefore sent the former U.S. Secretary of State (under President Jimmy Carter) Cyrus Vance as his personal representative to Yugoslavia on 8 October. Vance had played no part in the deliberations at The Hague up to then. As soon as he entered into this field of conflict, however, he immediately joined efforts with Wynaedts, and both of them took approximately the same attitude toward Croatia and the "war for the barracks" as UN representatives in Bosnia would later take toward the Muslims, viz., that it would be damaging for peace and peace efforts, and even serve to expand the conflict, if those under attack were to manage some resistance or, worse yet, have some success in this. Once more there were some noteworthy events which did not cast a favorable light on the EC observers. In some places, they tried, with suspicious haste, to "mediate" a capitulation of Croatian combat forces, as soon as this was required by the Serbs.[69] Wynaendts' book registers the complaint already in September that the Croats were becoming increasingly "aggressive".[70] For his part, Vance never tired of explaining how "saddened" he was because of the blockade of the army barracks; only after the conquest of Vukovar did he come to the realization that the army had "lied" to him.[71] Of the many mediators who tried their luck in Yugoslavia, Vance was probably one of the weakest. The judgment of his adversary from the Carter era, Zbigniew Brzezinski, seems apt; in Brzezinski's view, Vance was especially weak when he had to confront "the thugs of this world".[72]

For Slovenia, participation in the conference at The Hague was a problem, because it had decided for complete independence but found itself under pressure to collaborate "constructively" in efforts for a political settlement. In his speech at The Hague on 18 October 1991, Kučan emphasized, after he had confirmed Slovenia's intention of "cooperating constructively", that his republic saw the task of the conference primarily in terms of bringing the disaggregation of Yugoslavia to a close.[73] Slovenia stood firm as to its recognition as an independent state; he had explained this quite explicitly to Lord Carrington in a letter of 11 October. Slovenia's decision concerning independence was irreversible. Slovenia had nonetheless made some concrete proposals as to how its relations with the other republics might be constituted in future, namely on the basis of a free-trade zone. The last illusions, so said Kučan, that Yugoslavia might be resurrected had evaporated. Slovenia proposed that the relations between the republics be grounded "on the foundation of international law and on the rules of the CSCE". After the *coup d'état* in Belgrade on 4 October 1991, there was no longer any organ from the former federation which could claim any kind of legitimacy. It would be useful if the Yugoslav presidents would be advised concerning the mutual recognition of their states and borders; aside from that, the questions of the succession would finally have to be taken up seriously. For that purpose, the Yugoslav conference should have set up an additional commission.

The Slovenian statement was received with displeasure by the organizers of the conference. Moreover, the fact of the *coup d'état* in Belgrade alone should have sufficed to bring home the realization that the SFRY was finished once and for all, and that this result was Serbia's fault; but instead, there was now a wave of pressure on Slovenia, not the least from the conference's Commission for Economic Questions, which was chaired by Jean Durieux, a Belgian EC functionary. On 24 October 1991, Kučan reported in the Slovenian republic presidency,[74] that Durieux was constantly saying that Slovenia could not exist alone and would therefore have to join some sort of economic common market. Serbia was trying to endow the rump presidency with legitimacy and was clearly encountering goodwill on the part of the EC authorities for this endeavor. It was therefore necessary to register an energetic protest with Lord Carrington. Rupel added that there was a danger that this plea for the republic's inclusion in some economic zone could serve as a roundabout means of robbing Slovenia of her independence; Durieux's activities were, at any rate, harming Slovenia. Also injurious to Slovenia was the fact that it was constantly being tossed into the same pot with Croatia. It was imperative, Rupel underlined, to finally bring it home to the EC and others that

Slovenia and Croatia were no "Siamese twins". The Serbs were against Carrington's document; the danger now existed that the EC would yield to them and once more search for some sort of federal organ with which they could then associate Slovenia.

In response to these statements, a critical debate ensued in the Slovenian republic presidency concerning the role of the Slovenian representative in the Yugoslav state presidency, Drnovšek. Drnovšek had been a member of the Slovenian delegation in The Hague, together with Kučan and Rupel, but he had already indicated, on his arrival in The Hague, that he was also taking part, as a member, in the state presidency. Drnovšek conceded that, while in The Hague, he had been present for a meeting of the state presidency and had signed a "declaration for peace". Had he not done so, Slovenia would have been open to the charge of not having behaved "constructively".[75]

To this, Defense Minister Janša replied that Drnovšek's signature could be interpreted as signifying that Slovenia was still acting within a Yugoslav framework. Drnovšek had to admit that misunderstandings were possible. To that, Kučan replied that Drnovšek was part of the Slovenian delegation at The Hague, and that if he had taken part in a session of the Yugoslav state presidency, he had, in that event, taken part in the work of an organ of another state. Drnovšek defended himself by arguing that he had not signed anything which obliged Slovenia to anything.

Indeed, the question of the state presidency at The Hague was settled rather speedily on 18 October, when Kostić tried to speak as "chair" of this body; Lord Carrington balked at this, with the result that Kostić and the rest of the Serbian bloc left the room. In spite of this, Drnovšek's behavior at the conference had provided some occasion for misunderstandings. Zimmermann himself characterizes Drnovšek, albeit with some exaggerations, as having been prepared, almost to the very end, to work to save Yugoslavia.[76]

The pressure against Slovenia came not only in the conference's Commission for Economic Questions, but also in the Commission for institutions of a future new Yugoslav community. The Slovene delegate had to complain that the Slovenes' views had not been taken into account at all in the document of 18 October 1991. Slovenia was, after all, an independent legal actor and would, he said, only adhere to an agreement which considered its interests. Above all, Slovenia could not accept the Serbian standpoint that those who no longer wanted to take part in the Yugoslav community were "seceding". The fact was that Yugoslavia, as a subject of international law, no longer existed.

Slovenia felt that the status of the Serbian minority in Croatia and of the Albanians in Kosovo alike should be regulated by a special statute. This provoked a storm of protest from the Serbian representative. The Slovenian proposal, to establish a further commission for questions of succession, including the division of federal property and the sharing of the country's debts, was not taken into consideration.[77] Lord Carrington and his co-workers were also reluctant to take up the question of the blocking of Yugoslavia's foreign currency reserves, which remained in the accounts of the Yugoslav National Bank and which could, at Serbia's discretion, be used for its own purposes. I heard from Kučan at the time that Slovenia had approached Lord Carrington about this point several times, but received only the answer that the question was "too complicated" to be taken up. The U.S. was more cooperative. Eagleburger told Slovenia's representative in Washington D.C. and later ambassador personally, in mid-October, that Serbia had wanted to buy $300 million worth of rockets from China from these currency reserves.[78] It had been possible to prevent this transaction from taking place, but as a result of Lord Carrington's non-chalance, nevertheless, almost the entire currency reserves of the Yugoslav National Bank came into Serbian hands anyway and could be used, in large part, for weapons purchases.

On 25 October 1991, Lord Carrington presented a new draft at The Hague, containing some clear specifications concerning the former autonomous provinces. Under his proposal, these provinces would be assured of the constitutional status they had enjoyed before 1990. A position paper of the Slovenian foreign ministry[79] for this session stated that Slovenia would continue to take a "cooperative attitude", but in view of the fact that the EC continued to look for some sort of "general model" for Yugoslavia, had to state clearly that while the other republics could do as they pleased, for its own part, Slovenia had no interest in taking part in any new association of Yugoslav republics. In order to avoid any misunderstandings, Drnovšek would not attend the session in The Hague, though he could meet with Van den Broek elsewhere and inform him about Serbian manipulations in connection with the Yugoslav state presidency. Even if Slovenia's independent status was, in the meantime, more or less recognized de facto, it would still be confronted with new pressures, especially from the side of the Dutch Chair Van den Broek. The Slovenian foreign ministry's paper expressed great concern about the as yet uncurtailed attacks on Croatia by the army and Serbian insurgents; this situation could create new security problems for Slovenia.

Lord Carrington's new draft of 25 October 1991 won the approval of five of the six republics – curiously also from Montenegro; Serbia declared itself as often in agreement "in principle", but with fundamental reservations. Montenegrin President Momir Bulatović admitted, in the BBC television series of 1995, that his behavior had been inspired not least by offers of Italian financial assistance. But he later had to give up this independent line. As a result of Serbia's negative attitude, Lord Carrington allowed himself to be seduced into seeking to save his mission through fresh concessions to Milošević. While he abandoned the attempt to prescribe a specific form of "association" and, instead, offered three alternatives, he still insisted on a customs and currency union.[80]

The British pursued the goal of obtaining Serbia's agreement to the Carrington Plan, through concessions and promises, as if they were willing to pay almost any price. I heard a lot of angry rumblings about Slovenia at the time from British and other foreign diplomats in Belgrade; in their view, by creating its own currency, Slovenia had largely destroyed chances for any kind of loose union, to say nothing of a "tight and efficacious federation", which was, for Serbia, the only alternative to a Greater Serbian program.[81] On 28 October, the EC Council of Ministers had, at the demand of the British, the Dutch, and even the French, allowed itself to be deflected from imposing sanctions on the Serbs; Lord Carrington wanted to avoid any appearance of exerting pressure.

Nonetheless, this had the contrary effect to what had been intended. The Serbian media celebrated this as a great victory; Milošević had succeeded in convincing the EC that Serbia was not at war and was not responsible for the events taking place in Croatia. The result was a broad intensification of armed attacks, including against Dubrovnik and Vukovar. Van den Broek even threatened *the Slovenes* with sanctions on 28 October, because they would accept only a free trade zone. The Belgrade daily, *Borba*, wrote that some participants at The Hague only now grasped for the first time, with Drnovšek's failure to appear, that Slovenia's desire for independence was in earnest.[82]

The weightiest concession which Lord Carrington, at the last minute, thought he had to grant the Serbs was to strike from his plan, in his second draft of 25 October 1991, any reference to the restoration of the autonomy of Kosovo and Vojvodina in line with the status of 1990. With this, the custom was established of treating the question of Kosovo as an internal Serbian affair, at most as a question of minority rights or human rights. The actions of Lord Carrington, Van den Broek, and their collaborators at the end of October 1991 must be earnestly reviewed to consider whether the policy of the EC *vis-à-vis* the former Yugoslavia had been abandoned, much more so than earlier on Brioni, in favor of one-sided resolutions, without consultation with the other members.

The political situation became utterly surreal when, on 5 November 1991, Serbia declined even to respond to the new draft and Lord Carrington quietly ceased any further mediation. For this ambivalent behavior, he was reproached from various sides, because in this way he avoided a situation in which Serbia would be seen to be solely responsible for the collapse of the conference.[83] For many problems, especially those most directly connected with state succession, solutions could have been found between republics who were prepared to cooperate. But Lord Carrington conveyed the impression that once it was clear that the attempt to restore some sort of Yugoslav unity had failed, he saw no point in any further diplomatic activity for himself or for British interests either.

The recognition of Slovenia and Croatia

With regard to subsequent allegations that Germany had been "unilateral" and "premature" in its efforts in late 1991 to resolve the question of the recognition of Slovenia and Croatia, one may also raise the contrary question as to what the advocates of a restoration of Yugoslavia and a so-called "global solution" had to offer after Serbia's rejection of the final draft proffered by The Hague conference. I later asked this of the then-American ambassador, Zimmermann.[84] He had once more stepped forward in autumn 1991 with a plan for a new Yugoslavia, and one had the impression that he was speaking now more for himself than in the name of the government in Washington. Zimmermann's answer was "Continue to negotiate." With whom and about what, he did not know. Besides, the unclear situation in the Yugoslav area threatened to hinder political stabilization even where it was possible. Aside from that, Serbia's goals were now quite explicit and one could readily see with what means they were being realized. The restoration schemes represented and advocated by Van den Broek, Lord Carrington, and others seemed to throw into question the right of the Yugoslav peoples to determine their own future, which the EC had earlier explicitly affirmed.

It was only logical that after the collapse of efforts in The Hague, the question of the recognition of Slovenia and Croatia would seem ripe for resolution. Germany did not exert much influence in the conference at The Hague; nowhere is there any proof that Germany encouraged, much less supported, the resistance against a third Yugoslavia on the part of the two western republics. Croatia, which had always pinned its hopes on the EC and the international community, found itself now in such a bad situation that it had to accept many of Lord Carrington's proposals, even though some of them went against Croatia's interests.

Foreign Minister Genscher says[85] that the recognition of Croatia and Slovenia "came of age" through the objective course of events; even Germany's partners could not shut out reality. For him, the decisive criteria were still the rejection and condemnation of the use of force. On 5 October 1991, the EC foreign ministers had condemned the *coup d'état* in Belgrade, i.e., the Serbian manipulations of the state presidency, and had emphasized that the recognition of the other republics had to come as the fruit of a "negotiation process". That was the first time that the recognition, albeit under certain conditions, had been set before the entire EC for discussion.

That this was by no means only a German-inspired development is shown in two statements made by Van den Broek, even before the second conference at The Hague, in which the Dutch foreign minister and chair of the EC Council of Ministers even set an interval for the resolution of the recognition question. After meetings with Tudjman and Milošević he said on 10 October that "with the conclusion of the political process, hopefully within a month or so, at most in two months", the time would come to decide about the recognition of those republics which wanted it.[86] Van den Broek was even clearer on 18 October 1991 when he told the Austrian newspaper, *Die Presse*, that if there were no political agreement by 10 December and if the Yugoslav Army had not withdrawn completely from Croatia by that date, it would be time for the EC to decide on the recognition of Slovenia and Croatia. One could not deny their right to independence much longer, said Van den Broek. The Dutch foreign minister even added that there was no intention of forcing a "unified Yugoslavia" on the republics.[87] How he reconciled these statements with the attempt to threaten Slovenia with sanctions merely because this republic wanted to limit its ties within the Yugoslav area to a free-trade zone is something which only Van den Broek himself can explain.

Aside from that, the EC itself had already created at the beginning of September 1991 an instrument whose assignment was to set down the presuppositions for the recognition of those Yugoslav republics seeking independence, in order to clear the path for their subsequent recognition. This commission was chaired by French constitutional jurist Robert Badinter, and came to be known, thus, as the "Badinter Commission". Germany even deferred to the other EC states in the composition of this commission. But, through its ambassador, Gert Ahrens, Germany had shown an especial readiness to take up minority questions and was exerting pressure on Croatia to bring about a better solution within the framework of its own constitution. At base, it was Bonn which wanted to link the recognition of Croatia with the resolution of its minority question. To the question whether it was at all admissible under international law to make the recognition of a state contingent upon a concrete law on minorities, Genscher said that that had been a political decision of the EC. One suspected at the time that the uprising of the Serbs in Croatia had its roots, above all, in the ungracious attitude of the Tudjman regime towards its minority and that this question, as with many other questions in the Balkans, would be solved by giving more protection to minorities. The principles worked out by the EC conference on minorities, in Copenhagen, had been adopted as a guideline.[88]

After the final rejection of the Carrington Plan by the Serbs on 5 November 1991, a general impression was formed that the possibilities for the negotiation of a "global" solution in Yugoslavia had been exhausted. As early as 8 November, the 12 ministers declared that "the negotiation process was imperilled" and called for sanctions.[89] On 12 November, Genscher could affirm his agreement with Lord Carrington's declaration, which concerned the necessity of granting recognition to those republics which desired it.[90] On 25 November, Genscher would recall that the two-month delay, which the Dutch chair of the EC Council of Ministers had suggested, would expire on 10 December.[91]

In these days a second argument began to be heard in favor of recognition, alongside the abovementioned question of the use of force. It was, rather obviously, Serbia which had intentionally refused to negotiate.

Federal Chancellor Helmut Kohl brought this argument before the *Bundestag* for the first time on 27 November. The recognition of the Yugoslav republics who wanted this, he said, could not be put off through a blockade of negotiations. German policy-makers now found it necessary to set a deadline for recognition. Kohl said that this should be accomplished "before Christmas". The Badinter Commission supported this standpoint insofar as it established, in its first decision (on 7 December 1991), that Yugoslavia found itself "in the process of dissolution". The republics would carry over the problems connected with state succession and solve them "in accord with the procedures of international law".[92] How could the Yugoslav republics manage this, Slovenian President Kučan asked, as long as they were not recognized as subjects of international law?

Before the EC ministers could decide definitely about recognition, they engaged, following the initiative of Britain and France, in a doubtful endeavor. As a response to Serbia's destruction of Lord Carrington's efforts at negotiation, they imposed "sanctions", not only on the responsible republics, Serbia and Montenegro, but on all the Yugoslav successor states, thus also on Slovenia and Croatia. These sanctions consisted in essence of the suspension of the agreement reached earlier between the EC and Yugoslavia concerning trade and cooperation. Indeed, the ministers declared that they would be happy to lift these sanctions against republics which showed themselves "ready to cooperate", only they took their time about it. Then, well past the turn of the year, the trade agreement at least was reinstated for Croatia and Slovenia, but even here some EC states, among them France and Belgium, tried to push through some limitations to the earlier agreement with Yugoslavia.

When I spoke with Slovenian President Kučan at the end of November 1991, he had tough words about the EC's behavior.[93] The constant postponement of international recognition of Slovenia had brought the republic into an unendurable situation, he said; it was hindering political and economic consolidation, creating security problems, and endangering democratic development. The EC sanctions hurt export-intensive Slovenia, not blameworthy Serbia, most of all. Slovenia did not want to gain advantages at Croatia's expense, but if the EC had problems with the recognition of Croatia, then Slovenia should not suffer as a result. Kučan also complained that the EC and the rest of the Western community of states not only tolerated, but even cooperated, in Serbian endeavors to obstruct air traffic to and from Slovenia and Croatia. As for the dispatch of UN peacekeeping troops to Croatia, one should not always leave the initiative to Milošević. As long as Croatia was requesting such troops, nothing happened; now that Serbia had also demanded this, in order to use the UN presence to consolidate its own military conquests, the international community gave in to the demand.

In many circles, especially in Anglo-Saxon countries, the claim has been made that the recognition of Slovenia and Croatia was "premature" and that it made a "global solution" more difficult and seriously stoked the war; this claim became almost conventional wisdom, even an article of faith and a boundary marker between right and left. Given the facts, it is hard to understand this. Certainly, it was often said in Serbian propaganda emissions during autumn 1991 that, in the event of recognition, there would be "real war", but as far as one can determine from available documents and other sources, it never occurred to Lord Carrington and other British diplomats at the time to operate on the basis of this argument or to take Serbian threats seriously.

In reality, the events developed quite differently. The entire Serbian offensive, in which the army had readily offered a "helping" hand, took place in the summer and autumn of 1991, not later. Vukovar fell on 18 November 1991. The army and the Montenegrin volunteers had encircled Dubrovnik in mid-October, and even representatives of the Serbian opposition were describing Dubrovnik as "not Croatian" and demanding that it be converted, at a minimum, into a "free zone". The Serbian offensive had, for all practical purposes, cut Croatia in three. All in all, one can say, the Serbian offensive had attained all of its goals around the beginning of November 1991, even if the outer limit desired by extremists – from Virovitica in western Slavonia to Karlobag on the Adriatic (near Rijeka) – remained a fantasy. Kadijević apparently wanted to get more and blames difficulties with recruitment, above all in Serbia, for his failure to do so.[94]

In November 1991, Serbian operations came to a standstill. There were several reasons for this. First, the Serbs had, by now, reached purely Croatian districts on almost all fronts; thus, the army and the insurgents could no longer count on any local support. Second, Croatian defenses had finally attained a professional and effective level. And third, the Yugoslav Army was in a critical phase, as it was being transformed from a *Yugoslav* force into a *Serbian* army. The problems with the mobilization of Serbian reservists, mentioned by Kadijević, were real; neither Serbs from Serbia nor Montenegrins showed much enthusiasm at the time to fight in the Serbian districts in the west. In December 1991, the Croatian army in western Slavonia began a successful counteroffensive. General Anton Tus, the then Croatian Chief of the General Staff, told me in 1992 that in his opinion the truce reached at the end of 1991, on the basis of the Vance Plan for Croatia, was indeed favorable for the Serbs, since the Yugoslav Army was, at the time, showing clear signs of disintegration; at a minimum, Tus believes, Croatia could have completely liquidated the Serbian bridgehead in West Slavonia and should have enlarged its connections with Dalmatia. As Jović openly says, it was Serbia which now needed the UN to provide a cordon.[95]

It is correct and has never been disputed that Germany played a leading role in the process of recognition, but if the "rejection front" had still had any arguments on hand, after the failure at The Hague, these would certainly have been provided. It is noteworthy, and even characteristic, that opponents of the recognition of Slovenia and Croatia often do not even mention the fact that the Serbs had definitely rejected Lord Carrington's peace plan on 5 November.[96] One noticed, of course, the anonymous dilatory maneuvers. Perez de Cuellar warned, evidently on the "inspiration" of rejectionists, against any "premature recognition", lest the conflict spread – to which Genscher replied to him, that the very opposite was the case.[97] In reality, there were efforts in the UN Security Council, with regard to the conclusion of on-going negotiations of a truce within the framework of the Vance Plan, to postpone recognition once more. It would soon be shown that recognition did not damage the conclusion of negotiations concerning the Vance Plan in the least.

Genscher succeeded in obtaining a consensus within the EC that the question of the recognition of Croatia and Slovenia should not burden the EC conference at Maastricht, which was set for 19 December 1991. That meant that the decision should be taken before then. On 3 and 5 December, in Bonn, Kučan and Tudjman were given unambiguous assurances concerning recognition. On 7 December, the aforementioned first decision (p. 237) lay before the Badinter Commission and finally, on 15 December, Genscher succeeded in proposing, together with France, some "general guidelines" for the recognition of new states in southeast Europe, which were then brought before the determinative session of the 12 EC foreign ministers on 16 December and which set out the framework, so to speak, for the recognition of Croatia and Slovenia. Genscher says that he paid particular attention, in those days, to coordinating his actions with France.[98]

According to Genscher's own impression, he met with little resistance at this session in Brussels. Denmark and Belgium had shared the German point of view from the beginning. The only objection came from Greek Foreign Minister Antonis Samaras, because of Macedonia, but, upon being reassured that every case of recognition would be reviewed separately and that the current deliberations were not about Macedonia, he withdrew his opposition. Genscher expected that Van den Broek would still show some opposition. Indeed, Van den Broek, for his part, had expected Samaras to put up more of a fight and was visibly disappointed when this proved not to be the case. British Foreign Secretary Douglas Hurd said at the time that Germany had refrained from unilateral action, and that one had to respect this and, accordingly, come to an agreement now.[99] It was decided that recognition would formally take effect on 15 January 1992, though Genscher had announced already at the session that Germany would declare formal recognition as early as 18 December.

This, one should add, was perhaps not entirely unnecessary, because one could not exclude the possibility that individual EC ministers might look for loopholes, as had happened before, perhaps in connection with the final negotiations over the Vance Plan. This was in fact signed in Sarajevo on 2 January 1992; it consisted of a truce, an agreement on the dispatch of UN troops to the Croatian war zone, and a series of stipulations about the reconstitution of Croatian territorial integrity and the return of refugees. The truce held, more or less, but the UN could not find the will to carry out the other clauses.

The absurdities in the EC policy *vis-à-vis* the former Yugoslavia did not, however, come to an end with the recognition of Croatia and Slovenia. To be sure, the Badinter Commission vindicated the EC decision with its own determination, on 15 January 1992, that Slovenia had fulfilled all conditions as regards democracy and the protection of minorities; by the same virtue it also gave Croatia passing marks, though with some reservations with regard to the treatment of the Serbian minority. Croatia provided the appropriate guarantees, through President Tudjman's letter of 13 January 1992, and later, if with a bit of a delay, adopted the necessary constitutional amendments and changes to existing laws.

The Badinter Commission also found that Macedonia met all the preconditions for recognition; the clarifications which the Commission requested as regards Macedonia's relations to its neighbors were immediately provided by Macedonia, in the form of constitutional changes. In spite of that, the EC declined to offer diplomatic recognition to Macedonia, because of Greek objections, but did nothing to stop Greece from imposing an economic blockade against Macedonia and thereby seriously obstructing the consolidation of conditions in the southern Balkans.

One can cite a few possible reasons for the whispering campaign against Germany's policy in connection with the recognition of Croatia and Slovenia, which continues to be waged in many Western countries, both in political and in academic circles; but it can scarcely be understood in rational terms. In view of the political and moral catastrophe produced by Western policy in Bosnia – determined largely by Britain and France, but under the mantle of the UN – it became convenient to look for scapegoats. The Slovenes, Croats, and Germans were thus saddled with the "blame". While those British officials who spoke for their government in an official capacity remained fair and correct even after recognition – Lord Carrington defended the action quite explicitly in a talk at Chatham House on 10 March 1992 and Foreign Secretary Douglas Hurd did likewise in an interview on 14 July 1993[100] – other signals came soon enough from the French side. Already on 2 February 1992, France proposed that one should expressly acknowledge the "constructive attitude" adopted by Serbia and Milošević with respect to the EC and then, after his resignation, former Foreign Minister Roland Dumas criticized the decision on recognition, in which he himself had had a hand.

A second consideration is that the question of recognition was the first political question of any importance in Europe since the end of the Second World War in which Britain and France had had to accommodate German concepts. For France, this may well have seemed to threaten Paris' claim to the leading political role in the EC, while for a typical representative of the British ruling class such as Hurd, the situation must have seemed, at the very least, "unusual". Now one must acknowledge that Genscher and Kohl had chosen the moment cleverly, viz., at that moment when the other side was, quite simply, lacking any viable counter-arguments.

Hand in hand with this went the *idée fixe* that Croatia and Slovenia lay within the "traditional" German sphere of influence and would do so once again, in which case one should oppose this "German influence". In Paris and London, it was hoped that this influence might be obstructed, first, once it proved impossible to hold Yugoslavia together, by backing their traditional ally, Serbia, and second, as British Foreign Secretary Hurd would later demonstrate, by adopting an especially hostile attitude toward Croatia. The German sphere of interests in western Yugoslavia was, however, pure fiction; in regard to Slovenia it was, in historical terms, arrant nonsense. Austria was tangibly more interested in the question of Slovenia's and Croatia's recognition, and politically also more active, as it, quite understandably, wanted peace and stability along its southern border. Moreover, after the recognition of Croatia and Slovenia, the Germans had practically no Balkan policy at all, much to the dismay especially of the Croats. Nevertheless, there were always new attempts on the part of France, Britain, and their allies to make Germany "responsible" for Croatia; German policy-makers, especially where Foreign Minister Kinkel was concerned, from time to time yielded to this pressure, whether out of *naïveté* or out of some conviction about European solidarity. Precisely because of its inactivity after recognition, Germany's policy toward Croatia remained without further successes of any importance; the Germans were unable to deflect Tudjman from his catastrophic policy *vis-à-vis* the Bosnian Muslims or from his increasingly undemocratic behavior.

Various representatives of the "rejection front" of that time are prepared to concede today that the recognition of Slovenia was "possibly" justified, but when it comes to Croatia, they continue to grit their teeth.[101] In support of their thesis that the recognition of Croatia was unjustifiable they sometimes even claim that, according to the customs of international law, a state which does not exercise authority throughout its entire territory should not be accorded recognition. But this argument too can easily be refuted. In terms of sovereignty, there were no differences between Slovenia and Croatia; the old Yugoslav constitution had conceded both republics the distinction of "statehood". The fact that a national minority of 14 per cent existed in a state and raised a clamor has never, in the history of international law, been taken as a pretext for contesting the international legal status of such a state. Even the demand for fixed borders slips, in this case, into the void. To begin with, the EC itself as well as the Badinter Commission had recognized the borders between the Yugoslav republics as state boundaries. Second, it is not at all necessary for recognition, according to the valid precepts of international law, that a newly emerging subject of international law be already in control of firm boundaries. It is sufficient if "a secure space is available, on which the politically organized nation exercises its effective rule, independently of other states, with a view to continuance".[102] No one can dispute that this condition applied to Croatia in December 1991.

All of the attempts to slight Croatia under international law may have sprung from an emotional revulsion against certain events in the Croatian past and toward certain specific features of Tudjman's regime. It may also have troubled some people that, in certain milieus, recognition, especially of Croatia, was demanded because this country was strongly Catholic and therefore "European", while the Serbs, being Orthodox and under "Byzantine" influence, were considered natural antagonists.

Occasionally the reproach of a "premature" recognition is connected with the fact that Germany undertook this on 18 December, while the rest of the EC did not do so until 15 January. In this timeframe, or so these critics maintain, one might "perhaps" have worked out better conditions for the protection of minorities. This supposition does not seem to have any real basis. Finally, Germany had promised the recognition "before Christmas" and the entire EC had happily left the minority problems to the Badinter Commission. Moreover, regulations about minority rights in Croatia made very little sense at the time since all of the Serbian districts were already occupied.

Finally, some critics of Genscher's action in December 1991 happened upon the notion that this had contributed in some essential way to the outbreak of the war in Bosnia-Herzegovina. This reproach strikes me as especially absurd. As already mentioned, the war in Croatia ended on 2 January 1992 and the war in Bosnia began in April 1992 on the basis of separate development. This last notion does not take into consideration the fact that it was the United States, and not Germany, which led the way to the recognition of Bosnia-Herzegovina in spring 1992. As Genscher has noted, Germany did not oppose this policy, but it has not urged it.[103] In early spring 1992, American policy-makers came to the conclusion that it was senseless to wait for a "global solution" for all Yugoslavia. The alternative of independent states on the foundation of the former republic boundaries seemed to have established itself; in the case of Slovenia, it seemed to be expressly successful. So the view may have taken shape in Washington that one should continue on this path and solve the Bosnian problem accordingly. The Badinter Commission had prescribed a referendum in the case of Bosnia-Herzegovina.

Zealous advocates of European unification naturally bewail the tragedy of European policy in Bosnia, but they trace it back to the notion that the entire conflict in Yugoslavia broke out "too early", before the European Community had developed the necessary institutions for a common policy. In reality, individual countries acted on the basis of their own real or imagined national interests and viewed collective bodies such as the EC, the UN, and NATO essentially only as instruments under whose flags they could pursue these interests. After the American intermezzo in the recognition question, France and Britain tried to monopolize Western policy in Bosnia. The visit of French President François Mitterrand to Sarajevo on 28 June 1992 was interpreted at the time, throughout the Balkans, as signifying that Mitterrand, with his affirmation of purely humanitarian assistance, wanted to preempt the possibly more active interventionist intentions of other states, particularly the United States.[104] The long-lasting, almost emotional refusal to take any kind of armed action of significance or even to lift the arms embargo against the Muslims can scarcely have been dictated only by concern for the UN forces stationed there, as Britain and France repeatedly claimed. Once more those European states which had not wanted to acknowledge the collapse of Yugoslavia, which had then seen in Serbia a "counter-weight" to some purported "German sphere of influence", and which, at last, wanted to prove to the United States that this was "the hour of Europe", found themselves together in Bosnia again.

Epilogue

As I write this epilogue – in October 1998 – the crisis in the former Yugoslavia is still not at an end, more than seven years after the outbreak of open hostilities. Certainly, a truce and provisional peace for Bosnia-Herzegovina were realized through the Dayton Peace Accord in November 1995, but in early 1998 the smouldering conflict in Kosovo came into the open. It appears even now that this new center of crisis will necessitate once more a lasting political, financial, and perhaps also military engagement of the Western state community, and engender difficult complications in the absence of the termination of the international engagement in Bosnia within the foreseeable future.

The question as to why that should be the case is the question about the quality and correctness of Western policy in the Balkans. This cannot be characterized, for the entire period since 1991, as other than too little, too late, and always with the gaze fixed firmly on the status quo ante. To be sure, American special ambassador Richard Holbrooke deserves full credit for the style and manner in which he finally achieved an agreement in Dayton, but he himself describes the problems and obstacles he had to overcome in the process in his memoirs (*To End a War*, 1998). Among these problems were, not the least, the divergent views of America's European allies. But even Holbrooke, the great "doer", could not free himself from certain dubious archetypes of Western policy in the Balkans, which had become visible in the years since 1991. He took over, uncritically, theses and concepts which had been erected before him, from the reproach against Germany for its allegedly "premature" recognition of Slovenia and Croatia to the uncritical acceptance of the Bosnian partition plan worked out by the so-called "Contact Group", which assigned the Serbs (31.4 per cent of the republic's population on the eve of the war) 49 per cent of the territory of Bosnia-Herzegovina, even to the endorsement of the merger of the Muslim and Croat districts in the so-called "Federation". Similarly, he proceeded from the necessity of constructing a unified Bosnian state – here, however, supported by the Muslim leadership, which hoped and still hopes to be able to lay claim to this common state, thereby monopolizing foreign policy as well as the administration of foreign credits. The Muslim leadership seemed to aspire to something similar in regard to the "Federation". Yet another problem was that things had to move along quickly in Dayton, because Clinton's election campaign was already underway.

I am not suggesting that a new war is developing on the basis of the shortcomings of Dayton. But the political map of Bosnia-Herzegovina will end up looking entirely different from what was planned in Dayton and from that alone certain tensions and conflicts may arise. As for the unified Bosnian state, this is hardly more than a fiction, serving as an alibi for Western policy-makers. At the elections in late September 1998, the people of Bosnia served notice, by a large majority, that they see their futures bound up with their separate national communities and view the "Federation" as an artificial construction. Thanks to Western generosity to the Serbian entity in the apportionment of land and to Croatia's continuing pressure within the Federation, hemming in the Muslims, one will finally end up with precisely the kind of Muslim ghetto which Western policy-makers wanted to avoid and to which a general return of refugees is unthinkable.

With regard to Kosovo, the international community has declined to grant the independence sought by the majority of the province's Albanians. The international community has, of course, recognized that the province was illegally deprived of its autonomy, but it is nonetheless not prepared, at the present moment, even to engage itself decisively for a restitution of the level of autonomy provided under the Yugoslav constitution of 1974. The first attempt at an armed uprising ended in August 1998 in catastrophe, accompanied by a wave of refugees in misery similar to that earlier in Bosnia. Of course, at the beginning of the fighting, Western politicians announced almost unanimously that they would not permit a "second Bosnia". At Dayton, Holbrooke could use the threat of military intervention to obtain an at least partly usable even if unsatisfactory political solution. In the case of Kosovo, he obtained in October 1998, using similar methods, only a rather uncertain and nebulous agreement, which scarcely amounted to anything more than the barest beginning of a political solution of this problem. At the time of going to press, the only point that seems to be certain is another long-lasting political, economic and military engagement of the West.

Bibliography

Ajanovski, Vangel. *Egejski buri* (Skopje, 1975).

Alexander, Stella. *Church and State in Yugoslavia since 1945* (Cambridge, 1979).

Avdić-Vlassi, Nadira. *Za obranu Azema Vlasija* (Ljubljana, 1989).

Baker, James A. *The Politics of Diplomacy* (New York, 1995).

Banac, Ivo. *The National Question in Yugoslavia: Origins, History, Politics* (Ithaca, N.Y., 1984).

Behschnitt, Wolf Dietrich. *Nationalismus bei Serben und Kroaten 1830–1914: Analyse und Typologie der nationalen Ideologie* (Munich, 1980).

Biber, Dušan. *Nacizem in nemci v Jugoslaviji, 1933–1941* (Ljubljana, 1966).

Boban, Ljubo. *Sporazum Cvetković–Maček* (Belgrade, 1965).

—— *Maček i politika hrvatske seljačke stranke*, 2 vols. (Zagreb, 1974).

Bogdanov, Vaso. *Historija političkih stranka u Hrvatskoj* (Zagreb, 1958).

Bor, Matej *et al. Veneti* (Ljubljana, 1989).

Brey, Thomas. *Die Logik des Wahnsinns* (Freiburg i B., 1993).

Calić, Marie-Janine. *Der Krieg in Bosnien-Hercegowina* (Frankfurt, 1995).

Ćirković, Sima. *Istorija Bosne* (Belgrade, 1964).

Čubrilović, Vasa. *Istorija političke misli u Srbiji XIX veka* (Belgrade, 1958).

Čulinović, Ferdo. *Jugoslavija izmedju dva rata*, 2 vols. (Zagreb, 1961).

—— *Dokumenti o Jugoslaviji* (Zagreb, 1968).

Dedijer, Vladimir. *Josip Broz Tito* (Belgrade, 1953).

De Jong, Jutta. *Der nationale Kern des makedonischen Problems* (Frankfurt-am-Main, 1982).

Djaković, Spasoje. *Sukobi na Kosovu* (Belgrade, 1984).

Djilas, Milovan. *Tito: The Story from Inside* (New York, 1980; London, 1981).

—— *Wartime: With Tito and the Partisans*, trans. by Michael B. Petrovich (New York and London, 1977).

Doder, Duško. *The Yugoslavs* (New York, 1978).

Drnovšek, Janez. *Meine Wahrheit*, German ed. (Kilchberg, 1998).

Eger, Thomas. *Das regionale Entwicklungsgefälle in Jugoslawien* (Paderborn, 1980).

Ferenc, Tone. *Nacistićka politika denacionalizacije u Sloveniji u godinama od 1941 do 1945*, trans. from Slovenian by Ivo Tominc (Rijeka, 1979).

Furkes, J. and K. H. Schlarp. *Jugoslawien – Ein Staat zerfällt* (Reinbek, 1991).

Gasper, Gjini. *Skopsko–Prizrensko Biskupija kroz stoljeća* (Zagreb, 1986).

Gelhard, Susanne. *Ab heute ist Krieg* (Frankfurt-am-Main, 1992).

Glenny, Misha. *The Fall of Yugoslavia: The Third Balkan War* (London, 1992).

Grdešić, Ivan *et al. Hrvatska u izborima 1990* (Zagreb, 1990).

Gross, Mirjana. *Povijest Pravaške ideologije* (Zagreb, 1973).
—— *Vladavina Hrvatsko-srpske Koalicije* (Zagreb, 1960).
Grotzky, Johannes. *Balkankrieg* (Munich, 1993).
Grulich, Rudolf. *Die unierte Kirche in Mazedonien* (Würzburg, 1977).
Gutman, Roy. *A Witness to Genocide* (New York, 1993).
Halperin, Ernst. *Der siegreiche Ketzer* (Köln, 1957).
Hasani, Sinan. *Kosovo: Istine i zablude* (Zagreb, 1986).
Hodža, Hajredin. *Afirmacija albanske nacionalnosti u Jugoslaviji* (Priština, 1984).
Hoffmann, George W. and Fred Warner Neal. *Yugoslavia and the New Communism* (New York, 1962).
Holbrooke, Richard. *To End a War* (New York, 1998).
Hoptner, Jacob. *Yugoslavia in Crisis, 1934–1941* (New York, 1962).
Horvat, Josip. *Politička povijest Hrvatske* (Zagreb, 1936).
Horvat, Rudolf. *Najnovija doba hrvatske povijesti* (Zagreb, 1906).
Hory, Ladislaus and Martin Broszat. *Der kroatische Ustascha-Staat* (Stuttgart, 1964).
Hösch, Edgar. *Geschichte der Balkanländer* (Munich, 1993).
Isaković, Alija. *O nacionaliziranju Muslimana* (Zagreb, 1990).
Janković, Dragoslav. *Jugoslovensko pitanje i Krfska deklaracija* (Belgrade, 1967).
—— *Srbija i jugoslovenska pitanje* (Belgrade, 1973).
Janša, Janez. *Premiki* (Ljubljana, 1992).
Jelić-Butić Fikreta. *Hrvatska Seljačka Stranka* (Zagreb, 1983).
—— *Ustaše i NDH 1941–1945.* (Zagreb, 1978).
Jiriček, Konstantin. *Istorija Srba*, 2 vols. (Belgrade, 1952).
Jović, Borisav. *Poslednji dani SFRJ*, 2nd ed. (Belgrade, 1996).
Judah, Tim. *The Serbs: History, Myth and the Destruction of Yugoslavia* (New Haven, Conn., 1997).
Kadijević, Veljko. *Moje vidjenje raspada* (Belgrade, 1993).
Kardelj, Edvard. *Die Vierteilung, Nationale Frage der Slowenen*, German ed. (Vienna, 1971).
Kind, Christian. *Krieg auf dem Balkan* (Zürich, 1994).
Klaic, Nada. *Povijest Hrvata* (Zagreb, 1971).
Kleinert, Detlev. *Inside the Balkans* (Vienna, 1993).
Kočović, Bogoljub. *Žrtve drugog svetskog rata u Jugoslaviji* (London, 1985).
Kofos, Evangelos. *Nationalism and Communism in Macedonia* (Thessaloniki, 1964).
Kohl, Christine von. *Jugoslawien* (Munich, 1990).
—— and Wolfgang Libal. *Kosovo* (Vienna and Zürich, 1992).
Krizman, Bogdan. *Ante Pavelić i Ustaše* (Zagreb, 1978).
—— *Pavelić izmedju Hitlera i Mussolinija* (Zagreb, 1980).
—— *Ustaše i Treći Reich*, 2 vols. (Zagreb, 1983).
Ladas, Stephen. *The Exchange of Minorities: Bulgaria, Greece and Turkey* (New York, 1932; reprinted 1956).
Lendvai, Paul. *Zwischen Hoffnung und Ernüchterung* (Vienna, 1994).
Libal, Michael. *Limits of Persuasion* (Westport, Conn., 1997).
Libal, Wolfgang. *Das Ende Jugoslawiens. Chronik einer Selbstzerstörung* (Vienna, 1993).
—— *Mazedonien Zwischen den Fronten* (Vienna, 1993).
Lončar, Dragutin. *Političko življenje Slovencev* (Ljubljana, 1921).
Maček, Vladko. *In the Struggle for Freedom*, trans. by Elizabeth and Stjepan Gazi (University Park, Pa., 1957).
Magaš, Branka. *The Destruction of Yugoslavia: Tracking the Break-up 1980–92* (London, 1993).

Malcolm, Noel. *Bosnia: A Short History* (London, 1994).

—— *Kosovo: A Short History* (London, 1998).

Marković, Svetozar. *Sabrani spisi*, 4 vols. (Belgrade, 1960).

Mesić, Stipe. *Kako smo srušili Jugoslaviju* (Zagreb, 1992).

Meštrović, Ivan. *Uspomene na političke ljudi i dogadjaje* (Zagreb, 1969).

Mirić, Jovan. *Sistem i kriza* (Zagreb, 1984).

Mišović, Miloš. *Ko je tražio republiku: Kosovo 1941–1985.* (Belgrade, 1987).

Mitić, Ilija. *Dubrovačka država* (Zagreb, 1988).

Neubacher, Hermann. *Sonderauftrag Südost* (Göttingen, 1956).

Nuši, Pajazit. *Prizrenska Liga* (Priština, 1978).

Obradović, Djordje. *Stradanje Dubrovnika* (Dubrovnik, 1992).

Ostrogorsky, Georg. *Geschichte des byzantinischen Staates* (Munich, 1963).

Pavelić, Ante Smith. *Dr Ante Trumbić* (Munich, 1979).

Pirjevec, Jože, *Jugoslavija 1918–1992.* (Koper, 1995)

Pribičević, Svetozar. *Diktatura kralja Aleksandra*, trans. from French by Andra Milosavljević (Belgrade, 1953).

Pribichevich, Stoyan. *Macedonia: Its People and History* (University Park, Pa., 1982).

Prunk, Janko. *Slovenski narodni programi* (Ljubljana, 1986).

Radić, Stjepan. *Politicki spisi* (Zagreb, 1971).

Ramet, Sabrina P. *Balkan Babel: The Disintegration of Yugoslavia from the Death of Tito to Ethnic War*, 2nd ed. (Boulder, Colo., 1996), 3rd ed. forthcoming in Sept. 1999.

Rathfelder, Erich. *Sarajevo und danach* (Munich, 1998).

Reuter, Jens. *Die Albaner in Jugoslawien* (Munich, 1982).

Roberts, Walter R. *Tito, Mihailović and the Allies 1941–1945* (New Brunswick, N.J., 1973; reprinted Durham, N.C., 1987).

Rupel, Dimitrij. *Skrivnost države* (Ljubljana, 1992).

Rusinow, Dennison I. *The Yugoslav Experiment, 1948–1974* (Berkeley and Los Angeles, 1977).

Selimović, Meša. *Sjećanja* (Belgrade, 1983).

Shoup, Paul. *Communism and the Yugoslav National Question* (New York, 1968).

Silber, Laura and Allan Little. *The Death of Yugoslavia* (London, 1995).

Skendi, Stavro. *The Albanian National Awakening, 1878–1912* (Princeton, N.J., 1967).

Stadtmüller, Georg. *Geschichte Südosteuropas* (Vienna, 1950).

Stambolić, Ivan. *Put u bespuće* (Belgrade, 1995).

Starčević, Ante. *Politički spisi* (Zagreb, 1970).

Stojadinović, Milan. *Ni rat, ni pakt* (Buenos Aires, 1963).

Strossmayer, Josip Juraj and Franjo Rački. *Politički spisi* (Zagreb, 1971).

Suljević, Kasim. *Nacionalnost Muslimana* (Rijeka, 1981).

Sundhausen, Holm. *Geschichte Jugoslawiens* (Stuttgart, 1982).

Supilo, Frano. *Politički spisi* (Zagreb, 1970).

Šabanović, Hazim. *Bosanski pašuluk* (Sarajevo, 1959).

Šišić, Ferdo. *Pregled povijesti hrvatskoga naroda* (Zagreb, 1975).

Tašić, Predrag. *Kako sam branio Antu Markovića* (Skopje, 1993).

Tolstoy, Nikolai. *The Minister and the Massacres* (London, 1986).

Tomac, Zdravko. *The Struggle for the Croatian State* (Zagreb, 1993).

Tomaševich, Jozo. *War and Revolution in Yugoslavia, 1941–1945: The Chetniks* (Stanford, Calif., 1975).

Troebst, Stefan. *Die bulgarisch-jugoslawische Kontroverse um Makedonien 1967–1982* (Munich, 1993).
Tudjman, Franjo. *Bespuća povijesne zbiljnosti* (Zagreb, 1989).
Udovički, Jasminka and James Ridgeway (eds.). *Burn This House: The Making and Unmaking of Yugoslavia* (Durham, N.C., 1997).
Vacalopoulos, Apostolos. *History of Macedonia* (Thessaloniki, 1973).
Vavić, Milorad *et al.* (eds) *Tragom isdaje i zločina* (Zagreb, 1985).
Verdoss, Alfred and Bruno Simma. *Universelles Völkerrecht* (Berlin, 1981).
Vllasi, Azem. *Majstori mraka* (Zagreb, 1990).
Vukmanović-Tempo, Svetozar. *Memoari*, 2 vols. (Belgrade, 1971).
—— *Borba za Balkan.* (Zagreb, 1980).
Vuković, Ilija. *Autonomaštvo i separatizam na Kosovu* (Belgrade, 1971).
Wynaendts, Henry. *L'engrenage* (Paris, 1993).
Žečević, Momčilo. *Slovenska ljudska stranka i jugoslovensko ujedinjenje* (Belgrade, 1973).
Zimmermann, Warren. *Origins of a Catastrophe* (New York, 1996).
Zulfikarpašić, Adil (ed.). *Sarajevski proces 1983* (Zürich, 1987).
Žebot, Ćiril. *Neminljiva Slovenija* (Celovec [Klagenfurt], 1988).

Anonymous/collective. *Istorija na Makedonskiot Narod*, 3 vols. (Skopje, 1969). Published in English as *A History of the Macedonian People* (Skopje, 1979).
—— *Mali ključ povijesti crkve u Hrvata* (Zagreb, 1978).
—— *Pregled. Storija Saveza Komunista Jugoslavije* (Belgrade, 1963).

Newspapers and periodicals

Borba (Belgrade)
Danas (Zagreb)
Delo (Ljubljana)
Ekonomska Politika (Belgrade)
Mladina (Ljubljana)
NIN (Belgrade)
Nova Makedonija (Skopje)
Politika (Belgrade)
Oslobodjenje (Sarajevo)
Tanjug-Bulletin Wien (Vienna)
Vjesnik (Zagreb)

Notes

Foreword

1 Regarding Natural Law, see: Robert P. George (ed.), *Natural Law Theory: Contemporary Essays* (Oxford: Clarendon Press, 1992); Robert P. George (ed.), *Natural Law, Liberalism, and Morality: Contemporary Essays* (Oxford: Clarendon Press, 1987); Norberto Bobbio, *Thomas Hobbes and the Natural Law Tradition*, trans. from Italian by Daniela Gobetti (Chicago: University of Chicago Press, 1993); and Immanuel Kant, *The Metaphysics of Morals*, trans. from German by Mary Gregor (Cambridge: Cambridge University Press, 1991). For an interpretation of *political* legitimacy in terms of political succession, see Guglielmo Ferrero, *The Principles of Legitimacy*, trans. by Theodore R. Jaeckel (New York: G. P. Putnam Sons, 1942). For my own statements on the subject of legitimacy, see Sabrina P. Ramet, *Whose Democracy? Nationalism, Religion, and the Doctrine of Collective Rights in Post-1989 Eastern Europe* (Lanham, Md.: Rowman & Littlefield, 1997); and Sabrina P. Ramet, *Balkan Babel: The Disintegration of Yugoslavia from the Death of Tito to Uprising in Kosovë*, 3rd ed. (Boulder, Colo.: Westview Press, 1999), epilogue.
2 For my views concerning secession, see Sabrina P. Ramet, "Profit Motives in Secession", in *Society* 35: 5 (July/August 1998), pp. 26–29.

1 Fateful weaknesses after Tito's death

1 Revealed to me by the since-deceased Professor George Hoffmann.
2 Conversation with Mitja Ribičič, Ljubljana, March 1994.
3 Jovan Mirić, *Sistem i kriza* (Zagreb, 1984), p.15. Predrag Matvejević (in *Jugoslovenstvo danas*, Zagreb, 1982) tried to find a new definition of Yugoslav consciousness, based on a cultural foundation, though this was unrealistic since it was precisely in this sphere that the sense of belonging to a community of Yugoslav peoples was, from the beginning, especially weak.
4 Conversation with Mitja Ribičič, Ljubljana, March 1994.
5 On this point see Ernst Halperin, *Der siegreiche Ketzer* (Köln, 1957), p. 45.
6 Conversation with Milan Kučan, November 1987. For further information concerning the session of army cadres, see J. Furkes and K. H. Schlarp, *Jugoslawien – ein Staat zerfällt* (Reinbek, 1991), together with the sources cited there. Concerning the role of the army, see also Anton Bebler, "The Armed Conflicts on the Balkans", in *Balkan Forum* (Skopje), Vol. 1, No. 4 (September 1993).
7 Conversation with Ribičič, Ljubljana, March 1994.
8 Conversation with Janko Smole, Ljubljana, March 1994.
9 Mirić, *Sistem i kriza*, p. 19.

10 The constitution of the time cited according to the version published in the Yugoslav official bulletin, *Službeni list SFRJ*, No. 9 (21 February 1974).

11 According to *Politika* (12 February 1984), it ran as follows: Macedonia, Bosnia-Herzegovina, Slovenia, Serbia, Croatia, Montenegro, Vojvodina, Kosovo. This resulted in the fact that, at the time of Tito's death, a Macedonian (Koliševski) came to this distinction and was soon succeeded by a deputy from Bosnia-Herzegovina (Mijatović).

12 Conversation with Ribičič, Ljubljana, March 1994.

13 Veljko Kadijević, *Moje vidjenje raspada* (Belgrade, 1993).

14 According to Čiril Ribičič and Zdravko Tomac, *Federalizam po mjeri budućnosti* (Zagreb, 1989), p. 171.

15 V.M., "Zwei verschiedene Konzepte über die künftige Wirtschaftspolitik Jugoslawiens", in *Frankfurter Allgemeine Zeitung (FAZ)* (6 August 1980), and "Der Fehler liegt im System", in *Frankfurter Allgemeine* (7 February 1981).

16 "Zasto smo se zaduživali", in *NIN* (10 February 1985).

17 See his interview in *NIN* (16 November 1980).

18 Stevan Doronjski, interview for *Komunist*, as reported in V.M., "Jugoslawiens Partei will nicht an der Wirtschaftsmisere schuld sein", in *FAZ* (21 October 1980).

19 V.M., "Nur eine Analyse der Vergangenheit", in *FAZ* (28 June 1982).

20 It concerned the expression "World-Bank Socialism". See V. M. "Die zwei Seiten von Ostkrediten", in *FAZ* (10 November 1980).

21 *NIN* (10 February 1985).

22 V. M., "Sloweniens Angst vor Isolierung", in *FAZ* (26 October 1981).

23 V. M., "In Belgrad glaubt man an einem neuen Anfang", in *FAZ* (5 June 1982).

24 V. M., "Jugoslawische Wirtschaftskommission bekennt sich zum Prinzip des Marktes", in *FAZ* (27 July 1983); and conversation with Professor Oskar Kovač, 2 September 1983.

25 For the results of these talks, see V. M., "Die Republik Slowenien kämpft für offene Grenzen", in *FAZ* (20 November 1982).

26 From conversations in Belgrade, November 1982. See V. M. "Wirtschaftskrise in Jugoslawien", in *FAZ* (25 November 1982).

27 V. M., "Wenig Sympathien für Belgrads Pläne zur Umschuldung", in *FAZ* (26 November 1984).

28 V. M., "Vereinbarungen zwischen Belgrad und IWF günstig aufgenommen", in *FAZ* (28 March 1984).

29 V. M., "Zagreb heute Zentrum der jugoslawischen Parteidogmatiker", in *FAZ* (10 July 1984).

30 Conversation with Alexandar Bajt, March 1995. It is difficult to say whether these assessments are entirely correct. Certainly outlays to service the debt leveled out at $5 billion but the regime considered that it could handle only about $3–3.5 billion.

31 V. M., "In Slowenien herrscht Unmut", in *FAZ* (4 February 1986), and "Ein Gesetz, das nicht funktioniert", in *FAZ* (15 May 1986).

32 Government statement of Branko Mikulić, German text, 15 May 1986.

33 Talk at the CC Plenum; see V. M., "Steht die jugoslawische Partei vor der Aufsplitterung?", in *FAZ* (21 March 1985).

34 Indictment against Marko Veselica, Zagreb, September 1981; and V. M., "Kampagne gegen Oppositionelle in Jugoslawien", in *FAZ* (30 July 1980).

35 *FAZ* (30 July 1980).

36 Bogoljub Kočović, in *Žrtve drugog svetskog rata u Jugoslaviji* (London, 1985), esimates just over one million.

37 V. M., "In Jugoslawien nichts mehr verloren", in *FAZ* (5 October 1990), and the sources cited there.

38 Conversation with Franjo Tudjman, Vienna, March 1991.
39 V. M., "Bischöfe ermutigen Dissidenten und Opposition", in *FAZ* (3 June 1981), "Zwei Jahre für Gotovac", in *FAZ* (6 June 1981), and "Die Anklage stützt sich auf Aussagen zweier älterer Damen (Prozess Veselica)", in *FAZ* (11 September 1981).
40 See V. M., "Der neue Streit um Kardinal Stepinac", in *FAZ* (28 March 1981).
41 *Vreme* (Belgrade), 24 January 1994.
42 For the charges against Dr Šešelj, see *NIN* (8 July 1984).
43 Prof. Ivan Janković (April 1984), as cited in V. M., "Gefangenenbehandlung in Belgrad diskutiert", in *FAZ* (18 April 1984).
44 Lecture at the University of Skopje, *Tanjug Bulletin* (9 January 1984).
45 Cited from Slobodan Stanković, "Yugoslavia's Census – Final Results", in *RFE/RL Research Bulletin* (10 March 1982).
46 *Politika* (21 August 1983); and V. M., "Feindliche Propaganda und Sympathie für Chomeini", in *FAZ* (1 August 1983).
47 *Tanjug Bulletin*, Vienna (6 April 1981).
48 Detailed discussion in *NIN* (12 April 1981) and "Zašto smo bili neobaveštini", in *NIN* (19 April 1981).
49 *Tanjug Bulletin*, Vienna (15 April 1981).
50 Slobodan Stanković, "Yugoslavia One Year after Tito's Death", in *RFE/RL Research Bulletin* (6 May 1981).
51 See the polemic with the Albanian party organ *Zeri i Popullit*, in *Politika* (10 April 1981).
52 See the detailed discussion in Gjini Gasper, *Skopsko-prizrensko Biskupija kroz stoljeća* (Zagreb, 1986), pp. 97ff.
53 *Tatsachen über Jugoslawien*, official publication (Belgrade, 1983).
54 Christine von Kohl and Wolfgang Libal, *Kosovo* (Vienna and Zürich, 1992), p. 9.
55 Cf. Pajazit Nuši, *Prizrenska Liga* (Priština, 1978).
56 Cf. V. M., "Die Rückkehr der Serben auf das Amselfeld", in *FAZ* (24 June 1989).
57 For details concerning Xhaver Deva, see the informative essay by Milorad Vavić, in M. Vavić *et al.* (eds.), *Tragom izdaje i zločina* (Zagreb, 1985).
58 Svetozar Vukmanović-Tempo, *Memoari* (Belgrade, 1971), vol. 1, p. 322.
59 *Ibid.*, p. 378.
60 Extensive confirmations in: Enver Hoxha, *Die Titoisten* (Tirana, 1983), p. 130; and Spasoje Djaković, *Sukobi na Kosovu* (Belgrade, 1984), p. 210.
61 Cf. Ilija Vuković, *Autonomaštvo i separatizam na Kosovu* (Belgrade, 1985), p. 111 and the sources cited there.
62 *Ibid.*, p. 111.
63 Djaković, *Sukobi*, pp. 260ff.
64 Hajredin Hodža, *Afirmacija albanske nacionalnosti u Jugoslaviji* (Priština, 1984), p. 62.
65 *Ibid.*, p. 51.
66 Cf. *NIN* (11 December 1983).
67 Hodža, *Afirmacija albanske*, p. 70.
68 *Ibid.*, p. 71.
69 *Ibid.*, p. 73.
70 Miloš Mišović, *Ko je tražio republiku: Kosovo 1945–1985* (Belgrade, 1987), p. 69.
71 *Ibid.*, p. 141.
72 *Ibid.*, p. 163.
73 *Ibid.*, p. 162.
74 According to Mahmut Bakalli and Stane Dolanc, *Tanjug Bulletin* (Vienna), 6 April 1981.
75 Mišović, *Ko je tražio*, p. 97.

76 Speech in Jajce (30 November 1968).
77 Jože Pirjavec, *Jugoslavija* (Koper, 1995), p. 346; and Ivan Stambolić, *Put u bespuće* (Belgrade, 1995), pp. 55ff.
78 Conversation with Mahmut Bakalli, Priština, June 1978.
79 Cf. Thomas Eger, *Das regionale Entwicklungsgefälle in Jugoslawien* (Paderborn, 1980); and Jens Reuter, *Die Albaner in Jugoslawien* (Munich, 1982), pp. 54ff.
80 Reuter, *Die Albaner*, p. 74.
81 *NIN* (10 May 1981).
82 *Ekonomska politika* (19 January 1981); and Reuter, *Die Albaner*, p. 61.
83 Repeated conversations with Azem Vllasi, Priština, 1982–90.
84 Conversation with Sofokli Lazri, Tirana, 6 April 1982.
85 V. M., "Im Kosovo vergißt man schwer", in *FAZ* (29 December 1984).
86 See Spiro Galović, in *NIN* (10 May 1981).
87 Defense Committee of the Yugoslav Assembly, in *Politika* (14 May 1981).
88 Zdenko Antić, "Exodus of Serbs from Kosovo", in *RFE/RL Research Report* (18 May 1981), presented on the basis of official Yugoslav statements.
89 Statistical Office of Serbia, as reported in *NIN* (23 September 1984).
90 *NIN* (23 September 1984).
91 V. M., "Lieber in Belgrad betteln, als im Kosovo umgebracht werden", in *FAZ* (16 July 1982).
92 V. M., "Konkrete Vorwürfe können die Serben im Kosovo gegen ihre albanischen Mitbürger kaum vorbringen", in *FAZ* (2 December 1986).
93 *FAZ* (28 December 1985).
94 V. M., "Das Kosovo wehrt sich gegen Serben", in *FAZ* (31 December 1984).
95 V. M., "Drohungen auf dem Amselfeld", in *FAZ* (13 December 1986).
96 *Ibid.*

2 The turning point: 1986–7

1 Cf. "Nova izborna pravila", in *NIN* (16 March 1986).
2 V. M., "Je tiefer die Krise, desto mehr Feinde", in *FAZ* (12 May 1987).
3 *Ibid.*
4 "Reći i dela", in *NIN* (11 May 1986).
5 V. M., "Konkrete Vorwürfe können die Serben im Kosovo gegen ihre albanischen Mitbürger kaum vorbringen", in *FAZ* (2 December 1994).
6 *Politika* (27 February 1986).
7 See Aleksa Djilas, "A Profile of Slobodan Milošević", in *Foreign Affairs*, Vol. 71, No. 4 (Summer 1993).
8 V. M., "Ausnahmemaßnahmen im Kosovo", in *FAZ* (28 July 1986).
9 V. M., "Demonstrationen in Belgrad", in *FAZ* (29 June 1987).
10 *Politika* (16 January 1987).
11 *Politika* (28 June 1987).
12 Concerning the course of the session and the reports of the Eighth Serbian Plenum, see *Politika* (24/25/26 September 1987). The introductory report was presented by Zoran Sokolović; the most ferocious of Milošević's adherents were Aleksandar Mitrović, the new chief of television, and Belgrade Mayor Aleksandar Bakočević. Former Defense Minister General Ljubičić and many others could be numbered among his allies. See also V. M., "Kämpfe in der serbischen Führung", in *FAZ* (25 September 1987).
13 V. M., "Serbische Akademie folgt der Kritik der kommunistischen Führung nicht", in *FAZ* (20 December 1986).
14 Special edition of *Duga* (Belgrade), June 1989.
15 V. M., "Milošević und seine Kohorten", in *FAZ* (30 September 1987).
16 *Ibid.*

17 Conversation with Warren Zimmermann, Washington D.C., April 1994.
18 See the session of the Central Committee of the LC Bosnia-Herzegovina, in *Politika* (2 September 1987); V. M., "Skandal bei Agrokomerc weitet sich aus", in *FAZ* (2 September 1987), and "Der jugoslawische Finanzskandal", in *FAZ* (7 September 1987).
19 V. M., "Bosniens Prestige ist erschüttert", in *FAZ* (2 October 1987).
20 Conversation with Milan Kučan, Ljubljana; see also V. M., "Jeder vierte Soldat Jugoslawiens ein Albaner", in *FAZ* (3 November 1987).
21 V. M., "Nationalitätenpolitik nach altem Muster", in *FAZ* (14 October 1987).
22 V. M., "Jugoslawien und der Währungsfonds", in *FAZ* (23 January 1987).
23 V. M., "Jugoslawische Zeitungen kritisieren Mikulić", in *FAZ* (15 August 1987).
24 V. M., "Zweifel an der Kraft zur Selbsterneuerung", in *FAZ* (24 March 1987).
25 V. M., "Der dogmatische Untersatz erschwert die notwendige Erneuerung", in *FAZ* (26 February 1987).
26 Vasa Čubrilović, *Istorija političke misli u Srbiji 19. veka* (Belgrade, 1958), pp. 22ff.
27 *Ibid.*
28 *Delo* (Belgrade), no. 38 (1906), pp. 321ff.
29 "Socijalizam ili društveno pitanje", cited from Svetozar Marković, *Sabrani spisi* (Belgrade, 1960–).
30 Mihailo Polit-Desančić, *Die orientalische Frage und ihre organische Lösung* (Vienna, 1862).
31 Svetozar Marković, "Srbija na Istoku", in Marković, *Sabrani spisi.*
32 The *Sporazum* was received as a state ordinance (*uredba*) on 26 August 1939 and published in the official bulletin. The text may be found in Ferdo Čulinović, *Dokumenti o Jugoslaviji* (Zagreb, 1968), p. 340.
33 Vladko Maček, *In the Struggle for Freedom*, trans. by Elizabeth and Stjepan Gazi (University Park, Pa., 1957), p. 220.
34 Cf. Svetozar Pribičević, *Diktatura Kralja Aleksandra*, trans. from French by Andra Milosavljević (Belgrade, 1953), p. 174.
35 Special edition of *Duga* (Summer 1989), pp. 36ff.
36 According to Roy Gutman, in *Večernji list* (Zagreb), 8 June 1994.
37 Edvard Kardelj (Sperans), *Razvoj slovenskega narodnega vprašanja* (Ljubljana, 1957). German ed.: *Die Vierteilung, nationale Frage der Slowenen* (Vienna, 1971), pp. 61ff.
38 Milovan Djilas, *Der Krieg der Partisanen* (Vienna, 1978), p. 439.
39 Dragutin Lončar, *Političko življenje Slovencev* (Ljubljana, 1921). English edition: *The Slovenes: A Social History* (Cleveland, Ohio, 1939), p. 30.
40 Kardelj, *Razvoj*, pp. 148ff.
41 Only a small district in the Prekmurje region belonged to Hungary.
42 Janko Prunk, *Slovenski narodni programi* (Ljubljana, 1986).
43 *Nova Revija*, No. 57 (February 1987).
44 Prunk, *Slovenski narodni*, p. 425.
45 Of 30 May 1917, text in Momčilo Žečević, *Slovenska ljudska stranka i jugoslovensko ujedinjenje* (Belgrade, 1973), p. 71.
46 *Ibid.*, p. 76.
47 *Ibid.*, pp. 80ff.
48 *Ibid.*, p. 168.
49 Cited and interpreted in Žečević, *Slovenska ljudska stranka*, p. 357.
50 Maček, *In the Struggle*, p. 93.
51 "Bonafica del confine".
52 V. M., "Anknüpfungspunkte an den Westen gesucht", in *FAZ* (19 October 1987).
53 Tone Ferenc, *Nacistička politika denacionalizacije u Sloveniji u godinama od 1941 do 1945*, trans. from Slovene by Ivo Tominc (Maribor, 1968), p. 293.
54 Concerning the activities of the ethnic Germans in Slovenia before the war, see Dušan Biber, *Nacizem in nemci v Jugoslaviji, 1933–1941* (Ljubljana, 1966).

55 Čiril Žebot, *Neminljiva Slovenija* (Celovec [Klagenfurt], 1988), p. 241.
56 Estimates of the exact number vary slightly; the figure cited comes from President Kučan.
57 V. M., "Slowenien Vorreiter einer jugoslawischen Liberalisierung?", in *FAZ* (9 February 1985).
58 Contributions to a Slovenian national program in *Nova Revija*, No. 57 (February 1987).
59 Matej Bor *et al.*, *Veneti* (Ljubljana, 1989); also conversation with Professor Bogo Grafenauer, Ljubljana, 1989.
60 *Nova Revija*, No. 57 (February 1987).
61 V. M., "Pseudorevolution in Slowenien", in *FAZ* (2 March 1987).

3 The beginning of the end

1 Conversation with Milan Kučan, Ljubljana, July 1994.
2 Borisav Jović, *Poslednji dani SFRJ* (Belgrade, 1995).
3 Martin Špegelj, foreword to the Croatian edition of Janez Janša, *Pomači* (Zagreb, 1993).
4 Veljko Kadijević, *Moje vidjenje raspada* (Belgrade, 1993), especially chap. 1, pp. 9ff.
5 Conversation with Milan Kučan, Ljubljana, July 1994.
6 Materials from the 66th session of the P CC LCY, 4 February 1988, in the Archives of the Republic of Slovenia.
7 *Ibid.*
8 *Delo* (Ljubljana), 17 February 1988.
9 Archives of the Republic of Slovenia, concerning the CC LCY.
10 See the chronology of the conflict between Slovenia and the army, put together by the Slovenian presidency on 11 July 1989, in Archives of the Republic of Slovenia.
11 *Politika* (29 January 1988); and, with sharper tones, *Politika* (14 March 1988).
12 V. M., "Eine Villa für Mamula", in *FAZ* (14 March 1988).
13 *Politika* (30 March 1988).
14 V. M., "Eine Villa".
15 *Ocene i stavovi o povećanoj ugroženosti ustavnog poretka i bezbednosti zemlje*, papers of Kučan concerning the army, in Archives of the Republic of Slovenia.
16 Predsedništvo CK SKJ, Radna grupa, *Ocene i stavovi o akuelnim idejno-političkim pitanjima u vezi napada na koncepciju ONO i JNA i zadacima SKJ* (March 1988), concerning Presidium of the CC LCY, materials from the 72nd session (29 March 1988), in Archives of the Republic of Slovenia.
17 For Kučan's report, see Presidium of the CC LCY, materials from the 72nd session (29 March 1988), in Archives of the Republic of Slovenia. His report first became known in the West; see *Nova Hrvatska* (London), May 1988.
18 Conversation with Kučan, Ljubljana, July 1994.
19 *Ibid.*
20 Materials of Kučan concerning the army, in Archives of the Republic of Slovenia.
21 Janša, *Pomaci*, p. 9.
22 *Ibid.*, p. 18.
23 Document dated February 1989, among the materials of Kučan concerning the army, in Archives of the Republic of Slovenia.
24 Conversation with Kučan, Ljubljana, November 1993.
25 Conversation with Kučan, Ljubljana, November 1993.
26 See the overview in V.M., "In Slovenien wächst die Empörung über die Aktivitäten der Militärjustiz", in *FAZ* (13 June 1988).

27 *Delo* (29 June 1988); see also V. M., "Slowenischer Parteiführer nennt Militärprozeß verfassungswidrig", in *FAZ* (29 July 1988).
28 Note from Kučan; supplemental materials concerning the army (22 July 1988), in Archives of the Republic of Slovenia.
29 Kučan's speech: in *Delo* (29 June 1988).
30 V. M., "Militärgericht verhängt Haftstrafen", in *FAZ* (28 July 1988).
31 V. M., "Die Gefähr geht vom Zentrum aus", in *FAZ* (8 July 1988).
32 Conversation with Jože Smole, Ljubljana, June 1988.
33 V. M., "Zwei Konzepte von Jugoslawien", in *FAZ* (14 October 1988).
34 Session of the presidency of the Socialist Republic of Slovenia (16 February 1988), in Archives of the Republic of Slovenia.
35 Supplemental Slovenian materials concerning the army, in Archives of the Republic of Slovenia.
36 *Ibid.*
37 Kadijević, *Vidjenje*, p. 102.
38 *Ibid.*, p. 102.
39 Conversation with Vllasi, July 1994.
40 V. M., "Gesslerhüte im Kosovo", in *FAZ* (19 February 1988).
41 V. M., "Die Universität als Kopf der Schlange", in *FAZ* (12 February 1988).
42 *Politika* (27 May 1988).
43 V. M., "Energisch und fest", in *FAZ* (15 November 1988).
44 Materials from the 77th session of the presidium of the CC LCY (23/24 May 1988), in Archives of the Republic of Slovenia.
45 *Politika* (25 June 1988).
46 *Danas* (Zagreb), 5 July 1988, p. 23.
47 *Politika* (12 June 1988).
48 *Ibid.*
49 Boško Krunić in front of the CC LCY, in *Politika* (31 July 1988).
50 *Politika* (19 July 1988).
51 *Politika* (31 July 1988).
52 V. M., "Jugoslawisches Zentralkomitee wendet sich gegen die Agitation der serbischen Führung", in *FAZ* (1 August 1988).
53 V. M., "In Slowenien erwartet man, daß Milošević seine Agitation fortsetzt", in *FAZ* (3 August 1988).
54 Materials from the 91st session of the presidium of the CC LCY (11 August 1988), in Archives of the Republic of Slovenia.
55 V. M., "Pressionen und Demonstranten in Jugoslawien", in *FAZ* (5 September 1988).
56 *Politika* (27 September 1988).
57 Materials from the 96th session of the presidium of the CC LCY (16 September 1988), in Archives of the Republic of Slovenia.
58 Materials from the 98th session of the presidium of the CC LCY (30 September 1988), in Archives of the Republic of Slovenia.
59 *Politika* (1 October 1988).
60 Conversation with Kučan, Ljubljana, 21 July 1988.
61 *Politika* (7 October 1988).
62 *Politika* (10 October 1988).
63 *Tanjug Bulletin* (Vienna), 12 October 1988.
64 V. M., "Beschwichtigung auf Kosten der Slowenen und Albaner", in *FAZ* (12 October 1988).
65 *Politika* (18–20 October 1988); and V. M., "Milošević mit dem ZK unzufrieden", in *FAZ* (22 October 1988).
66 *Politika* (18 October 1988).
67 V. M., "Nur Marktwirtschaftler sollen aufrücken", in *FAZ* (20 October 1988).

68 *Politika* (6 November 1988).
69 Materials concerning the 104th session of the presidium of the CC LCY (27 October 1988), in Archives of the Republic of Slovenia.
70 Materials from the 106th session of the presidium of the CC LCY (9 November 1988), in Archives of the Republic of Slovenia.
71 *Ibid.*; and materials from the 107th session of the presidium of the CC LCY (15/16 November 1988), in Archives of the Republic of Slovenia.
72 *Politika* (20 November 1988).
73 Conversation with Vllasi, July 1994.
74 Conversation with Kolgezi, Priština, early 1989.
75 V. M., "Auf Druck Miloševićs tritt die Parteiführung des Kosovo zurück", in *FAZ* (19 November 1988).
76 *Ibid.*
77 *Politika* (20 November 1988).
78 Materials from the 10th session of the presidium of the CC LCY (23 November 1988), in Archives of the Republic of Slovenia.
79 *Politika* (14 January 1989).
80 Materials from the 119th session of the presidium of the CC LCY (16 January 1989).
81 *Ibid.*
82 V. M., "Milošević als Spalter", in *FAZ* (13 February 1989).
83 *Mladina* (10 March 1989).
84 *Danas* (31 January 1989).
85 *Politika* (31 January–2 February 1989).
86 V. M., "Niederlage Miloševićs im jugoslawischen Zentralkomitee", in *FAZ* (31 January 1989).
87 *Politika* (24 February 1989).
88 *Ibid.*
89 *Politika* (28 February 1989).
90 *Ibid.* (25 February 1989).
91 *Ibid.*
92 *Politika* (27 February 1989).
93 Materials from the 121st session of the presidium of the CC LCY (29 January 1989), in Archives of the Republic of Slovenia.
94 *Danas* (7 March 1989).
95 See the chronology of events in *NIN* (5 March 1989).
96 *Politika* (28 February 1989).
97 Conversation with Janez Stanovnik, Ljubljana, March 1989.
98 Materials from the 129th session of the presidium of the CC LCY (28 February 1989), in Archives of the Republic of Slovenia.
99 Materials concerning the session of the presidency of the Socialist Republic of Slovenia (20 March 1989), in Archives of the Republic of Slovenia.
100 Materials concerning the 129th session of the presidium of the CC LCY (28 February 1989), in Archives of the Republic of Slovenia.
101 *Ibid.*
102 Text in *NIN* (5 March 1989).
103 Text in *NIN* (5 March 1989).
104 *Politika* (3 March 1989).
105 See *Danas* (7 March 1989).
106 *Tanjug Bulletin* (Vienna), 2 March 1989.
107 V. M., "Verteidigung oder die letzten Tage", in *FAZ* (20 March 1989).
108 Materials concerning the session of the presidency of the Socialist Republic of Slovenia (20 March 1989), in Archives of the Republic of Slovenia.
109 *Danas* (7 March 1989).

110 Materials concerning the 132nd session of the presidium of the CC LCY (21 March 1989), in Archives of the Republic of Slovenia.
111 V. M., "Die Verteidigung oder die letzten Tage", in *FAZ* (20 March 1989).
112 V. M., "Besorgnis über die Lage im Kosovo", in *FAZ* (20 March 1989).
113 V. M., "Das Parlament des Kosovo begibt sich einer Regionalautonomie", in *FAZ* (25 March 1989); also *Politika* (24 March 1989).
114 Cf. *FAZ* (29 March 1989).
115 Materials concerning the 133rd session of the presidium of the CC LCY (28 March 1989), in Archives of the Republic of Slovenia; and V. M., "In Belgrad ist das Bundesparteipräsidium zusammengetreten", in *FAZ* (29 March 1989).
116 *Politika* (29 March 1989).
117 *NIN* (31 March 1989).
118 V. M., "Nach dem Sieg im Kosovo greift Milošević auf ganz Jugoslawien aus", in *FAZ* (31 March 1994).
119 *Politika* (7 April 1989).
120 V. M., "In Priština gilt die Sprache des Siegers", in *FAZ* (19 April 1989).
121 V. M., "Wir sind überrollt worden", in *FAZ* (22 April 1989).
122 *Politika* (18 April 1989).
123 *Danas* (20 June 1989).
124 The contemporary leadership of Kosovo had obtained the right to equal dialogue. See *Politika* (20 May 1989).
125 *Tanjug Bulletin* (Vienna), 24 May 1989.
126 See the Amnesty International report of June 1989; also V. M., "Die serbische Kosovo-Politik droht Jugoslawien zu spalten", in *FAZ* (13 May 1989).
127 *Politika* (23 May 1989).
128 *Politika* (29 June 1989).
129 V. M., "Serbien in einem Zustand nationalen Fiebers", in *FAZ* (8 July 1989).
130 V. M., "Auch in der Partei und in der Staatsführung ist von einem politischen Prozeß die Rede", in *FAZ* (31 October 1989); see also Azem Vllasi, *Majstori mraka* (Zagreb, 1990); and his wife, Nadira Avdić-Vllasi, *Za obranu Azema Vllasija* (Ljubljana, 1989).
131 V. M., "Auch die Albaner wollen Grundrechte", in *FAZ* (10 November 1989).
132 *Ibid.*
133 V. M., "In Angelegenheiten des Kosovo verweigert Serbien den Dialog", in *FAZ* (2 February 1990).
134 V. M., "Die Politik Serbiens im Kosovo spaltet Jugoslawien", in *FAZ* (2 April 1990).
135 *Borba* (3 May 1991).
136 V. M., "Im Streit um den Kosovo sucht Serbien den Konflikt", in *FAZ* (21 July 1990).
137 *Ibid.*
138 Stipe Mesić, *Kako smo srušili Jugoslaviju* (Zagreb, 1992), p. 12.
139 *Ibid.*, p. 26.
140 *Ibid.*, p. 11.
141 V. M., "Eine Unterdrückung wie das nicht einmal in Südafrika der Fall ist", in *FAZ* (21 September 1990).
142 V. M., "Die Albaner des Kosovo bleiben den Wahlurnen fern", in *FAZ* (10 December 1990).
143 *Vjesnik* (26 August 1991).

4 Western Yugoslavia reacts

1 V. M., "Jugoslawien ersucht um Umschuldung", in *FAZ* (1 October 1987).
2 *Ibid.*

3 *Politika* (20 October 1987).
4 V. M., "Jugoslawiens Regierung verliert Vertrauen", in *FAZ* (7 November 1987).
5 V. M., "Belgrads Umschuldungsgesuch und antiwestliche Manifestationen", in *FAZ* (22 December 1987).
6 V. M., "Kein Wirtschaftsplan in Jugoslawien", in *FAZ* (8 January 1988).
7 V. M., "Eine fragwürdige Einigung zwischen Belgrad und dem Währungsfonds", in *FAZ* (29 April 1988).
8 V. M., "Schwierige Schuldner auf dem Balkan", in *FAZ* (29 April 1988).
9 *Politika* (15 May 1988).
10 V. M., "Auch Kroatien gegen die Regierung Mikulić", in *FAZ* (13 May 1988).
11 *Ibid.*
12 V. M., "Jugoslawiens Kommunisten bekennen sich jetzt zur Marktwirtschaft", in *FAZ* (30 May 1988).
13 *Ibid.*
14 Materials concerning the session of the presidium of the CC LCY (29 March 1988), in Archives of the Republic of Slovenia.
15 V. M., "Eine Zerreißprobe für die jugoslawischen Kommunisten", in *FAZ* (17 October 1988).
16 *Politika* (8 November 1988).
17 V. M., "Zwei Konzepte von Jugoslawien", in *FAZ* (14 October 1988); and V. M., "Slowenen setzt sich durch", in *FAZ* (26 October 1988).
18 *NIN* (3 July 1988).
19 V. M., "Wirtschaftsreform in Belgrad umstritten", in *FAZ* (29 December 1988).
20 V.M., "Jugoslawische Regierung nach Abstimmungsniederlage zurückgetreten", in *FAZ* (31 December 1988).
21 See Marijan Korošić, *Jugoslovenska kriza* (Zagreb, 1988).
22 Veljko Kadijević, *Moje vidjenje raspada* (Belgrade, 1993), p. 106.
23 *Danas* (7 March 1989), p. 15.
24 V. M., "Belgrad entdeckt Europa", in *FAZ* (10 January 1989).
25 V. M., "Marković fordert neue Moral für Jugoslawien", in *FAZ* (18 March 1989).
26 *Politika* (17 March 1989).
27 V. M., "Marković fordert neue Moral" (see note 25).
28 Predrag Tašić, *Kako sam branio Antu Markovića* (Skopje, 1993), p. 16.
29 *Ibid.*, p. 17.
30 Belgrade, July 1989. See V. M., "Der Regierung Marković schlägt der Widerstand Miloševićs entgegen", in *FAZ* (24 July 1989).
31 V. M., "Marković will Jugoslawien mit einem Notprogramm retten", in *FAZ* (23 December 1989).
32 *NIN* (24 December 1989).
33 Tašić, *Kako sam branio*, p. 18.
34 Conversations with Bajt, December 1989 and September 1994.
35 Materials concerning the session of the presidency of the Socialist Republic of Slovenia (20 March 1989), in Archives of the Republic of Slovenia.
36 V. M., "Eine Kluft zwischen Belgrad und Zagreb", in *FAZ* (21 April 1989).
37 Conversations with Kučan, Ljubljana, July 1994. For the statements of Dolanc, see the records of the Archives of the Republic of Slovenia concerning the session of the presidency of the Socialist Republic of Slovenia (20 March 1989). Concerning the legal basis for a state of emergency, see D. Zagrac, in *Danas* (7 March 1989).
38 *Politika* (22 April 1989).
39 See Jens Reuter, "Konfligierende politische Ordnungsvorstellungen als Hintergrund zur Krise in Jugoslawien", in *Südosteuropa* (1989), no. 1.

40 Speech of Kadijević before the party organization of the Defense Ministry. See V. M., "Jugoslawiens Armee gegen Pluralismus", in *FAZ* (17 July 1989).

41 V. M., "Wahlüberraschung in Slowenien", in *FAZ* (5 April 1989); and V. M., "Ein ruhiger Slowene", in *FAZ* (11 May 1989).

42 V. M., "Jugoslawien braucht eine Beruhigungsperiode", in *FAZ* (18 April 1989).

43 Draft and commentary in materials from the 139th session of the presidium of the CC LCY (9 May 1989), in Archives of the Republic of Slovenia.

44 Materials from the 139th session of the presidium of the CC LCY (9 May 1989), in Archives of the Republic of Slovenia.

45 Janez Janša, *Pomaci* (Zagreb, 1993), p. 27.

46 *Delo* (23 June 1989).

47 *Ibid.*

48 Janša, *Pomaci*, p. 27.

49 Text in *Borba* (19 June 1988). See also V. M., "Wenn wir uns nicht einigen können, sollten wir auseinandergehen", in *FAZ* (1 July 1989).

50 *Ibid.*

51 V. M., "Serbien in einem Zustand nationalen Fiebers", in *FAZ* (8 July 1989).

52 Materials concerning the session of the presidency of the Socialist Republic of Slovenia (2 June 1989), in Archives of the Republic of Slovenia.

53 Materials concerning the 142nd session of the presidium of the CC LCY (30 May 1989), in Archives of the Republic of Slovenia.

54 Declaration of the new chairman of the LCY presidium, Macedonian Milan Pančevski, at the 145th session of the presidium of the CC LCY (20 June 1989), in Archives of the Republic of Slovenia.

55 V. M., "Slowenien beharrt auf neuer Verfassung", in *FAZ* (19 September 1989).

56 Exposé by Miran Potrč before the Slovenian parliament, in *Politika* (28 September 1989).

57 Materials from the 153rd session of the presidium of the CC LCY (30 August 1989), in Archives of the Republic of Slovenia.

58 *Politika* (30 August 1989); and *FAZ* (11 September 1989).

59 Conversation with Kučan, July 1994, as well as earlier conversations; reports concerning the session in *Delo* (27/28 September 1989).

60 Text of the speech in *Delo* (28 September 1989).

61 Conversation with Kučan, July 1994.

62 *Danas* (3 October 1989).

63 V. M., "Slowenien hat sich durchgesetzt", in *FAZ* (3 October 1989).

64 Conversation with Kučan, Ljubljana, 21 July 1994.

65 Kadijević, *Vidjenje*, p. 108.

66 Materials concerning the 152nd session of the presidium of the CC LCY (22 August 1989), in Archives of the Republic of Slovenia.

67 V. M., "Spontan stimmen Abgeordnete und Besucher das patriotische Trinklied", in *FAZ* (29 September 1989).

68 V. M., "Slowenien hat sich durchgesetzt", in *FAZ* (3 October 1989).

69 *Danas* (7 November 1989).

70 *Politika* (19 October 1989).

71 V. M., "Eingreifen der Armee in die Politik Jugoslawiens nicht mehr auszuschließen", in *FAZ* (26 October 1989).

72 *Danas* (7 November 1989).

73 Materials concerning the session of the presidency of the Socialist Republic of Slovenia (1 December 1989), in Archives of the Republic of Slovenia.

74 *Ibid.* (5 December 1989).

75 *Politika* (6 December 1989).

76 *Politika* (1 December 1989).
77 *Ibid.*
78 V. M., "Marković will Jugoslawien mit einem Notprogramm retten", in *FAZ* (23 December 1989).
79 *Tanjug Bulletin* (Vienna), 16 January 1990.
80 *Borba* (27 February 1990).
81 V. M., "Die serbische Kosovo-Politik droht Jugoslawien zu spalten", in *FAZ* (13 May 1989).
82 V. M., "Eine Kluft" (see note 36).
83 "Obrana ili poslednji dani", in *Danas* (7 March 1989).
84 V. M., "Eine Kluft" (see note 36).
85 *Ibid.*
86 *Danas* (25 July 1989).
87 *NIN* (3 September 1989).
88 See Ferdo Šišić, *Pregled povijesti hrvatskoga naroda* (Zagreb, 1975), pp. 327ff.
89 V. M., "Ein Bischof des Jugoslawismus", in *FAZ* (26 July 1983).
90 See Vaso Bogdanov, *Historija političkih stranka u Hrvatskoj* (Zagreb, 1958), p. 626.
91 Text in *Ibid.*, p. 625.
92 Ante Starčević, *Izabrani spisi* (Zagreb, 1971), pp. 61ff.
93 *Ibid.*, p. 475.
94 Tomislav Ladan in the preface to *A. Starčević – politički spisi* (Zagreb, 1971), p. 49.
95 Frano Supilo, *Politika u Hrvatskoj* (Zagreb, 1953), p. 49.
96 Vladko Maček, *In the Struggle for Freedom*, trans. by Elizabeth and Stjepan Gazi (University Park, Pa., 1957), p. 51.
97 See Mirjana Gross, *Vladavina Hrvatsko-srpske Koalicije* (Belgrade, 1960).
98 See Josip Horvat, *Politička povijest Hrvatske* (Zagreb, 1936), p. 465.
99 *Ibid.*, p. 488.
100 Maček, *In the Struggle*, p. 105.
101 *Ibid.*, p. 122.
102 Concerning the establishment of the *Ustaše* movement and its history in exile, see Bogdan Krizman, *Ante Pavelić i Ustaše* (Zagreb, 1978).
103 Hermann Neubacher, *Sonderauftrag Südost* (Göttingen, 1956), p. 31, attributes the citation directly to Pavelić.
104 For obvious reasons, the identity of this conversation partner must remain undisclosed.
105 See *Mali ključ povijesti crkve u Hrvata* (Zagreb, 1978).
106 Fikreta Jelić-Butić, *Ustaše i NDH 1941–1945* (Zagreb, 1978), p. 220.
107 *Ibid.*, p. 220.
108 *Ibid.*, p. 219.
109 Maček, *In the Struggle*, p. 235.
110 *Ibid.*, p. 187.
111 *Ibid.*, p. 229.
112 Neubacher, *Sonderauftrag*, p. 128.
113 See V. M., "In Banja Luka wollen die Serben ihren eigenen Staat", in *FAZ* (9 August 1991).
114 V. M., "Nochmals eine Türkenherrschaft wollen wir nicht", in *FAZ* (16 June 1979).
115 Milovan Djilas, *Der Krieg der Partisanen*, trans. from Serbo-Croatian (Vienna, 1977), p. 413.
116 The number is hard to specify even today, since many of these people were not allowed to cross the borders. Holm Sundhausen, *Geschichte Jugoslawiens* (Stuttgart, 1982), p. 136 cites a figure of 100,000. I have, from various

sources, often heard a figure of 18,000 Croatian combatants turned over. These were partly liquidated in Carinthia.

117 Conversation with Radovan Karadžić, Sarajevo, March 1991.
118 Franjo Tudjman, *Bespuća povijesne zbiljnosti* (Zagreb, 1989).
119 V. M., "Eine neue Konstellation in Belgrad", in *FAZ* (24 May 1989).
120 *Politika* (13 July 1989).
121 *Danas* (3 October 1989).
122 Conversation with Ivica Račan, Zagreb, November 1994.
123 Conversation with Zdravko Tomac, Zagreb, November 1994.
124 Conversation with Račan, November 1994.
125 Interview in *Novi Vjesnik* (Zagreb), 12 September 1992.

5 Irreconcilable positions

1 *Borba* (23 January 1990).
2 V.M., "Die jugoslawischen Kommunisten können sich über nichts mehr einigen", in *FAZ* (24 January 1990).
3 *Borba* (23 January 1990).
4 *Ibid.*
5 Conversation with Račan, Zagreb, 14 November 1994.
6 V.M., "ZK der jugoslawischen Kommunisten beschlußunfähig", in *FAZ* (2 April 1990).
7 Conversation with Račan, Zagreb, 14 November 1994.
8 *Ibid.*
9 *Ibid.*
10 Conversation with Josip Manolić, Zagreb, 14 November 1994.
11 Borisav Jović, *Poslednji dani SFRJ* (Belgrade, 1995), pp. 118ff.
12 Veljko Kadijević, *Moje viđenje raspada* (Belgrade, 1993), p. 107.
13 Jović, *Poslednji dani*, p. 135.
14 *Ibid.*
15 V. M., "Vorgehen der Armeeführung mißbilligt", in *FAZ* (24 January 1990).
16 Misha Glenny, *The Fall of Yugoslavia: The Third Balkan War* (London, 1992), p. 61.
17 V. M., "Jugoslawien braucht die Partei nicht mehr", in *FAZ* (14 April 1990).
18 Records of the session of the presidency of the Socialist Republic of Slovenia (2 March 1990), in Archives of the Republic of Slovenia.
19 Conversation with Jože Pučnik, Ljubljana, October 1994.
20 See records of the session of the presidency of the Socialist Republic of Slovenia (8 January 1990), in Archives of the Republic of Slovenia.
21 Records of the session of the presidency of the Socialist Republic of Slovenia (18 January 1990), in Archives of the Republic of Slovenia.
22 As cited in *Borba* (24 March 1990).
23 V. M., "Slowenien erstrebt die Selbständigkeit", in *FAZ* (17 March 1990); and V. M., "Die Konföderation als letzte Rettung", in *FAZ* (26 March 1990).
24 V. M., "Nicht Loslösung, aber Selbständigkeit", in *FAZ* (26 March 1990).
25 For the electoral results, see *Delo* (13 April and 25 April 1990).
26 Conversation with Josip Manolić, Zagreb, 14 November 1994.
27 V. M., "Frei sein in einem freien Volk", in *FAZ* (6 April 1990).
28 Publications of the Croatian election office; and *Tanjug Bulletin* (Vienna), 27 April 1990, with the title, "Durchbruch der Rechtskräfte in Kroatien"; also *Vjesnik* (8 May 1990).
29 *Delo* (30 May 1990).
30 *Politika* (28 April 1990).
31 Conversation with Franjo Tudjman, Zagreb, 7 May 1990. See also V. M., "Sieg der Kroatischen Demokratischen Gemeinschaft", in *FAZ* (9 May 1990).

32 Conversation with Boris Malada, 7 May 1990.
33 V. M., "Auch Slowenien wünscht eine Konföderation", in *FAZ* (12 May 1990).
34 *Ibid.*
35 Conversation with Kučan, Ljubljana, 17 July 1994.
36 *Borba* (14 May 1990).
37 V. M., "Widerspruch gegen Belgrader Zentralismus", in *FAZ* (28 May 1990).
38 Records of the session of the presidency of the Republic of Slovenia (17 May 1990), in Archives of the Republic of Slovenia.
39 Janez Janša, *Pomaci* (Zagreb, 1993), p. 39.
40 Records of the session of the presidency of the Republic of Slovenia (18 May 1990), in Archives of the Republic of Slovenia.
41 Janša, *Pomaci*, p. 40.
42 *Ibid.*
43 Conversation with Stipe Mesić, Zagreb, 15 November 1994.
44 Janša, *Pomaci*, p. 40.
45 Conversation with Jelko Kacin, Ljubljana, October 1994.
46 Letter of 16 May 1985, in materials from the 72nd session of the presidium of the CC LCY (29 March 1988), in Archives of the Republic of Slovenia.
47 Janša, *Pomaci*, p. 40.
48 Kadijević, *Vidjenje*, p. 94.
49 *Borba* (29 May 1990).
50 *Ibid.*
51 *Tanjug Bulletin* (Vienna), 28 May 1990.
52 V. M., "Slowenien und Kroatien wollen ein neues Jugoslawien", in *FAZ* (15 June 1990).
53 V. M., "Jugoslawiens Zukunft steht zur Debatte", in *FAZ* (23 June 1990).
54 V. M., "Ministerpräsident Marković will Jugoslawiens Retter sein", in *FAZ* (6 August 1990).
55 V. M., "Gedenkfeier für die Domobrancen", in *FAZ* (10 July 1990); and V. M., "Praktizierte Versöhnung", in *FAZ* (4 July 1990).
56 Conversation with Kacin (see note 45).
57 Martin Špegelj, foreword to Janša, *Pomaci*.
58 *Documenta Croatica* (Zagreb, 1982), p. 129.
59 Revelation by Tudjman, autumn 1990.
60 See Tudjman's conversation with Rašković, full text in *Danas* (31 July 1990).
61 V. M., "Das Serbien Miloševićs setzt sich über Bundesverfassung hinweg", in *FAZ* (29 June 1990).
62 V. M., "Kroatien setzt dem Begehren der Serben Grenzen", in *FAZ* (11 August 1990).
63 V. M., "Kroatien fühlt sich nach dem mißglückten Aufstand in Knin gestärkt", in *FAZ* (23 August 1990).
64 V. M., "Der Glaube an Jugoslawiens Einheit schwindet", in *FAZ* (25 September 1990).
65 *Danas* (30 October 1990).
66 *Borba* (3 October 1990).
67 *Danas* (20 October 1990).
68 V. M., "Ertasten was Vernunft ist", in *FAZ* (6 February 1990).
69 Published in *Borba* (8 October 1990).
70 V. M., "Jugoslawiens Tage sind gezählt", in *FAZ* (4 October 1990).
71 V. M., "In Jugoslawien nichts mehr verloren", in *FAZ* (5 October 1990).
72 V. M., "Staatspräsidium über Neuordnung Jugoslawiens weiter uneins", in *FAZ* (12 October 1990).
73 Records of the sessions of the presidency of the Republic of Slovenia (17 July and 29 September 1990), in Archives of the Republic of Slovenia.

74 Records of the session of the presidency of the Republic of Slovenia (2 October 1990), in Archives of the Republic of Slovenia.
75 V. M., "Armee besetzt Militärgebäude in Slowenien", in *FAZ* (6 October 1990).
76 V. M., "Slowenien und Kroatien fühlen sich bedroht", in *FAZ* (26 November 1990). Kadijević's remarks became known through the notes which General Čad, commander of the army corps in Rijeka, a Slovenian, made.
77 *Borba* (5 November 1990).
78 Kadijević, *Vidjenje*, p. 111.
79 Records of the session of the presidency of the Republic of Slovenia (26 November 1990), in Archives of the Republic of Slovenia.
80 Records of the session of the presidency of the Republic of Slovenia (5 December 1990), in Archives of the Republic of Slovenia.
81 Predrag Tašić, *Kako sam branio Antu Markovića* (Skopje, 1993), pp. 69ff.
82 Kadijević, *Vidjenje*, p. 111.
83 Records of the session of the presidency of the Republic of Slovenia (5 December 1990), in Archives of the Republic of Slovenia.
84 V. M., "Vorsichtig und bedacht", in *FAZ* (6 December 1990).
85 V. M., "Die Serben haben sich für den Nationalismus ihres Führers Milošević entschieden", in *FAZ* (12 December 1990).
86 V. M., "Sie serbische Opposition klagt über Wahlfälschungen", in *FAZ* (13 December 1990).
87 V. M., "Belgrad droht Laibach", in *FAZ* (21 December 1990).
88 Tasic, *Kako sam branio*, pp. 58ff.
89 V. M., "Slowenen will eigene Währung schaffen", in *FAZ* (14 January 1991).
90 Tašić, *Kako sam branio*, p. 61.
91 V. M., "Ein Jugoslawien der sechs Präsidenten", in *FAZ* (10 April 1991).
92 See Laura Silber and Allan Little, *Brüderkrieg*, German ed. of *The Death of Yugoslavia*, trans. from English (Graz, 1995), p. 125. Regarding the meeting itself, see the records of 24 January 1991 in Archives of the Republic of Slovenia.
93 Kadijević, *Vidjenje*, p. 111.
94 V. M., "Kroatische Polizeireservisten haben ihre Waffen abgegeben", in *FAZ* (30 January 1991).
95 Kadijević, *Vidjenje*, p. 111.
96 Records of the session of the presidency of the Republic of Slovenia (22 January 1991), in Archives of the Republic of Slovenia.
97 V. M., "Kroatische Polizeireservisten" (see note 94).
98 *Ibid.*
99 Records of the session of the presidency of the Republic of Slovenia (4 March 1991), in Archives of the Republic of Slovenia.
100 Records of the session of the presidency of the Republic of Slovenia (10 March 1991), in Archives of the Republic of Slovenia.
101 Stipe Mesić, *Kako smo srušili Jugoslaviju* (Zagreb, 1992), pp. 23ff.
102 Conversation with Mesić, Zagreb, 25 November 1994.
103 Mesić, *Kako smo srušili*, p. 24.
104 *Ibid.*, p. 25.
105 *Ibid.*, p. 25.
106 *Ibid.*, p. 26. Mesić assured me that these statements during these sessions were reproduced according to protocol.
107 Records of the session of the presidency of the Republic of Slovenia (19 March 1991), in Archives of the Republic of Slovenia.
108 V.M., "Der serbische Führer Milošević erkennt das jugoslawische Staatspräsidium nicht mehr an", in *FAZ* (18 March 1991); and V. M., "In Jugoslawien gibt es kein institutionelles Vakuum", in *Ibid*.

109 *Ibid.*
110 Jović confirmed this in his memoirs. See Jović, *Poslednji dani*, p. 307.
111 Kadijević, *Vidjenje*, p. 114.
112 Conversation with Mesić, Zagreb, 15 November 1994.
113 *Ibid.*
114 *Ibid.*
115 *Borba* (23/24 March 1991).
116 Tašić, *Kako sam branio*, p. 75.
117 *Ibid.*, p. 78.
118 *Ibid.*, p. 69.
119 Glenny, *The Fall*, p. 61.
120 Conversations with General Anton Tus, Zagreb, 1992/93.
121 Tašić, *Kako sam branio*, p. 67.
122 *Ibid.*, p. 80.
123 V. M., "In Jugoslawien gibt es keine zentralistischen Lösungen mehr", in *FAZ* (3 May 1991).
124 Records of the session of the presidency of the Republic of Slovenia (18 February 1991), in Archives of the Republic of Slovenia.
125 V. M., "Keine Einigung über weitere Entwicklung in Jugoslawien", in *FAZ* (3 May 1991).
126 V. M., "Die jugoslawische Armee stellt den Kroaten ein Ultimatum", in *FAZ* (3 April 1991).
127 V. M., "Die jugoslawische Krise kann nur gemeinsam bewältigt werden", in *FAZ* (6 April 1991); and V. M., "Ein Jugoslawien der sechs Präsidenten", in *FAZ* (10 April 1991).
128 V. M., "EG-Delegation in Belgrad", in *FAZ* (5 April 1991).
129 V. M., "Milošević fühlt sich durch Erklärungen aus dem Westen bestärkt", in *FAZ* (20 April 1991).
130 Jović, *Poslednji dani*, pp. 319ff.
131 *Ibid.*, p. 322.
132 Mesić, *Kako smo srušili*, pp. 1–15.
133 V. M., "Kroatien zur Selbständigkeit entschlossen", in *FAZ* (22 May 1991).
134 Conversation with Kiro Gligorov, Skopje, October 1994.
135 *Borba* (22/23 June 1991).
136 Records of the session of the presidency of the Republic of Slovenia (15 May 1991), in Archives of the Republic of Slovenia.
137 Records of the session of the presidency of the Republic of Slovenia (5 June 1991), in Archives of the Republic of Slovenia.
138 Dimitrij Rupel, *Skrivnost države* (Ljubljana, 1992).
139 *Ibid.*, p. 130.
140 Records of the session of the presidency of the Republic of Slovenia (21 June 1991), in Archives of the Republic of Slovenia.
141 V. M., "Sloweniens Sorgen vor dem großen Sprung", in *FAZ* (8 May 1991).
142 V. M., "In Jugoslawien gibt es keine zentralistischen" (see note 123).
143 Records of the session of the presidency of the Republic of Slovenia (24 May 1991), in Archives of the Republic of Slovenia.
144 V. M., "Sloweniens Sorgen" (see note 141).
145 See Rupel, *Skrivnost*, p. 134.
146 Špegelj, foreword to Janša, *Pomaci*, p. iii.
147 Conversations with Kučan, summer 1991.
148 Rupel, *Skrivnost*, p. 132.
149 *Delo*, special issue (26 June 1991).
150 *Borba* (26 June 1991).

151 Records of the session of the presidency of the Republic of Slovenia (20 June 1991), in Archives of the Republic of Slovenia.
152 See especially Janša, *Pomaci*, passim.
153 Rupel, *Skrivnost*, p. 141.
154 Janša, *Pomaci*, p. 215.
155 Records of the session of the presidency of the Republic of Slovenia (1 July 1993), in Archives of the Republic of Slovenia; and Janša, *Pomaci*, p. 176.
156 Tašić, *Kako sam branio*, pp. 103ff.
157 Both texts in *Ibid.*, p. 116, enclosure.
158 Conversations with Kučan and Kacin, Ljubljana, October 1994.
159 Tašić, *Kako sam branio*, p. 120.
160 Silber and Little, *Brüderkrieg*, p. 176.
161 Warren Zimmermann, *Origins of a Catastrophe* (New York, 1996), p. 145.
162 Silber and Little, *Brüderkrieg*, p. 179.
163 Zimmermann, *Origins of a Catastrophe*, p. 71.
164 Janša, *Pomaci*, p. 207.
165 Špegelj, foreword to Janša, *Pomaci*, p. iv.
166 Kadijević, *Vidjenje*, pp. 120ff.

6 Unwanted independence – the fate of Macedonia and Bosnia-Herzegovina

1 Conversations with Mirče Tomovski (later the chief editor of the newspaper, *Puls*), Skopje, October 1994.
2 Demosthenes, *Dritte Philippika* (Stuttgart, 1985), pp. 173ff.
3 Georg Ostrogorsky, *Geschichte des byzantinischen Staates* (Munich, 1963), pp. 250ff.
4 Concerning the history of Macedonia, see the extensive discussion in: Wolfgang Libal, *Mazedonien zwischen den Fronten* (Vienna and Zürich, 1993).
5 *Istorija na Makedonskiot Narod* (Skopje, 1969).
6 Elizabeth Barker, *Macedonia: Its Place in Balkan Power Politics* (London, 1950).
7 V. M., "In Kumanovo ist der Balkan besonders kompliziert", in *FAZ* (11 May 1993).
8 For an extensive discussion of these movements including figures, see Stephen P. Ladas, *The Exchange of Minorities: Bulgaria, Greece, and Turkey* (New York, 1932). According to that source, about 62,000 "Bulgarians" emigrated from Greece to Bulgaria (pp. 15ff.) during and after the First World War, about 47,000 of them from eastern Thrace.
9 Ladas, *Exchange of Minorities*, p. 105. *Istorija na Makedonskiot Narod*, Vol. 3, p. 259 reports some 32,000 settlers from eastern Thrace between the end of the war and 1928.
10 Re. this event, see Evangelos Kofos, *Nationalism and Communism in Macedonia* (Thessaloniki, 1964), p. 48; and *Istorija na Makedonskiot Narod*, p. 258.
11 See Ladas, *Minorities*, passim. According to this census, more than 20,000 Muslim Albanians were also counted in the Camharija district in Epirus, who were expelled in 1945.
12 See his memoirs: *Memoare na Dimitar Vlahov* (Skopje, 1970).
13 On this point, see Libal, *Mazedonien*, pp. 59ff.
14 For the text, see *Istorijski Arhiv K.P.J.*, Vol. 7, p. 50. This decision of the Comintern was handled discretely by both sides for a long time.
15 For a Bulgarian presentation, see Zola Dragitschewa, *Von Niederlage bis zum Sieg*, German ed. (Vienna, 1983).
16 Svetozar Vukmanović-Tempo, *Revolucija koja teče*, 2 vols. (Belgrade, 1971).
17 Stoyan Pribichevich, *Macedonia: Its People and History* (University Park, Pa., 1982), p. 150.

18 *Ibid.*, p. 151.
19 Kofos, *Nationalism and Communism* (see note 10), p. 50.
20 *Ibid.*, p. 151.
21 Pribichevich, *Macedonia*, p. 154.
22 Vladimir Dedijer, *Josip Broz Tito* (Belgrade, 1953), p. 449.
23 *Ibid.*, p. 187.
24 V. M., notes from my trip to Macedonia (July 1990); also Dragoljub Stavrev, press conference, Ohrid, 22 May 1983.
25 V. M., "Mazedonien will nötigenfalls allein gehen", in *FAZ* (7 August 1990).
26 V. M., "Sofia in Sorge wegen der Instabilität auf dem südlichen Balkan", in *FAZ* (27 July 1992).
27 Disclosure by President Gligorov, Skopje, October 1994.
28 V. M., "Mazedonien will nötigenfalls" (see note 25).
29 *Ibid.*
30 Conversation, Skopje, October 1994.
31 Conversation with Gligorov, Skopje, October 1994.
32 V. M., "Europa hat die Wahl zwischen Athen und Skopje", a conversation with Mitsotakis, in *FAZ* (9 June 1992).
33 Conversation with Gligorov, Skopje, 12 June 1992.
34 Conversation with Stojan Andov, Skopje, October 1994.
35 Conversation with Ljubčo Georgijevski, Skopje, July 1990.
36 Conversation with Abdurahman Aliti (Party for Democratic Prosperity), Tetovo, October 1994.
37 V. M., "Trotz widriger Umstände schon viel erreicht", in *FAZ* (9 November 1993).
38 Figure from *Borba* (13 January 1992), relying on data from the Federal Office for Statistics still issued before the outbreak of the war.
39 These impressions are derived from my trip notes on the occasion of my visit to Sarajevo, 20–22 October 1989.
40 Conversation with Radovan Karadžić, Sarajevo, 21 October 1990.
41 Conversation with Alija Izetbegović, Sarajevo, 21 October 1990.
42 Conversation with Stjepan Kljuić, Sarajevo, 21 October 1990.
43 V. M., "Nation und Glaube", in *FAZ* (12 October 1990); and Adil Zulfikarpašić's interview with *Borba* (22 September 1990).
44 *Oslobodjenje* (21 November 1990).
45 *Ibid.* (22 November 1990).
46 *Vjesnik* (13 December 1990).
47 Data from *Vjesnik* (13 December 1990).
48 For example, Misha Glenny, *The Fall of Yugoslavia: The Third Balkan War* (London, 1992), p. 153.
49 Concerning the history of old Bosnia, see Sima Ćirković, *Istorija Bosne* (Belgrade, 1964).
50 See Noel Malcolm, *Geschichte Bosniens*, German ed. (Frankfurt-am-Main, 1996), p. 47.
51 Hazim Šabanović, *Bosanski Pašaluk* (Sarajevo, 1959), pp. 77ff.
52 Meša Selimović, *Sjećanja* (Belgrade, 1983), p. 42. For a cultural inventory of the Bosnian-Muslim world, see Smail Balić, *Das unbekannte Bosnien* (Köln and Vienna, 1992).
53 Cited in Kasim Suljević, *Nacionalnost Muslimana* (Rijeka, 1981), p. 150.
54 Conversation with him and with other Bosnian politicians, Sarajevo, 20–22 October 1991.
55 V. M., "Schwierige Mission Kinkels in Zagreb", in *FAZ* (15 May 1992).
56 Glenny, *Fall of Yugoslavia*, p. 140 makes the rather incomprehensible claim that "the majority of Muslims" had collaborated with the Croatian *Ustaše*.

57 Suljević, *Nacionalnost Muslimana*, p. 214.
58 *Ibid.*
59 Cited in *Ibid.*, p. 236.
60 *Ibid.*
61 Sulejman Grozdanić, in Alija Isaković, *O nacionaliziranju Muslimana* (Zagreb, 1990), p. 355.
62 Ćirković, *Istorija Bosne*, p. 109.
63 V.M., "In Banja Luka wollen die Serben ihren eigenen Staat", in *FAZ* (9 August 1991).
64 V.M., "In Bosnien regiert Mißtrauen", in *FAZ* (25 May 1991).
65 V.M., "Der Rest wird gleichgeschaltet", in *FAZ* (23 February 1991).
66 V.M., "Bosnien-Hercegovina ist blockiert", in *FAZ* (13 December 1991).
67 *Ibid.*; also trip notes.
68 Conversation with Ejup Ganić, Sarajevo, 10 December 1991.
69 Silber and Little, *Brüderkrieg*, p. 261.
70 V. M., "Kaum Behinderungen durch die Serben beim Referendum in Bosnien-Herzegovina", in *FAZ* (2 March 1992).
71 V. M., "Auch in Bosnien-Herzegovina machen die Serben gegen die Unabhängigkeit mobil", in *FAZ* (3 March 1992).
72 V. M., "Folgenschweres Zögern des Westens", in *FAZ* (30 March 1992).
73 James A. Baker, *The Politics of Diplomacy* (New York, 1995), p. 641.
74 Cited from *Voice of America* (16 June 1994).
75 V. M., "Das eigentliche Übel ist die Jugoslawische Volksarmee", in *FAZ* (13 April 1992).

7 From the Yugoslav tragedy to the tragedy of the West

1 Dimitrij Rupel, *Skrivnost Države* (Ljubljana, 1992), p. 159.
2 Conversation with Warren Zimmermann, Washington D.C., April 1994.
3 Conversation with Robert B. Zoellick, Washington D.C., April 1994.
4 Conversation with Ernest Petrič, Washington D.C., April 1994.
5 Conversation with Milan Kučan, Ljubljana, October 1994.
6 Rupel, *Skrivnost*, p. 134.
7 James A. Baker, *The Politics of Diplomacy* (New York, 1995), pp. 482ff.
8 Warren Zimmermann, *Origins of a Catastrophe* (New York, 1996), p. 137.
9 Baker, *Politics of Diplomacy*, p. 481.
10 Rupel, *Skrivnost*, p. 134.
11 Cited from Predrag Tašić, *Kako sam branio Antu Markovića* (Skopje, 1993), p. 116.
12 *Ibid.*, p. 112.
13 Conversation with Hans-Dietrich Genscher, Bonn, 19 December 1994.
14 Conversation with Zimmermann (see note 2).
15 *Ibid.* See also Warren Zimmermann, "Origins of a Catastrophe: Memoirs of the last American Ambassador to Yugoslavia", in *Foreign Affairs*, Vol. 74, No. 2 (March/April 1995).
16 Conversation with Kučan (see note 5).
17 Disclosure from Rupel, summer 1991.
18 V. M., "Zuviel nach Belgrad geschaut", in *FAZ* (15 April 1991).
19 Stipe Mesić, *Kako smo srušili Jugoslaviju* (Zagreb, 1992), p. 32.
20 *Ibid.*, p. 33.
21 Hans-Heinrich Wrede, "Die deutsche Balkanpolitik im Einklang mit den Partnern", in *Das Parlament*, No. 40 (1 October 1993).
22 Mesić, *Kako smo srušili*, p. 51.
23 Conversation with Genscher (see note 13).
24 Wrede, "Die deutsche Balkanpolitik", passim.

25 Conversation with Genscher (see note 13).
26 For example, James Steinberg, "The Response of International Institutions to the Yugoslav Conflict", in F. Stephen Larrabee (ed.), *The Volatile Powder Keg: Balkan Security after the Cold War* (Washington D.C., 1994), p. 194.
27 Kadijević, *Vidjenje*, passim.
28 Janez Janša, *Pomaci* (Zagreb, 1993), p. 161.
29 Records of the session of the presidency of the Republic of Slovenia (29 June 1991), in Archives of the Republic of Slovenia.
30 Rupel, *Skrivnost*, p. 153.
31 Records of the session of the presidency of the Republic of Slovenia (1 July 1991), in Archives of the Republic of Slovenia.
32 Janša, *Pomaci*, p. 165.
33 Rupel, *Skrivnost*, p. 152.
34 *Ibid.*, p. 153.
35 *Ibid.*
36 *Ibid.*, p. 159.
37 *Ibid.*, p. 147.
38 Records of the session of the presidency of the Republic of Slovenia (1 July 1991), in Archives of the Republic of Slovenia.
39 Mesić, *Kako smo srušili*, pp. 57ff.
40 *Ibid.*, p. 67.
41 Conversation with Genscher (see note 13).
42 Rupel, *Skrivnost*, p. 156.
43 *Ibid.*, pp. 155ff.
44 Cited from Steinberg, "The Response".
45 Cited from Rupel, *Skrivnost*, p. 162.
46 Conversation with Janez Janša, *(Ljubljana, 1992)*.
47 Disclosure by Kučan, summer 1991.
48 Borisav Jović, *Poslednji dani SFRJ* (Belgrade, 1995), p. 364.
49 Stenogram as cited in Mesić, *Kako smo srušili*, pp. 57ff.
50 *Ibid.*, pp. 121ff.
51 V. M., "Der Vermittlungsversuch der EG in Jugoslawien gescheitert", in *FAZ* (5 August 1991).
52 V. M., "Befürchtungen in Jugoslawien nach dem Scheitern der EG-Mission", in *FAZ* (6 August 1991).
53 *Ibid.*
54 Conversation with Genscher (see note 13); also Wrede, "Die deutsche Balkanpolitik", passim.
55 Henry Wynaendts, *L'engrenage* (Paris, 1993), p. 33.
56 *Ibid.*, pp. 82 and 94.
57 *Ibid.*, p. 77.
58 *Ibid.*, p. 13.
59 *Ibid.*, p. 71.
60 V. M., "EG-Debakel in Jugoslawien", in *FAZ* (16 September 1991).
61 For a chronology of events, see Steinberg, "The Response".
62 Text of the draft of 18 October 1991 in Rupel, *Skrivnost*, pp. 198ff.
63 Mesić, *Kako smo srušili*, p. 218.
64 Conversation with Kučan (see note 5).
65 Mesić, *Kako smo srušili*, pp. 262ff.
66 *Ibid.*
67 V. M., "Die Sirenen in Slowenien geben symbolisch Entwarnung", in *FAZ* (28 October 1991).
68 V. M., "Serbische Generäle führen den Krieg gegen Kroatien zunehmend auf eigene Faust", in *FAZ* (4 October 1991); also Kadijević, *Vidjenje*, p. 128.

69 V. M., "Die Sirenen" (see note 67).
70 Wynaendts, *L'engrenage*, pp. 93ff.
71 V. M., "Der Krieg geht underdessen weiter", in *FAZ* (16 December 1991).
72 Zbigniew Brzezinski, *Power and Principle: Memoirs of the National Security Advisor 1977–1981* (New York, 1985), p. 44.
73 Materials from the session of the presidency of the Republic of Slovenia (24 October 1991), in Archives of the Republic of Slovenia.
74 *Ibid.*
75 *Ibid.*
76 Zimmermann, *Origins*, pp. 99 and 126.
77 Materials from the session of the presidency of the Republic of Slovenia (24 October 1991), in Archives of the Republic of Slovenia.
78 Disclosure by Ernest Petrič to the Slovenian Foreign Ministry, in materials from the session of the presidency of the Republic of Slovenia (24 October 1991), in Archives of the Republic of Slovenia; and conversation with Petrič, Washington D.C., April 1994.
79 Materials from the session of the presidency of the Republic of Slovenia (24 October 1991), in Archives of the Republic of Slovenia.
80 Conversation with Kučan (see note 5).
81 V. M., "Die serbischen Medien feiern einen Sieg", in *FAZ* (30 October 1991); and V. M., "Carrington will Serbien zufriedenstellen", in *FAZ* (4 November 1991).
82 *Ibid.*
83 Wrede, "Die deutsche Balkanpolitik".
84 Conversation with Zimmermann (see note 2).
85 Conversation with Genscher (see note 13).
86 Cited in Wrede, "Die deutsche Balkanpolitik".
87 *Ibid.*
88 Conversation with Genscher (see note 13).
89 Wrede, "Die deutsche Balkanpolitik".
90 *Ibid.*
91 *Ibid.*
92 *Ibid.*
93 V. M., "EG-Sanktionen und Verzögerung der Anerkennung schaffen eine schwere Lage", in *FAZ* (28 November 1991).
94 Kadijević, *Vidjenje*, pp. 136ff.
95 Jović, *Poslednji dani*, p. 410.
96 See, for example, Heinz-Jürgen Axt, "Hat Genscher Jugoslawien entzweit", in *Europa Archiv* (1993), no. 12.
97 Wrede, "Die deutsche Balkanpolitik".
98 Conversation with Genscher (see note 13). The claim by Silber and Little (in *Brüderkrieg*, p. 232), according to which British Foreign Secretary Douglas Hurd did not take part in this meeting at all, is difficult to verify since there was a constant coming and going at this meeting.
99 Conversation with Genscher (see note 13).
100 Disclosure by Genscher, December 1994.
101 So the former U.S. Ambassador to Yugoslavia, Warren Zimmermann, told me in April 1994 (see note 2).
102 Alfred Verdross and Bruno Simma, *Universelles Völkerrecht* (Berlin, 1981), p. 202.
103 Conversation with Genscher (see note 13).
104 See V. M., "Verwirrung über die UN und Mitterrand", in *FAZ* (3 July 1992).

Index of Names

Abdić, Fikret 41, 42, 197, 200
Adžić, Blagoje 99, 140, 155, 166, 225
Ahrens, Gert 236
Alexander (Karadjordjevic), King 46, 55, 130
Andov, Stojan 192, 193
Antall, Joszef 159
Arbasi, Aziz 91
Arifi, Ekrem 81, 86
Arkan (Zeljko Raznjatovic) 173
Avramović, Života 180
Azemi, Husamedin 81, 85, 88, 89

Babić, Milan 155
Badinter, Robert 236
Bajramovic, Sajda 99, 173
Bajt, Alexandar 11, 16, 109
Bakalli, Mahmut 24, 29, 30–1
Bakić, Miloš 62
Baker, James 176, 212, 215–16, 220
Baltić, Milutin 15, 18, 36
Barker, Elisabeth 184
Basileiros II, Emperor 183
Bauer, Archbishop Ante 127
Bavčar, Igor 67, 150, 177
Bilandžić, Dućan 41
Bilić, Jure 18, 36
Blaževic, Jakuv 19–20
Blum, Emerik 197
Boban, Mate 209
Bobetko, Janko 144–5
Bogićević, Bogić 161, 163, 164–5, 172, 173, 229
Bojanić, Milenko 15
Boljkovac, Josip 134, 154
Bor, Matej 58
Borštner, Ivan 66, 68–9
Botteri, Robert 66, 67
Branković, Vuk 44

Brovet, Stane 77–8, 139, 159, 165
Brzezinski, Zgibniew 231
Bućar, France 67, 177, 217
Budak, Mile 130
Budiša, Dražen 144
Bukoshi, Bujar 100
Bulatović, Kosta 38
Bulatović, Momir 83, 118, 159, 161, 233
Bulc, Marko 112
Bulgaranov, Bojan 187
Bush, George 218
Buxhovi, Jusuf 97

Cankar, Ivan 52
Čarnojevic, Patriarch Arsenije III 24
Carrington, Peter Lord 226, 228–9, 231, 232, 233–4, 236, 240
Castro, Fidel 2
Châtelais, Michel 217
Čičak, Ivan Zvonimir 144
Cingrija, Pero 127
Ćosić, Dobrica 21, 50, 96, 115
Crvenkovski, Branko 192
Crvenkovski, Krste 193
Cubrilović, Vasa 44
Cvetković, Dragiša 47
Cyril 182–3
Czartoryski, Prince Adam 45

Dabčević–Kučar, Savka 134, 144
Delors, Jacques 219
Demaqi, Adem 27
Deva, Veli 24, 29
Deva, Xhaver 25
Dimitrov, Filip 191
Dimitrov, Georgi 188, 189
Dimotrović, Dragutin (Drago) 36, 134–5

Dizdarević, Raif 64, 68, 84, 86, 104, 106, 159; army 70; collapse of LCY 83; Kosovo 89, 90–1; state presidency and Milošević 79–80, 81–2, 107
Djilas, Milovan 3, 4, 51, 83, 134
Djuranović, Veselin 12, 82
Dodik, Milorad 44
Dolanc, Stane 4, 13, 21, 23, 38, 63, 70, 77; arrest 66; Kosovo 88–9, 92, 110
Dolašević, Svetislav 79
Dragosavac, Dušan 18, 36
Drašković, Vuk 43, 44, 161
Drnovšek, Janez 109, 116, 119, 148, 152, 222; Brioni 224–5; Hague Conference 232, 233; state presidency 112–13, 143, 165–6
Družić, Ivo 136
Dumas, Roland 240
Durieux, Jean 231
Dusan the Mighty, Tsar 24

Eagleburger, Lawrence 218, 233
Ehrlich, Lambert 56
Eiff, Hansjörg von 217, 223
Ertl, Tomaz 63, 66
Erzen, Ivan 63, 66

Ferdinand, Archduke Franz 196
Ferenc, Tone 55
Florijančič, Jože 15
Frank, Josua 125–6
Friedman, Milton 106

Ganić, Ejup 200, 208
Garašanin, Ilija 44–5
Genscher, Hans-Dietrich 217, 221, 223–4, 226; recognition of Slovenia and Croatia 227, 235–6, 239, 241, 242
Georgijevski, Ljubčo 194
Glenny, Misha 141, 169
Gligorov, Kiro 11, 13, 43, 109, 182, 188, 190; compromise proposal with Izetbegović 174, 192, 207; independence for Macedonia 191–5 *passim*
Goldštajn, Slavko 135, 144
Gošev, Petar 181, 182, 192, 194
Gotovac, Vlado 19, 144
Gračanin, Petar 86, 107, 150, 159, 169
Grafenauer, Bogo 58

Grebo, Zdravko 20
Gregurić, Franjo 176
Grey, Edward 128
Gubec, Matija 51

Hall, Peter 217
Hasani, Sinan 37
Hebrang, Andrija
Herljević, Franje 20, 197
Hočevar, Ivan 148–9, 158
Hodza, Hajredin 26, 27–8
Holbrooke, Richard 244–5
Horvat, Branko 11, 105, 135
Hötzendorf, Conrad von 126
Hoxha, Enver 30
Hoxha, Fadil 26, 37
Hribar, Spomenka 58
Hurd, Douglas 228, 239, 240, 241

Isaković, Antonije 50
Izetbegović, Alija 173, 200, 203, 207, 208, 210, 211; compromise proposal with Gligorov 174, 192, 207; Islamic Declaration 22, 23, 199; Party of Democratic Action 197, 198–9; trial 22–3

Janša, Janez 56, 61, 113, 114, 150, 177, 179, 222, 232; arrest 66–7; Minister of Defense 144; TO 148–9, 158; trial 68–9
Jashari, Kaqusha 72–3, 76, 77, 79, 80, 81
Jelačić, Ban Josip 124
Jelinčić, Zmago 142
Jokanović, Vukašin 93
Jović, Borisav 60, 98, 143, 155, 170, 180, 219, 238; army 140, 224–5; efficacious federation proposal 157–8; expert group for economic questions 169; Mesić 158, 173; proposed for Prime Minister 107; Serbian constitutional reforms 72, 86, 93; Slovenia and Croatia 147–8, 150, 153, 163–7 *passim*; state presidency 7, 147, 172–3

Kacin, Jelko 149–50, 177, 179
Kadijević, Veljko 8, 61, 68, 106, 107, 120, 135, 139, 159, 221; Bosnia-Herzegovina 210, 213–14; constitution 119, 120; Croatia 163–4, 229–30, 238; demand for freedom of action for the army 172;

four-point program 140; March 1991 demonstrations 165–6, 167; Marković 108, 141; Moscow visit 166, 169; Slovenia 70–1, 180, 225; Territorial Defense 150, 160; Western diplomats and 227
Karadžić, Radovan 134, 198, 199, 204, 209, 210, 211, 212, 213,
Karadžić, Vuk 125
Karakushi, Jusuf 95
Kardelj, Edvard 1, 6, 8, 49, 51, 52, 53, 57, 190
Kasche, Siegfried 133
Kavaja, Burhan 91
Kavčič, Stane 35
Kelmendi, Aziz 42
Khuen-Hedervary, Count 126, 127
Kidrić, Boris 57
Kinkel, Klaus 241
Kljuić, Stjepan 199, 200, 207, 209
Kljušev, Nikola 182
Kocbek, Edvard 57, 58
Kocijančič, Janez 118
Kohl, Helmut 221, 237, 241
Kolgezi, Remzi 81, 82
Koliševski, Lazar 24, 181, 187, 193
Koljević, Nikola 200, 211, 213
Kolšek, Konrad 180
Korošec, Anton 53, 54, 55
Korošec, Stefan 81–2, 91, 138
Korošić, Marijan 105–6
Kossuth, Ferenc 127
Kosters, Johan 227
Kostić, Branko 229, 232
Kovač, Oskar 104
Kraigher, Sergej 11
Krek, Janez 52
Krunić, Bosko 60, 64, 65, 66, 74, 75
Kučan, Milan 35–43, 84, 104, 142, 170, 172; army against Slovenia 63–8 *passim*, 70; confederation 147, 152; independence of Slovenia 110, 111, 114, 116–20 *passim*, 164, 175–9 *passim*; Kosovo 77, 88–91 *passim*; negotiations with Milošević 162–3; Territorial Defense 148, 149; Western diplomats 215–16, 218, 222, 223, 229, 231–3 *passim*, 237, 239
Kuharić, Archbishop Franjo 19, 131
Kulin, Ban 201
Kvaternik, Slavko 132

Ladas, Stephen 186
Lasić, Miro 209
Lazaroski, Jakuv 90, 111
Lazri, Sofokli 30–1
Leškošek, Franc 57
Little, Allan 163, 179, 210
Ljubićić, Nikola 13, 60, 70
Lončar, Budimir 104, 107, 172, 175, 219, 221, 228
Lovrić, Jelena 123

Maček, Vladko 47, 54, 127, 129–30, 132–3
Malada, Boris 146
Malcolm, Noel 201
Mamula, Branko 13, 39, 61, 63, 66, 68, 136, 141, 159
Manolić, Josip 134, 139, 140, 144–5
Marinc, Andrej 66
Marković, Ante 9, 36, 84, 92, 119, 158, 167; accession as Prime Minister 106–10; borders 175–6; collapse of LCY 141; economic and monetary reforms 161–2; Kosovo 97; League of Reform Forces 151, 152, 197; military intervention in Slovenia 178–9, 215, 225; 'new Yugoslavia' proposal 174; precarious position 168–72 *passim*; Serbian economic blockade 121; Serbia's suspension of the constitution 99; Western diplomats 216–17, 219–20, 222, 228
Marković, Draža 21
Marković, Mihajlo 50
Marković, Mirjana 39, 92, 159
Marković, Svetozar 45–6, 186, 203
Matić, Petar 74
Matvejević, Predrag 135
Mesić, Stipe 99, 134, 144–5, 149, 153, 155, 156, 168, 225, 228; state presidency 158, 165–7 *passim*, 173, 222, 223, 229
Meštrović, Ivan 128
Metaxas, Ioannnis 189
Methodius 182–3
Michelis, Gianni de 221–3, 224, 227
Mihajlov, Vance 187
Mihajlović, Kosta 50
Mikelić, Boro 144
Mikulić, Branko 14, 16, 17, 20, 35, 39, 42–3, 70, 101–6, 197
Milošavljević, Miloš 104

Milošević, Slobodan 25, 35–43, 43–4,
    60, 69, 139, 154, 171, 172, 204,
    225; 'anti-bureaucratic revolution'
    49; Bosnia-Herzegovina 168, 207,
    210, 213, 214; candidate for Prime
    Minister 106–7; consolidation of
    power in Serbia 71–84;
    constitutional reform 72–8, 151;
    Croatia 123, 124, 135, 167–8; end
    of autonomy in Kosovo 84–100
    passim; Greater Serbia 162–3;
    independence of Slovenia 114, 115,
    120–1; last LCY Congress 136–7;
    Macedonia 181, 192, 193;
    Marković and 108; National Bank
    loan to Serbia 161–2; 1990
    elections 161; Socialist Party 151;
    state capitalism 105; state
    presidency 166–7; Western
    diplomats 218, 226, 233–4
Mirković, Stevan 159
Mišković, Miroslav 109
Mišović, Miloš 28
Mitrović, Aleksandar 107, 169
Mitsotakis, Konstantinos 193
Mitterand, FranÁois 243
Mladić, Ratko 155, 213
Mock, Alois 221
Mojsov, Lazar 64, 65, 68, 70, 91–2,
    102, 110, 111, 159, 193
Morina, Rahman 31, 81, 84–5, 86,
    88, 89, 93, 95, 96
Mužević, Boris 90, 119

Natlačen, Marko 55
Nikezić, Marko 50

Obrenović, Prince Milos 44
Oman, Ivan 111, 141
Orlandić, Marko 82
Ostrogorsky, Georg 183
Owen, David Lord 204

Palacky, František 124
Pančevski, Milan 41, 44, 64, 111,
    116, 138, 193
Paraga, Dobroslav 19, 144
Pašić, Najdan 95–6
Pašić, Nikola 46, 54, 128–9
Paul (Karadjordjević), Prince-Regent
    47, 55, 132
Pavelić, Ante 130, 204
Pavlović, Dragiša 40
Perez de Cuellar, Javier 230, 239

Perišin, Ivo 105
Perović, Latinka 50
Peterle, Lojze 56, 67, 141, 143, 152,
    175, 217
Petrić, Ernest 215, 216
Philip of Macedonia 182
Pinheiro, João D. 212
Planinc, Milka 13–14, 16, 17, 18, 36
Plavšić, Biljana 44, 200
Polit-Desanšić, Mihailo 45
Poos, Jacques 221–3, 224
Popit, France 35, 68, 116–17
Popović, Miladin 26
Potrč, Miran 115, 116, 117, 119
Pozderac, Hamdija 41–2
Pregl, Živko 107, 108
Preseren, Franc 52, 119
Pribičević, Svetozar 46, 47, 127, 128,
    129
Protić, Stojan 46
Prunk, Janko 53
Pucar, Djuro 196–7
Pučnik, Jože 58, 141, 142, 143
Puk, Marko 133

Račan, Ivica 67, 85, 90, 91, 135–7
    passim, 138–9, 144
Račić, Puniša 129
Radić, Antun 126, 129
Radić, Stjepan 46, 126, 129
Ranković, Aleksandar 27, 49
Rašković, Jovan 144, 146, 153–4, 155
Raznjatovic, Zeljko ('Arkan') 173
Renovica, Milenko 39
Ribičič, Ciril 137, 138
Ribičič, Mitja 2, 3, 5, 8, 11
Rožman, Bishop Gregorij 56
Rugova, Ibrahim 97, 100
Rupel, Dimitrij 52, 59, 141, 152;
    independence of Slovenia 174–7
    passim; Western diplomats 219, 222,
    223, 231–2
Rupnik, Leon 56
Rus, Veljko 58

Sachs, Jeffrey 109–10
Samaras, Antonis 239
Samuil, Tsar 183
Santer, Jacques 219
Sapunxhiu, Riza 98–9
Šatarov, Methodi (Sarlo) 187
Scanlan, John 41, 218
Scowcroft, Bent 218
Sekulić, Tomislav 95

Selimović, Meša 203
Šešelj, Vojislav 21
Šetinc, Franc 76
Shiroka, Kolj 37, 79
Shukrija, Ali 37, 85, 88, 89
Silber, Laura 163, 179, 210
Simić, Petar 90, 118
Simović, General 132
Sirotković, Jakov 101
Školc, Jozef 112, 142
Slapar, Janez 158, 229
Smole, Janko 5
Smole, Jože 23, 59, 62, 66, 68, 69, 88, 104; Socialist Alliance 111, 113, 142
Sogorov, Milovan 74
Sokol, Smiljko 57, 139
Spaho, Mehmed 203
Špegelj, Martin 152–3, 164, 176, 179, 180, 230
Špiljak, Mika 36
Stambolić, Ivan 38, 40
Stamboliski, Alexander 187
Stanovnik, Janez 68, 70, 88
Starčević, Ante 125, 126
Stepinac, Alojzije Cardinal 19–20, 132
Stojadinović, Milan 47, 48, 55, 132
Stojčević, Stanko 36, 123, 124, 136
Stojšić, Djordje 74
Strossmayer, Bishop Josip Juraj 124–5
Supilo, Frano 127, 128, 128–9
Surroi, Veton 97
Šušteršić, Ivan 53
Šuvar, Stipe 22, 37, 60, 67, 70, 91, 94, 123, 137, 148; attacks on 85, 122; and Milošević 75, 78–80, 82, 84, 87

Tašić, David 66, 68–9
Tašić, Predrag 108, 161–2, 169, 179
Tito, Josip Broz 18, 49, 111, 137, 204–5; Kosovo 26, 27, 28; Macedonia 187, 188, 189–90; political legacy 1–10
Tomac, Zdravko 136, 209
Tomšic, Franc 111
Trajković, Momčilo 98
Trifunović, Bogdan 77, 117
Tripalo, Miko 134, 144
Trubar, Primož 51
Trumbić, Ante 127, 128
Tudjman, Franjo 131, 134, 135, 149,

152–3, 171, 216, 223, 230; army's attempted coup 164; Bosnia-Herzegovina 168, 204, 207, 209–10; elections 1990 144–7; independence of Croatia 173, 176–7; meeting with Milošević 167–8; Serbs in Croatia 153–4, 156–7; trial 19; Western diplomats 227, 239, 241
Tupurkovski, Vasil 79, 81–2, 193, 229
Tus, Gen. Anton 169, 238
Tutwiler, Margaret 176
Tvrtko I, Ban and King 201, 205

Urbančić, Ivan 58–9
Uzelac, Gen. Nikola 193

Van den Broek, Hans 221–9 *passim*, 233, 234, 235, 239
Vance, Cyrus 204, 230–1
Vaphiades, Marko 189
Vento, Sergio 217
Veselica, Marko 19
Vidmar, Josip 57
Višnjić, Svetozar 62–3
Vittorio Emanuele III, King 82
Vlahov, Dimitar 186
Vllasi, Azem 21, 30, 33, 34, 35–43, 71–2, 79, 81; arrest 91; blamed for demonstrations 87, 89; trial 96
Vojnić, Dragomir 109
Vrhovec, Josip 18, 36, 37, 70, 75, 95, 122
Vukmanović-Tempo, Svetozar 25, 187, 188, 189

Wynaendts, Henry 227, 230

Yazov, Dimitry 166

Zach, Franjo 45
Žakelj, Viktor 114–15, 142
Žarković, Vidoje 66, 75, 76, 82, 83
Zavrl, Franc 66, 68–9
Žebot, Ćiril 56
Žečević, Momcilo 53
Zemljarić, Janez 16
Zimmermann, Warren 41, 115, 179, 213, 215, 216, 217, 218, 227, 232, 235
Zoellick, Robert B. 215
Zulfikarpašić, Adil 199, 203

Subject Index

Agrokomerc 41–2, 197
Albania 26, 30–1
Albanians 24–6; demonstrations
  28–32, 81–2, 86–9, 93–7; Kosovo
  27–34; Macedonia 194–5;
  repression in Kosovo 98–100
Albanological Institute 100
Anti-Fascist Council for the People's
  Liberation of Macedonia (ASNOM)
  188
army 5–6, 42, 120; against Slovenia
  60–71; attacks on Croatia 229–30;
  Bosnia-Herzegovina 207–8; clash
  with Slovenia in Central
  Committee 117–18; hegemonism
  and socialism 138–57;
  independence of Croatia and
  Slovenia 158–80 passim; Macedonia
  192–3; transformation into Serbian
  army 238; war in Slovenia 177–80;
  Western diplomats 222, 225,
  229–30
Association of Socialist Youth of
  Slovenia 112
asymmetric federation 119
Austria 221, 241
Austro-Hungarian empire 52–4,
  125–8, 203

Badinter Commission 210, 236, 237,
  239, 240, 241, 242
Balkan Wars 1912–13 46, 185
Bogomilism 201, 202
borders 178–9; deposits to cross
  14–15; tolls 12–13
Bosnia-Herzegovina 16, 21, 47–8,
  126, 242; Dayton Peace Accord
  244–5; financial scandal 41–2;
  Islamic renaissance 22–3; Tudjman

and Milošević 167–8; unwanted
  independence 195–214
Bosnian-Macedonian compromise
  plan 174, 192
Brioni Declaration 224–5
Britain 220, 240–1, 243
Bujan conference 1944 26
Bulgaria 183, 185, 186, 187, 189–90,
  191–2
Bulgarian Exarchate 184

Carrington Plan 228–34
Catholic Church 19–20, 131–2, 201
Central Committee, LCY 4, 75–6,
  79–80, 85, 117–18, 135–6
Chamber of Republics and Provinces
  6–7
Chetniks 48, 133–4, 204
Christian Democrats 142–3
Coalition of National Understanding
  144, 145
colonists, law on 111
Comintern 48, 187
Commission for Economic Questions
  231
Committee for Meetings 119–20
Committee for the Protection of
  Human Rights 67
confederation proposal 157–8
Congress of Berlin 184
constitution: Macedonia 191; 1974
  6–10, 49–50; Serbia's constitutional
  revision 72, 73–4, 85–6, 92–4, 97,
  108, 151–2; Slovenia's amendments
  116–19
contract economy 1
conversions, forced 131–2
coup d'état of 4 October 1991 229,
  231

Croatia 36–7, 47–8, 52; and
  Bosnia-Herzegovina 204, 208–10;
  'Croatian Spring' 18, 134; elections
  139, 144–7; independence 157–80;
  opposition to reforms 15, 18–22;
  overdue political change 122–37;
  recognition of 235–43; Serb
  rebellion 153–7; Western diplomats
  218–19, 225–6, 229–30
Croatia-Slavonia-Dalmatia, Kingdom
  of 128
Croatian Democratic Community
  (HDZ) 134, 139, 144–5, 199, 209
Croatian Peasant Party 126–7, 129, 132
CSCE Conference 1991 220
currency: law on hard 16–17
customs 176
Czechoslovakia 5–6

Dachau trials 58
Dalmatia 125, 127
Dayton Peace Accord 244–5
debt 10–11, 15, 101
Delo 143
democratic centralism 3
Democratic League of Croatia 135
Democratic League of Kosovo 97,
  100
Democratic League of Slovenia
  111–12
demonstrations: Kosovo 28–32, 81–2,
  86–9, 93–7; mass demonstrations in
  1989 88–91; mass demonstrations
  in 1991 164–5; Vojvodina 74
'Demos' coalition 141–2, 143, 152
'differentiations' 33, 71–2
disassociation 147
Domobranci (Home Guards) 56, 57
Dubrovnik, siege of 230
Duchy of Krain 51

EC 212; collapse of restoration efforts
  215–34; recognition of Slovenia and
  Croatia 235–43; troika 221–6
economic boycott 121–2
economic reforms 103–6, 108–10;
  opposition to 10–23
elections: Bosnia-Herzegovina
  197–200; Croatia 139, 144–7;
  Macedonia 182, 193–4; Serbia
  99–100, 160–1; Slovenia 139,
  140–4
emergency, state of 90–2, 110–11
Energoinvest 197

Federal Chamber 6–7
Federal Council for the Protection of
  the Constitutional Order 64
federalism 51–9
Féderation Balcanique 186
forced conversions 131–2
France 220, 240–1, 243
'Friedjung trial' 127–8
'Fundamental Charter of Slovenia'
  113–14

Gastarbeiter 10, 14–15
Germany 55–6, 132–3, 217–18, 220,
  221; credit package 12; recognition
  of Croatia and Slovenia 235–42
  passim
Greater Macedonia 189–90
Greater Serbia 43–50
Greece 182, 184, 185–6, 188–9,
  190–1, 193
Greek Civil War 189, 190

Habsburg Monarchy 52–4
Hague Conference 226–34
'Handshar Waffen-SS division 204
HDZ 134, 139, 144–5, 199, 209
hegemonism: Serbia and the army
  138–57; Yugoslav and Serbia
  43–50
Helsinki Charter 220
Hungary 125, 126, 127

'Ilinden' 191
Ilinden Uprising 1903 185
IMRO 130, 185, 187
IMRO-Democratic Party for
  Macedonian National Unity 194
inflation 102, 108
international law 241–2
International Monetary Fund (IMF)
  15, 16, 101, 102–3, 104
Islamic Declaration 22–3, 199
Italy 25, 53, 55–6, 220

Kalvov-Politis Protocol 186
Kingdom of Serbs, Croats and
  Slovenes 54
KOS 5, 66–7, 160, 179
Kosovo: constitutional status 6, 8–9,
  49, 71; end of autonomy 84–100;
  international community and 234,
  244, 245; 1981 unrest 17–18,
  23–34
Kraigher Commission 11, 13, 43

Law on Associated Labor 1, 15
LCY Presidium 4, 67, 116;
    endorsement of Milošević 74–5;
    Kosovo 78–9, 80–1, 89–91; March
    1988 64–6
League of Communists of Croatia
    136, 144
League of Communists – Movement
    for Yugoslavia 159
League of Communists of Slovenia
    119–20
League of Communists of Yugoslavia
    (LCY) 2–4; Central Committee 4,
    75–6, 79–80, 85, 117–18, 135–6;
    last Congress 136–7, 138–9; Party
    Presidium *see* LCY Presidium
League of Peasants 111
League of Prizren 24–5
League of Reform Forces 152, 197
League of the Yugoslav Democratic
    Initiative 135
Liberals 142
Liberation Front 57–8
loan to Serbia 161–2
London Agreement 1915 53, 128

Macedonia 111, 240; unwanted
    independence 181–95
Macedonian-Bosnian compromise
    plan 174, 192
'May Declaration' 1989 53, 113, 114
Memorandum of the Serbian
    Academy of Sciences and Art
    48–50
migrations 32, 205–6
Military Council 62–3, 65
miners' strike 86–8, 91–2
Mladina 62, 66, 84
Montenegro 82–4, 233
Muslims 22–3, 168, 195–6, 202–5

'Načertanje' 44–5
Narodna Zaščita (National Protection)
    150
National Bank 16–17, 161–2, 233
National Council of Slovenes, Croats
    and Serbs 54
National Movement for the
    Annexation of Kosovo to Albania
    27
'national program' of Slovenia 58–9,
    62
nationalities: peoples and 9
Netherlands 227

Neuilly Peace Treaty 186
Nova Revija 58–9, 61–2
Novi Sad rallies 74

opposition to reform 10–23
Osimo Accords 57
Ottoman Empire 202–3

parallel administration system 100
paramilitary forces 159, 163–4; *see
    also* Territorial Defense Forces
Partisans 133–4
Party of Democratic Action 197,
    198–9, 202
Party of Democratic Prosperity 194
Pašaluk of Belgrade 44
Pašaluk of Bosnia 202
peasant uprisings 51
peoples: nationalities and 9
People's Liberation Army (ELAS) 189
police 4–5, 94
political parties *see* elections
political reform: opposition to 10–23
Politika 73–4, 78
Posavina 209–10
Prečani Serbs 47–8
prisoners, treatment of 95
Priština 29
Prohor Pčinski, Monastery of 181
provincial parliament of Kosovo
    98

referendums: Bosnia 210–11, 212;
    Slovenia 160, 161
repression 21–2; Bosnia-Herzegovina
    196; Kosovo 94, 98–100
restoration schemes 215–34
Rijeka resolution 1905 127
Roman Catholic Church 19–20,
    131–2, 201

sanctions 237
Serbia, Kingdom of 128
Serbia 238; between Yugoslav
    hegemonism and Greater Serbia
    43–50; hegemonism and socialism
    138–57; loan from National Bank
    to 161–2; Milošević's consolidation
    of power 71–84; 1989 celebrations
    of return to Kosovo 25; revision of
    constitution 72, 73–4, 85–6, 92–4,
    97, 108, 151–2; status of Kosovo
    and Vojvodina 8–9; Western
    diplomats 225–6, 233–4

Serbian Democratic Party 153–4, 198, 199
Serbian National Council 155
Slavic-Macedonian National Liberation Front (SNOF) 189
Slavonia 125
'Slavophone' refugees 190
Slovenia: army against 60–71; defence of federalism 51–9; democracy and indep- endence 110–22; elections 139, 140–4; independence 157–80; opposition to reforms 14–15, 16–17; recognition 235–43; war 177–80; Western diplomats 215–17, 218–19, 221–5, 231–3, 234
Slovenian People's Party 52, 53, 54
Social Democratic Association 111
Social Democratic Union of Macedonia 182
Social-Liberal Alliance 135
socialism 138–57
Socialist Alliance 69
Socialist Party 142
Sporazum of 1939 47, 132, 203–4
state of emergency 90–2, 110–11
state presidency 7, 98–9, 112–13, 116; army coup of October 1991 229; Jović initiative 147–8; rendered incapable of functioning 172–4; setback for Milošević in March 1991 165–7; state of emergency 88–9

TAS 197
Territorial Defense Forces 6; Slovenia (TO) 148–9, 150, 158, 159, 163–4, 175, 180

tree–trunk rebellion 155–7
Trepča miners 86–8, 91–2
Trieste Memorandum 57
Turkish Croatia 202

UDBa (political police) 4, 27, 66–7
United Nations 208, 228, 230–1, 237, 239, 243
United States (US) 212, 242; collapse of restoration efforts 215–34 *passim*
University of Priština 23, 29, 30, 33
'unprincipled alliance' 79–80
Ustaše (Insurrectionary) movement 18, 20, 130–1, 133, 134

Vance Plan 238–9, 239–40
Vojvodina 47, 86, 234; constitutional status 6, 8–9, 49, 71; end of autonomy 78; Novi Sad rallies 74

'war for the barracks' 230
weapons: army procurement 169; confiscation of 148–9; embargo 228
World Bank 12, 15

Young Muslims 204
Yugoslav Committee 46, 128
Yugoslav Muslim Organization 203
Yugoslav National Bank 16–17, 161–2, 233
Yugoslav People's Army (JNA) *see* army
'Yugoslav synthesis' 123, 124
'Yugoslavism' 124–5

'Zajedno' 44
'Zveno' 187